Into the Garden

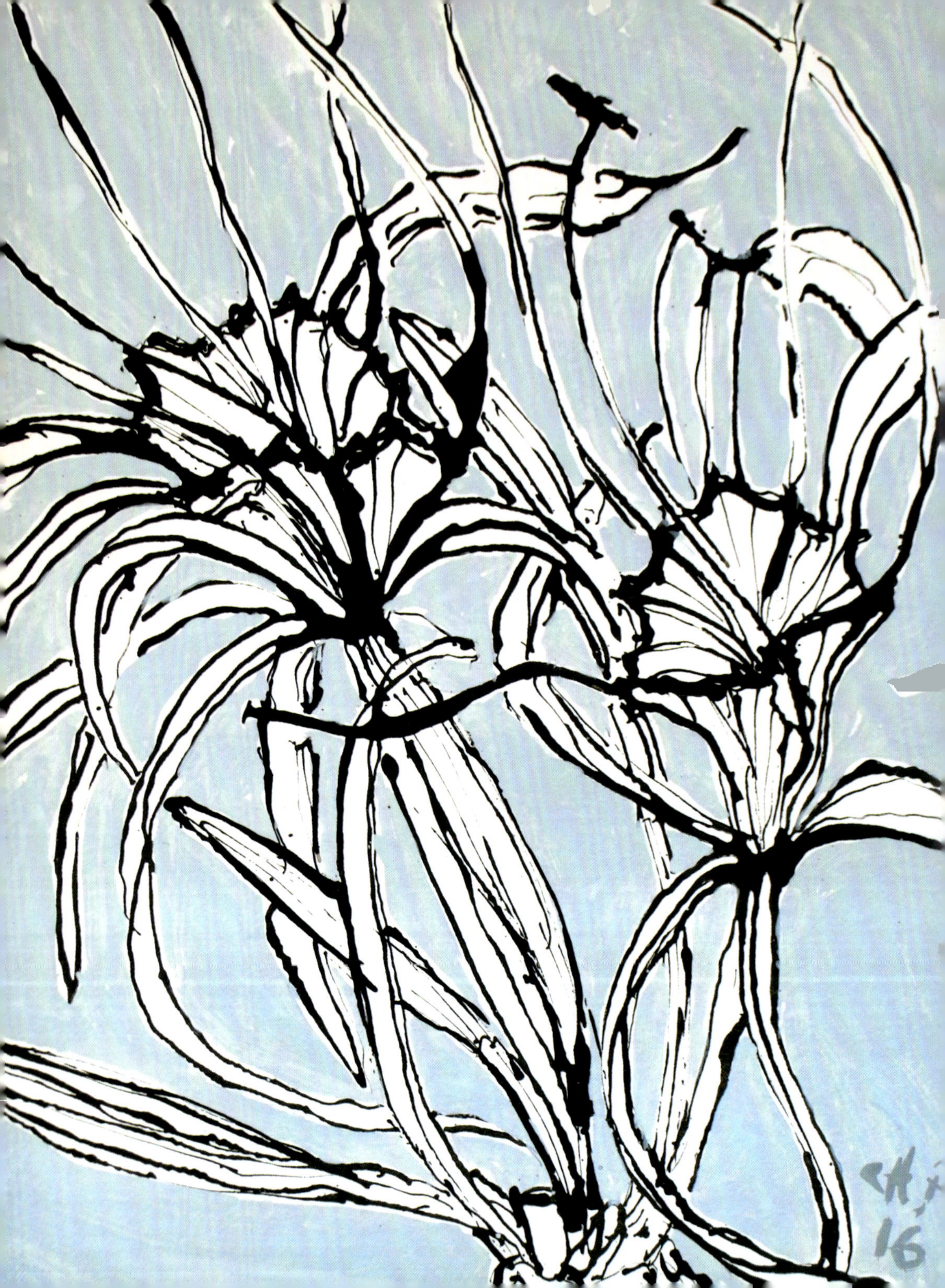

Into the Garden

CHRISTIAN PELTENBURG-BRECHNEFF

Foreword Bunny Williams

Essay Donald Kuspit

G ARTS | NEW YORK

First published in 2019 by

G Arts
311 West 43 Street
Floor 12
New York, New York 10036

www.glitteratieditions.com
media@glitteratieditions.com

First edition, 2019

Library of Congress Cataloging-in-Publication data is available from the publisher.

Hardcover edition
ISBN: 978-0-9992430-4-6

Printed and bound in China

10 9 8 7 6 5 4 3 2 1

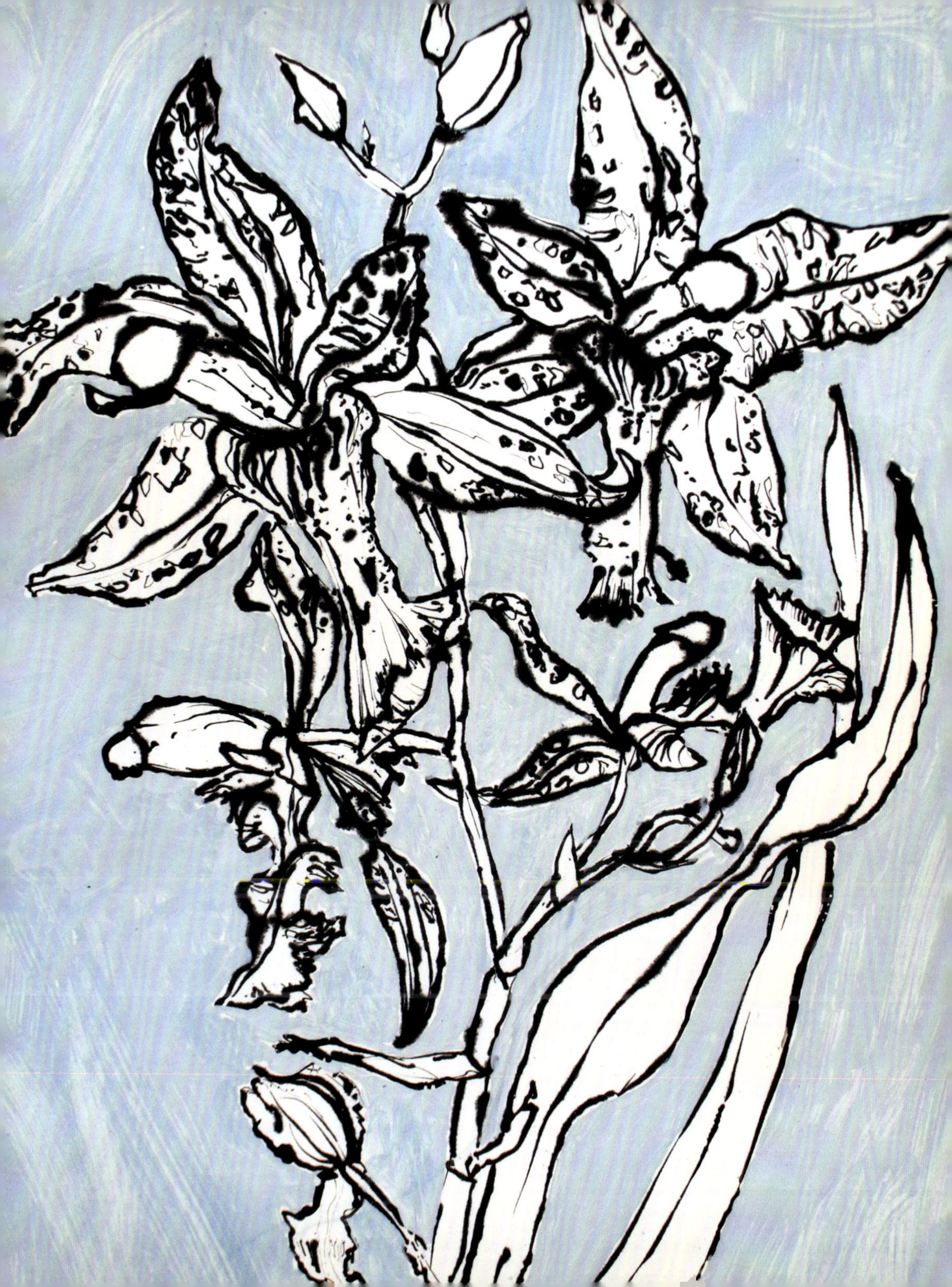

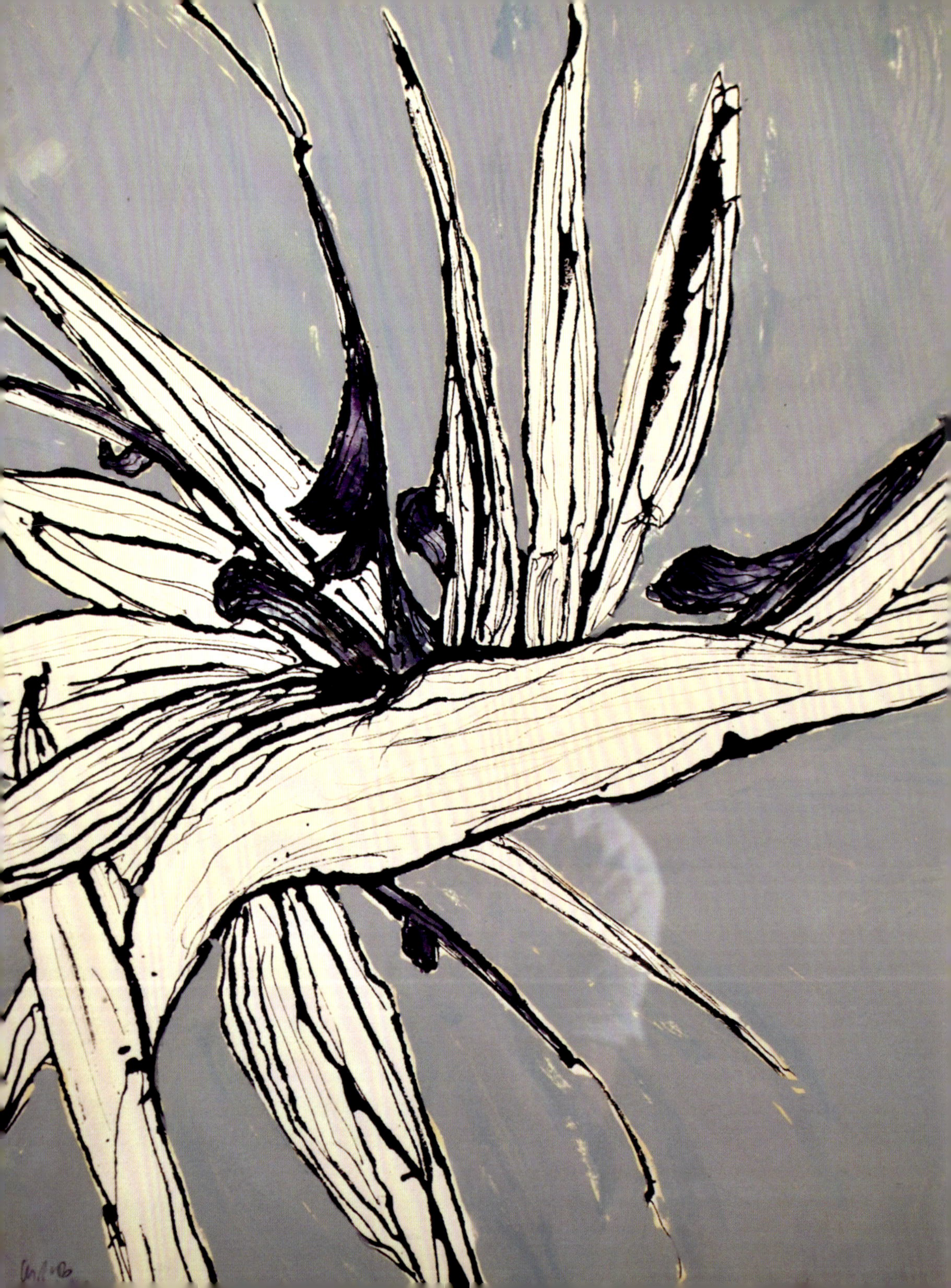

We must cultivate our garden.

—Voltaire

Contents

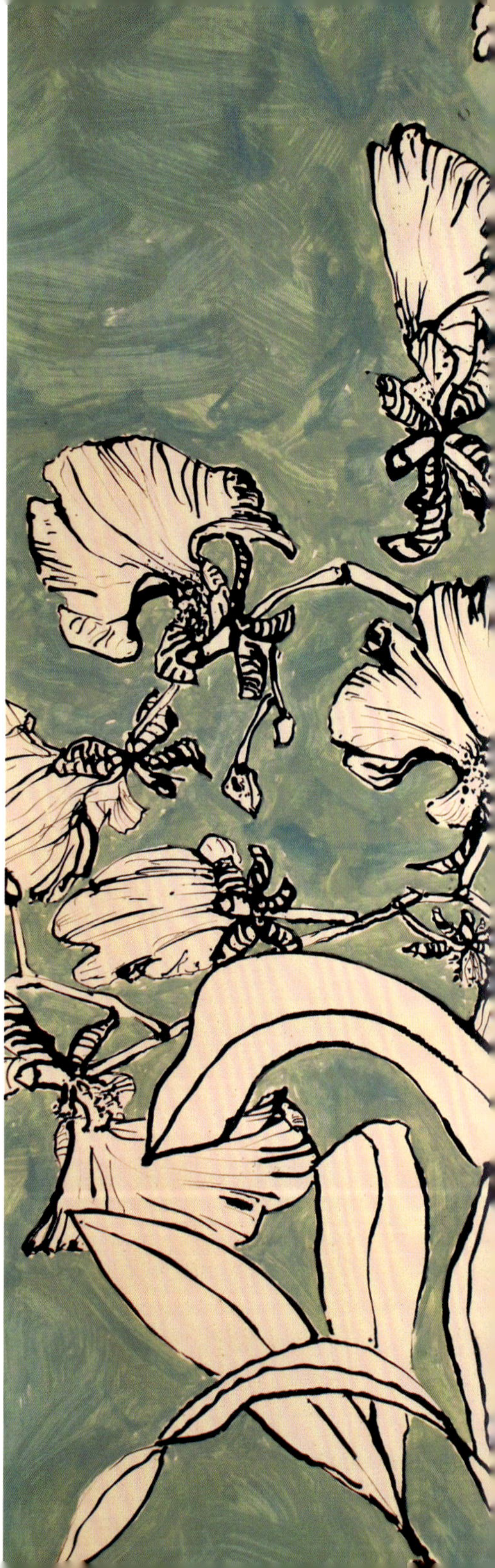

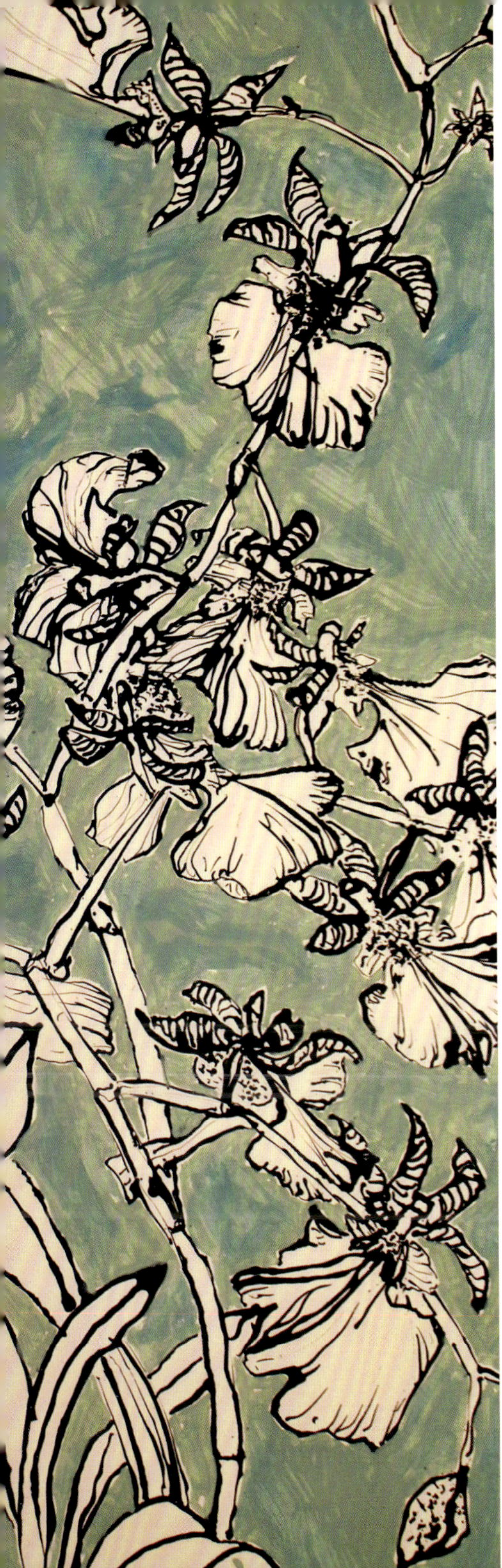

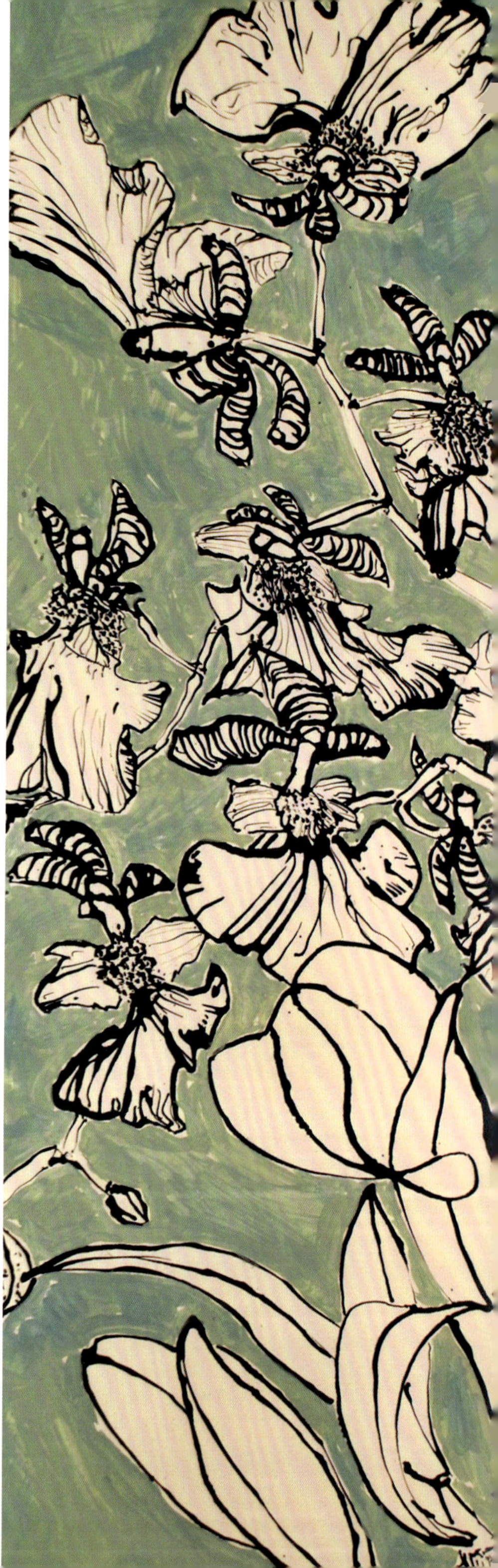

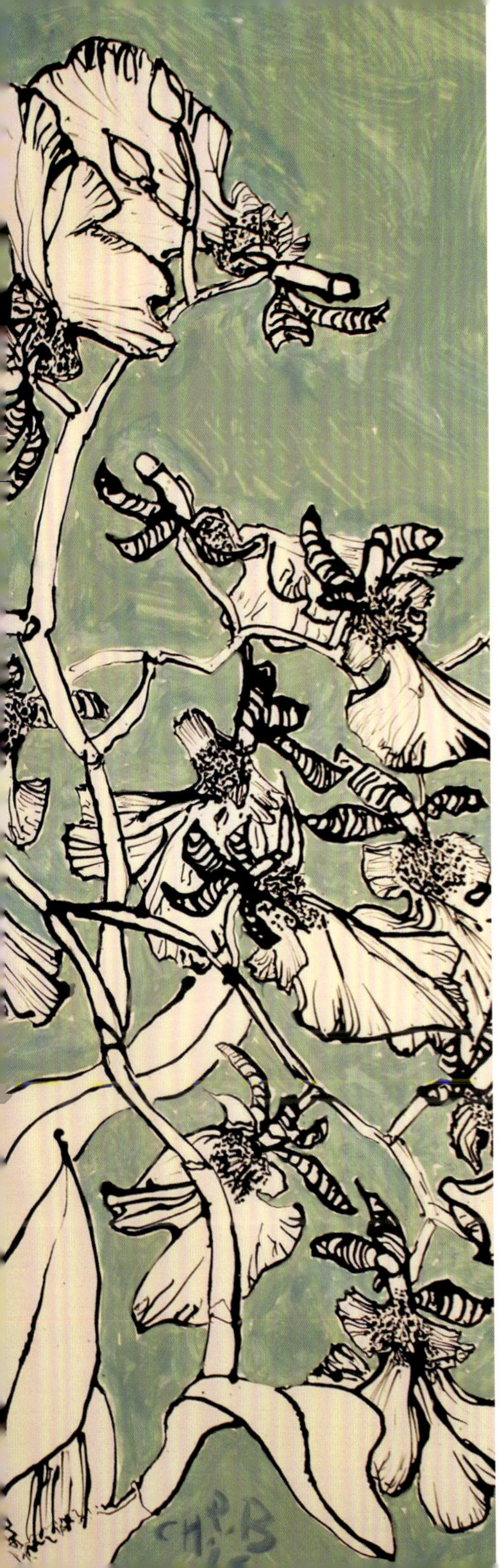

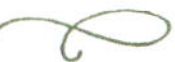

APPENDICES

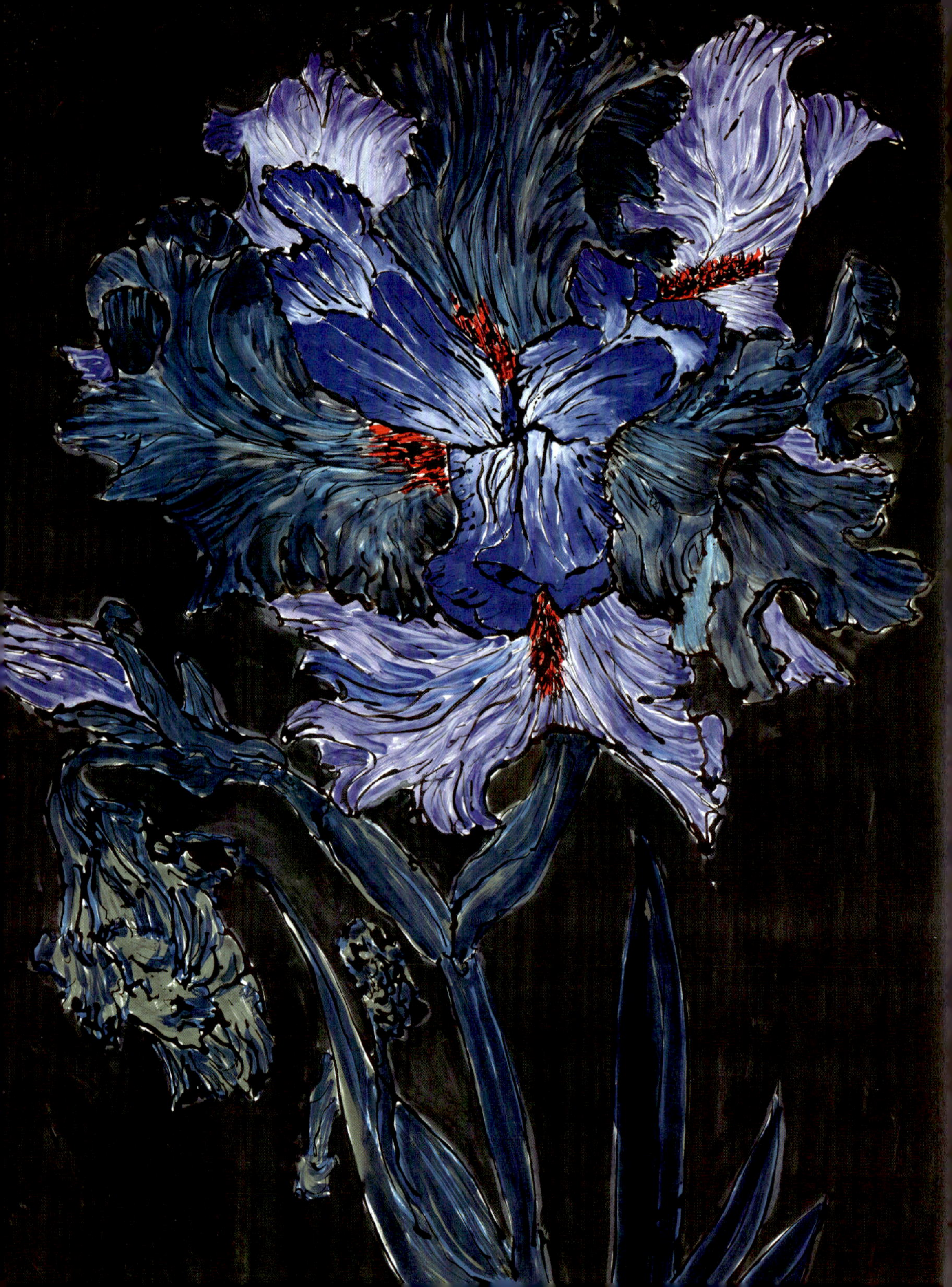

Foreword

Christian Peltenburg-Brechneff has been a dear friend of mine and my husband, John Rosselli, for 40 years. I knew of his large, beautiful landscapes, but when I first saw a pastel of an enormous hollyhock on a grey background, I gasped. I don't think I had ever seen a botanical drawing that was more exciting. The looseness of Christian's hand, his mastery of pastels, and his extraordinary color sense made me covet this picture. I have been a long-time gardener and thus a collector of prints, drawings, and paintings pertaining to the garden. But it is his subtle black ink drawings which are so modern and unusual that when John and I had shows for Christian at our shop, Treillage, they sold out.

What was always thrilling was to watch Christian paint in our own gardens. Whether they were in color or black and white ink, the gardens came alive on his paper. There was an electricity to his work. I sometimes felt that Vincent van Gogh was looking over his shoulder and waving approval. Christian would come for a visit and immediately peruse the garden, finding his spot to paint.

When in the Dominican Republic, Pablo, our house manager, would take us to the nursery on a quest for exotic orchids. Christian often stayed on after we had all returned home to paint in quiet, and I could not wait to see his interpretation of the gardens I had created. My gardens are my passion as they are Christian's, so to have him bring them to life in his unique way was thrilling. It was also always fun to talk of other gardens that I had not seen and books I had not read. Not only is he a gifted painter but an incredible friend. Over the years, Christian, Tim, John, and I have shared so many wonderful moments, many of them sitting in our gardens.

This book is filled with amazing paintings that take the reader from Connecticut to Greece, from New York to Sri Lanka, exploring some of the most exciting gardens created, and certainly through Christian's amazing eye, they have been given a new life. And with each flower drawing, one wonders if nature is a bit tame. This is a rare and special look at gardens around the world by a very talented artist . . . and friend.

Bunny Williams

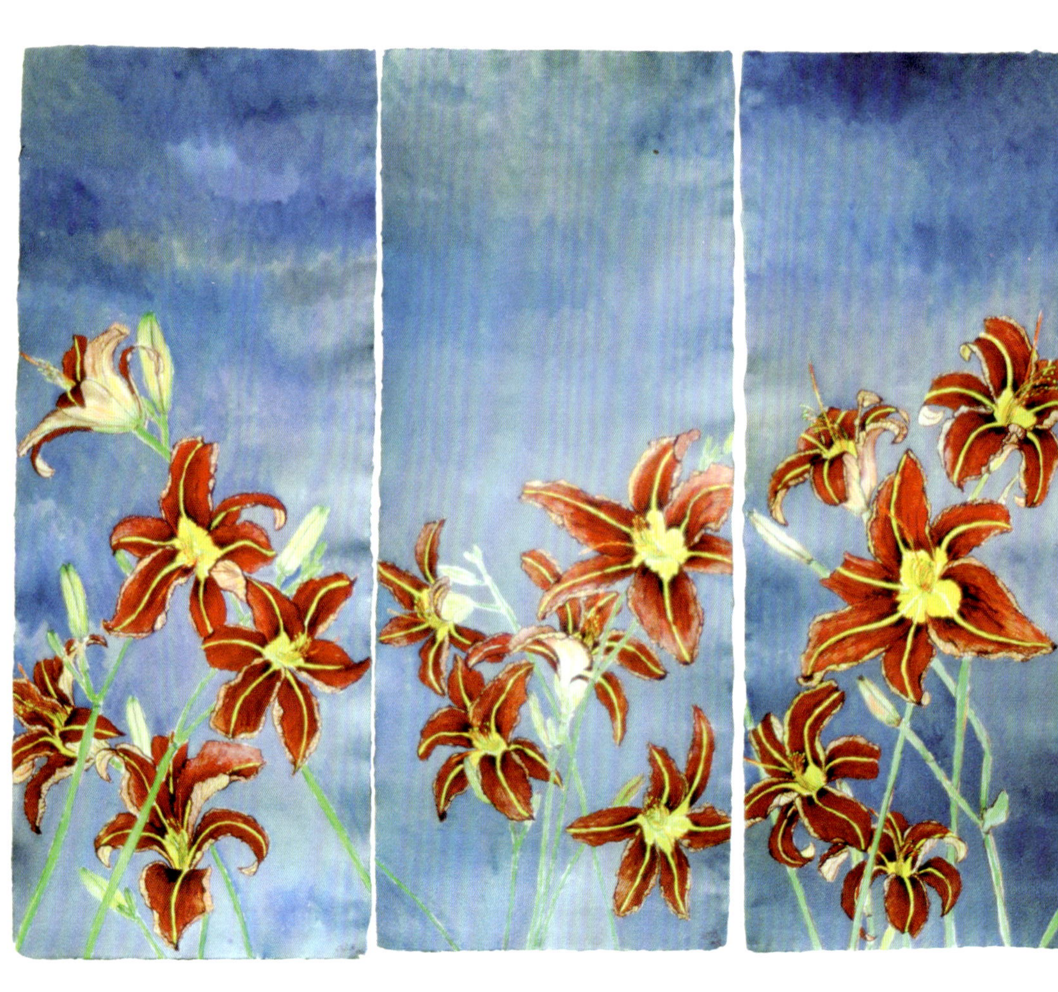

Introduction

When I was young, growing up in Basel, Switzerland, the only garden I really knew, ours, consisted of twelve wooden flower boxes on our apartment balcony that my mother filled every year with red and white geraniums—the Swiss colors.

My mother was very proud of her geraniums and with good reason as they seemed to be the fullest and lushest around and were much admired by our neighbors. I thought they were very pretty, but it was the largely neglected gardens of the mostly 19th-century uninhabited villas that surrounded our apartment block in an old-fashioned residential neighborhood called The Gellert, many of them about to be demolished to make room for more apartment blocks like ours, that left a profound impression on me. We children could play uninhibited in those magical gardens. I can still see them with their untrimmed boxwood bushes and hedges, lost winding paths lined with yew, a broken fountain hidden away here and there, a sculpture of a lady, or a lonely stone bench—a child's paradise. Wandering through them left me with a secret longing for half-ruined, almost wild gardens, and still today, Tim, my husband, and I would happily describe our garden as structured, yes, but with plenty of room for the wild.

In the early nineties, it was our own garden in the Connecticut River Valley that inspired me to do my first garden paintings, sitting right there in the middle of our new-found paradise in Hadlyme.

Our close friend, Mac Griswold, a well-known garden writer, saw the new work and invited me to come paint in the gardens at Sylvester Manor, where she was busy writing a history of the house and gardens, and my garden career was launched. I found I could sit there happily all day painting in this isolated, magical place surrounded by beauty, wonderful scents, butterflies, rabbits, and, truth to tell, the occasional snake. For me, it was, and is, a meditative experience.

Fortunately, other gardens began to open their gates to me so I could paint there, and I started getting commissions as well. After a year or two, I was invited to Sri Lanka by a collector friend who happened to be the Swiss ambassador there. I definitely enjoyed the little Swiss flag on the white Mercedes that picked me up at the airport in Colombo, but I loved the magic and lush world of Sri Lankan gardens and their aristocratic owners to whom the ambassador introduced me. I visited Sri Lanka three times to paint. Although he was a friend of the ambassador, getting permission from the world-famous architect Geoffrey Bawa to paint in his then very secret gardens at Lunuganga took quite a bit of diplomacy, and even when finally allowed to paint there, in spite of the many houses, guest cottages, and beds there, he wouldn't let me stay. Mr. Bawa only allowed me to nap there in the incredible afternoon heat in a room over the garage, a more stylish spot than it sounds because of his fabulous old Rolls Royce convertible that was parked below. It's probably the most beautiful place I have ever worked in. I was in heaven there, at least on the days his dog would not bite me.

With time Geoffrey began to be rather fond of my visits, inviting me to very long boozy lunches and dinners. Though they cut into my painting time there, I knew I was in the company of a great architect and landscape designer, and I was not about to complain. He also took me to see his then dying older brother Bevis with whom he had competed all his life over which of their neighboring gardens was the most beautiful. When I mentioned that I might like to paint Bevis's garden too—it was incredibly beautiful and full of visual jokes and whimsy—he said no way. I was "his."

These two strikingly handsome, seven-foot tall men barely talked to each other.

The heart of this book, I am sure, is probably Lunuganga and the other Sri Lankan gardens. They gave me the confidence to just go and "do it" in spite of the incredible heat and humidity, the daily rains and blazing sun, and all the other obstacles a painter experiences working outdoors—like whole families of chattering monkeys leaping from branch to branch above me, defecating on my paintings or actually throwing their stools at me.

Several visits to Mexico followed thanks to an introduction by a sculptor friend of mine to a grand marquess whose garden in Mexico City, in San Ángel, had been photographed for *Vogue* magazine and who was selling the property and commissioned me to paint there. The three pictures I did in her garden became her favorite Christmas card, and she also invited me to paint her walled gardens in Cuernavaca, a truly unforgettable experience. When we were not out in the club there drinking and dining, we would be sipping tequila in her garden with her telling me all about her remarkable life. When she died a few years later, Tim and I thought of changing our lives completely and buying her house, but we soon realized she had been the magic there and that, without her, the place seemed somehow walled in and sad.

Reached from a bridge high above a canal to a tower across the way, the gardens of the Palazzo Albrizzi in Venice, designed by the late Bruce Kelly for our friend Alessandro, was a treat for me to paint in even though Venice is not famous for its gardens and the skittering rats were a nuisance. Casetta Rossa was comparatively modest but had an amazing location next to the Accademia Bridge on the Grand Canal and was full of charm. Staying there was always a wonderful Venetian experience.

I often wish I had painted more in Italy, but there were so many American gardens that were there for me to paint. My dear friends Bunny Williams and John Rosselli created a paradise by the sea in Punta Cana in the Dominican Republic and another in northwestern Connecticut, and our friendship of many years allowed me to follow the growth of those two gardens over a long period of time.

Not only are Bunny and John's talents and hospitality legendary, but the beauty of those places is truly overwhelming, and I was fortunate to be able to be part of their magical world and paint in both places again and again.

Another highlight painting in America was working at "Woodyhouse" on Long Island. I was lucky enough to visit there often since the early eighties and was able to work there as well more recently. Sitting there in these amazing garden room follies full of butterflies, the constant breeze from the Atlantic keeping me cool, and having my kind hostess offering stimulating company and delicious food made working there in that dune garden totally magical.

I have never become tired of garden paintings, but somehow the large scale flower drawings and paintings have begun to take over. They seem to be an unconscious extension of my very detailed and tiny garden work. I enjoy working on them at home in my Connecticut studio, using flowers from the garden and tropicals I buy at the nursery.

Odile's wonderful house and garden on top of Pic Paradis in St. Martin, where we get to stay during winters or did until a hurricane two years ago nearly destroyed her garden and much of the rest of the island, has inspired me to produce my first large scale pastel flowers and my most recent and boldest impressions from a tropical garden. I cannot wait to return there.

The research for this book took me back to memories of the late eighties and early nineties, to all those wonderful places I have had the privilege to work in. Looking through these pages, I am humbled and grateful to have had the eyes, patience, energy, and the gift to paint the beauty of nature we take so often for granted. And I realize how lucky I have been to be able to watch our own garden here in Hadlyme grow, to feel its magic, listen to its sounds, and still be painting there in the garden almost 30 years later.

Christian Peltenburg-Brechneff

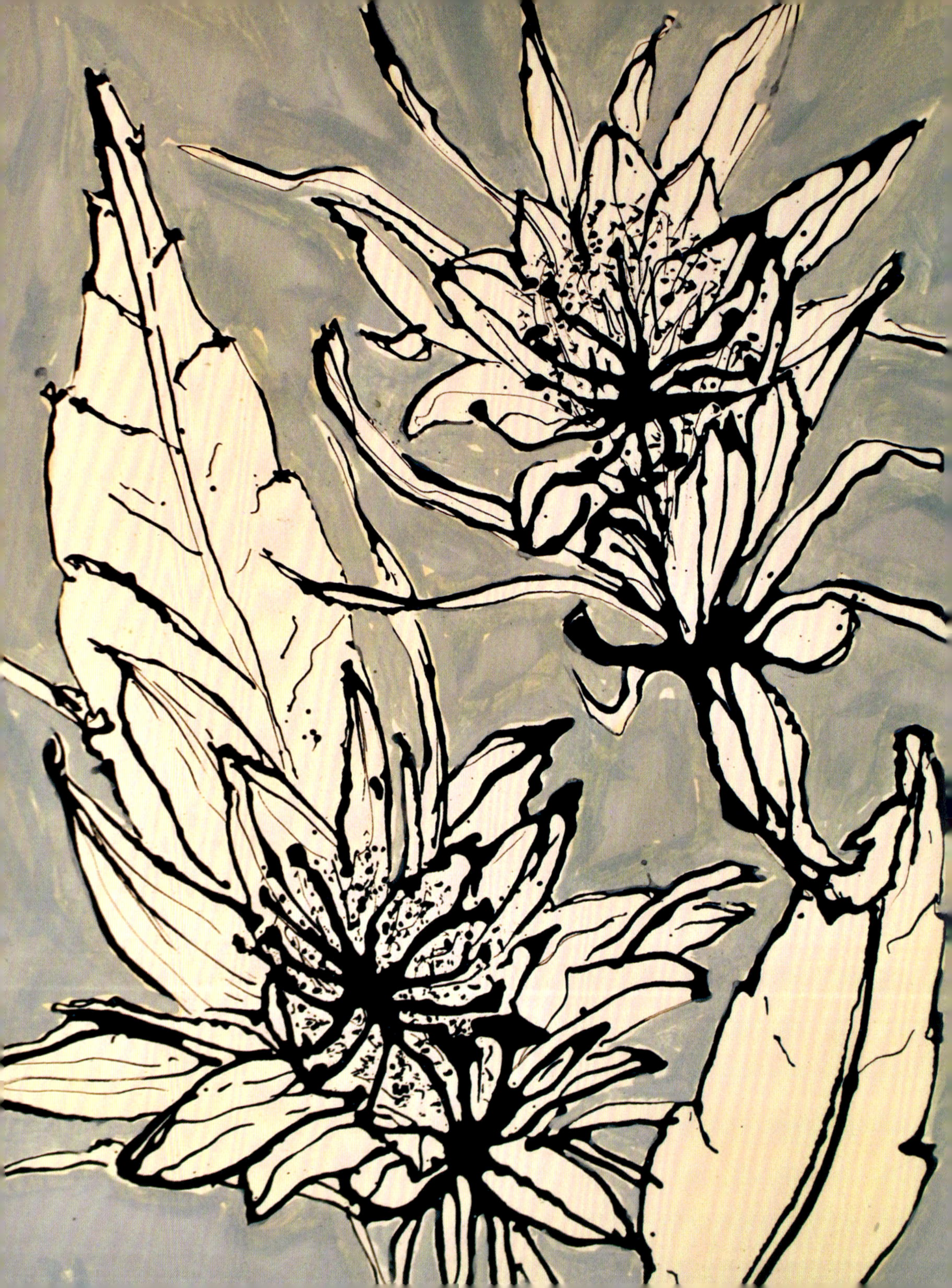

An Abundance of Beauty

"Learn to fathom what a flower infers."
—Rainer Maria Rilke

As though on a pilgrimage, not unlike that of the hero in John Bunyan's *Pilgrim's Progress*—he also was named Christian and in search of salvation, in our modern Christian's case through beauty—Peltenburg-Brechneff has made his way, with daring determination and obsessive eagerness, to various gardens, each a sort of sacred place, a space apart from the ugliness of the profane world. He has drawn and painted the lush gardens of Sri Lanka three times, a secret garden in Lunuganga—probably the most beautiful place he ever worked in, he says—as well as a garden in Mexico City, the garden of the Palazzo Albrizzi in Venice, a garden in Punta Cana in the Dominican Republic, a garden on the island of St. Martin, and a less remote garden in northwestern Connecticut. Christian and Tim's garden is in Lyme, Connecticut. All of them have been carefully designed by such masters as Geoffrey Bawa, Bruce Kelly, Bunny Williams, and John Rosselli—all major artists in their own right. Such gardens may have been commissioned by aristocrats, as Christian tells us in his preface, and it may be the privilege of aristocrats to have such sanctuaries from the world—the garden traditionally is a *hortus conclusus*—but, more to the point, they are edifying places, places not only of repose and self-restoration but of aesthetic transcendence, the beauty that blesses the self with its presence. And, strange as it may seem to say so, I suggest that opening their private gardens to the public by way of Christian's art is their owners' way of saying that the garden is a model for a harmonious society, for it is a harmonious gathering of different flowers. Society is conveyed by the architectural elements in many of Christian's works, but they are subsumed by the flowers, harmoniously together for all their differences—their individuality, paradoxically more evident, indeed emphatic the more they are integrated in the totality of the garden.

While Christian's garden pictures trace the changing dialectic of part and whole, his flower pictures are studies in individuality—sort of character portraits. His flowers are often grandly monumentalized, as though to immortalize them. While "a thing of beauty may be a joy forever," as Keats famously wrote, many of Christian's beautiful flowers seem to be seen as though through a glass darkly as his colorless flowers suggest. They may have a wild beauty—an expressionistic exuberance, suggestive of Sturm und Drang as well as *joie de vivre*, terror and suffering as well as ecstatic happiness—but they have a melancholy aura. *Into the Garden* opens with a display of five such singular, oddly manic, subliminally depressing flowers, for their radiantly white petals have black edges, limiting and containing their growth, suggesting that they are close to death, fated to die. However libidinously alive, the death instinct informs them—gives them a morbid edginess, an insidious intensity.

These five flowers are followed by an equally majestic seventh flower, more astonishing—eye-catching—and glorious by reason of its royal blue petals, marked with vein-like luminous striations, suggesting that it is illuminated from within, and its luridly red stigma and style. At its base is the ovary: "The biological function of a flower is to effect reproduction, usually by providing a mechanism for the union of sperm with eggs." Flower sperm—male gametophytes—are contained in the pollen grains produced by the stamen, and the eggs—female gametophytes—are contained in the ovules produced by the carpels. Flowers are "perfect," as botanists say, meaning they are bisexual or hermaphroditic, and thus, in a sense, self-sufficient. A flower may be a symbol of a vagina, as Georgia O'Keeffe's flowers have been said to be, but they are also phallic symbols, if one wants to separate what are biologically inseparable and complementary.

I suggest, perhaps absurdly, that the seventh image shows a self-fertilizing flower—and thus a symbol of what psychoanalysts call the "primary creativity" with which every individual is born—in orgasmic ecstasy. The darkness that surrounds it conveys the melancholy—let down—that Aristotle said follows sexual satisfaction. The flower is fraught with erotic meaning, which is one reason it is creatively inspiring—it is Christian's muse, that is, the mother of his art, and as such the first and lasting object of his love, as he implies by beginning his foreword with an account of his mother and her care for her geraniums, emulated by Christian, who mothers flowers with his art. More broadly, the flower is a symbol of elemental feelings—thus red roses are a symbol of love, beauty, and passion, lilies signify life and resurrection, daisies symbolize innocence, poppies convey consolation—suggesting that Christian's heart-felt flowers indicate his profound romanticism. His gardens are romantic places, places made for love, which is life-giving and inspiring.

They are more abstract than they appear at first exciting glance. Pages 138-139 are exemplary: the staircase is an inorganic man-made geometrical construction, the tree that triumphantly breaks through it conveys the inexhaustible power and innate expressivity of organic nature. The architecture on pages 162 through 165 dominates the natural growths, including the diminutive birds that seem humbled by the space, incidental to it yet subtly functioning as repoussoir devices emphasizing its grandeur, but their presence suggests that the space is not barren and sterile. It is a heavenly womb, as the grand arches that contain and surmount it suggest. Human beings are not present in Christian's gardens, except in the surrogate and idealized form of statues, as on pages 190, 191, 194, and 195 show. Animals are at home in it, as the cow on page 133 and the birds on pages 154 and 155 show. As the bust of Pan, the ancient god of the wilderness, on page 133 suggests, the garden is wilderness tamed, that is, made into art. In antiquity Pan's presence caused sexual panic—he was forever pursuing nymphs and often in the company of Dionysus—but civilized by art he remains peacefully in place in Christian's garden. Nonetheless, his presence there suggests that flowers are intoxicating. Perhaps the key to the book is the oscillation between standalone flowers, Apollonian in import, and Dionysian gardens, to play on Nietzsche's distinction, bringing with it the distinction between Apollonian sculpture—for Christian's flowers have a three-dimensional presence, swirling in space as they tend to do, to convey the whorl that is the arabesque-like character of the flower—and the Dionysian painting of his garden works. One might say that Apollonian flowers grow in his Dionysian garden. The one stands out of the many that produced it.

Each and every one of the works in Christian's garden book is a masterwork of its kind. His flowers more than hold their own in the grand tradition of flower painting traceable from Ambrosius Bosschaert's *Still Life with Flowers* (1641) through Emil Nolde's *Peonies and Irises* (1936) with many masterpieces in between. More particularly, I suggest that what began with Monet's impressionistic gardens—the garden as an atmospheric field painting, in which particular growths all but dissolve in the Heracleitean flow of the paint—climaxes in Christian's expressionistic gardens, paintings in which the patchwork of flowers form a kind of color field painting, abstract whatever it represents. To my eye the dazzling luminous yellow flowers on pages 192-193 are more than a match for Van Gogh's sunflowers—certainly hold their aesthetic own. They have an even greater confrontational integrity, for they spread across the entire canvas, filling the space to bursting, overrunning its edges and breaking through the picture plane into our space. Many of Christian's works have a similar "explosive"—and exploratory—character: the restless images on pages 168 and 169 seem eager to break the bounds of the picture.

Christian's gardens seem to expand infinitely, suggesting they are more English type landscape gardens than French type formal gardens—gardens that suggest the irrational character of nature in contrast to gardens that bring it under control, that is, "rationalize" it. More broadly, as landscape paintings—the designers of the gardens are landscape architects—they remind us that landscapes remain "a resurrection, the Easter of the eyes," as the Goncourt Brothers wrote in 1855, all the more necessary now as it becomes clearer and clearer that "eternal mother (nature)" is "condemned to death," as they presciently realized. Thus the therapeutic value of contemplative absorption in nature, with Christian's flower and garden art leading us into it. The larger issue—a core aesthetic issue—raised by Christian's art is whether the natural beauty of nature and the man-made beauty of art can converge. To my eye, they seem to in his flower and garden paintings.

Donald Kuspit

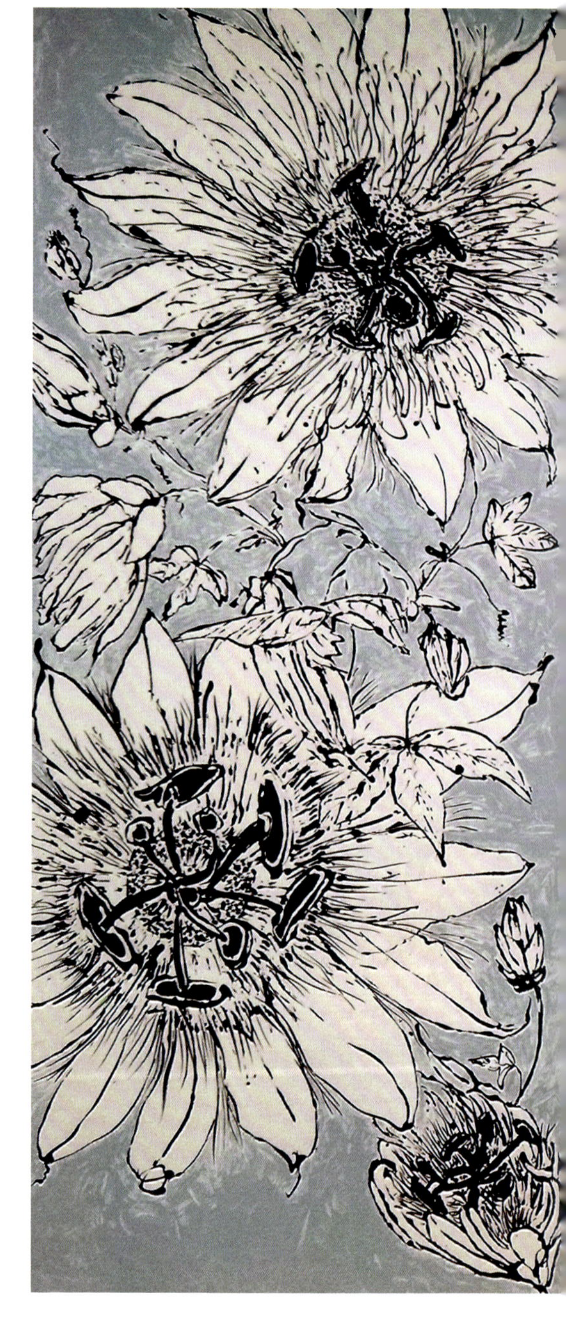

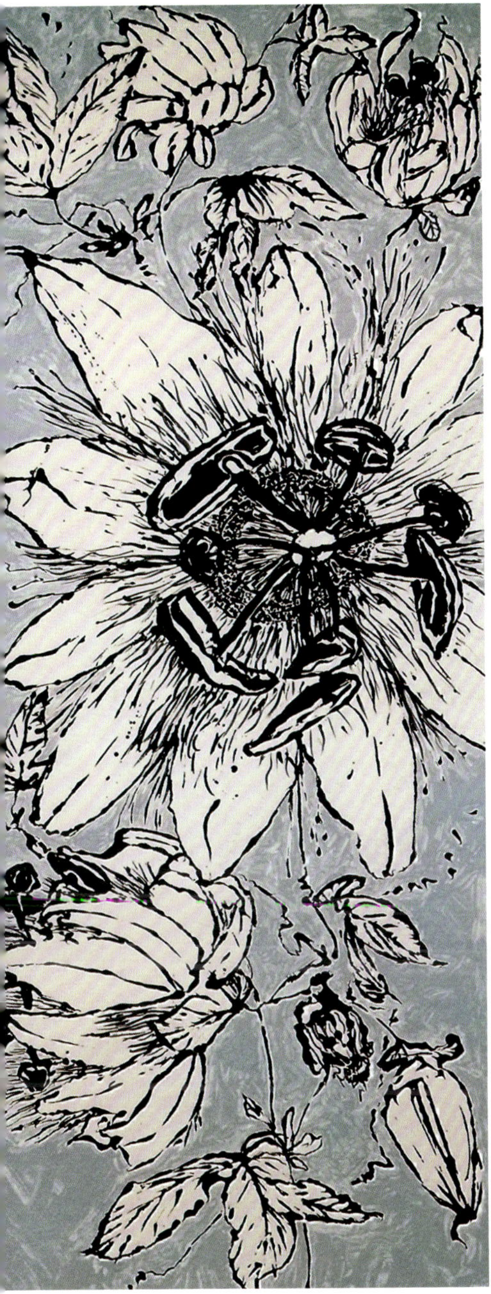

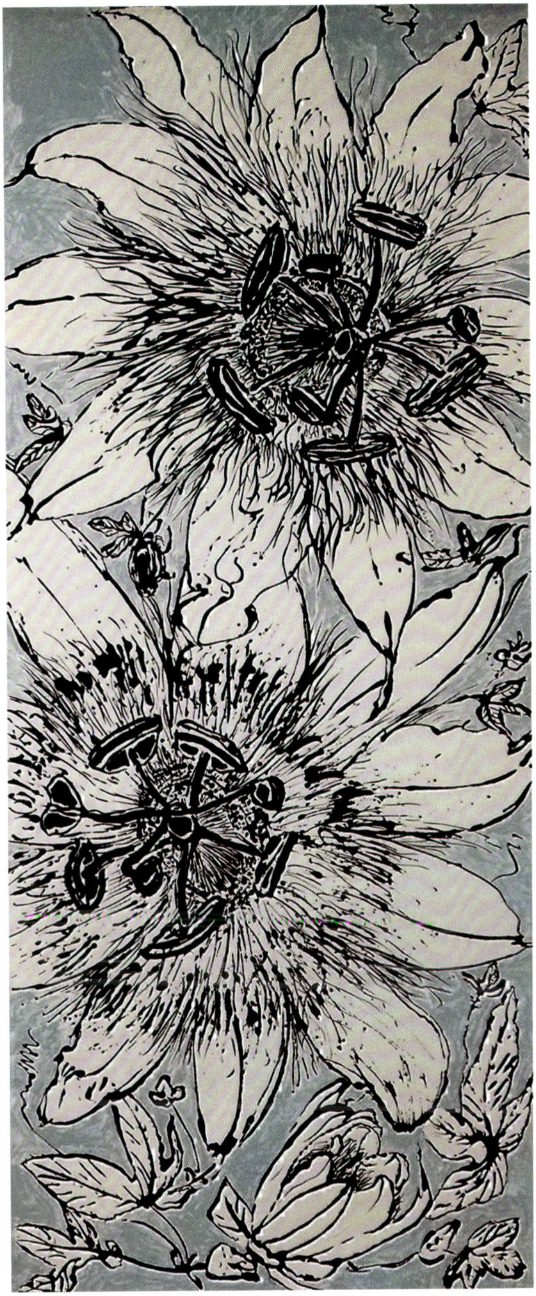

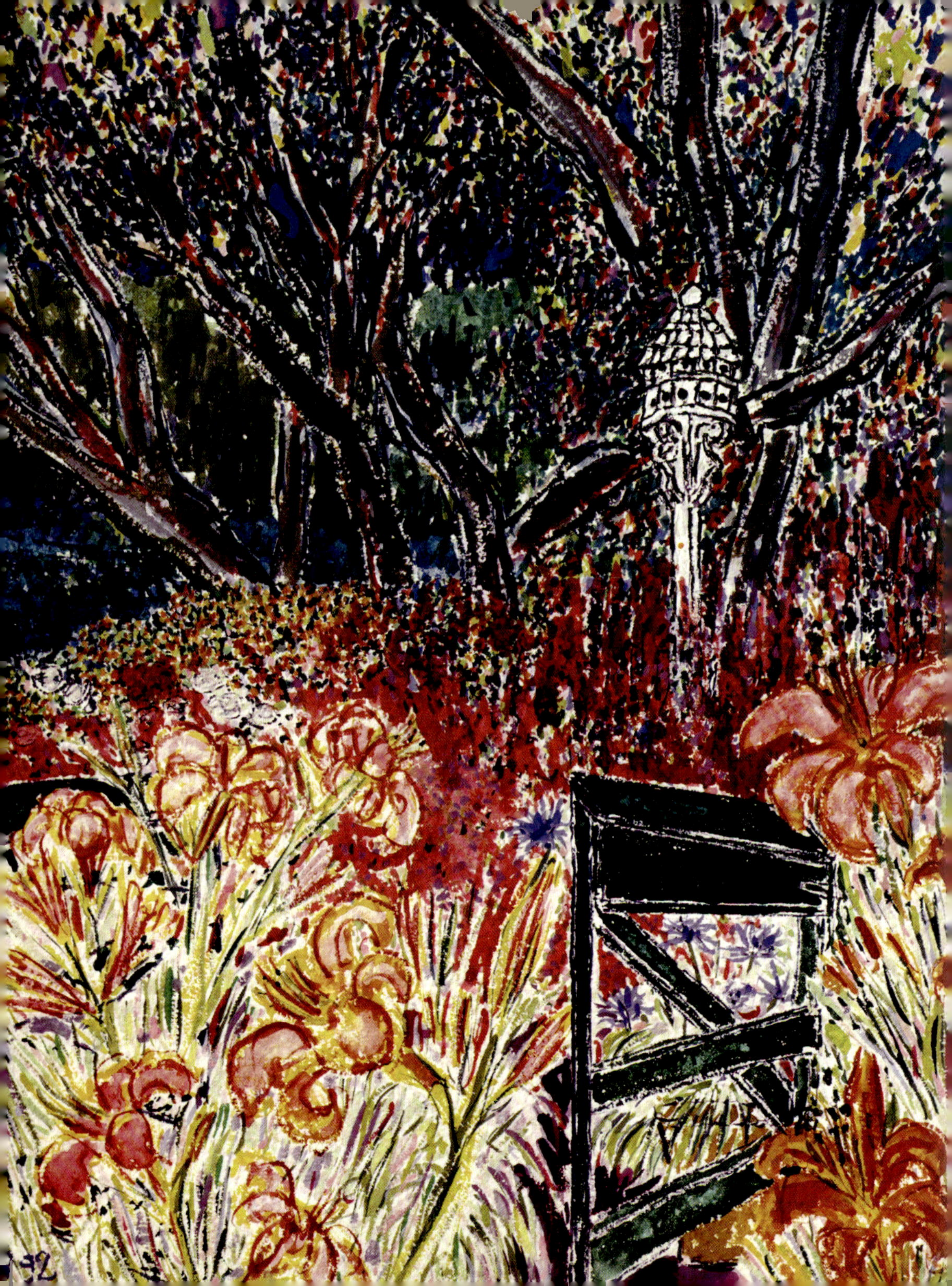
92

Tim and Christian's Garden

Hadlyme, Connecticut

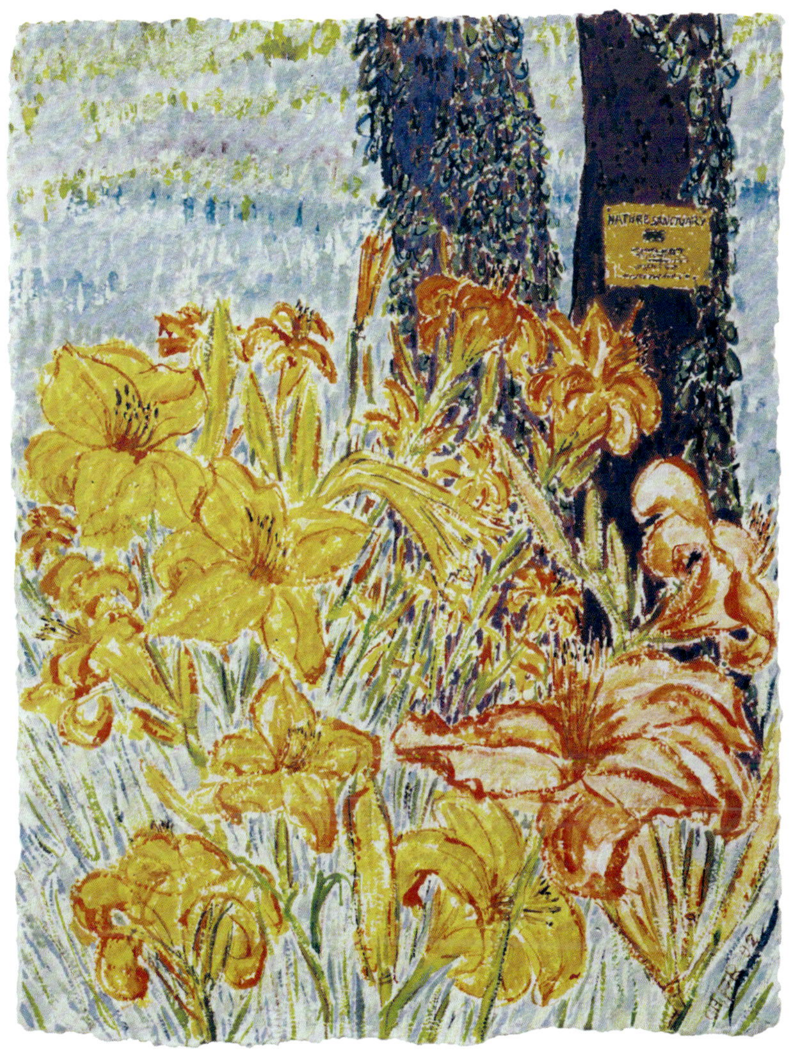

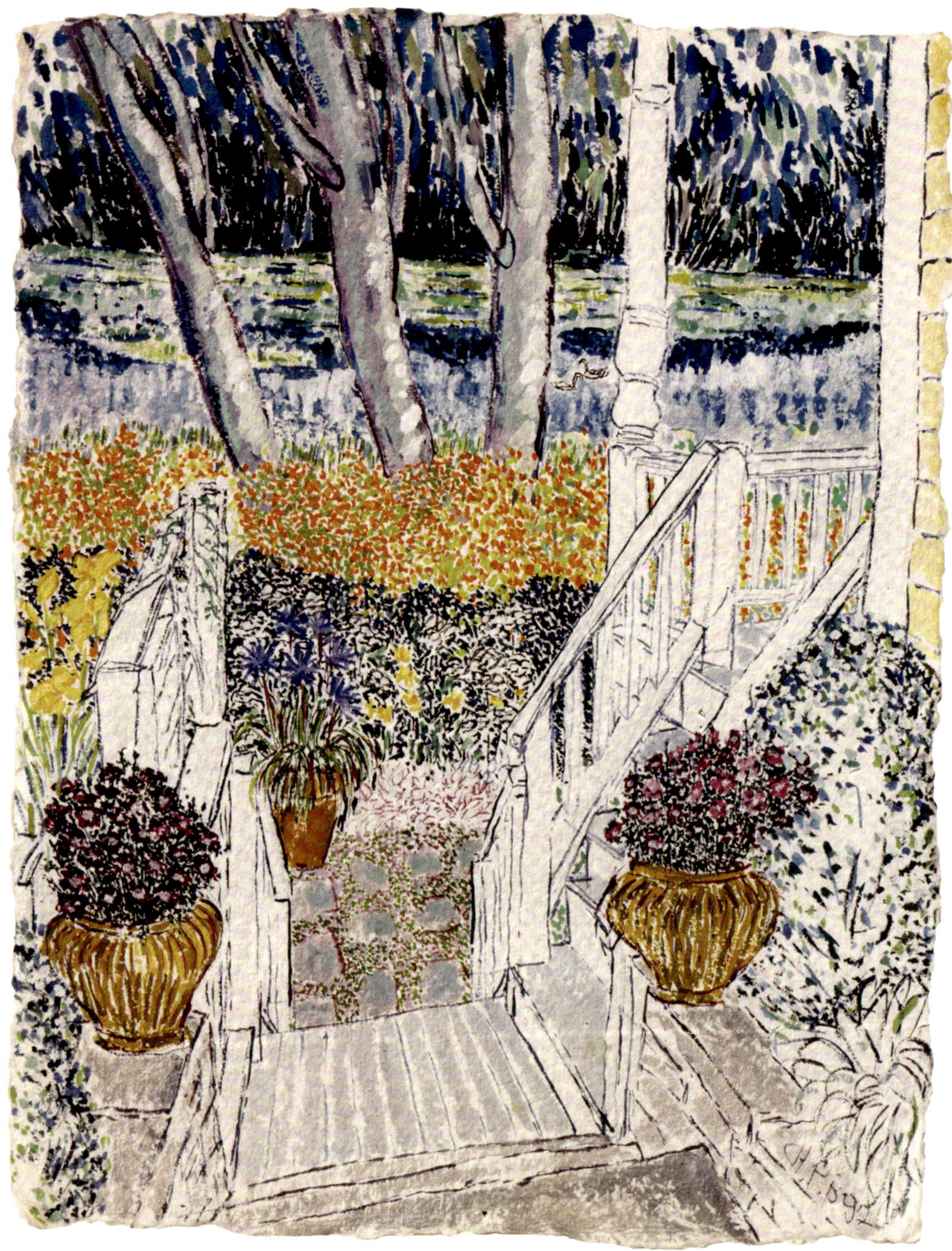

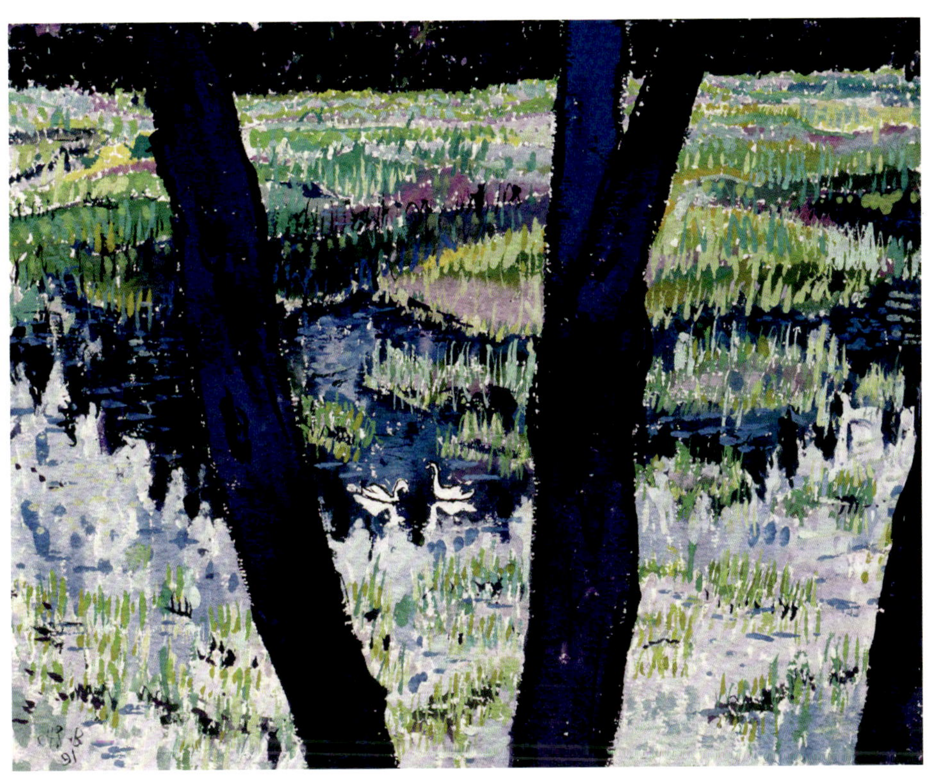

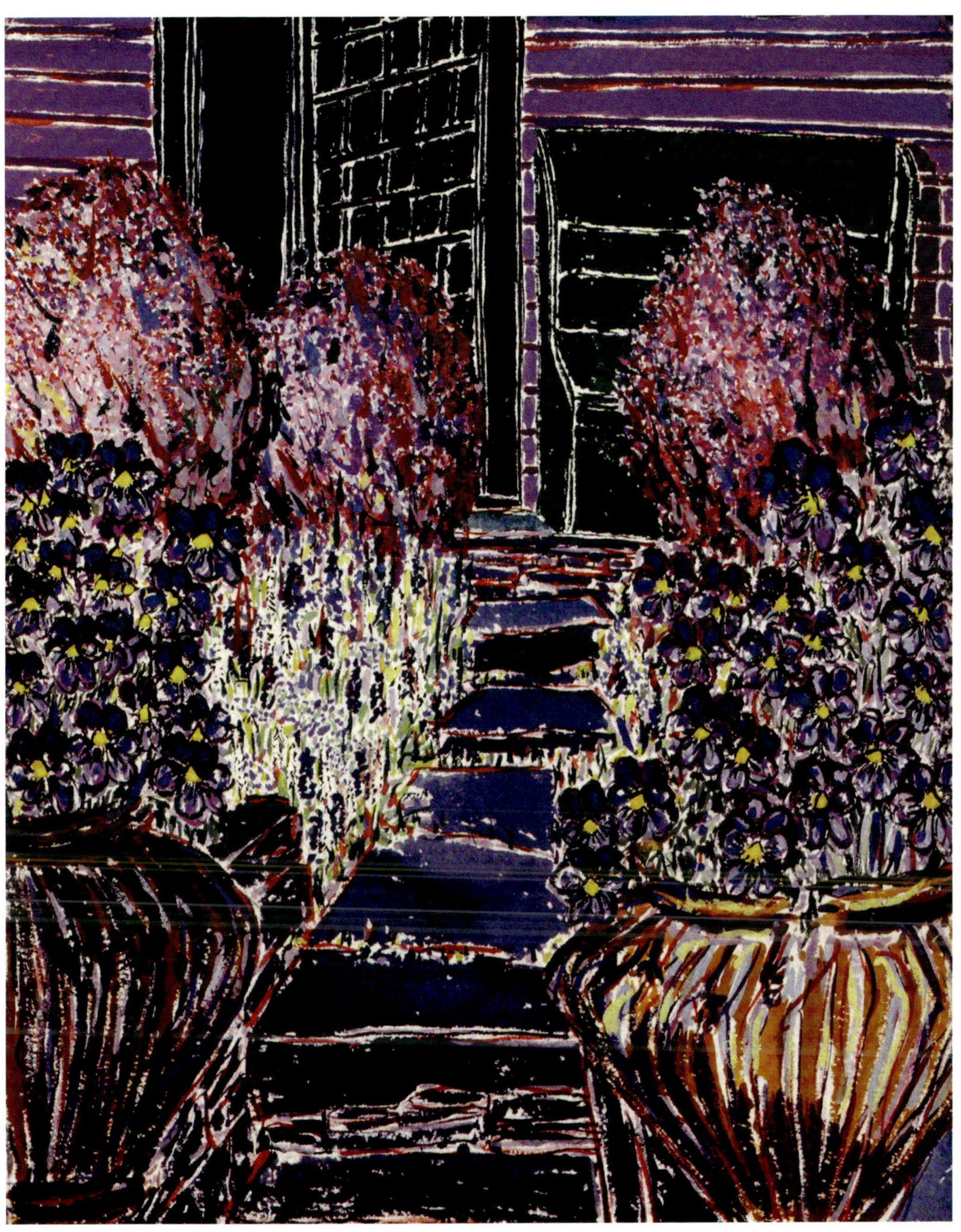

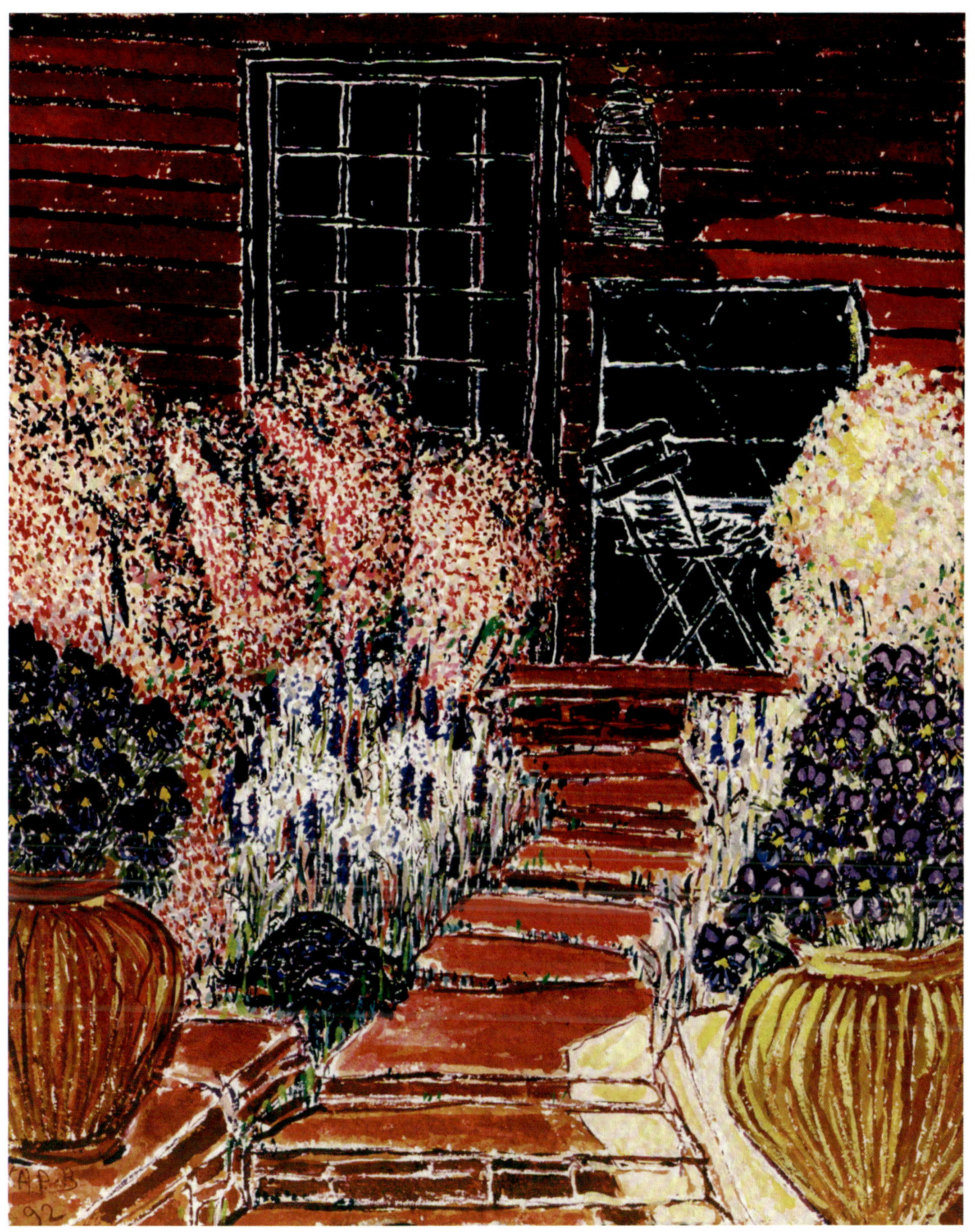

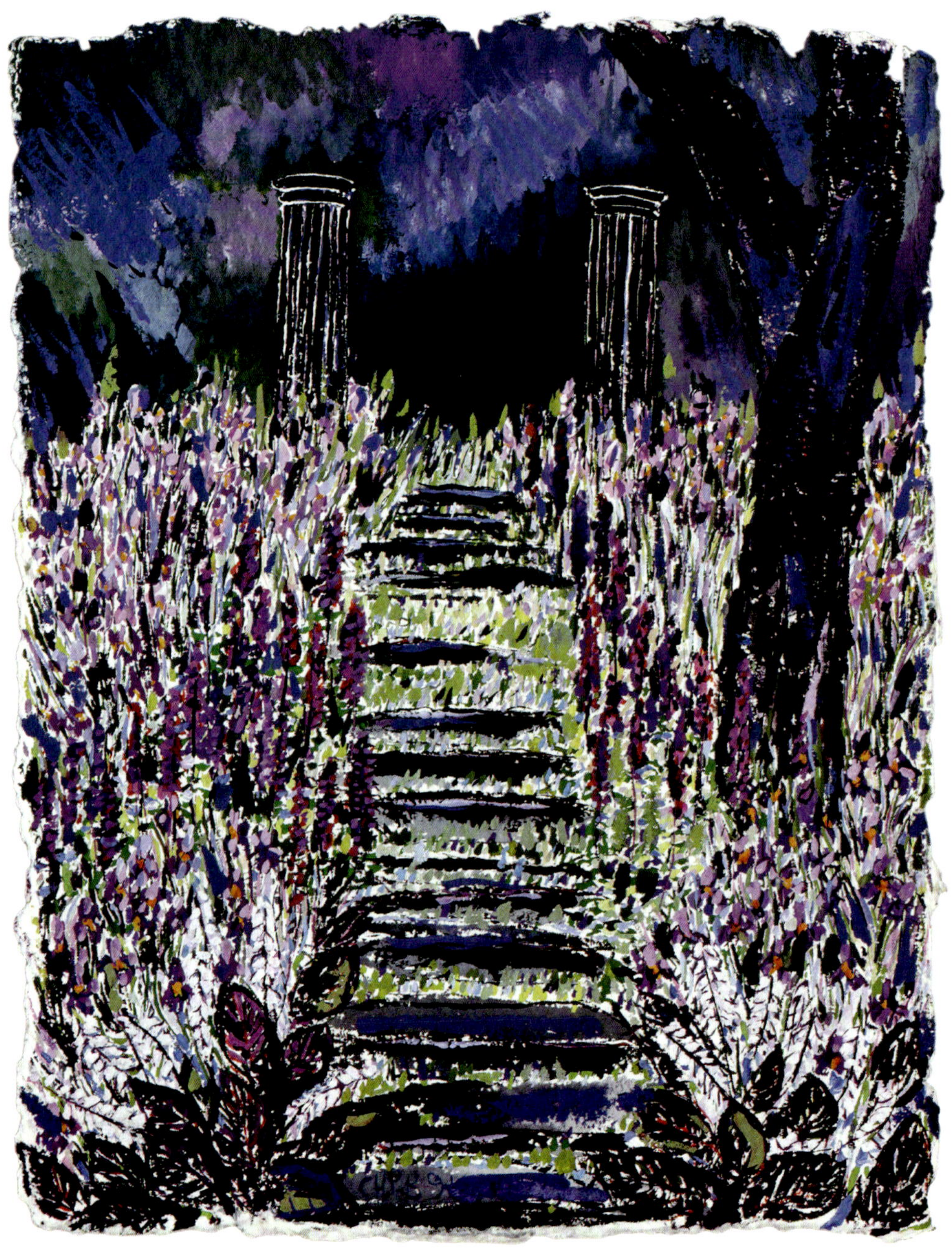

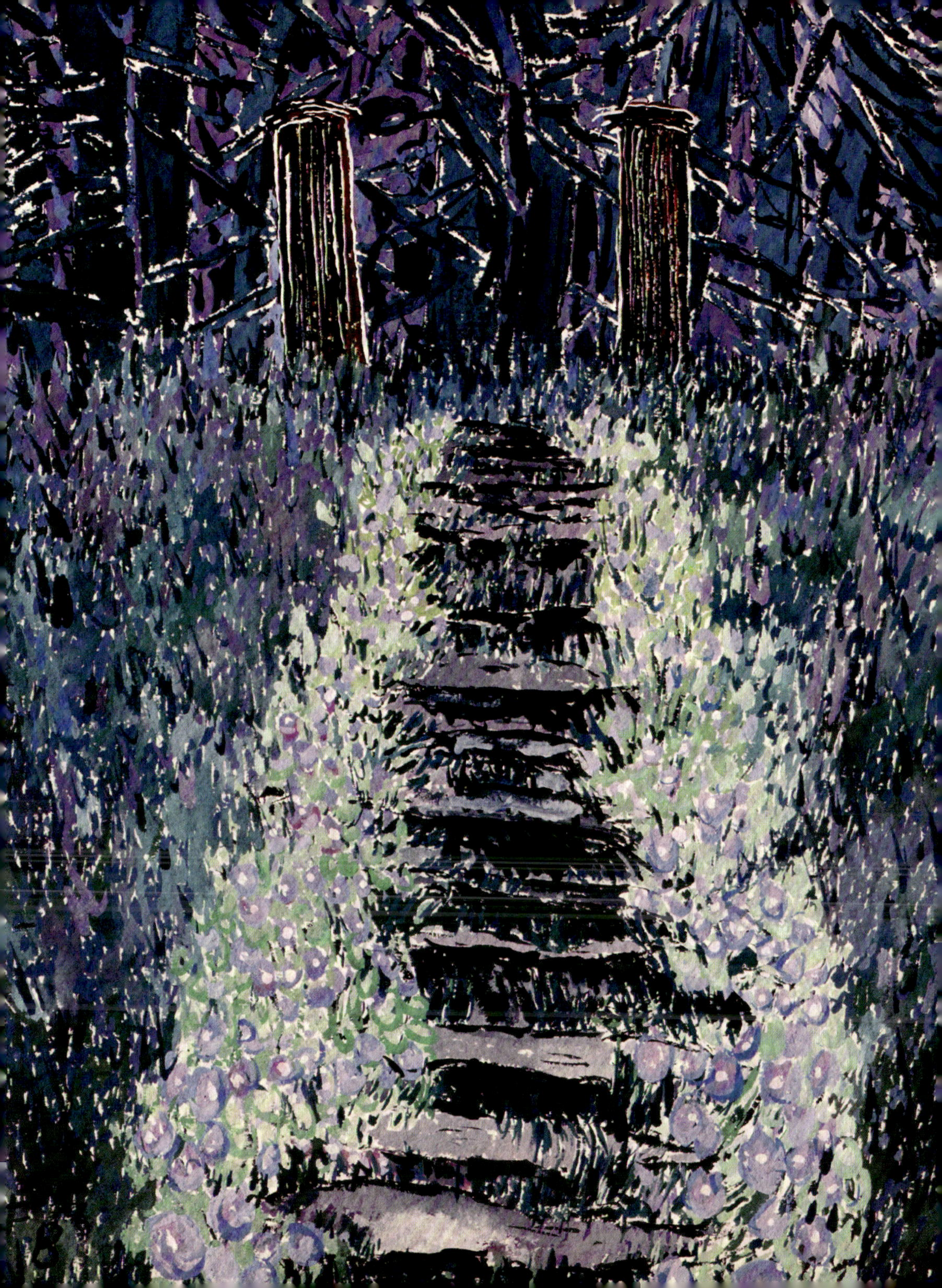

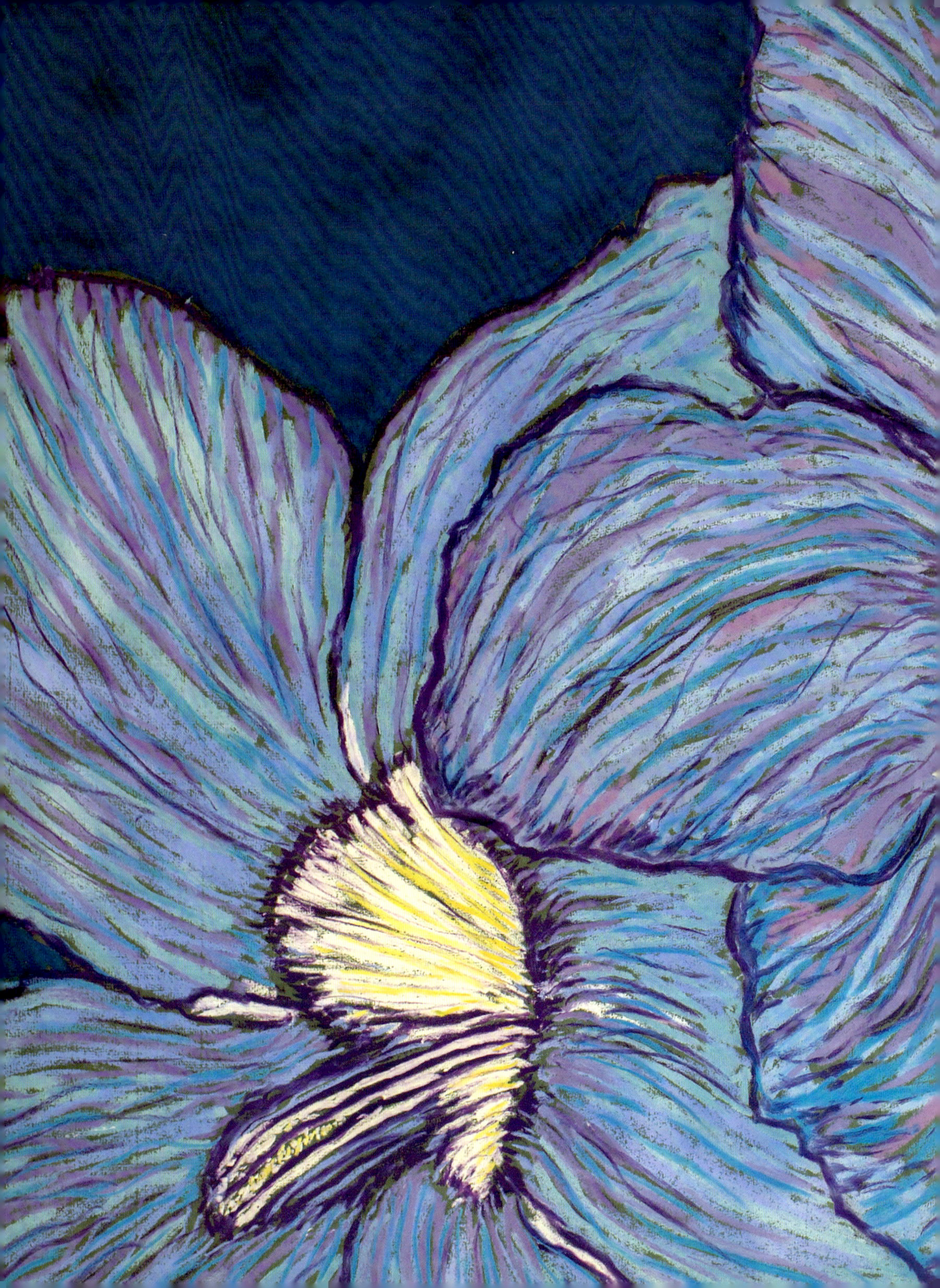

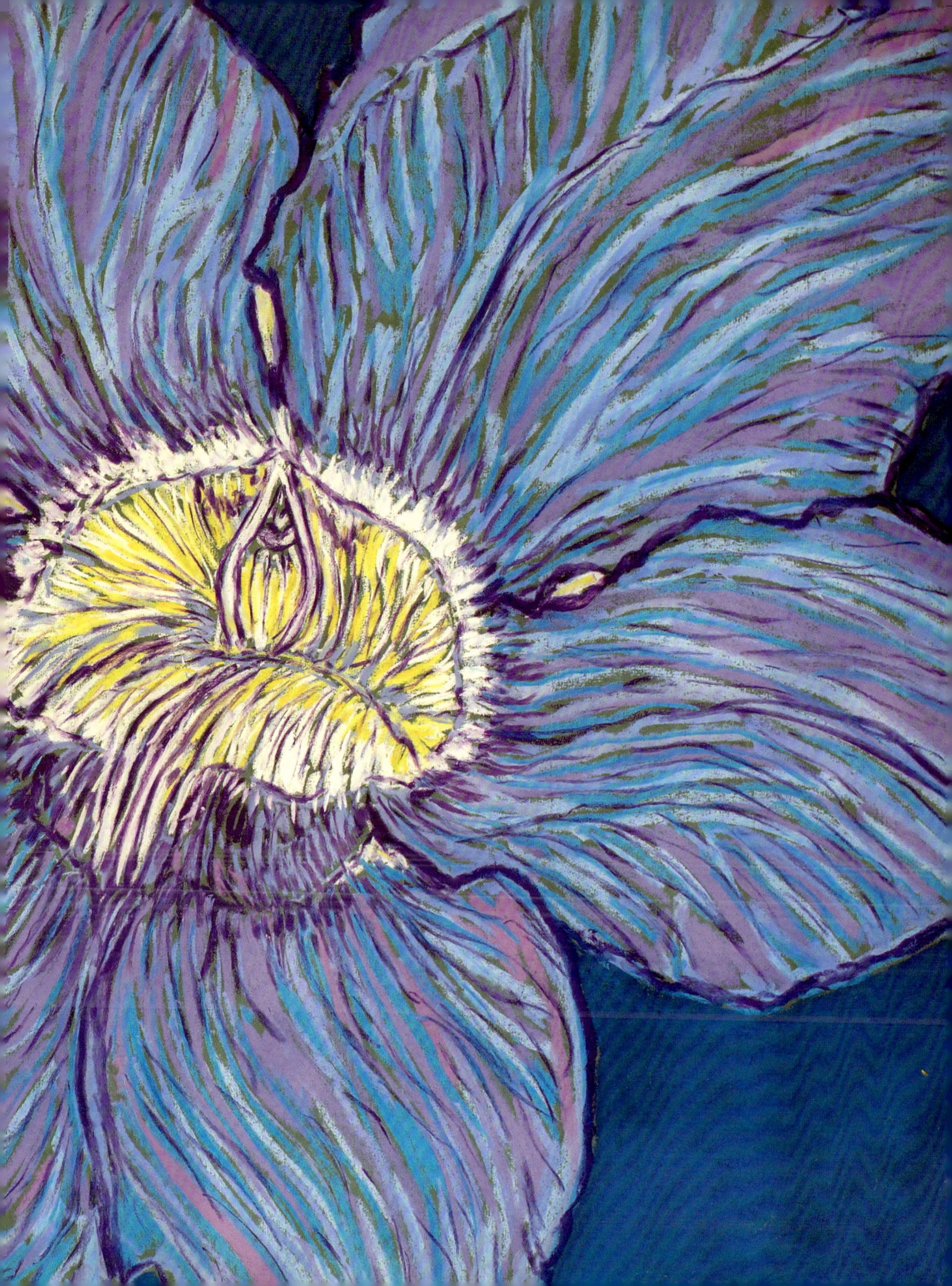

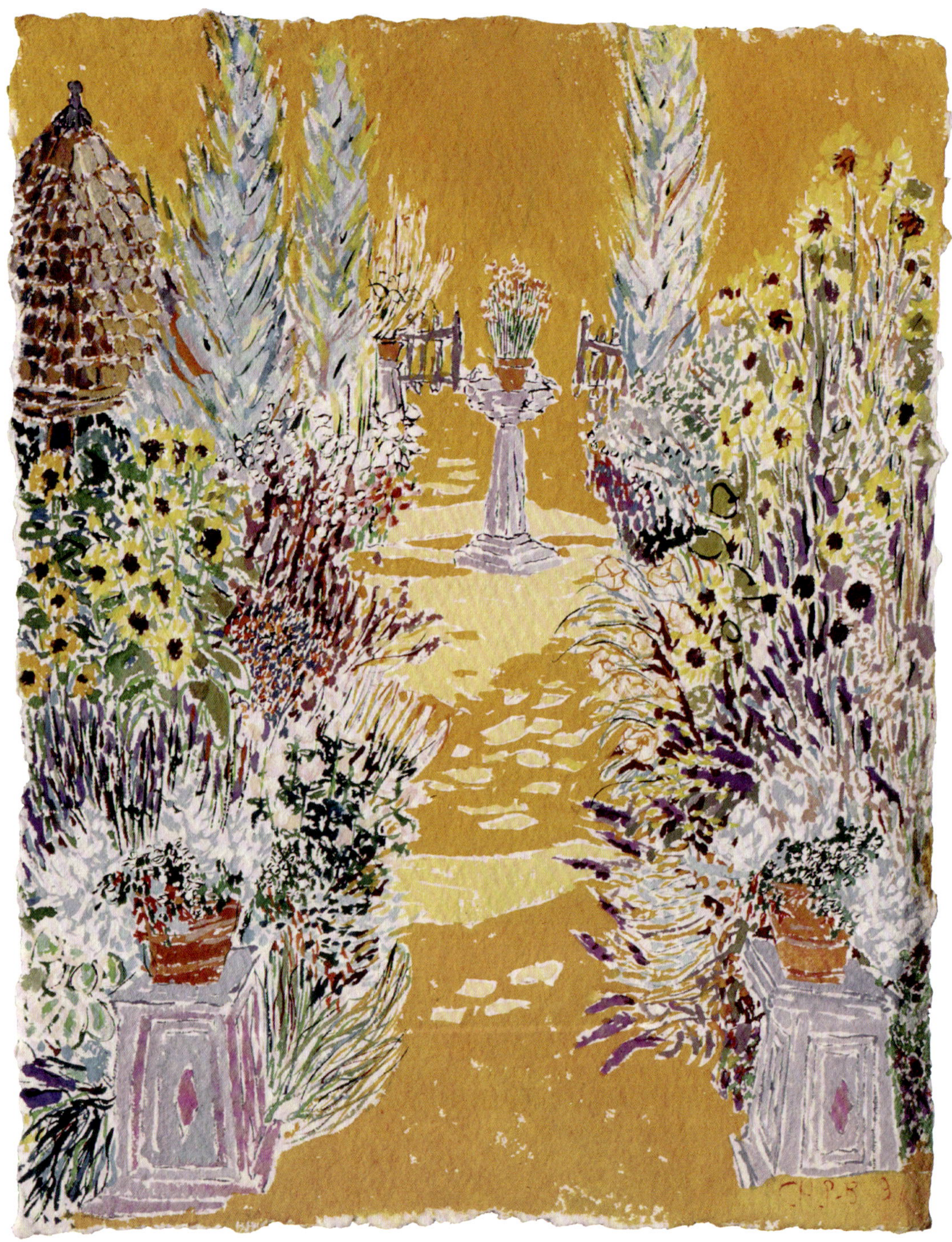

Peter's Garden

Roxbury, Connecticut

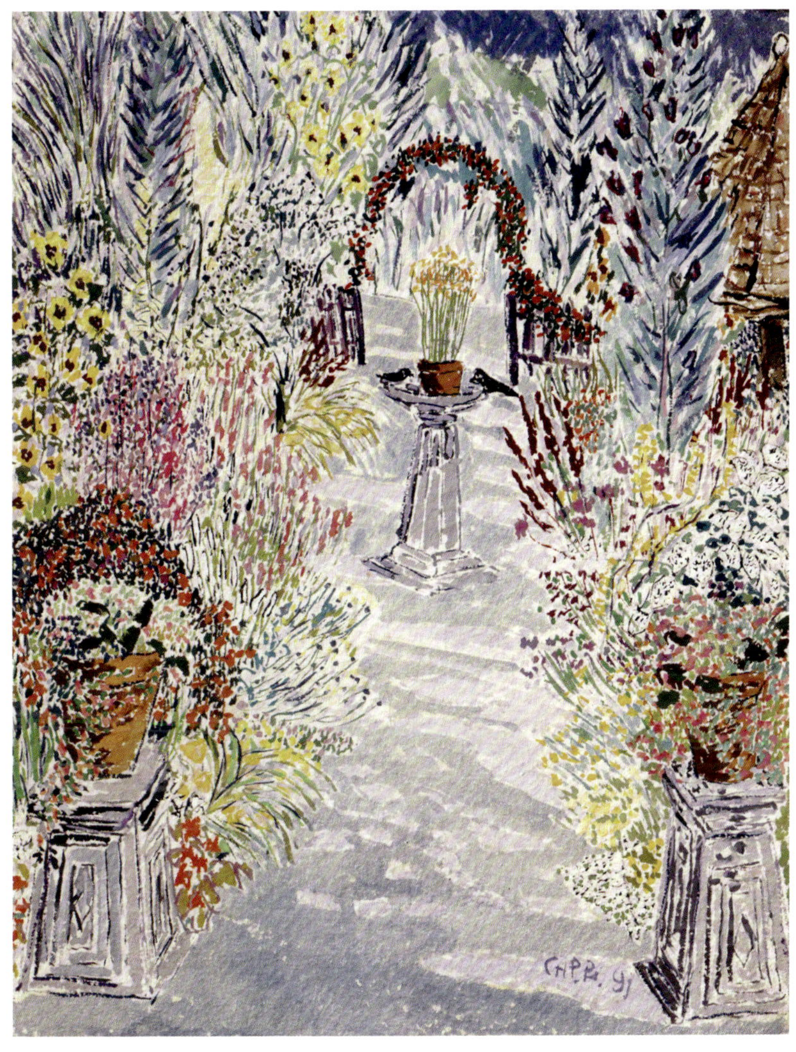

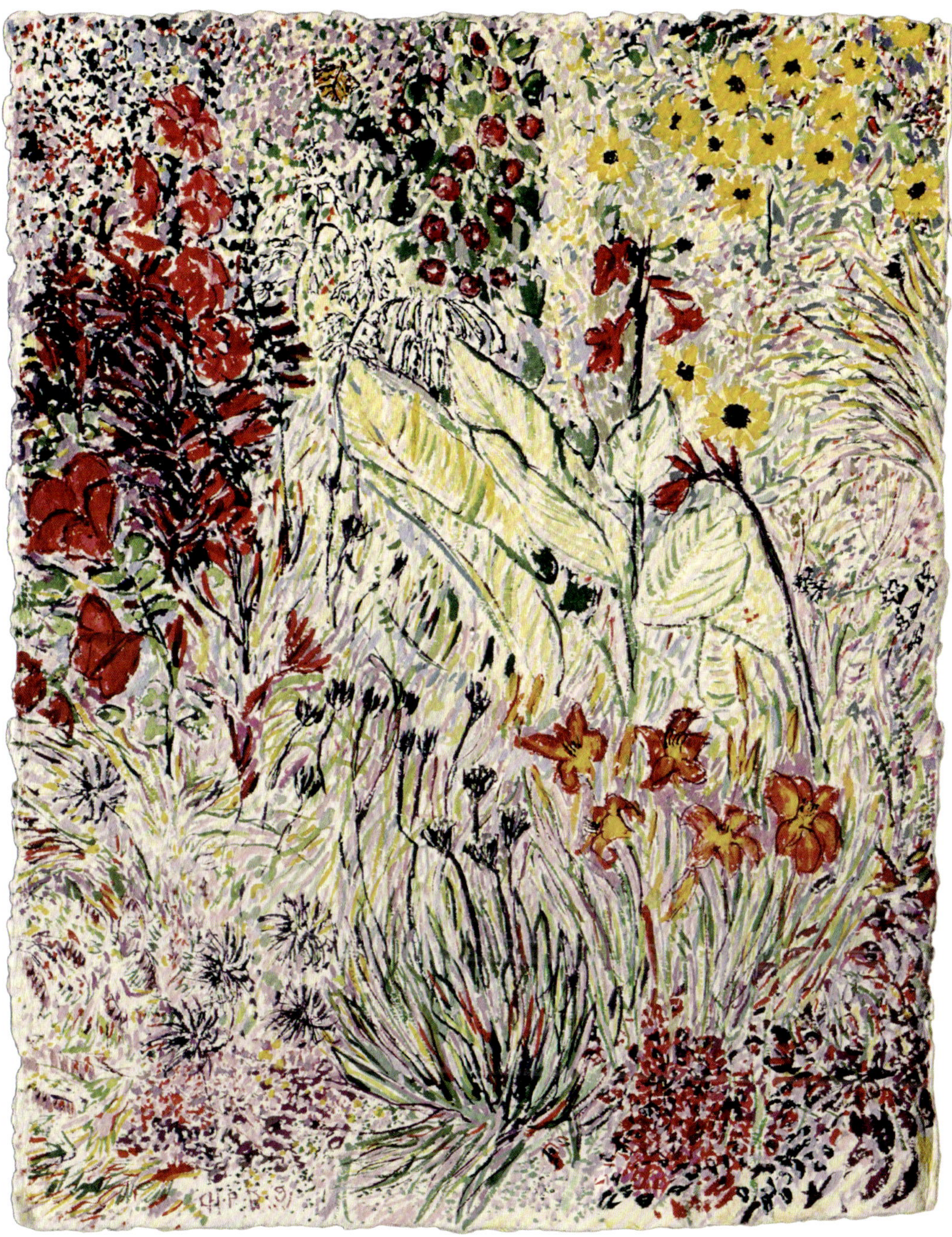

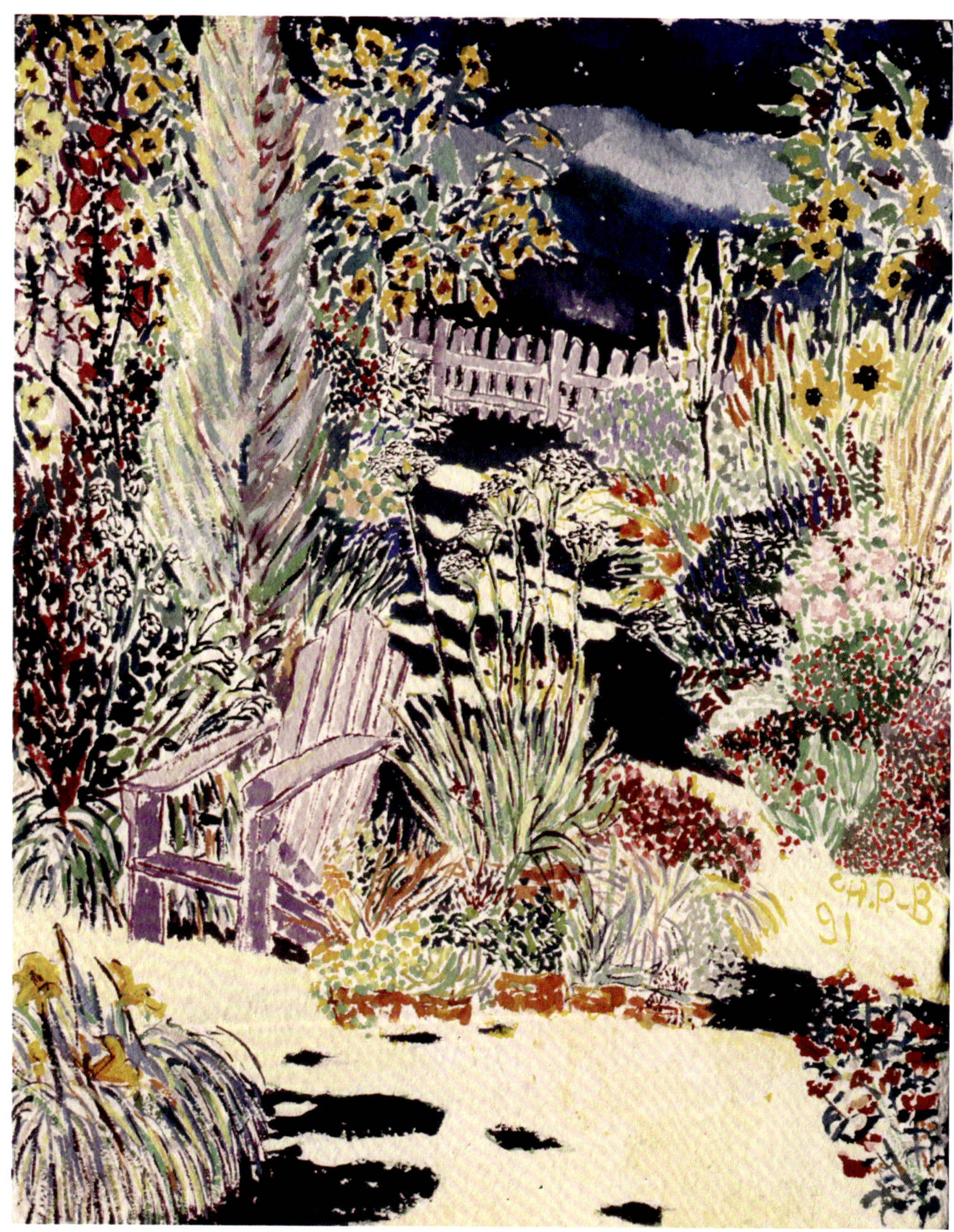
CH.P-B
91

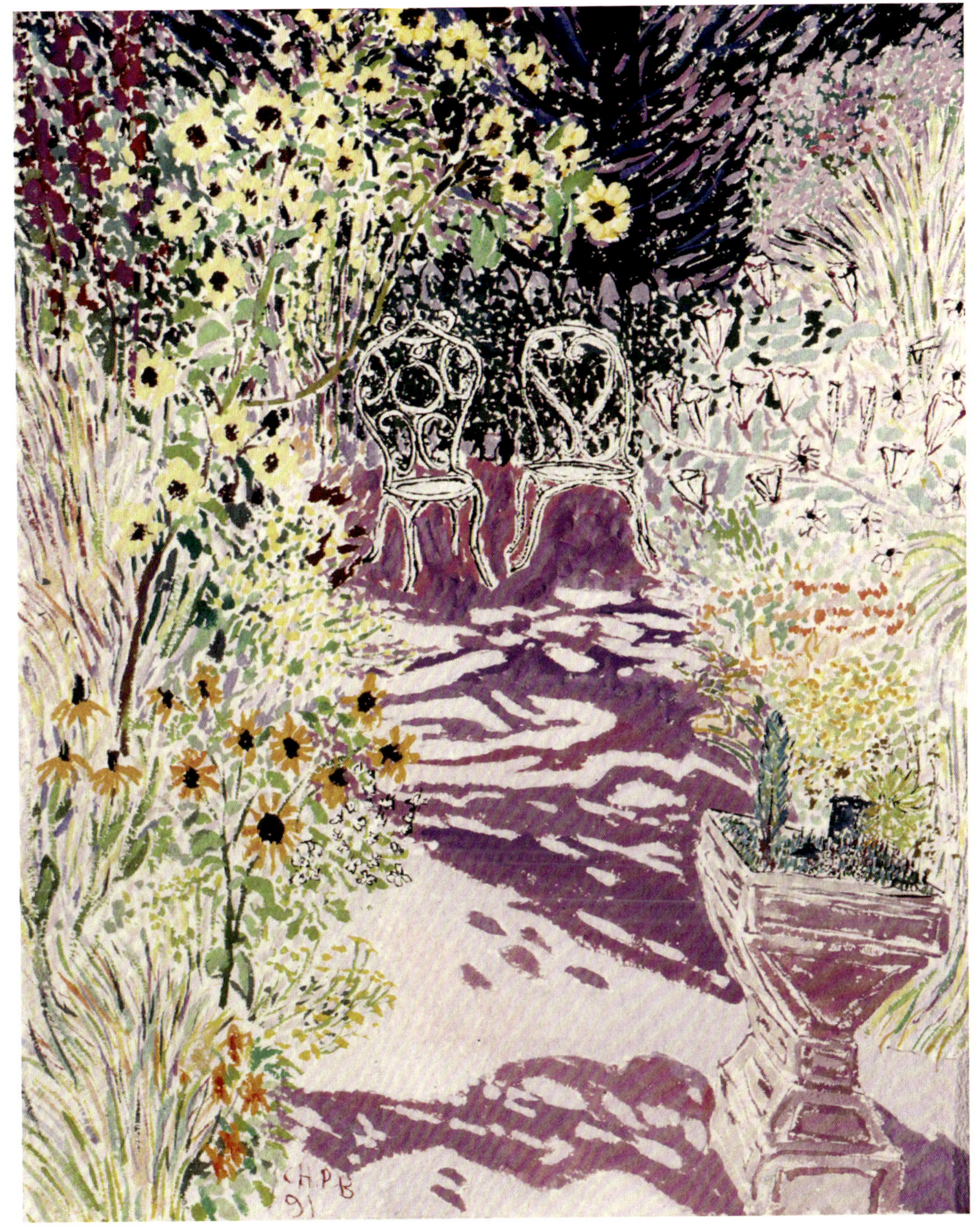
CHPB
91

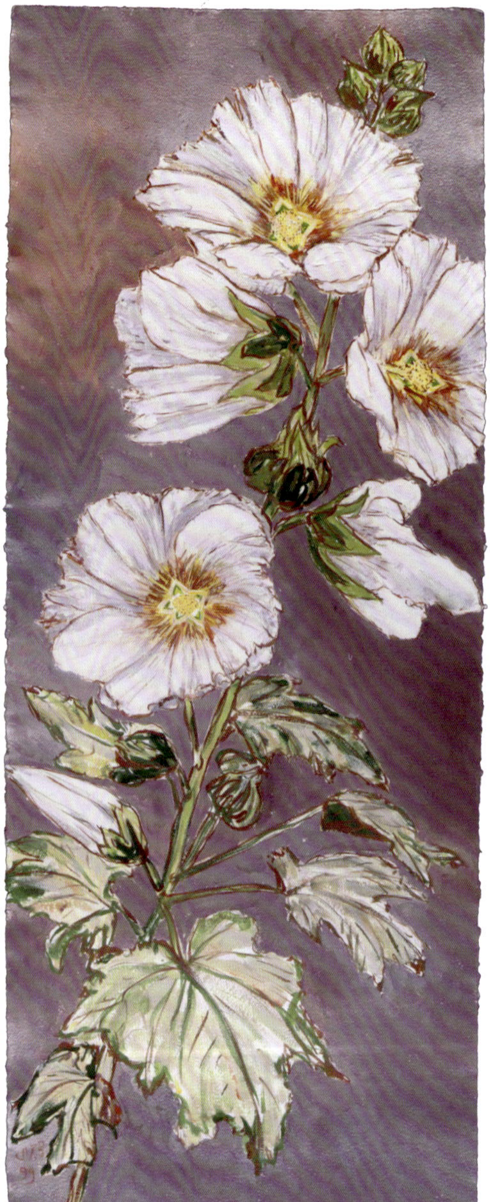

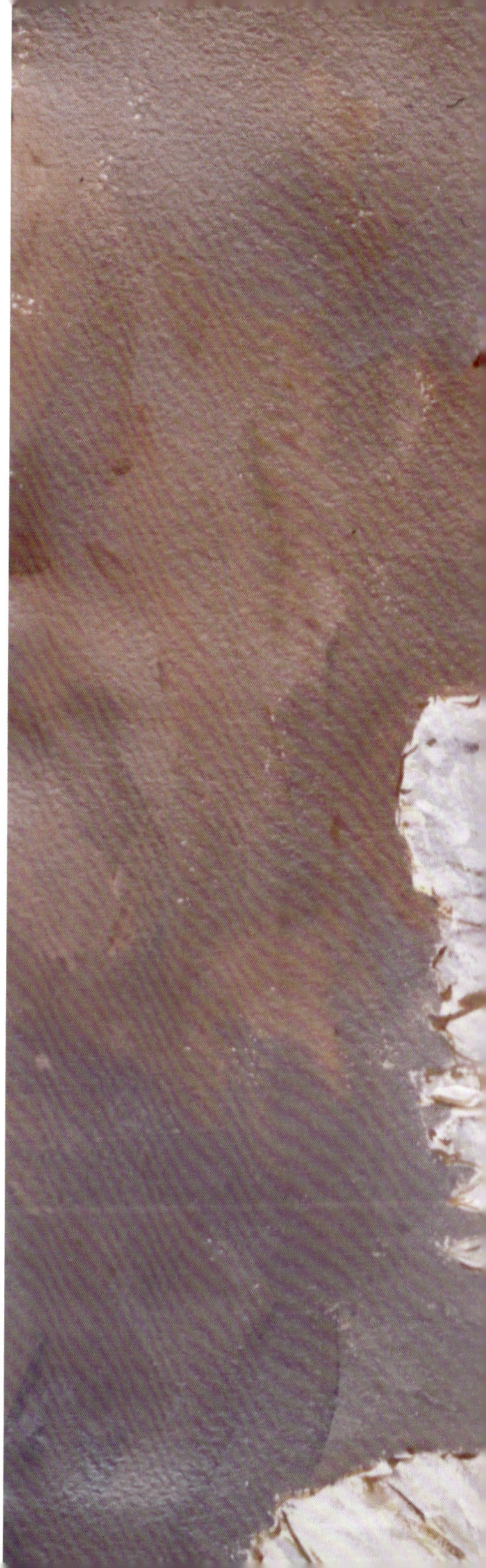

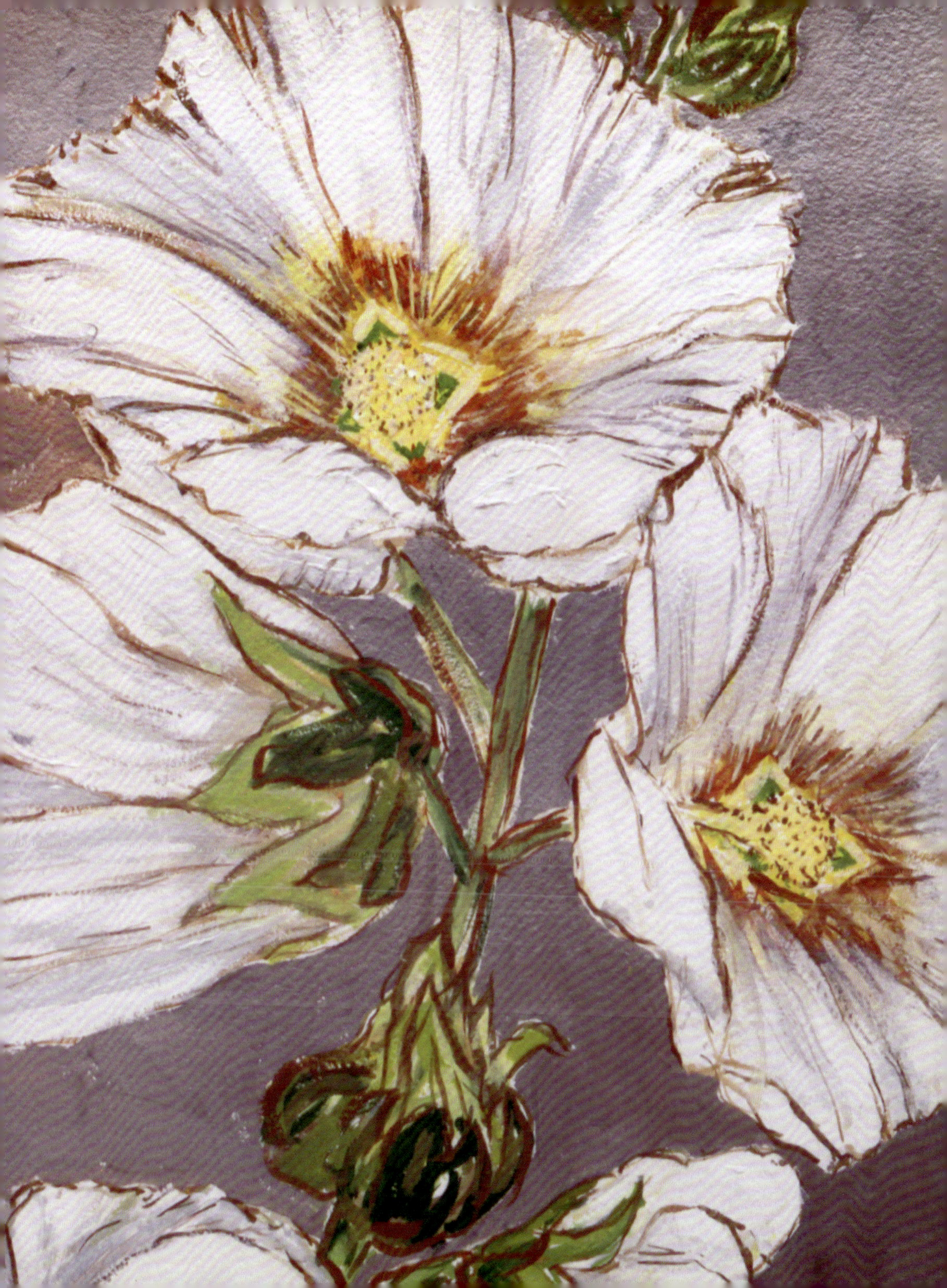

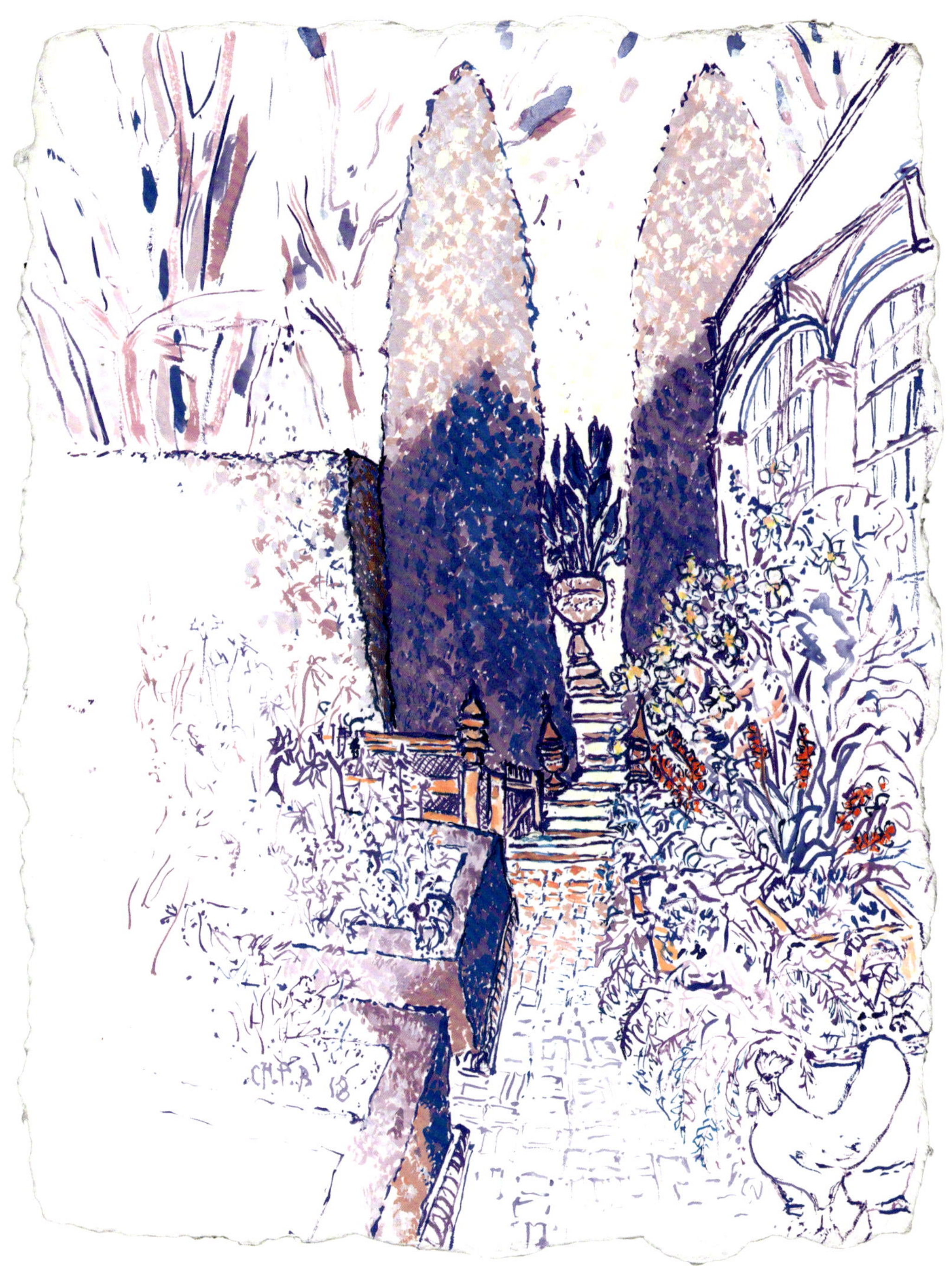

Bunny and John's Garden

Falls Village, Connecticut

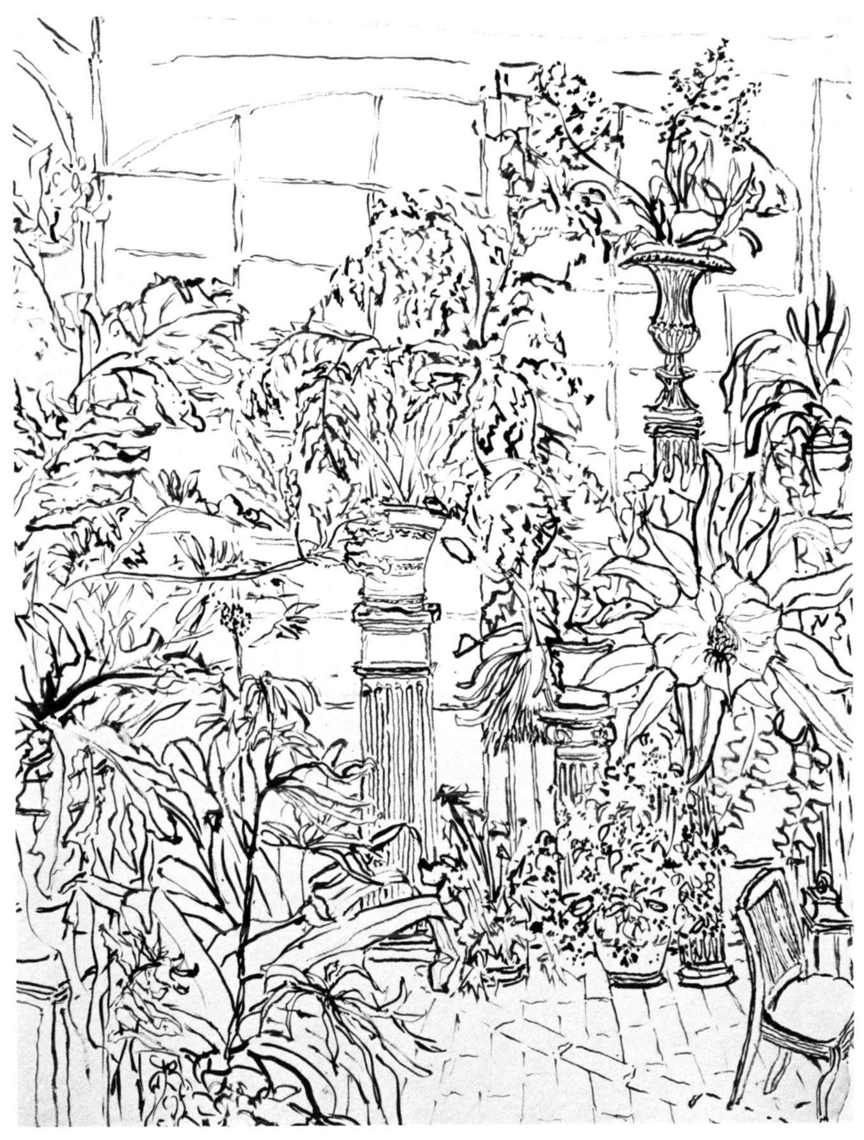

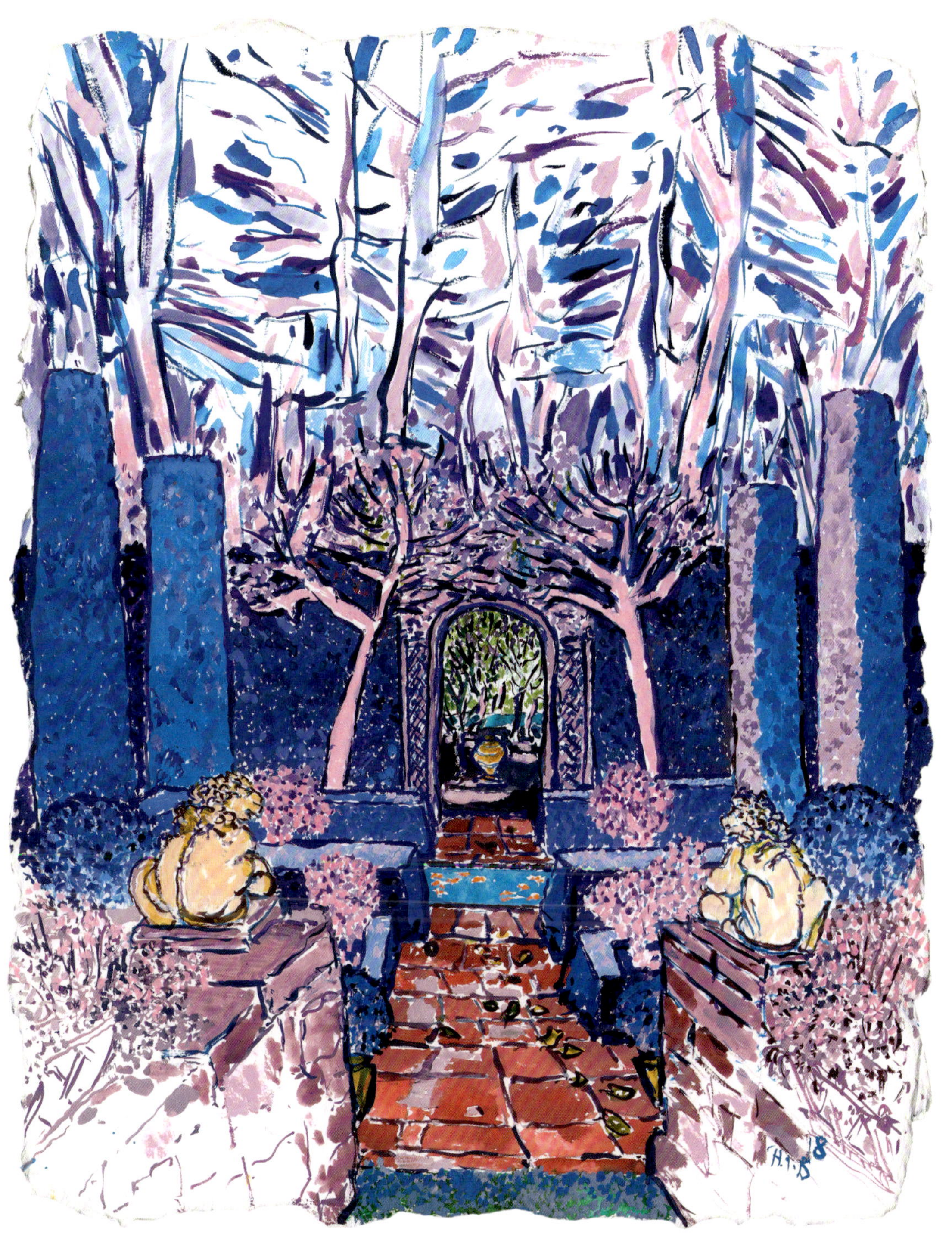

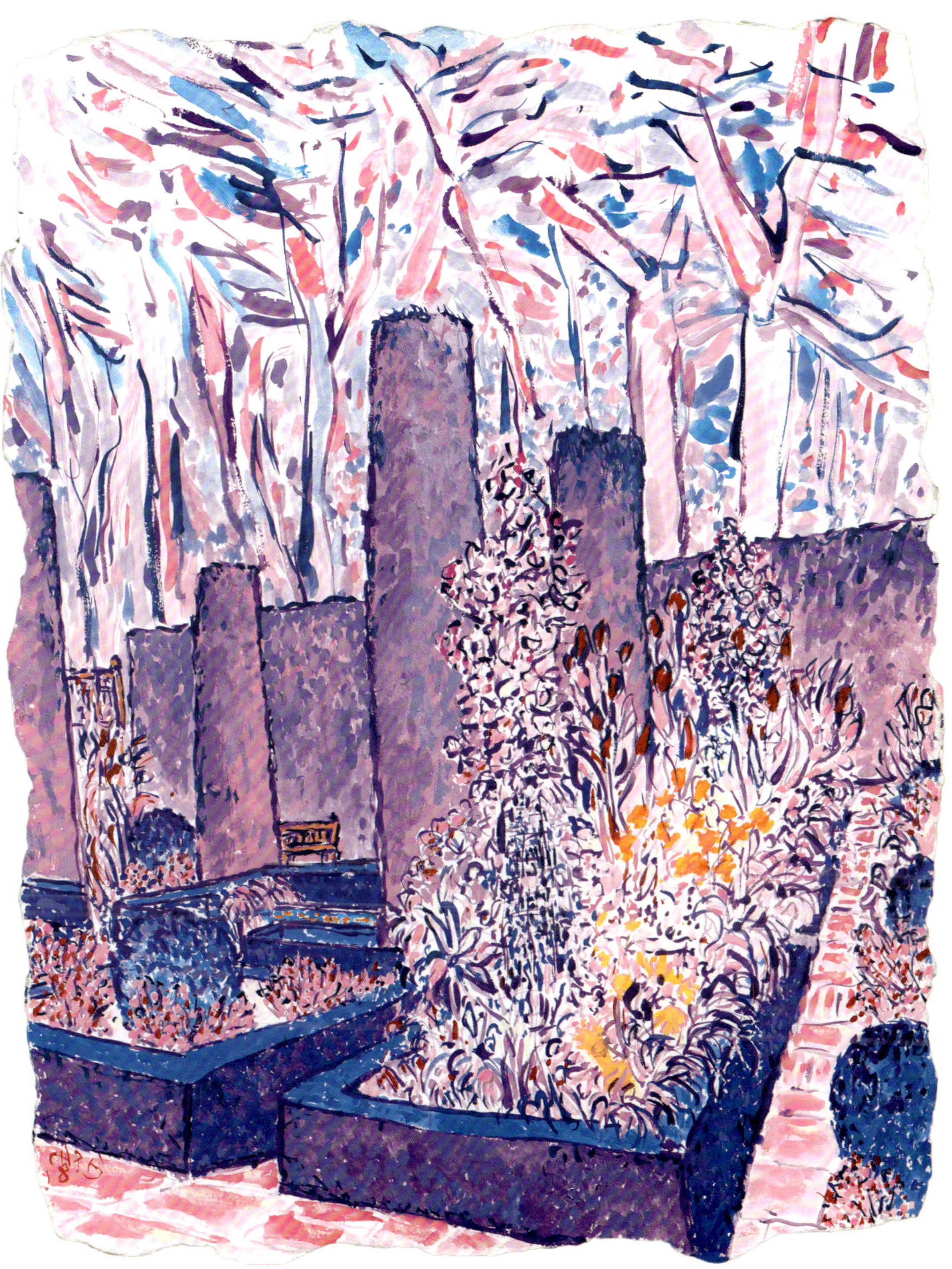

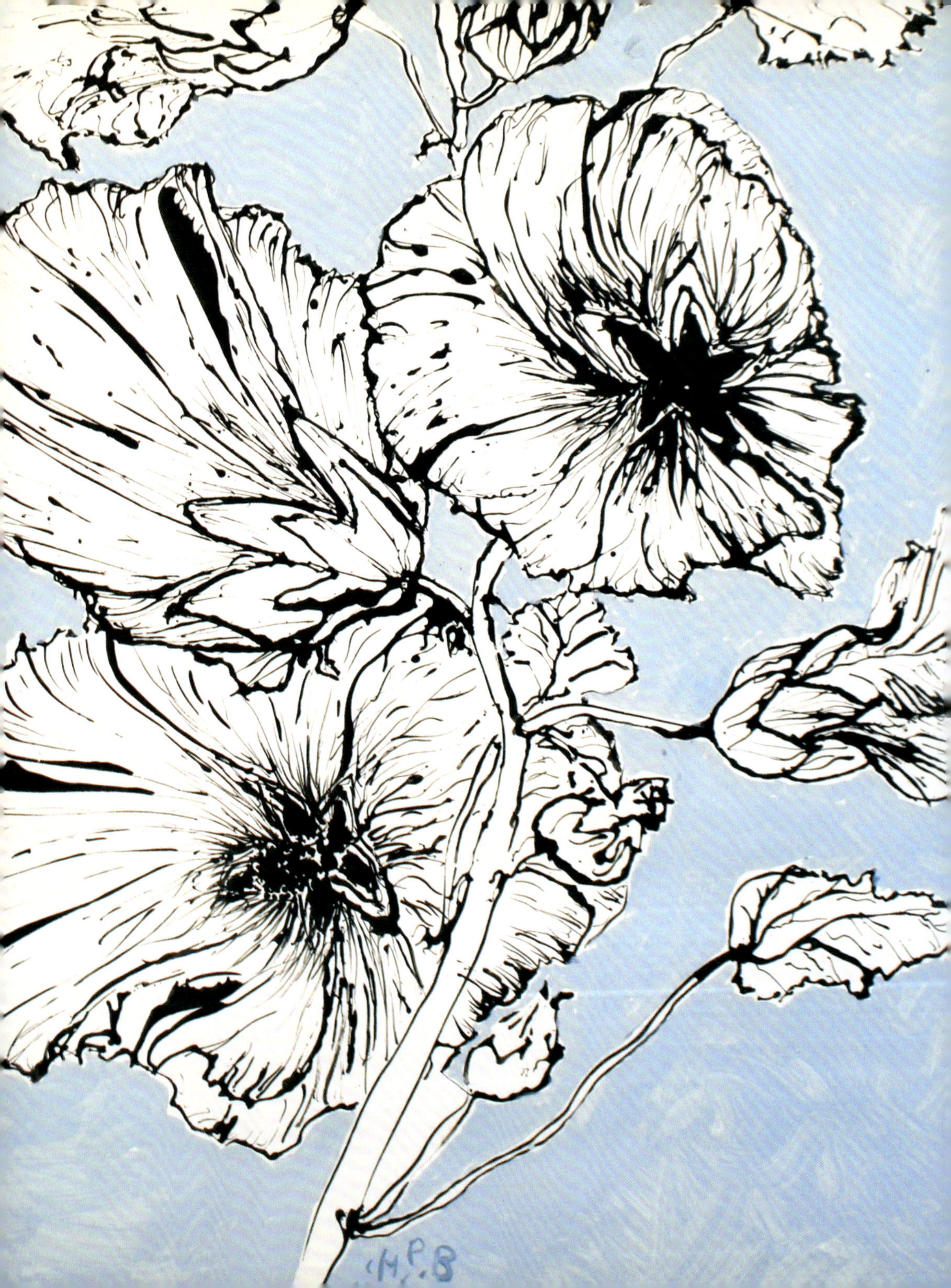

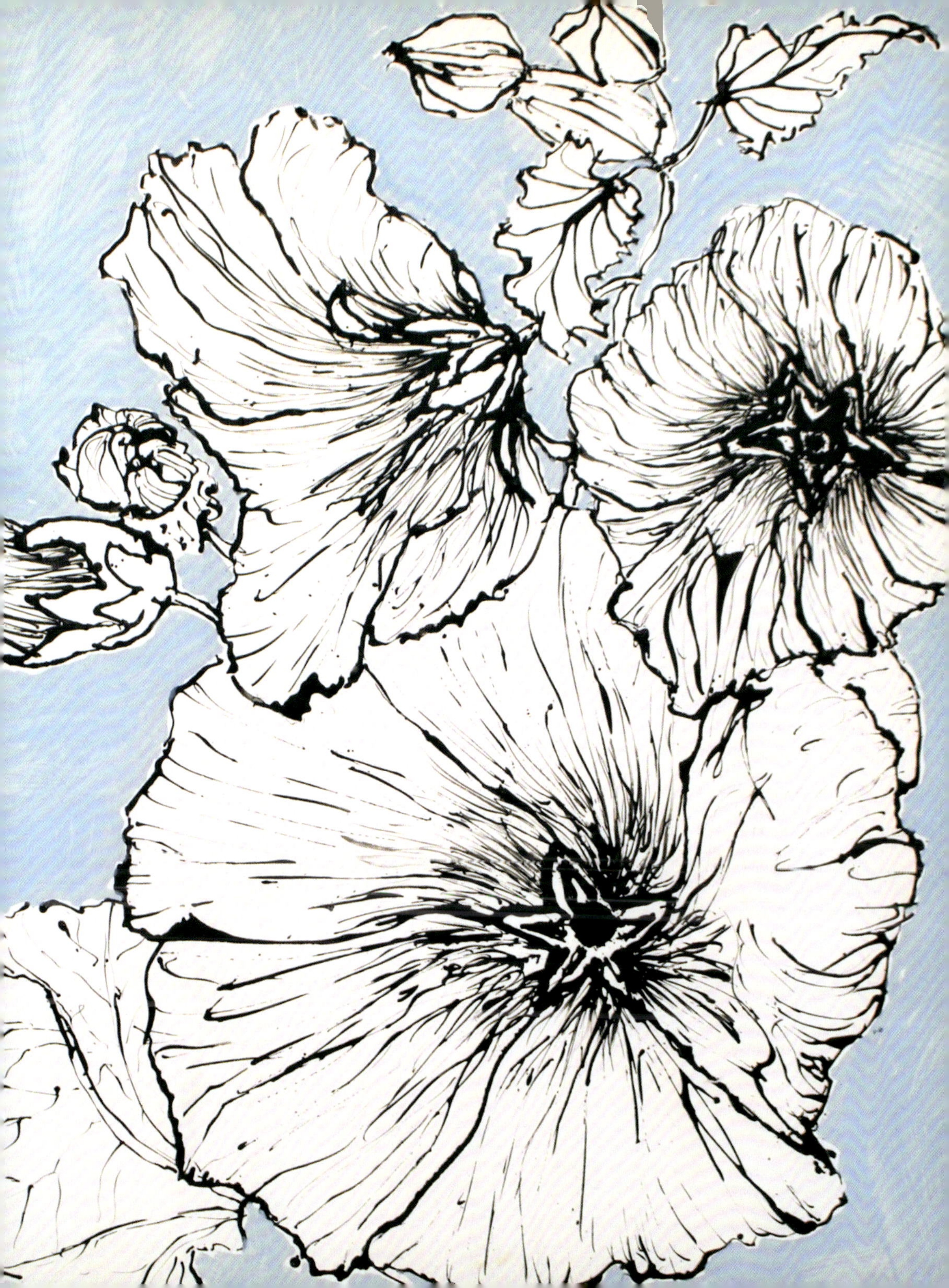

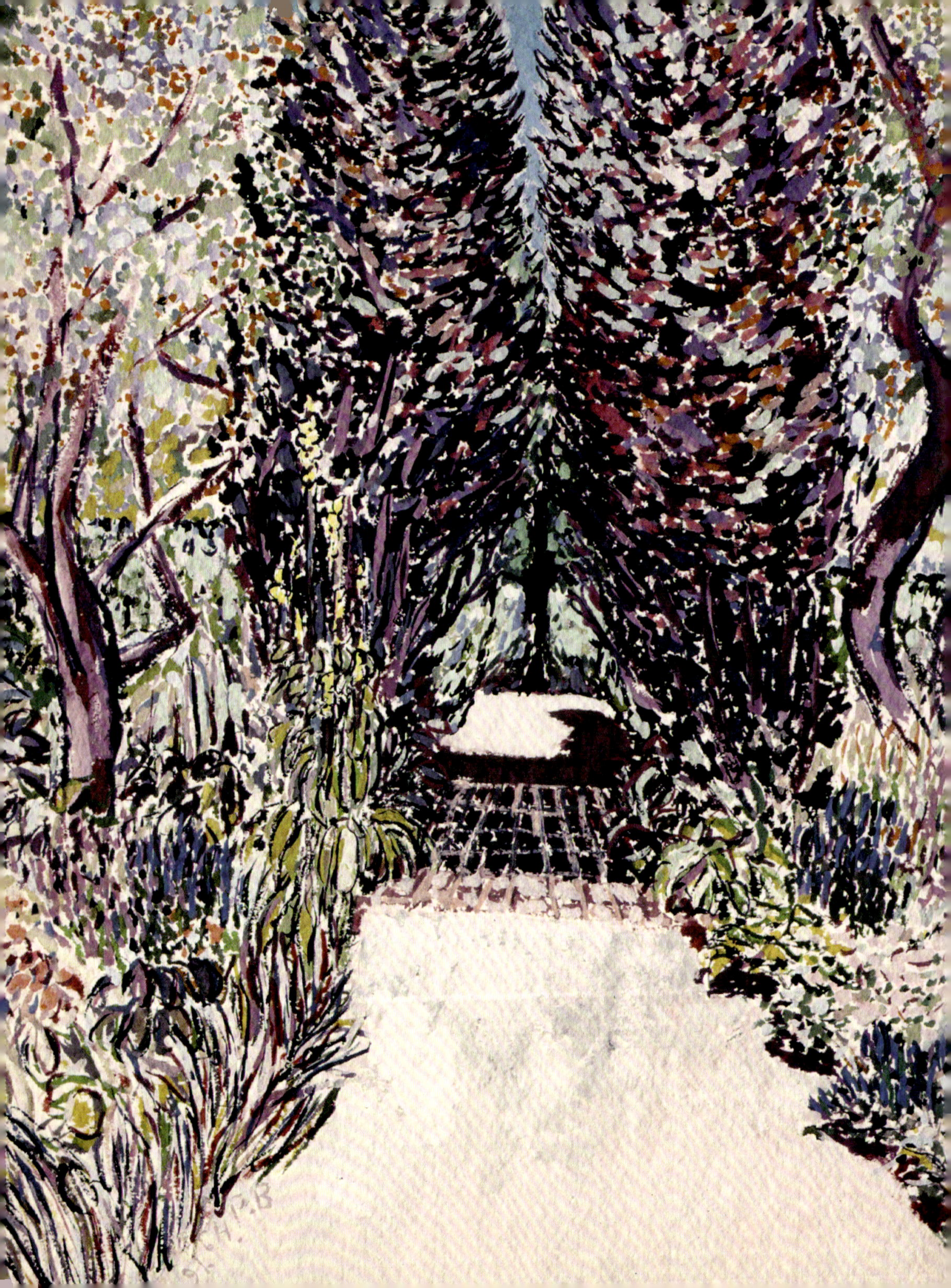

Sylvester Manor

Shelter Island, New York

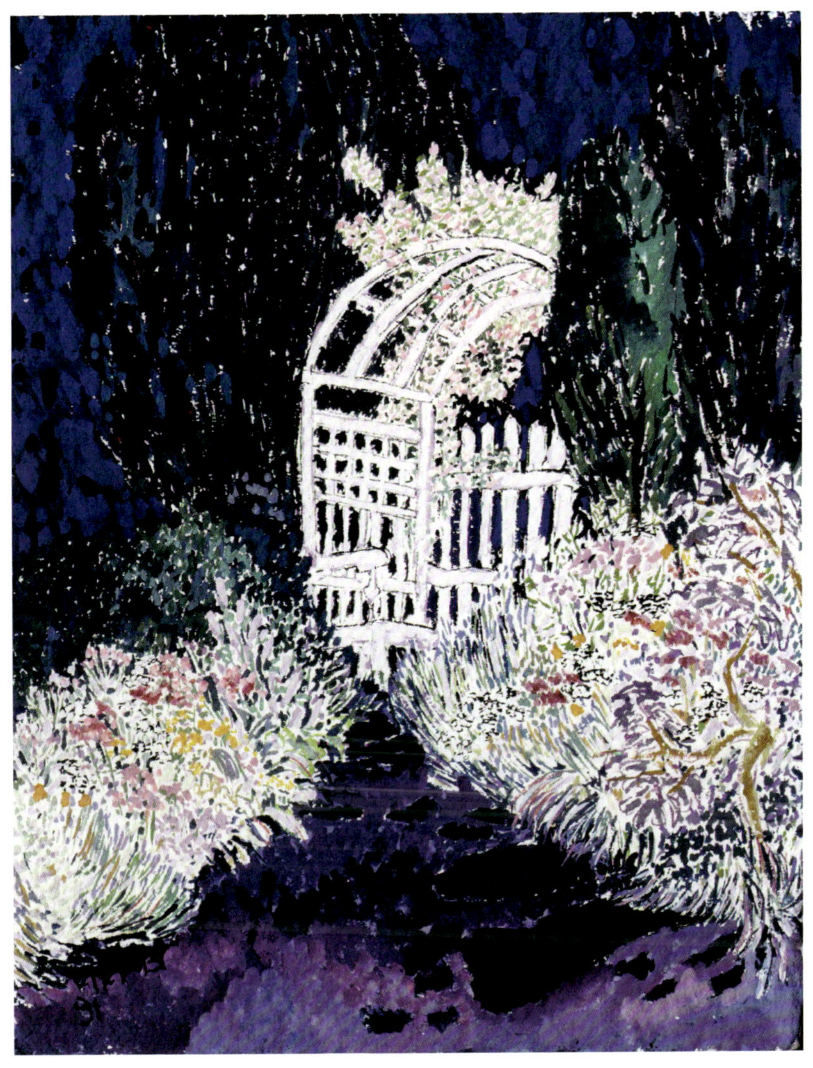

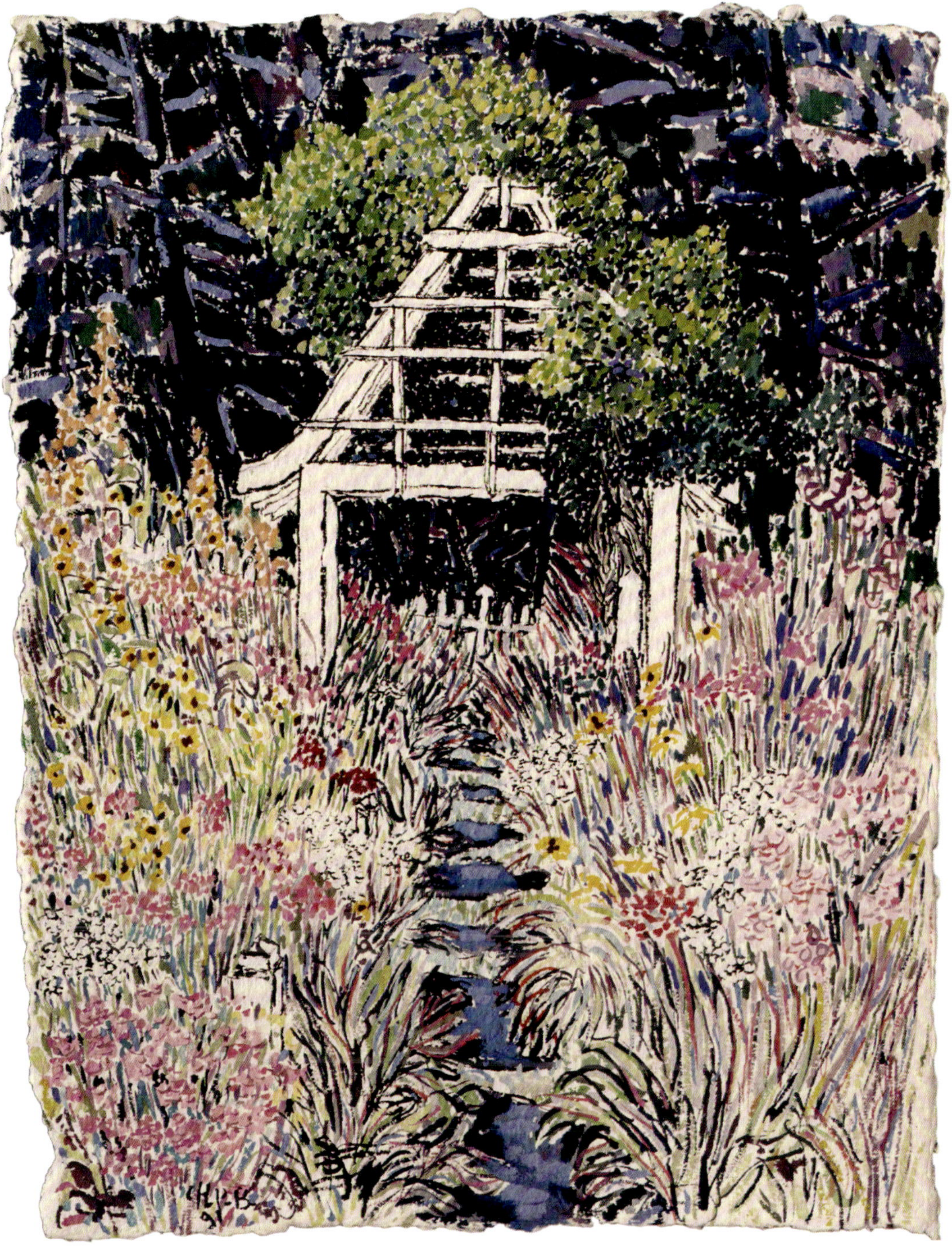

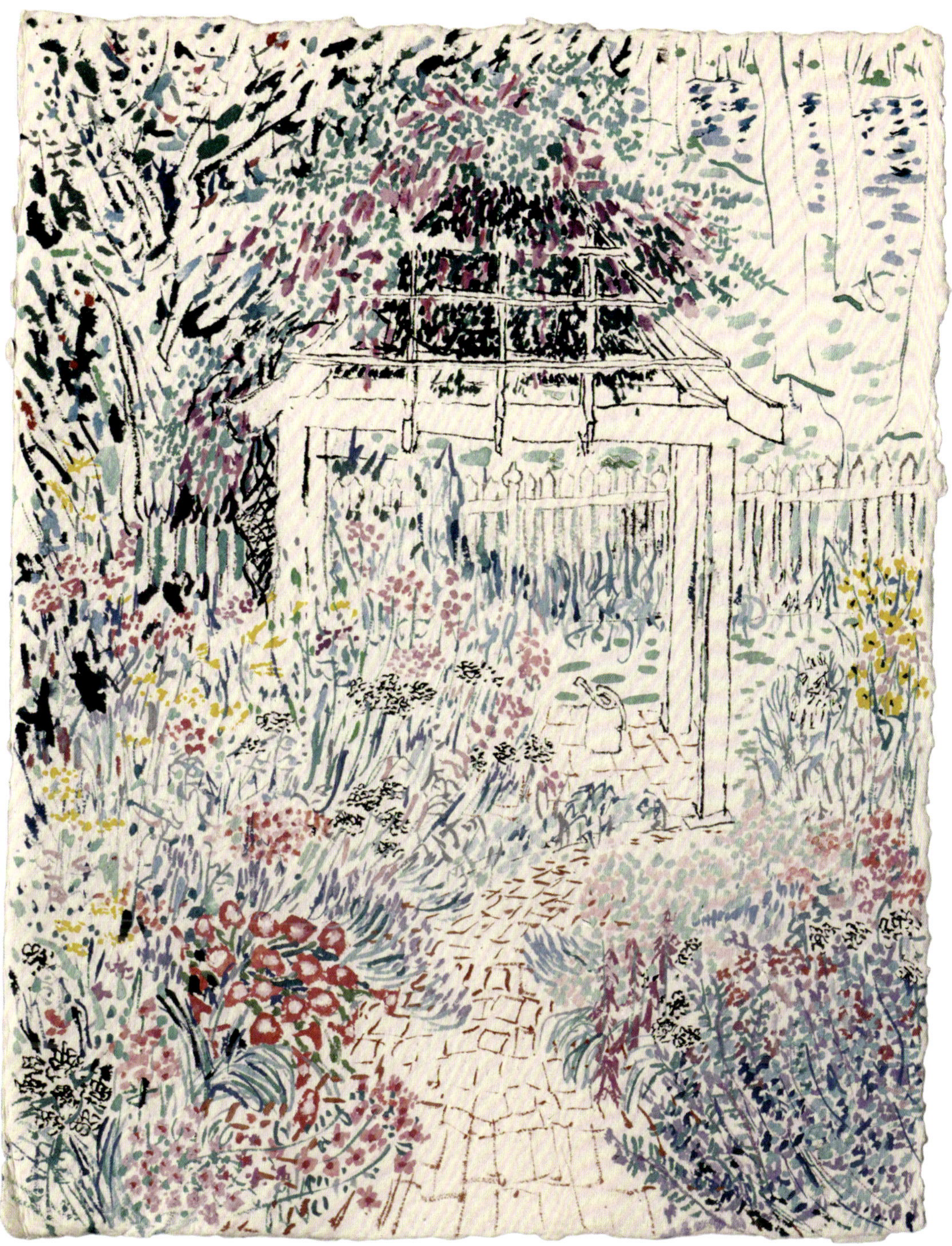

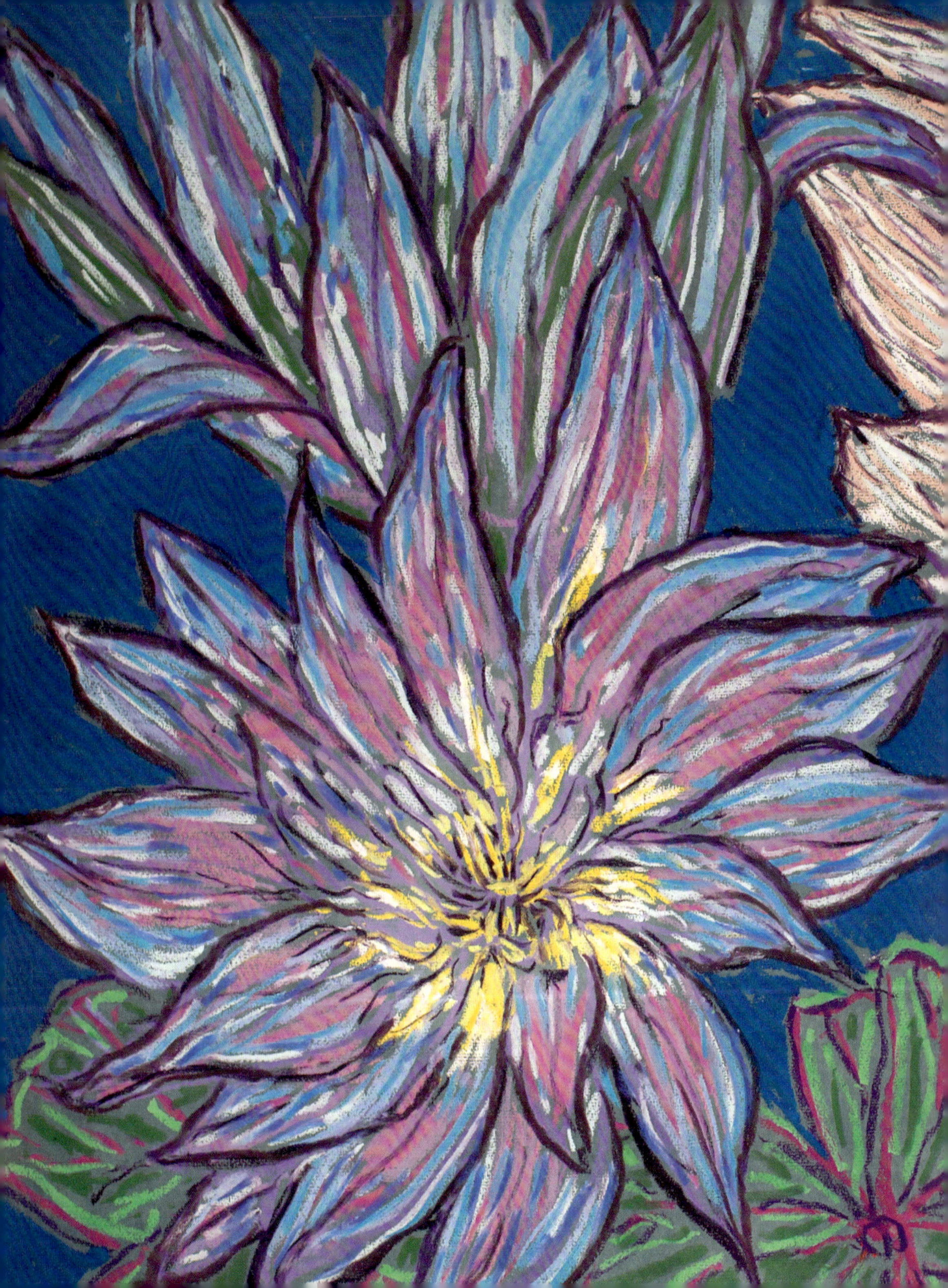

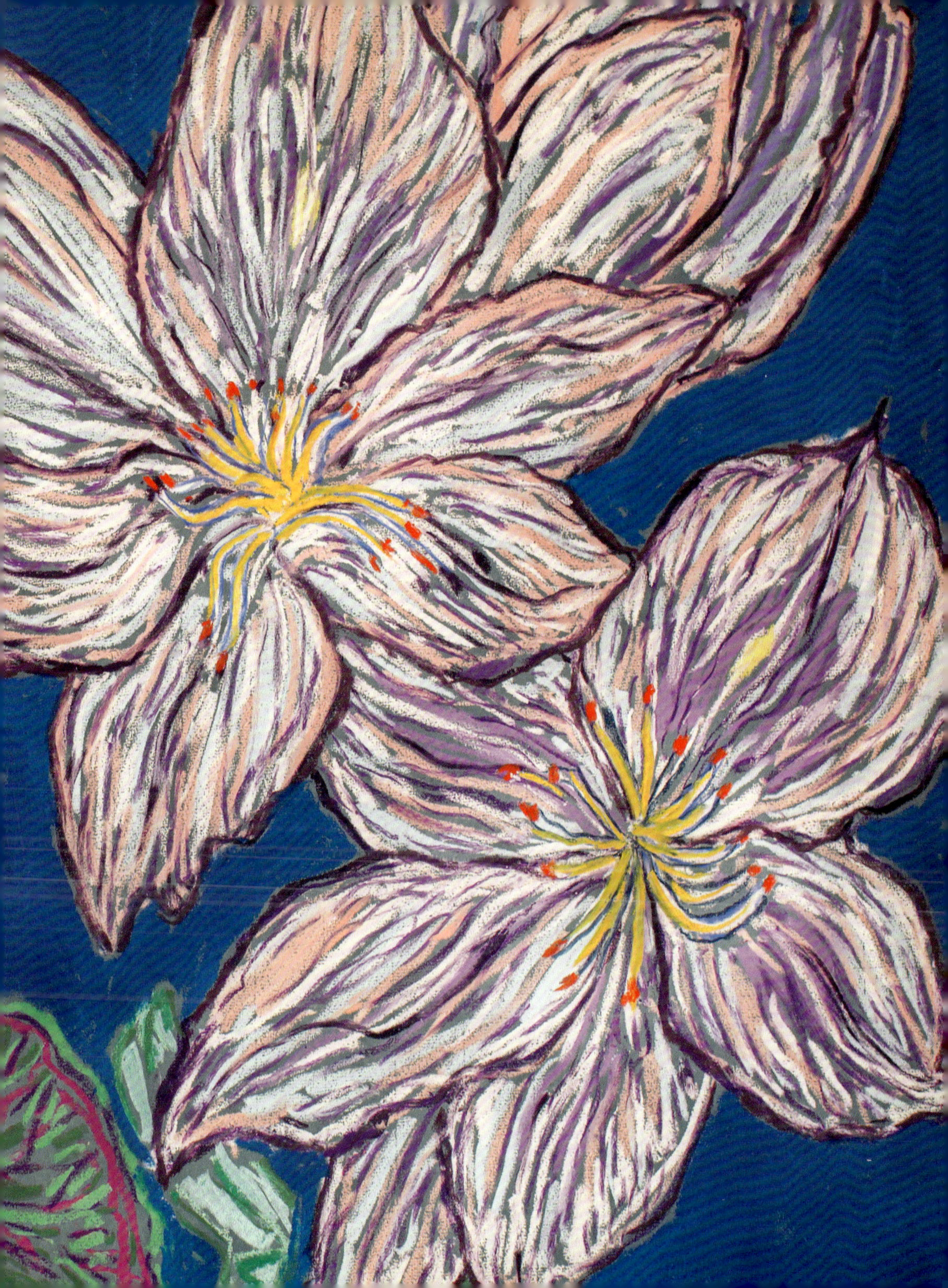

Madoo Conservancy

Bridgehampton, New York

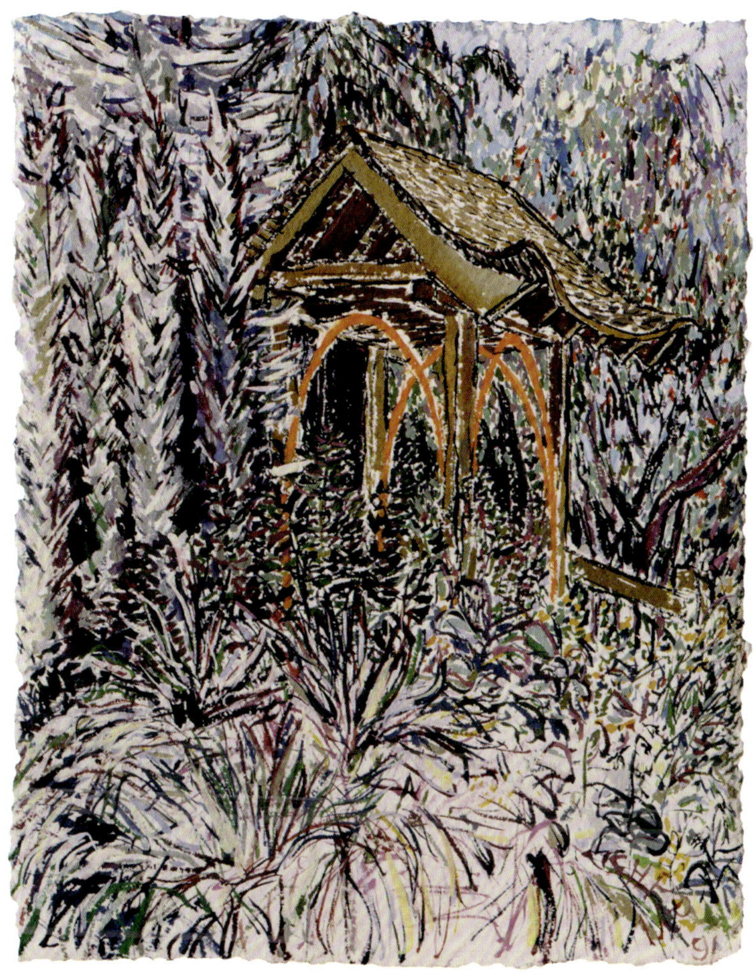

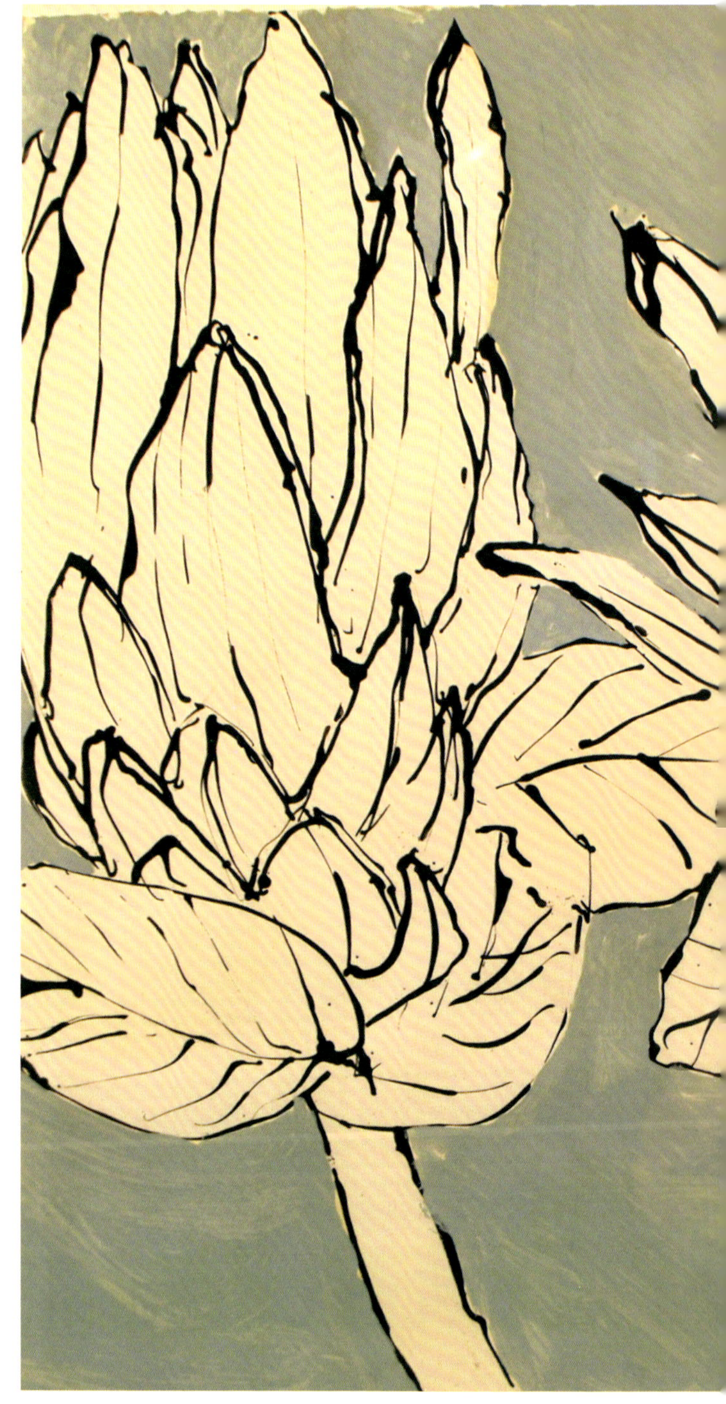

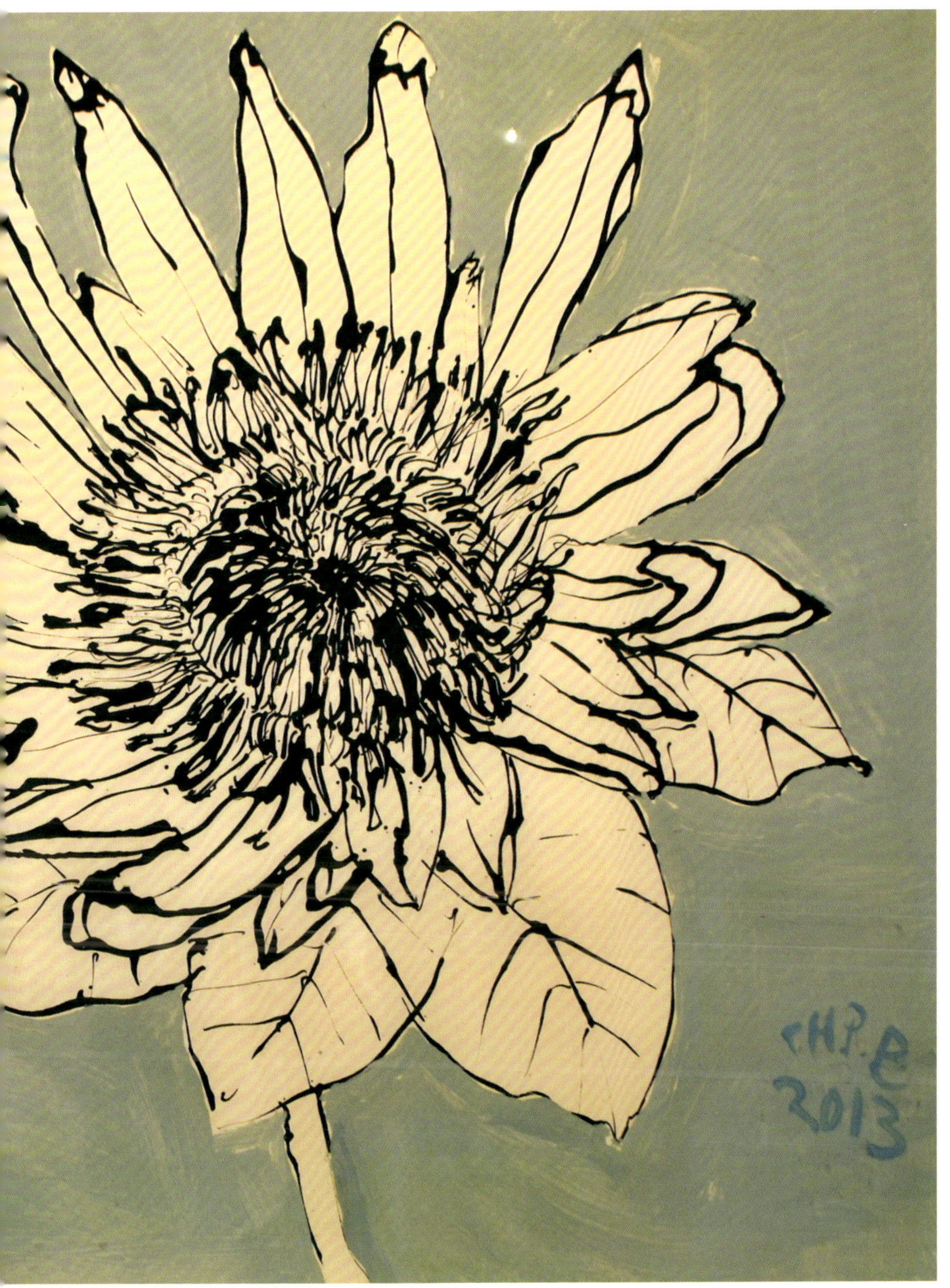
CHP.B
2013

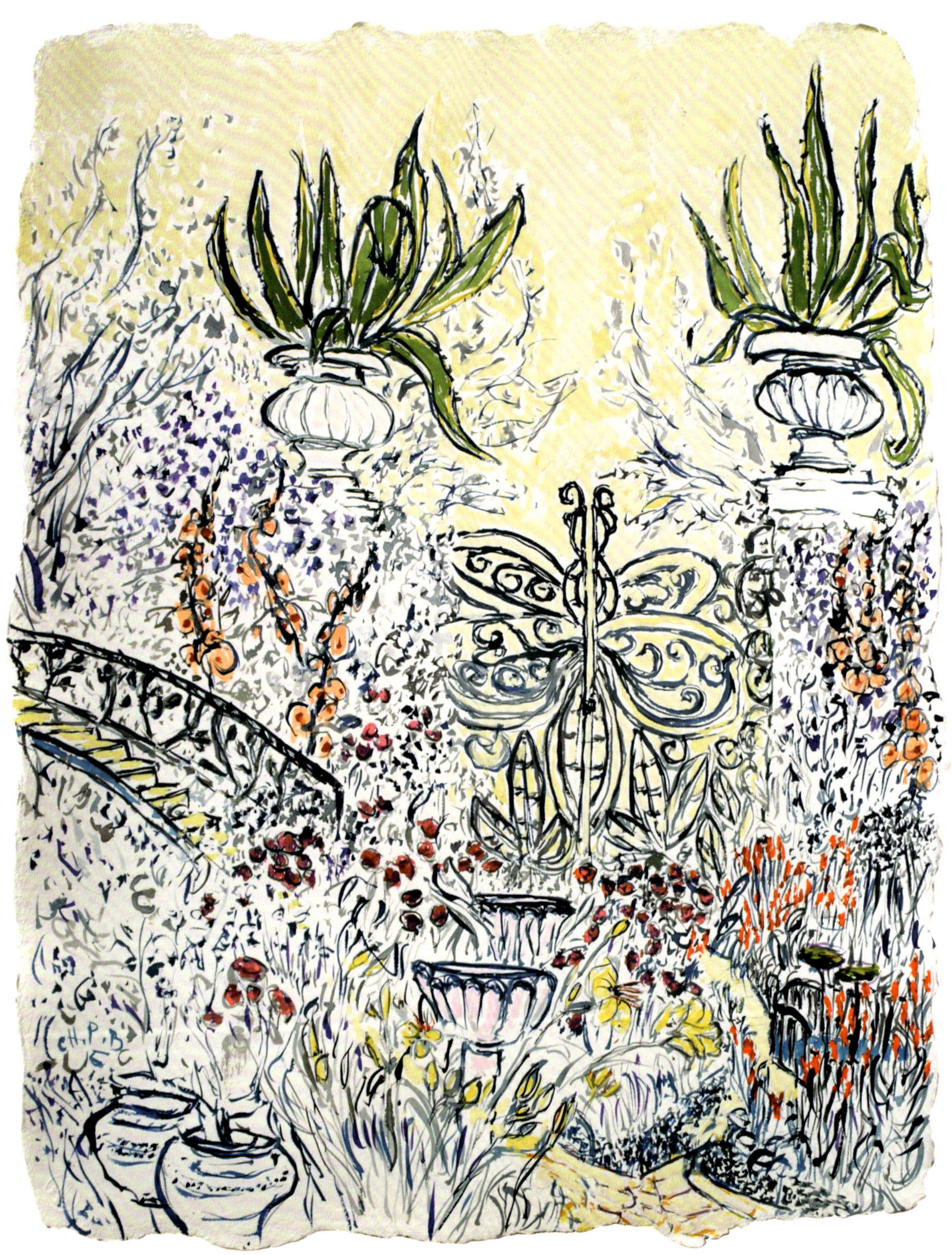

Woodyhouse

East Hampton, New York

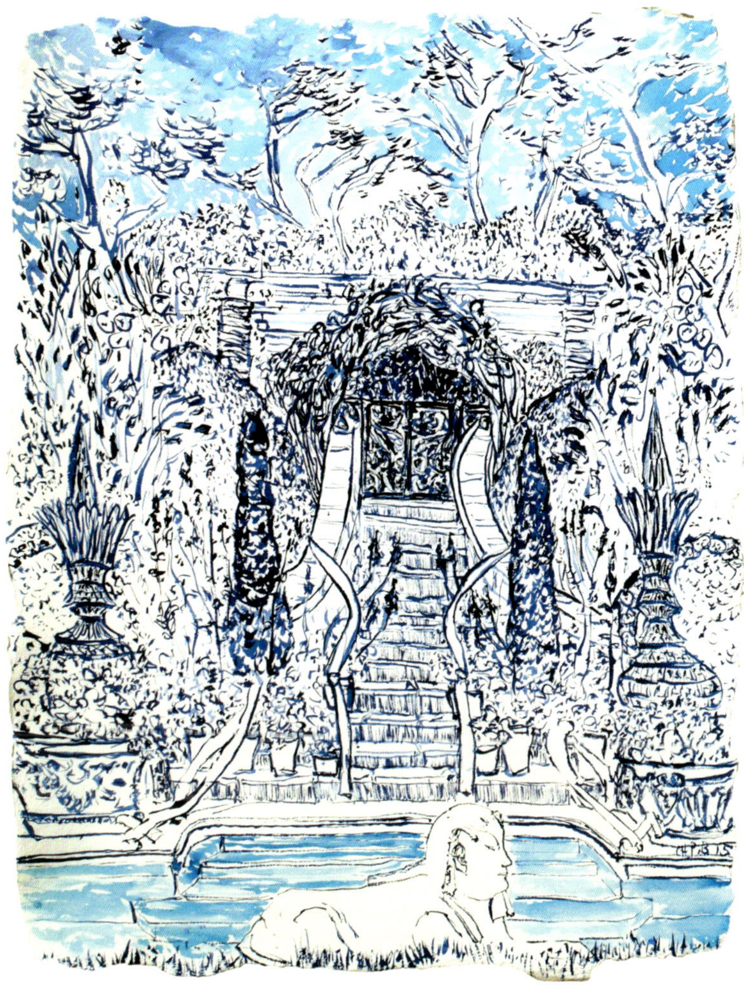

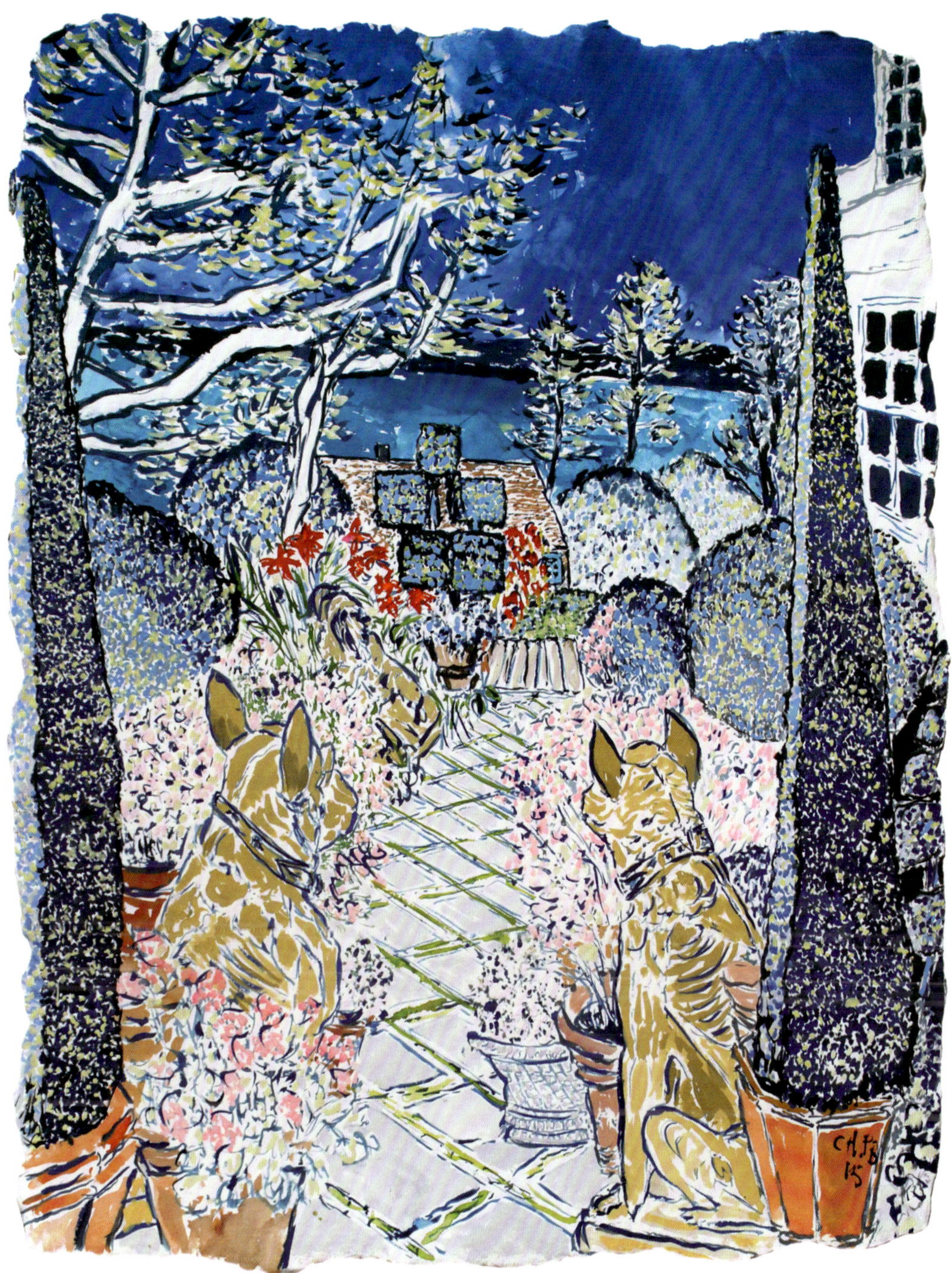

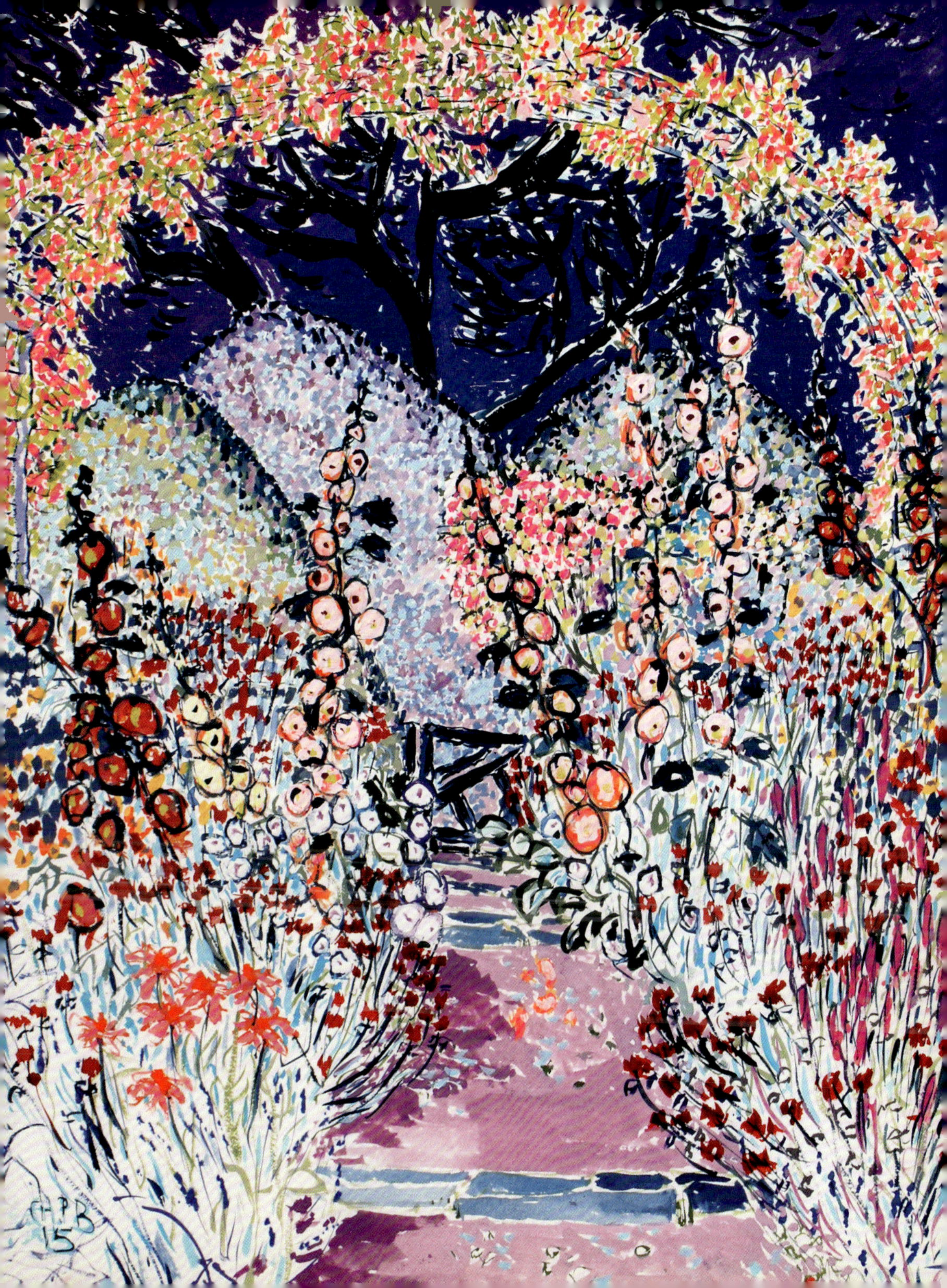

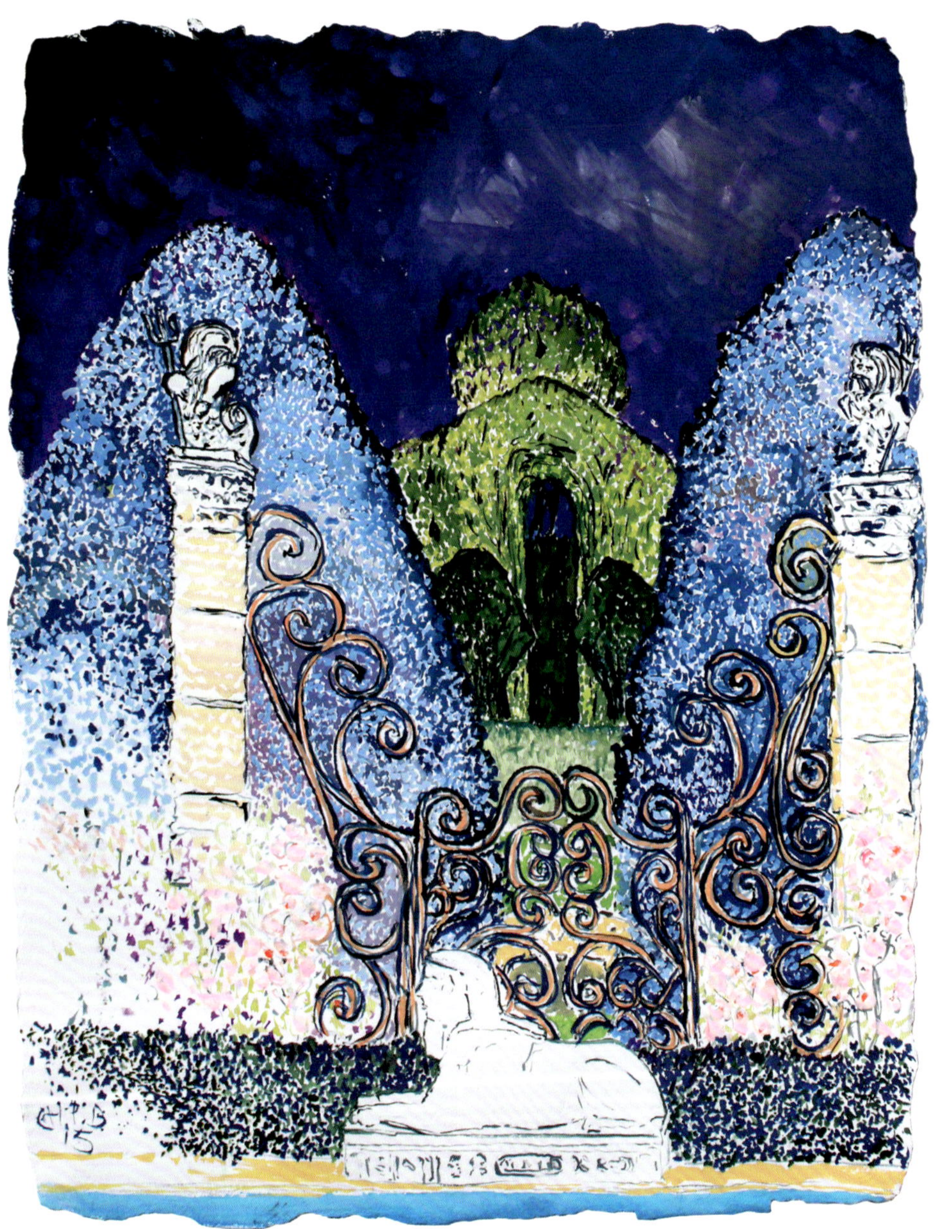

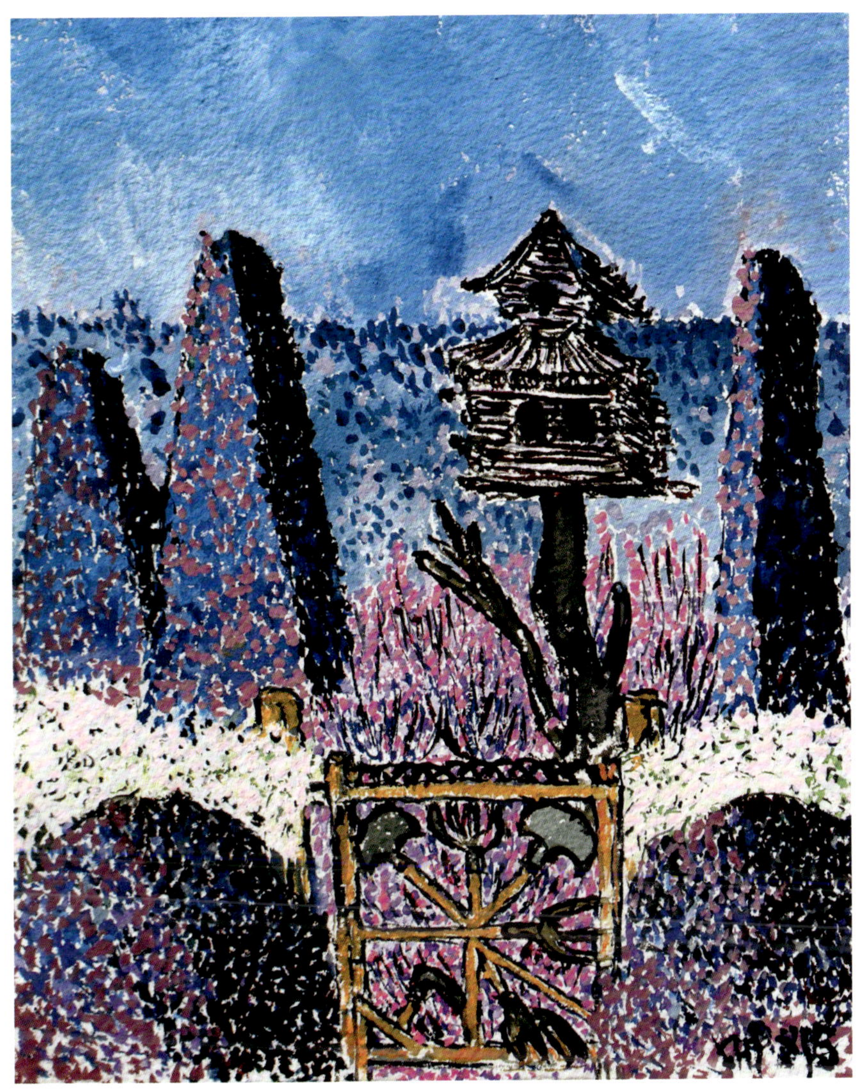

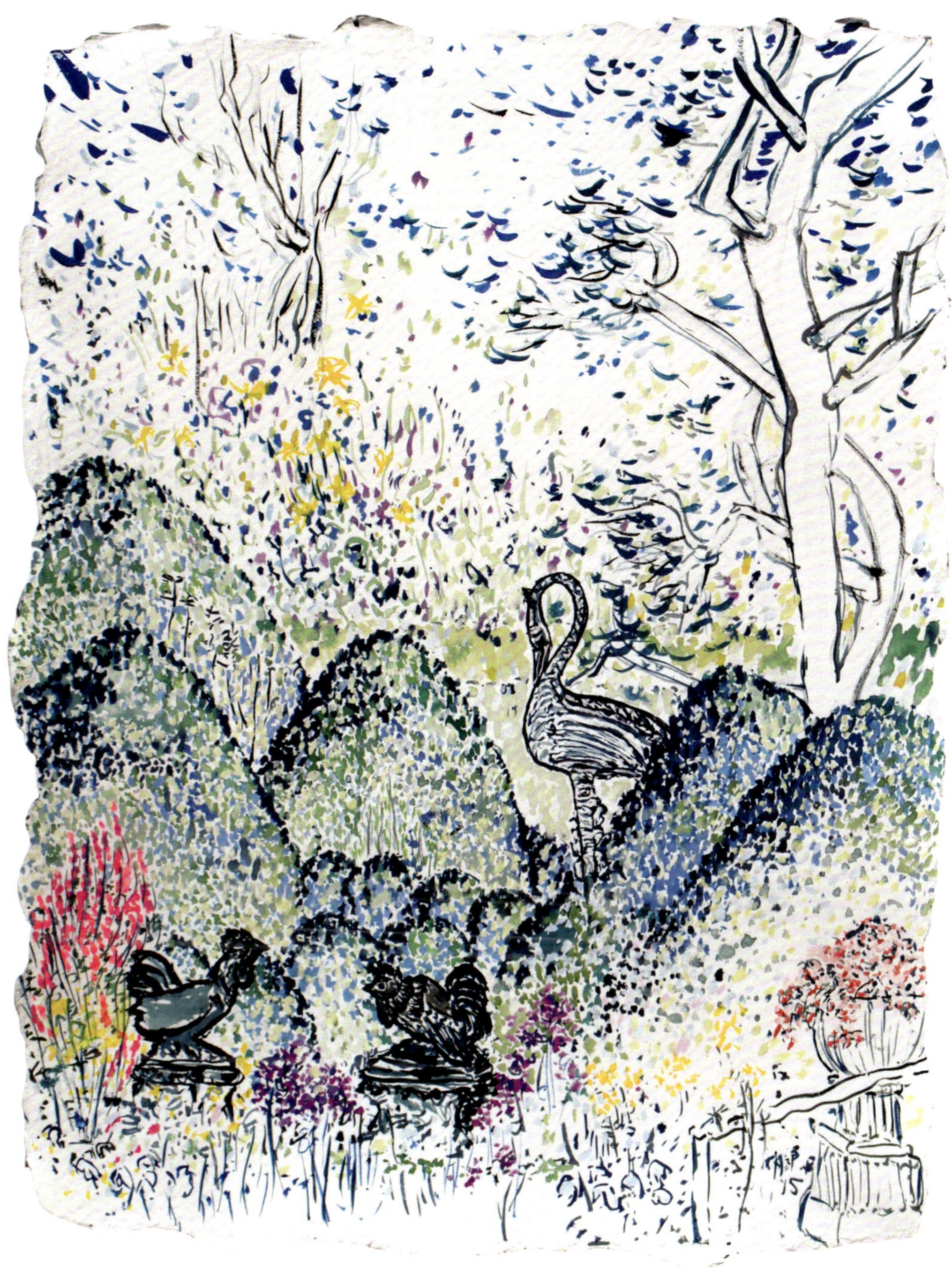

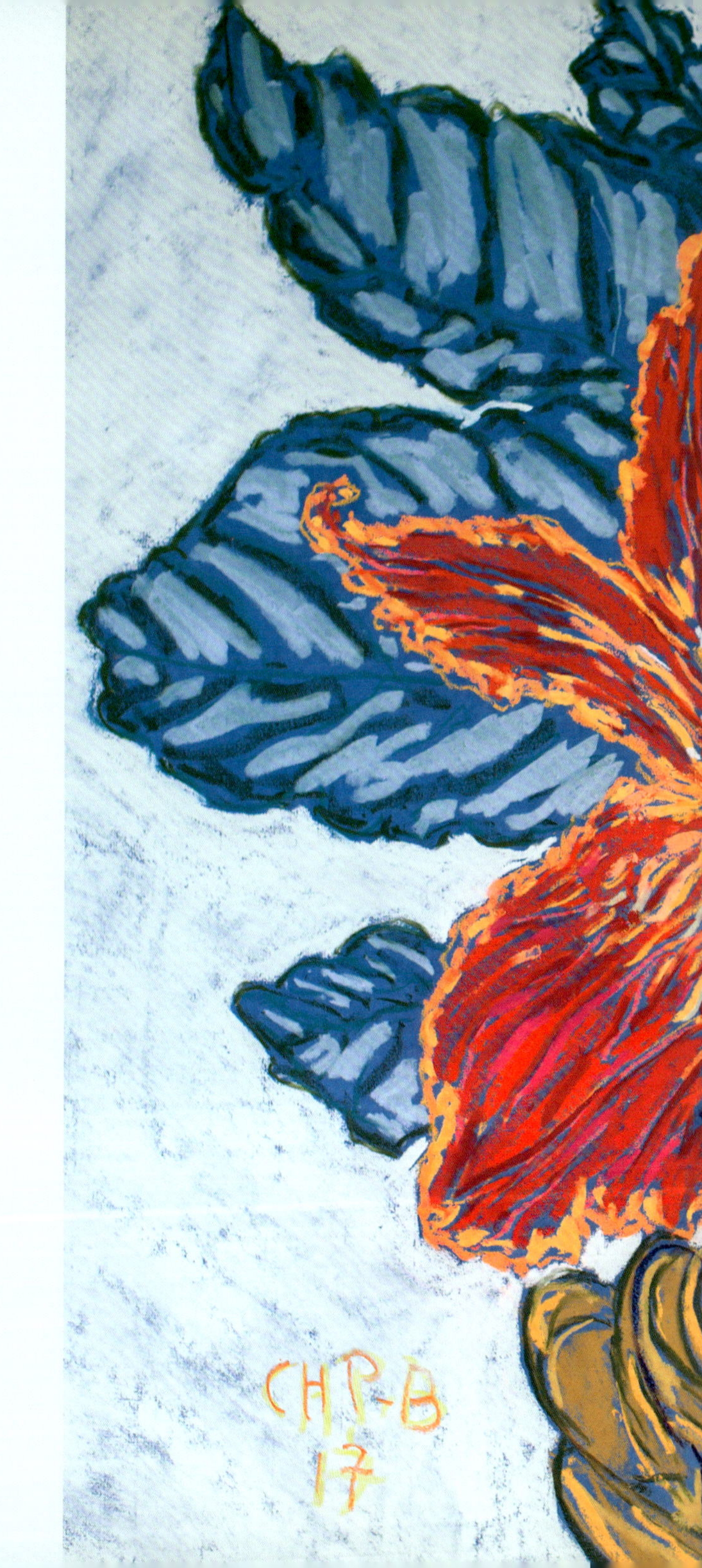
CHP-B
17

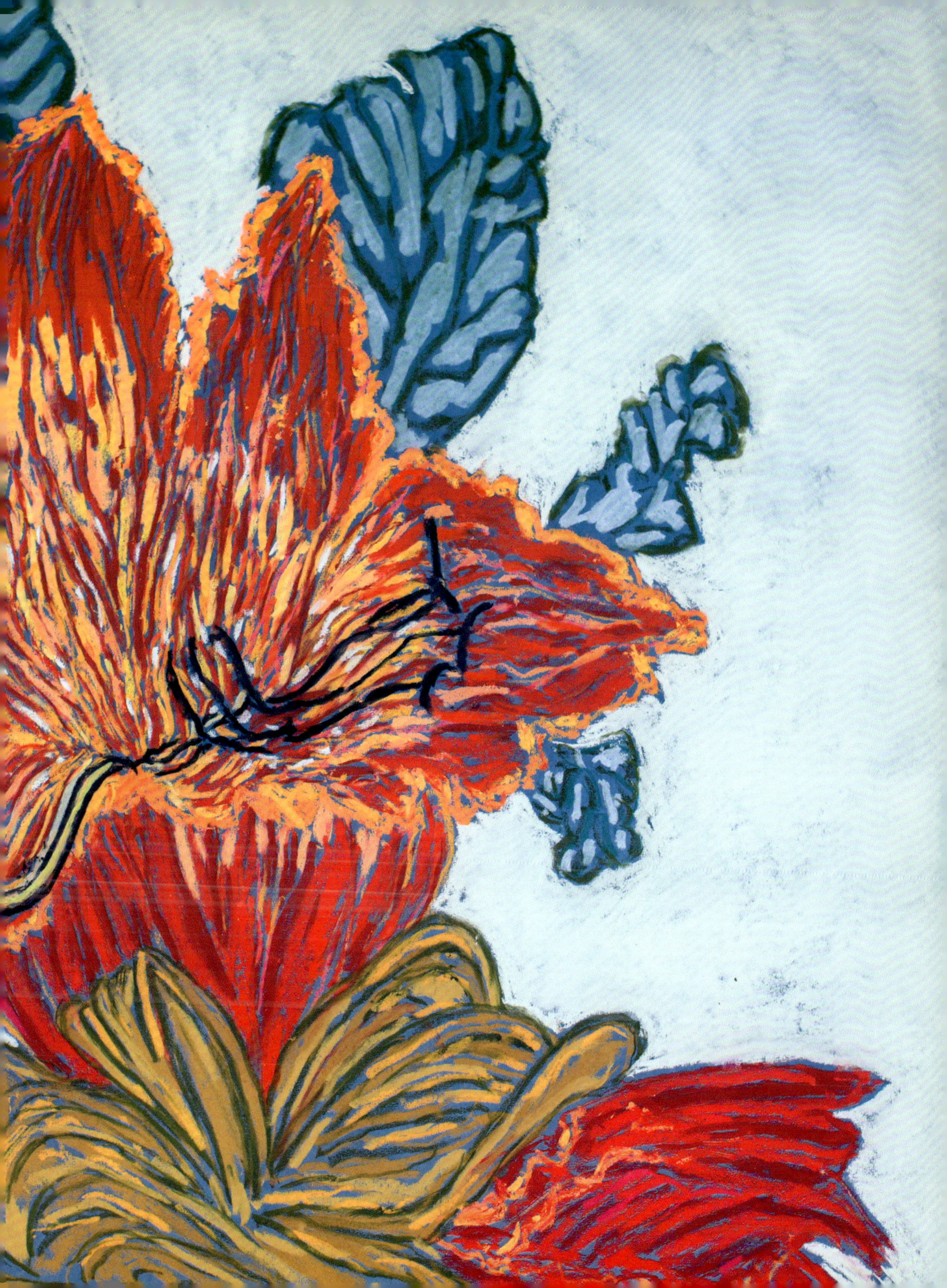

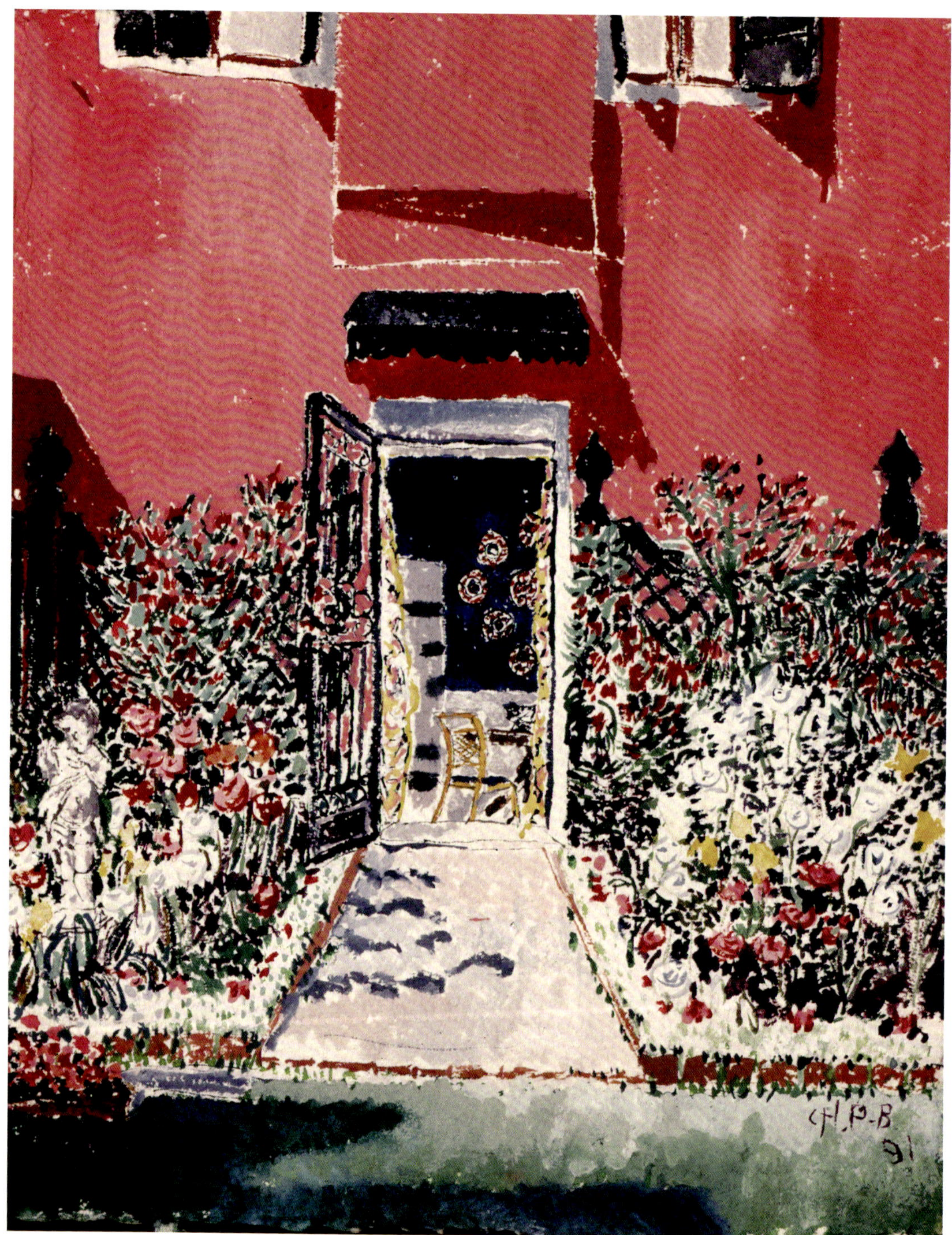
CH.P.B
91

Casetta Rossa

Venice, Italy

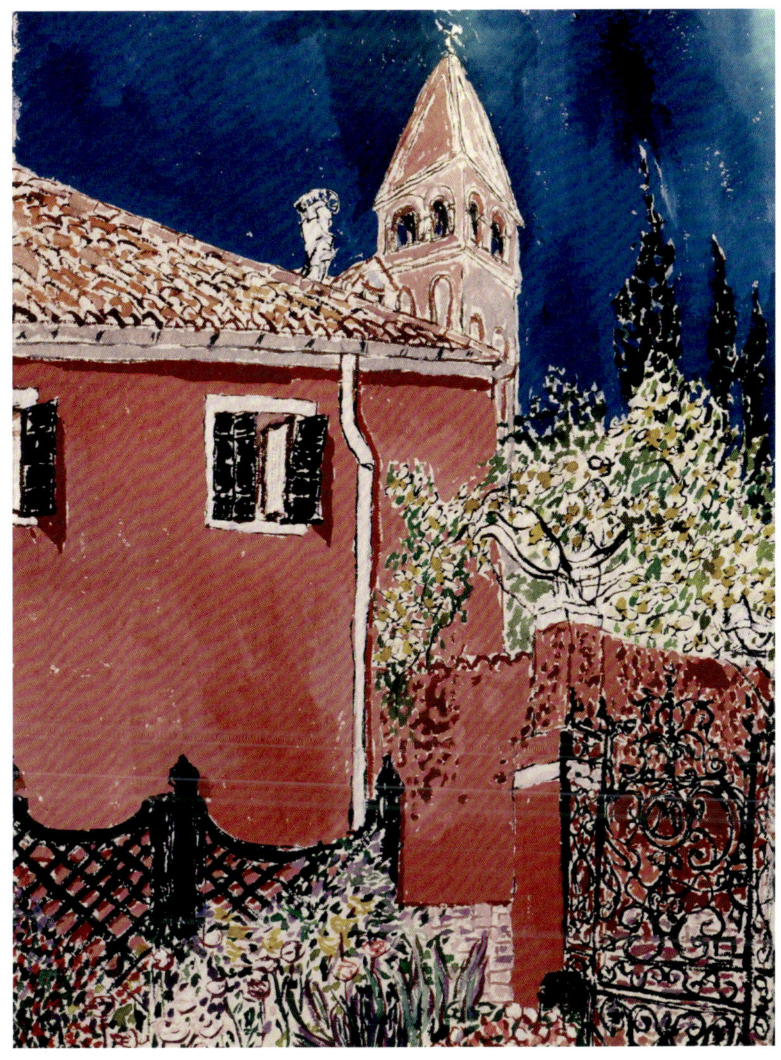

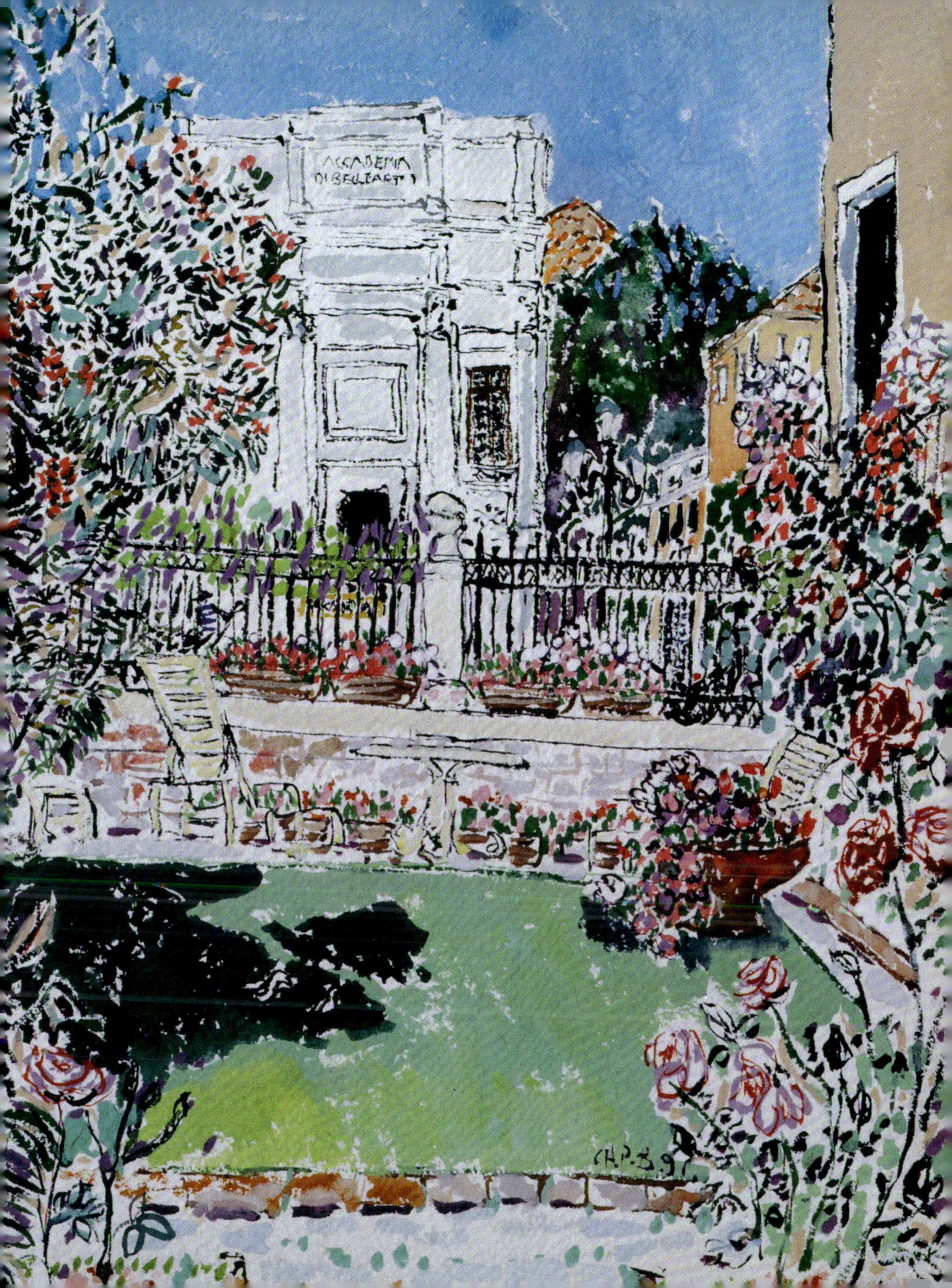
ACCADEMIA
DI BELLEARTI

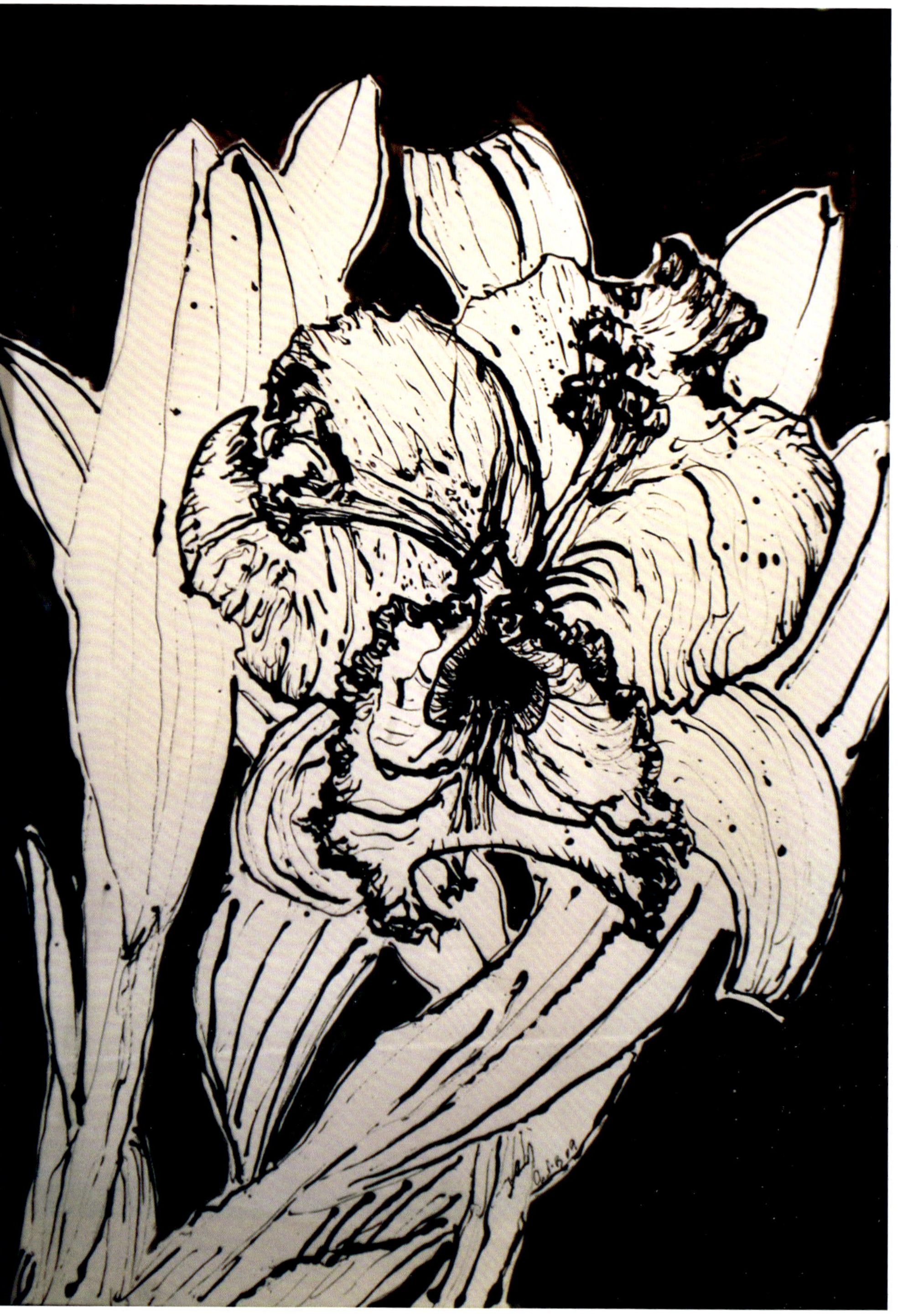

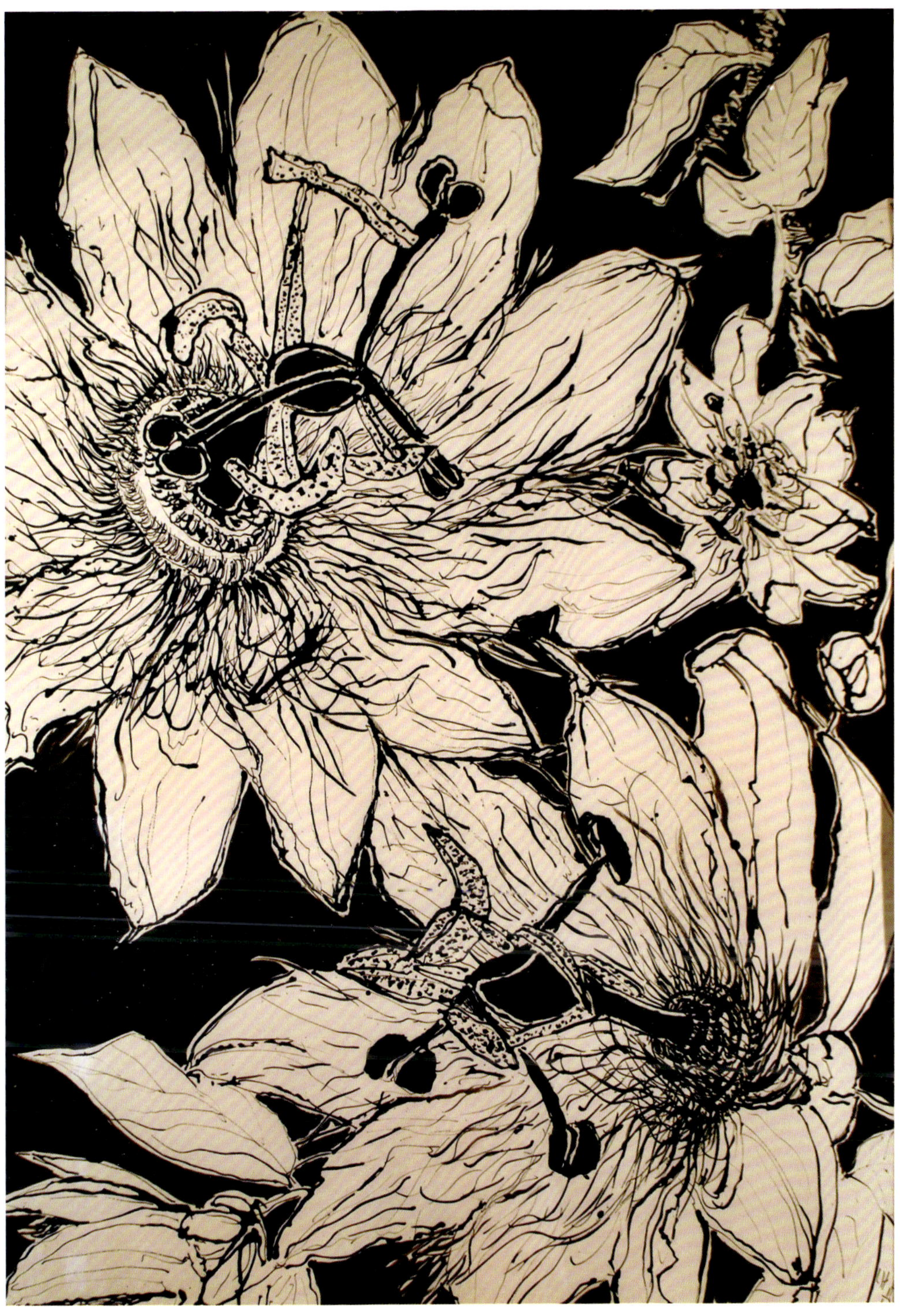

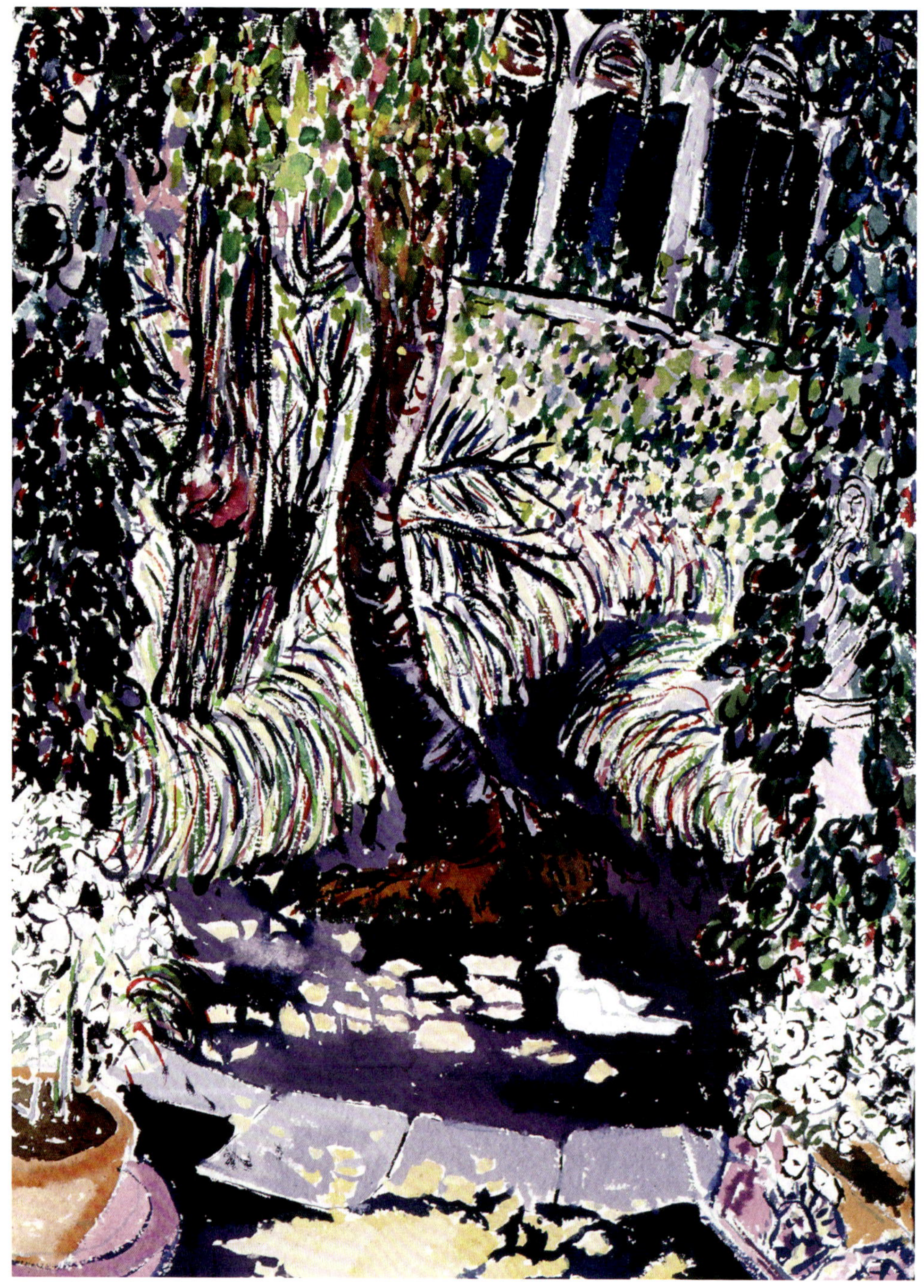

Palazzo Albrizzi Garden

Venice, Italy

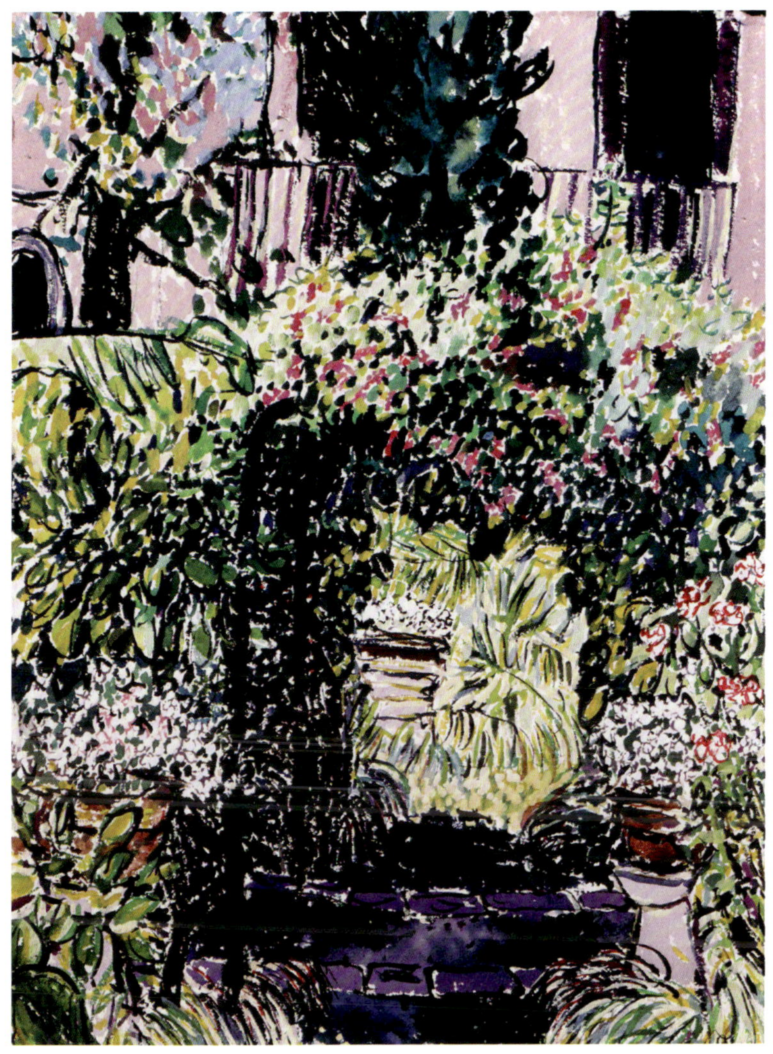

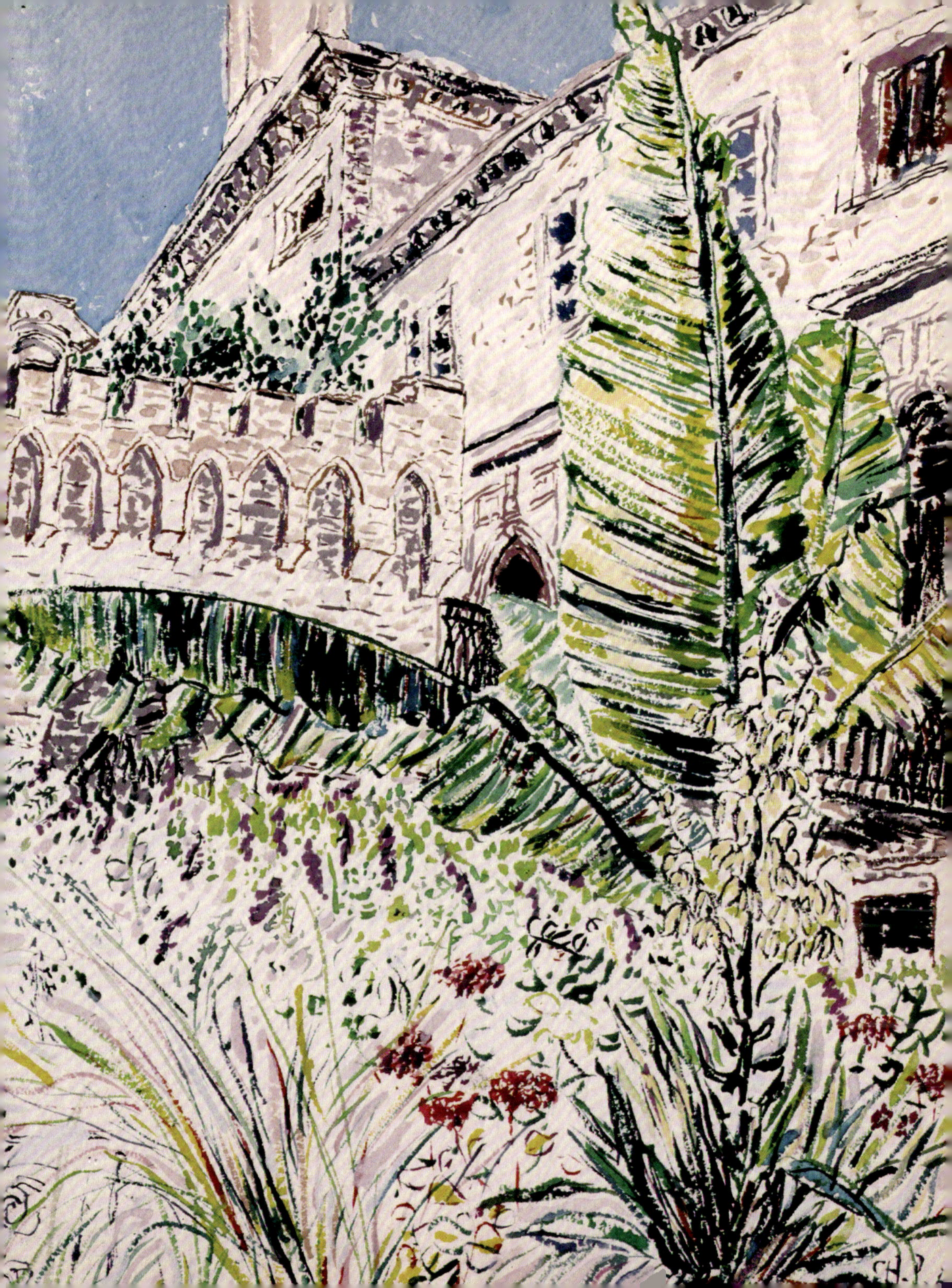

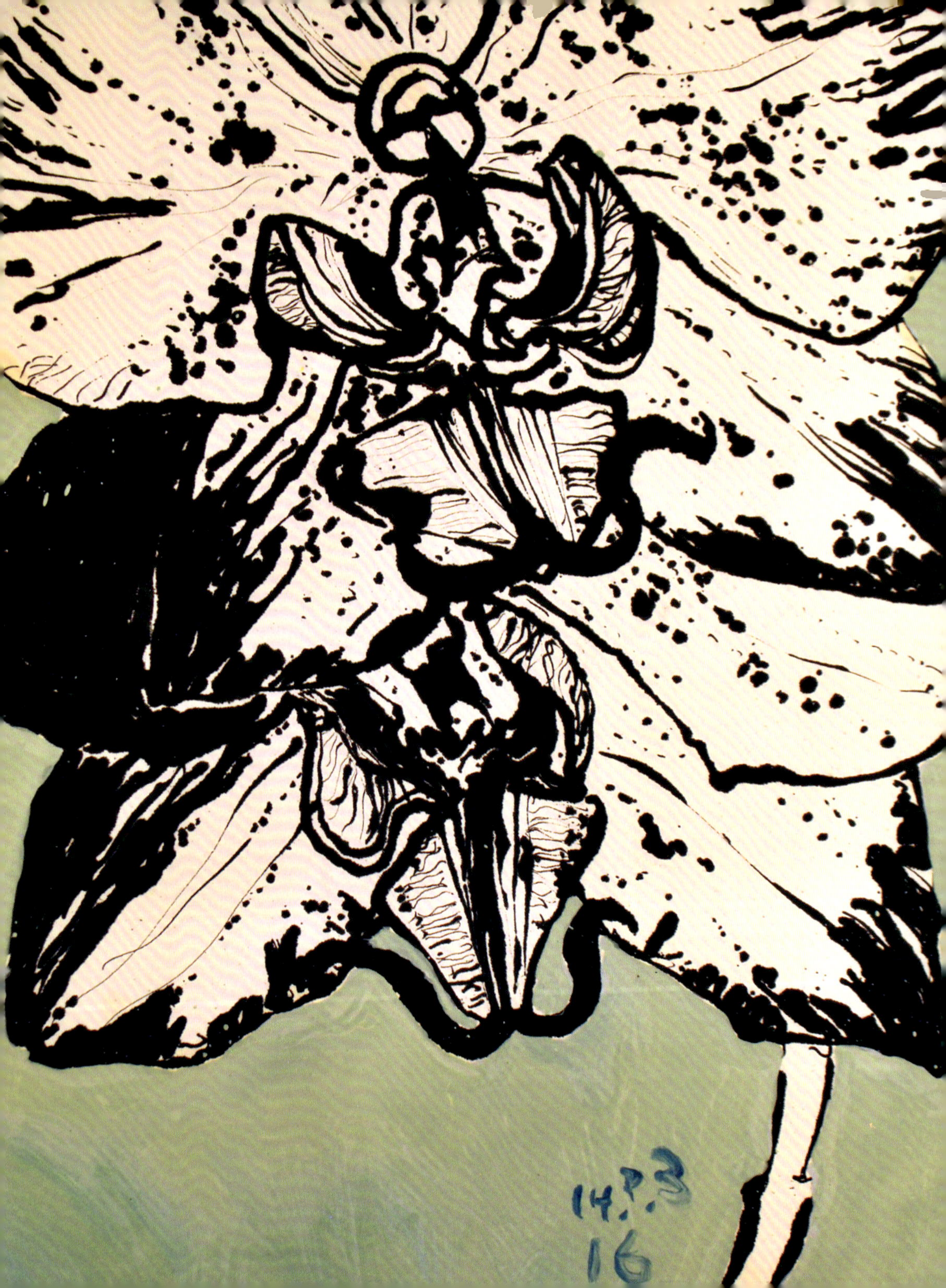

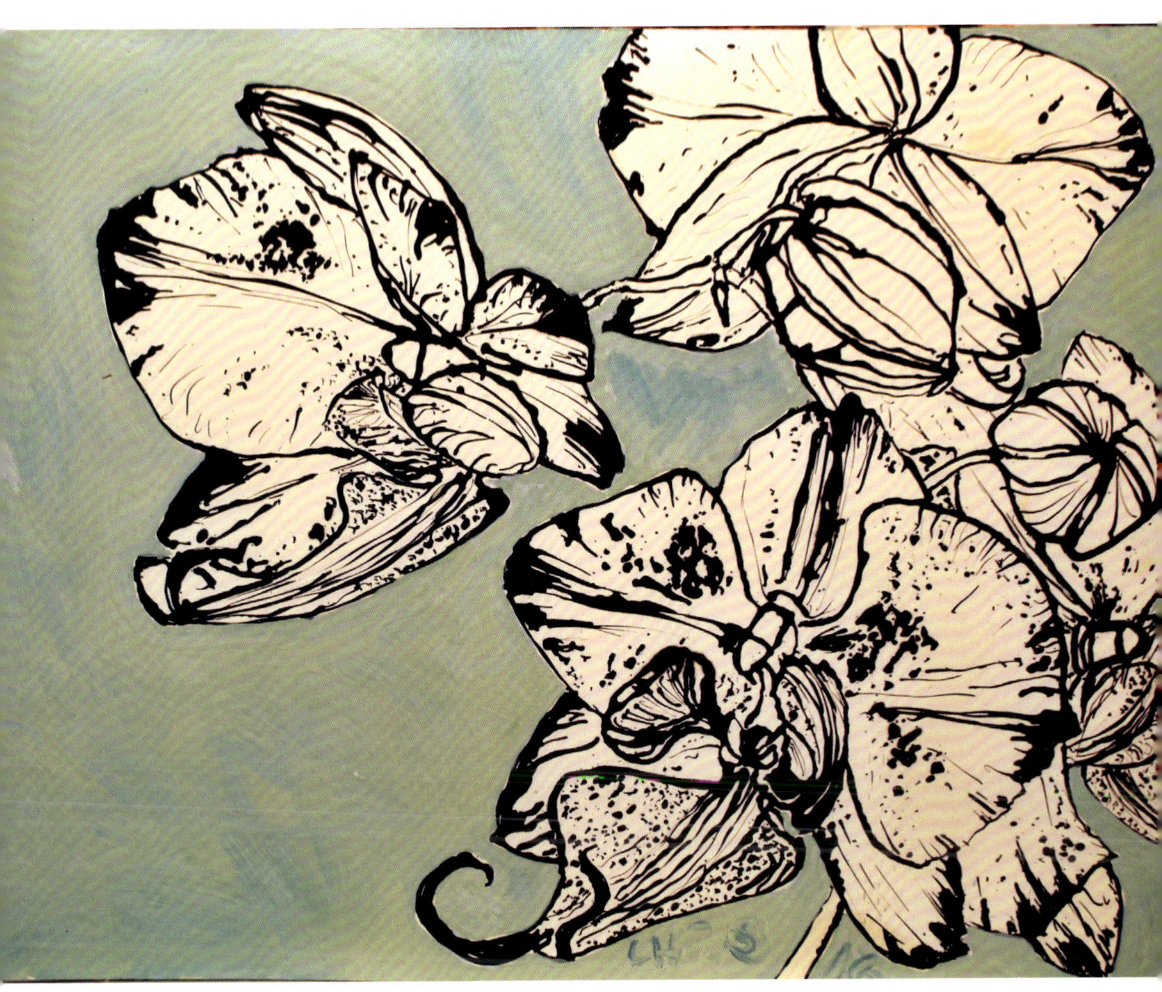

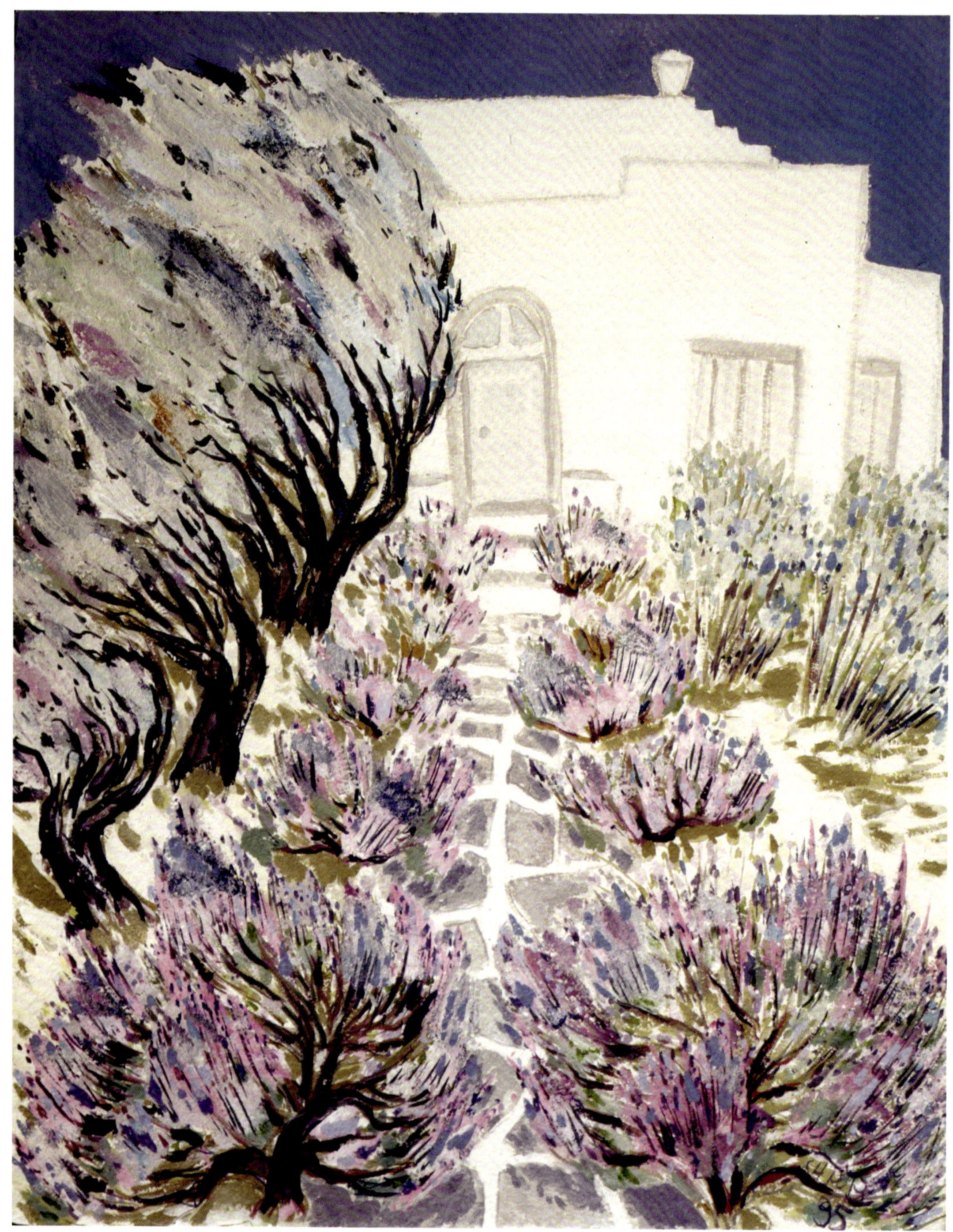

Sifnos Gardens

Sifnos, Greece

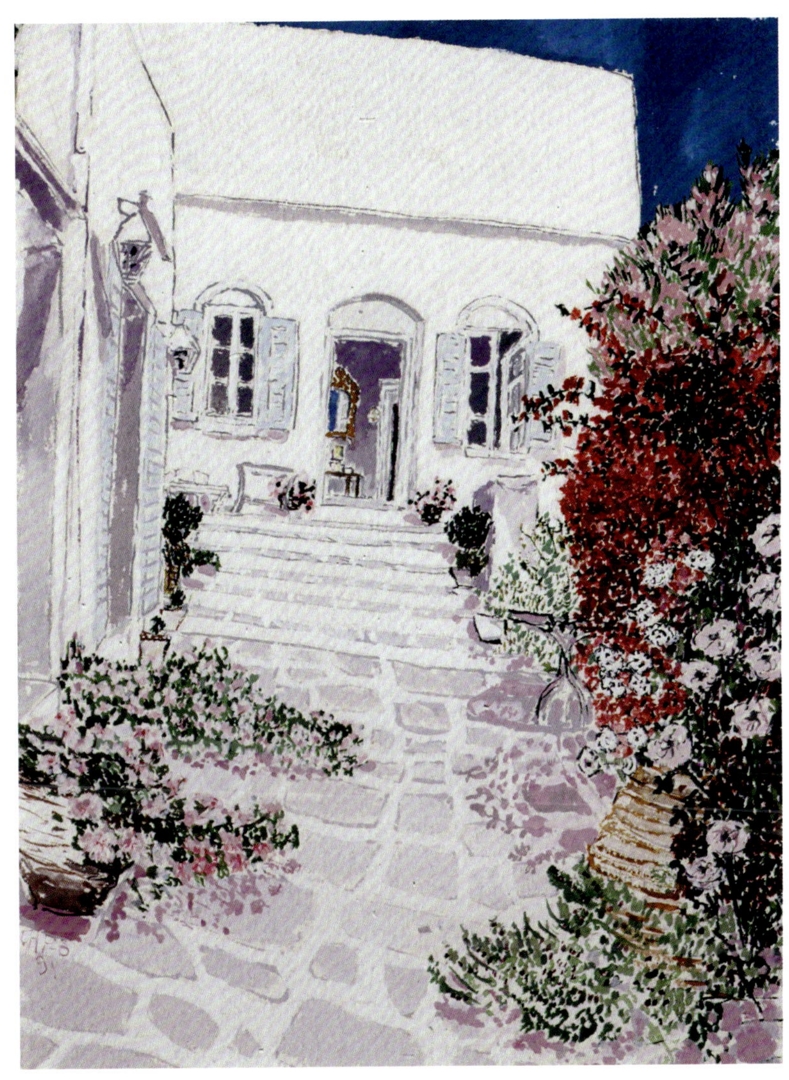

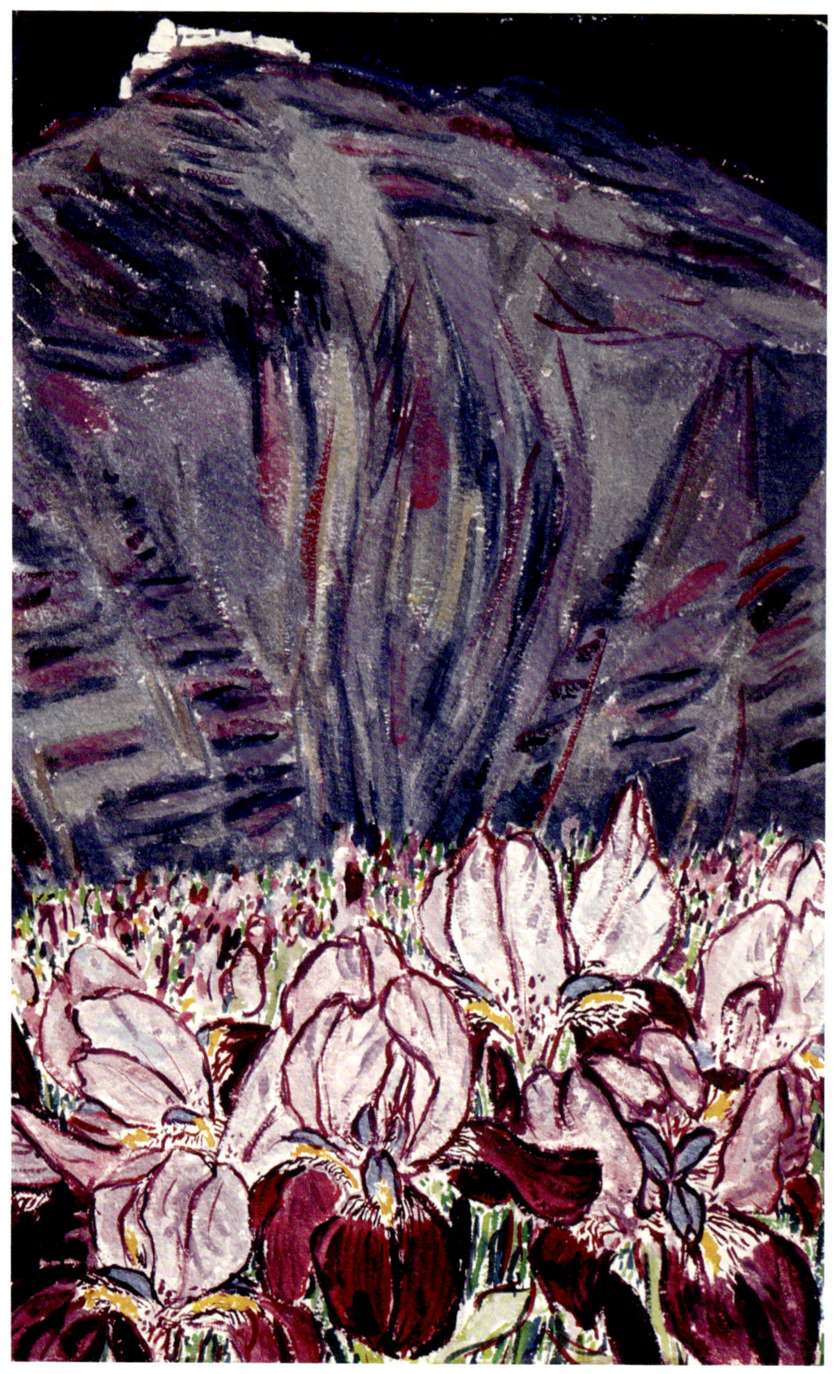

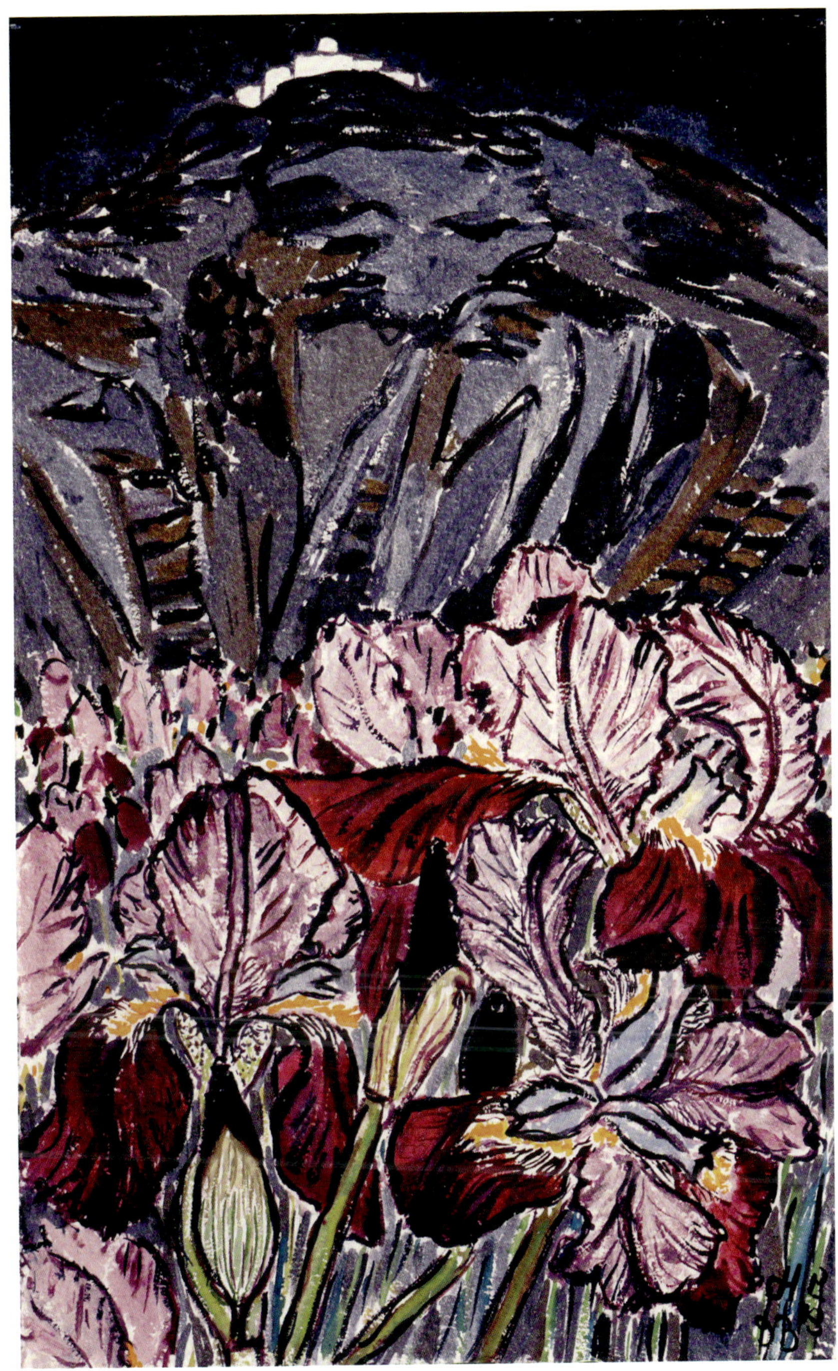

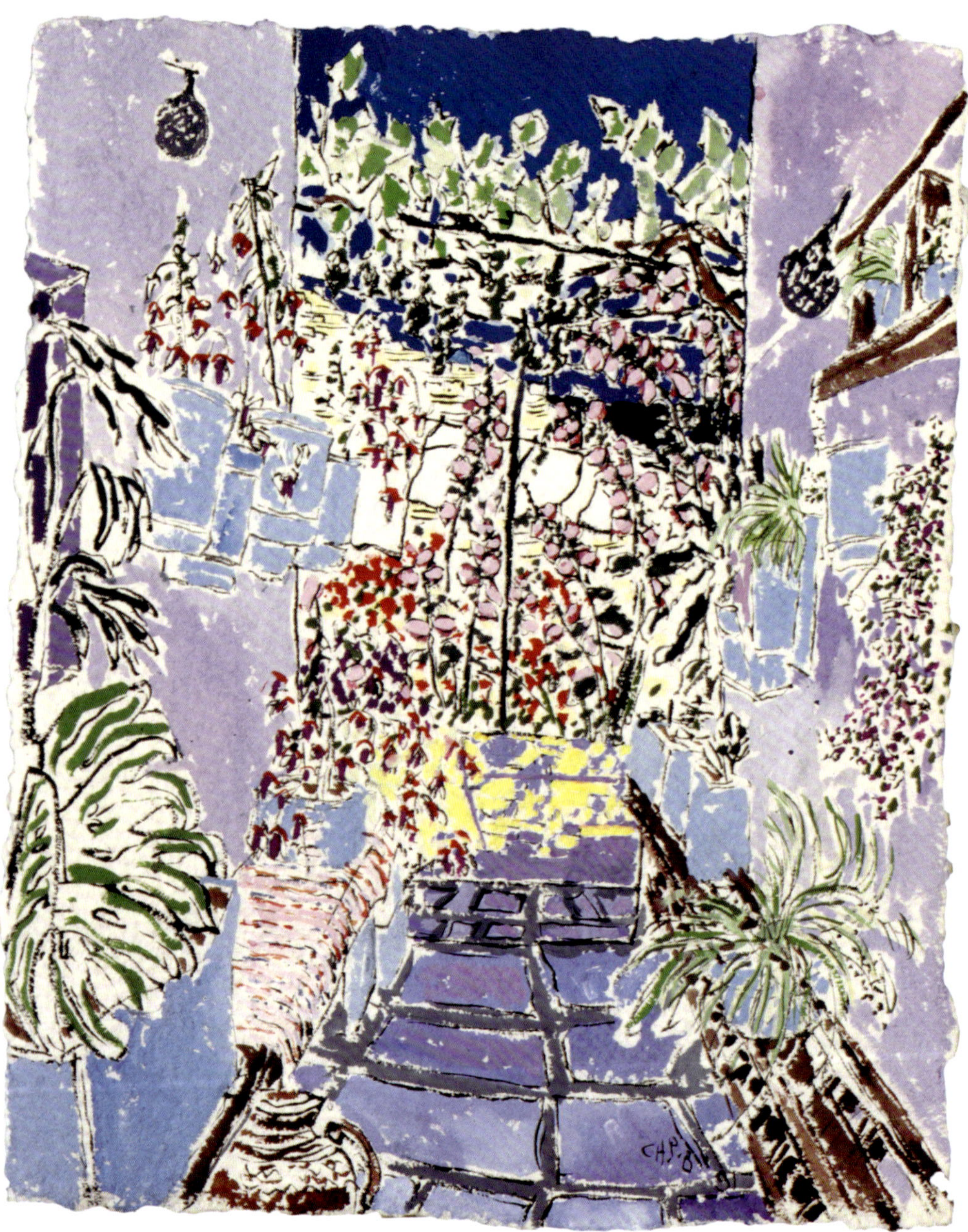

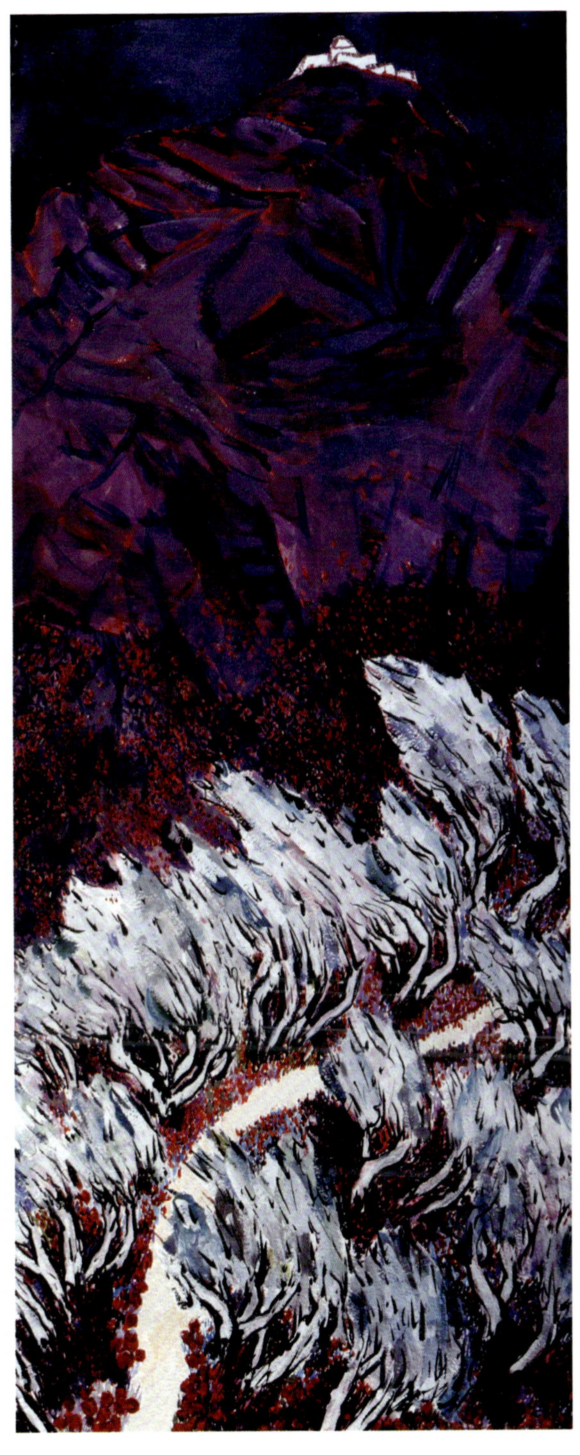

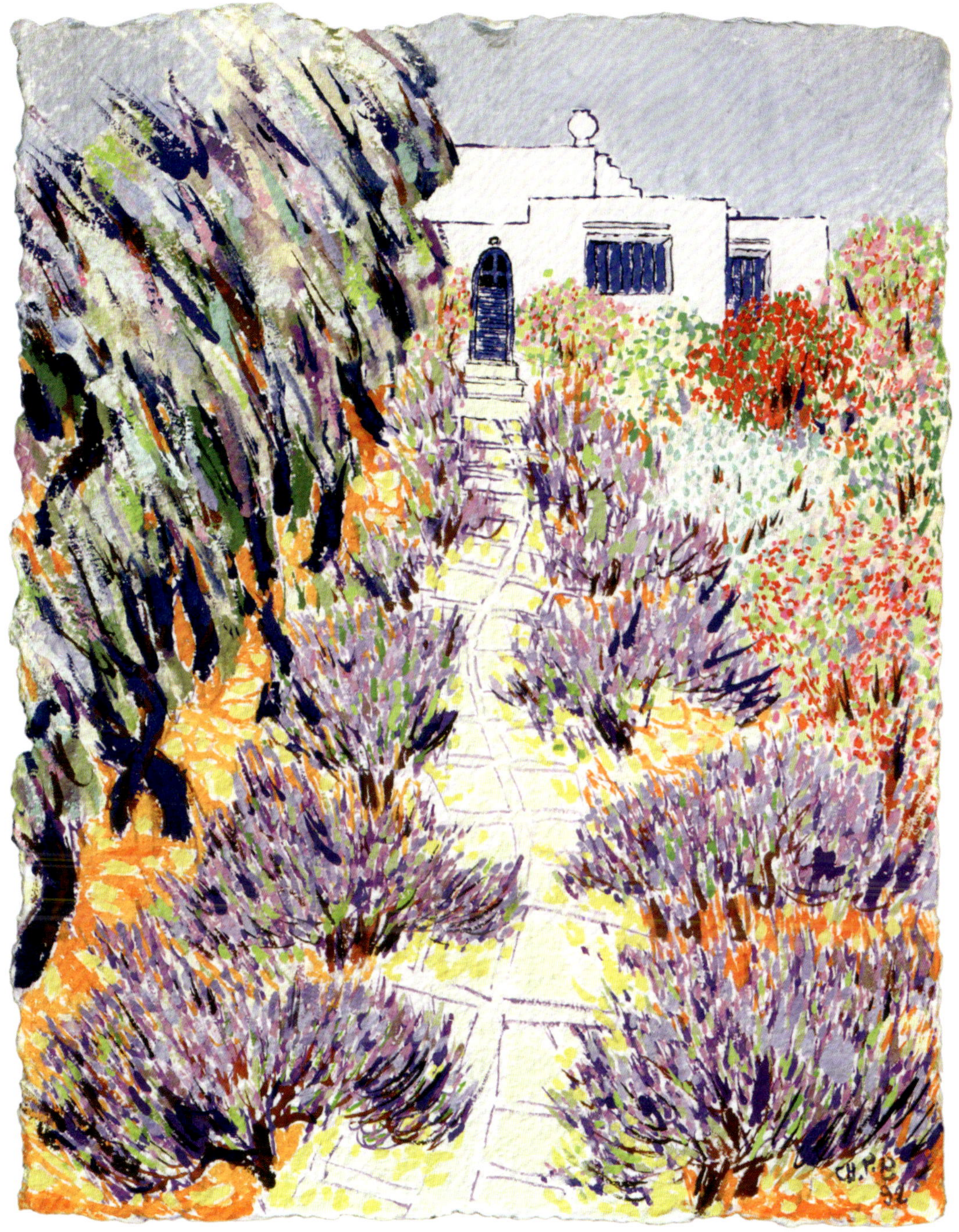

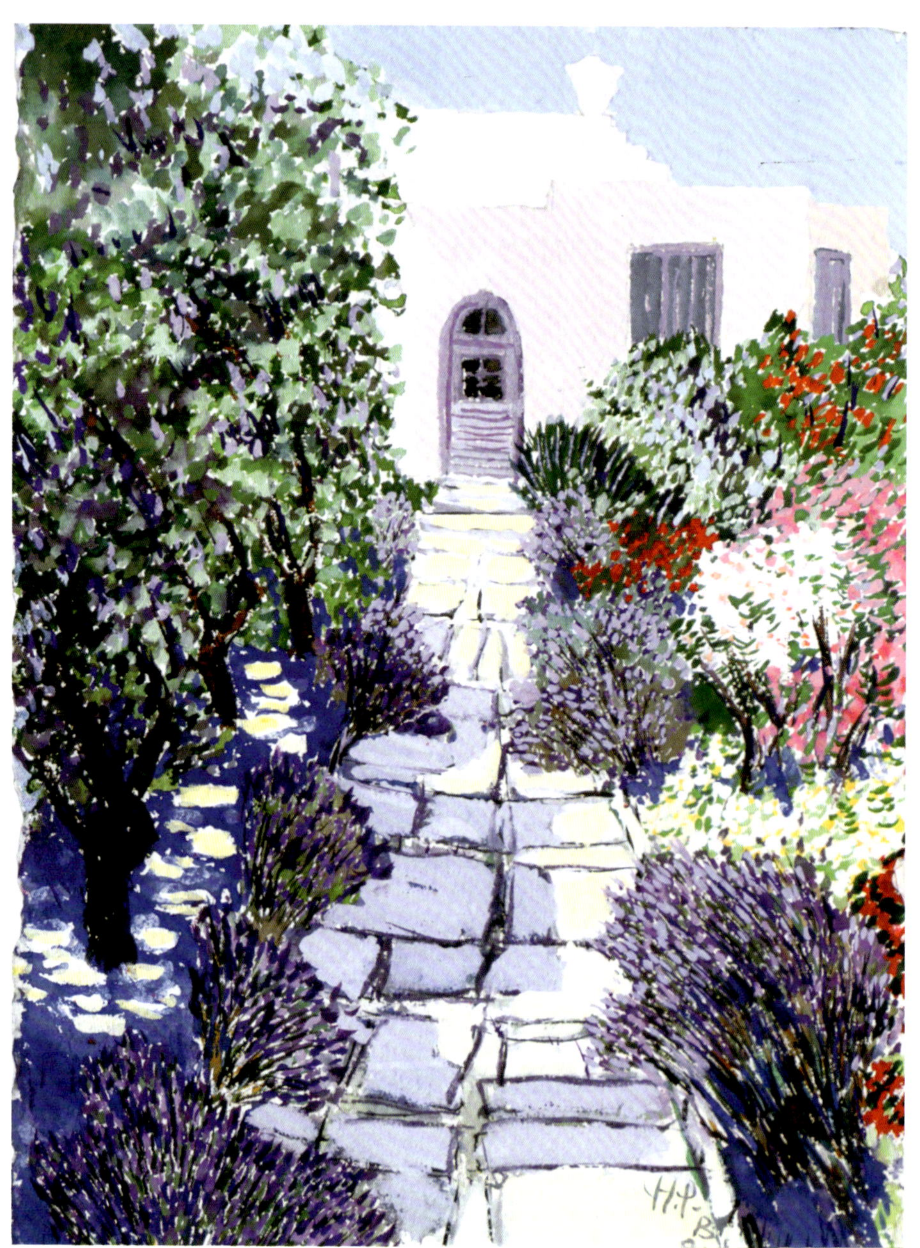

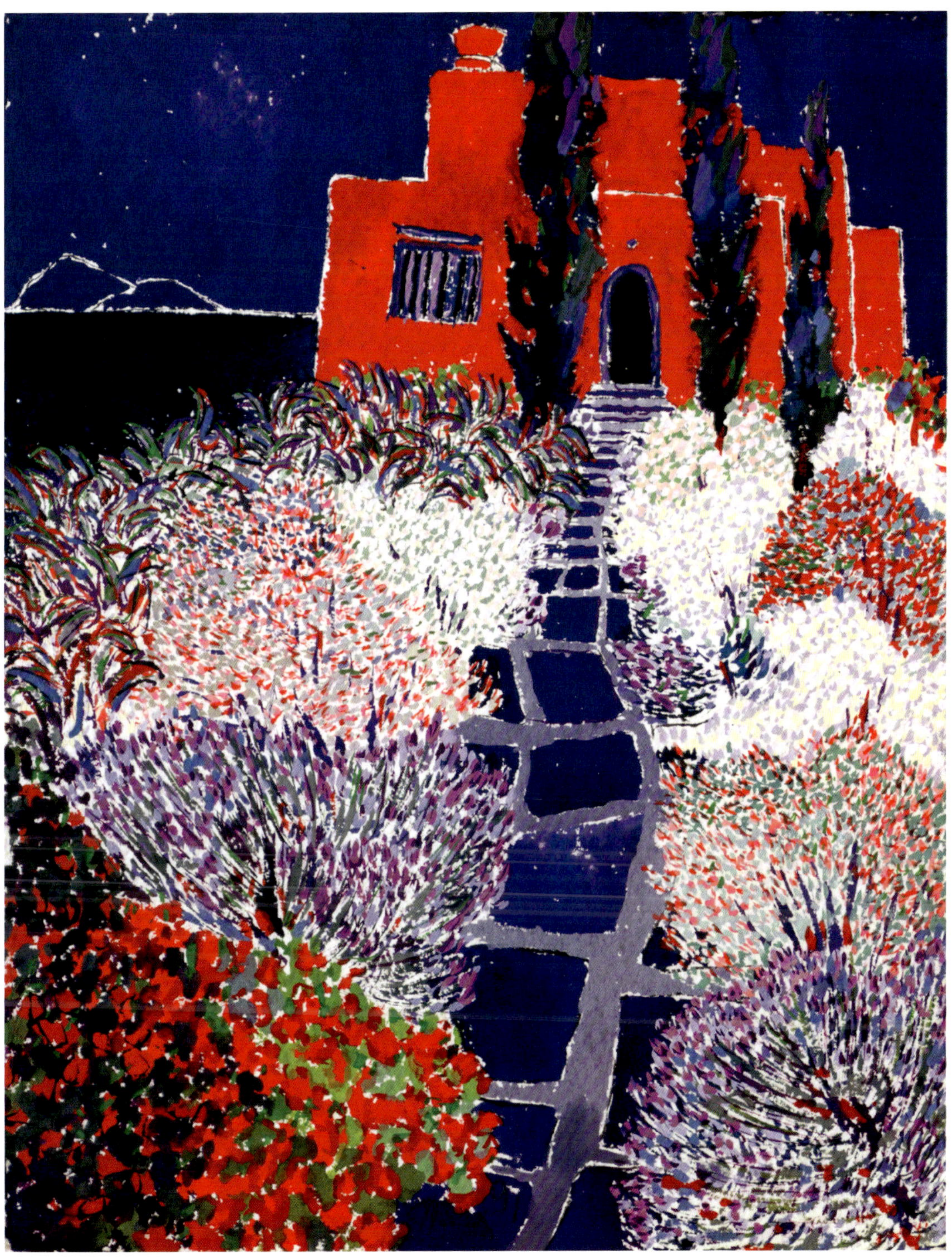

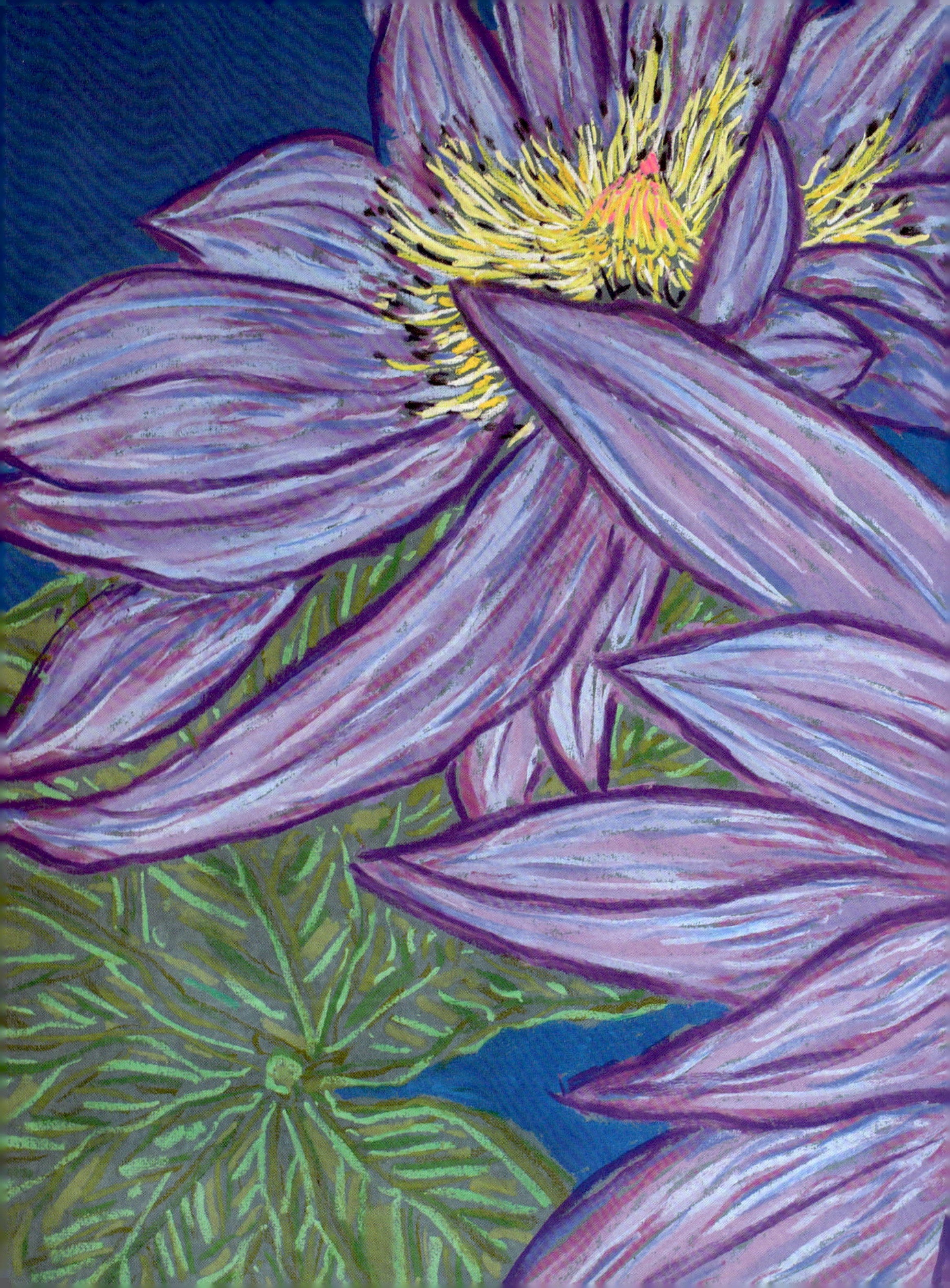

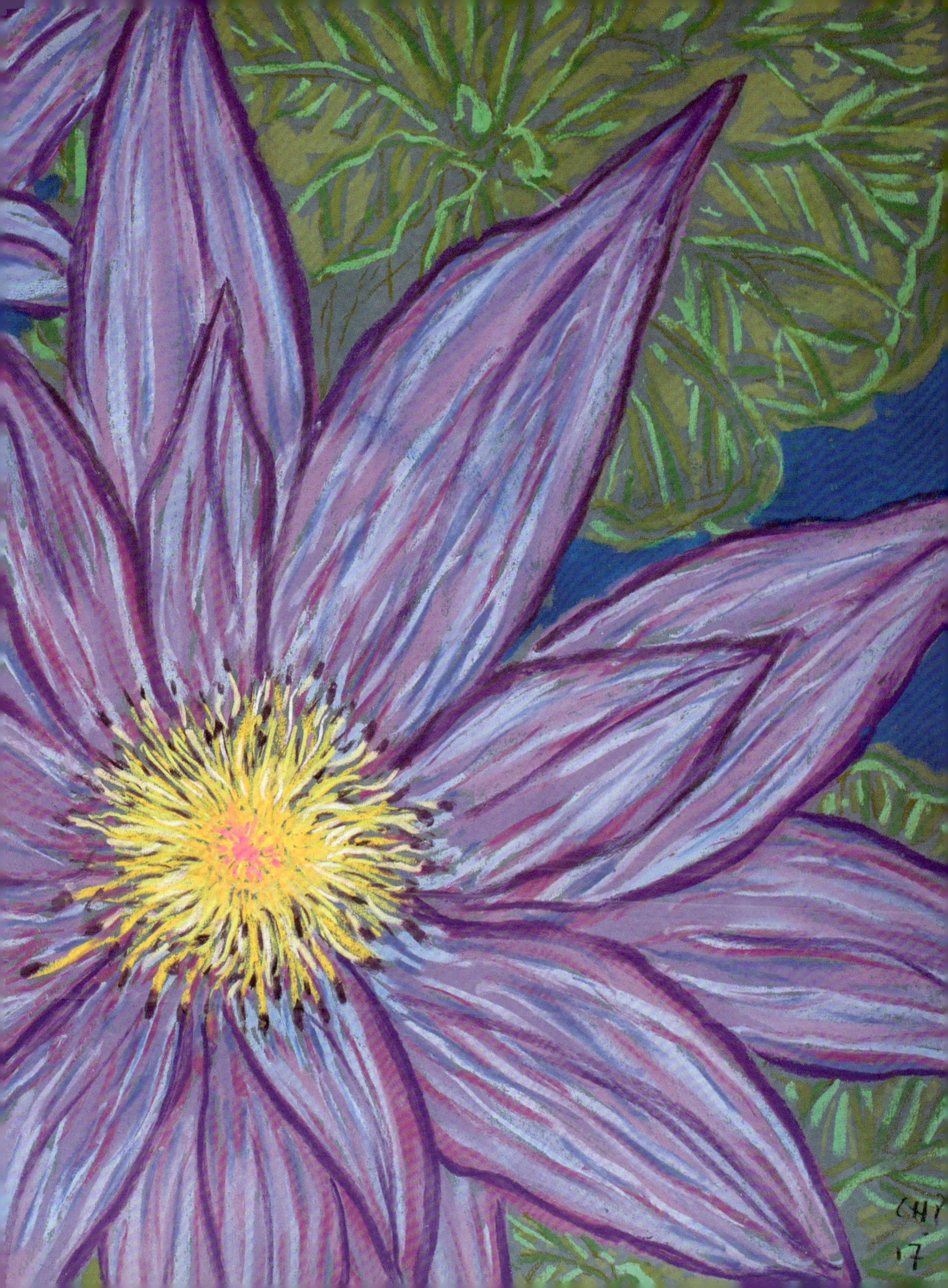

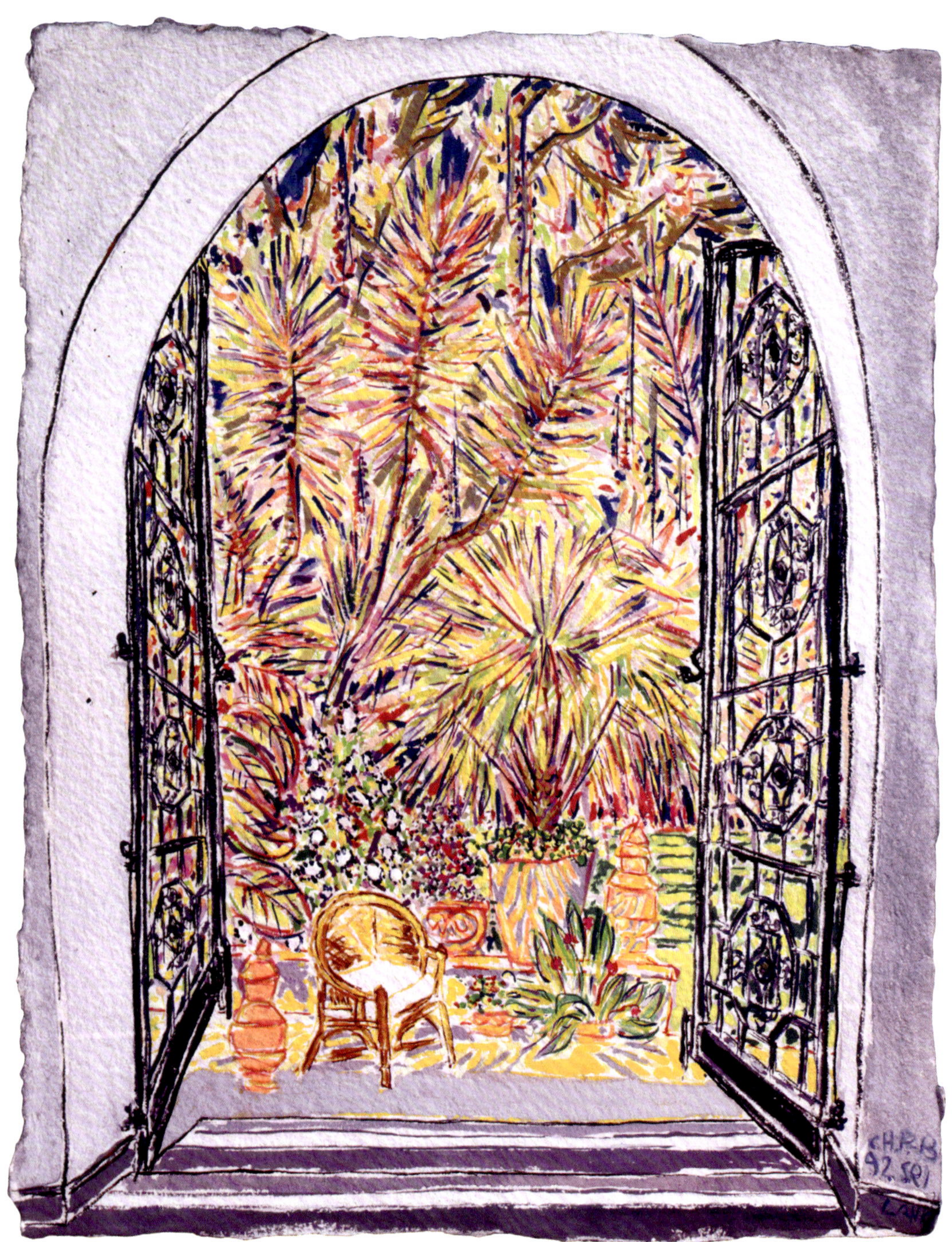
CH.P.B
92.SEI

Colombo Residence

Colombo, Sri Lanka

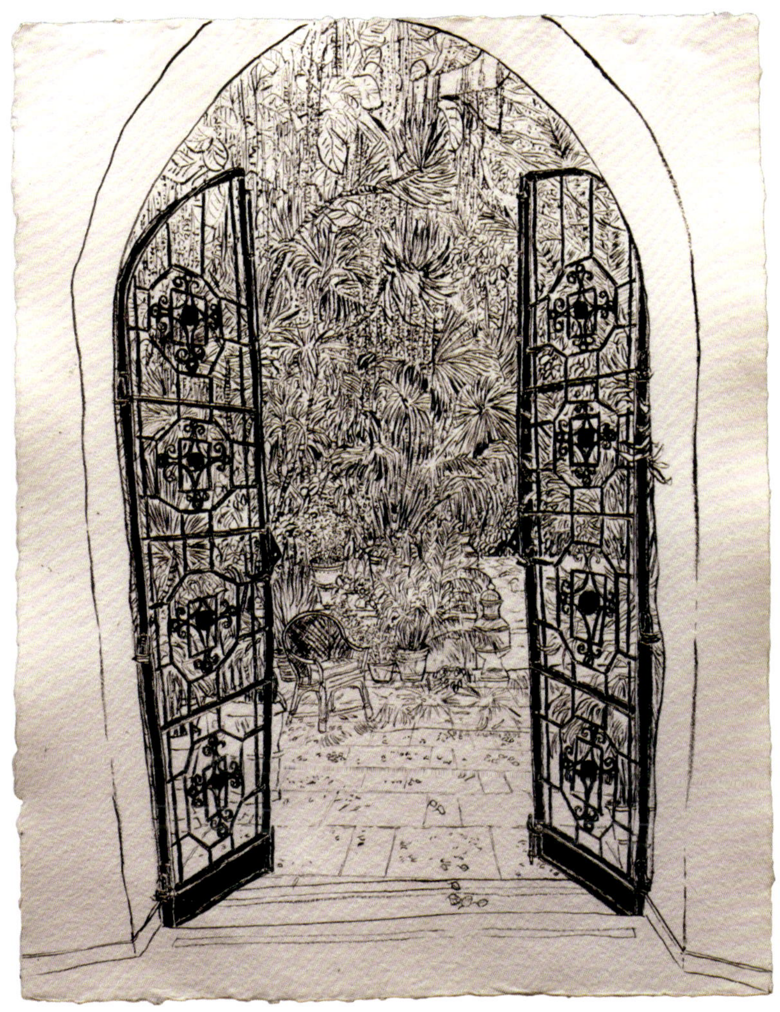

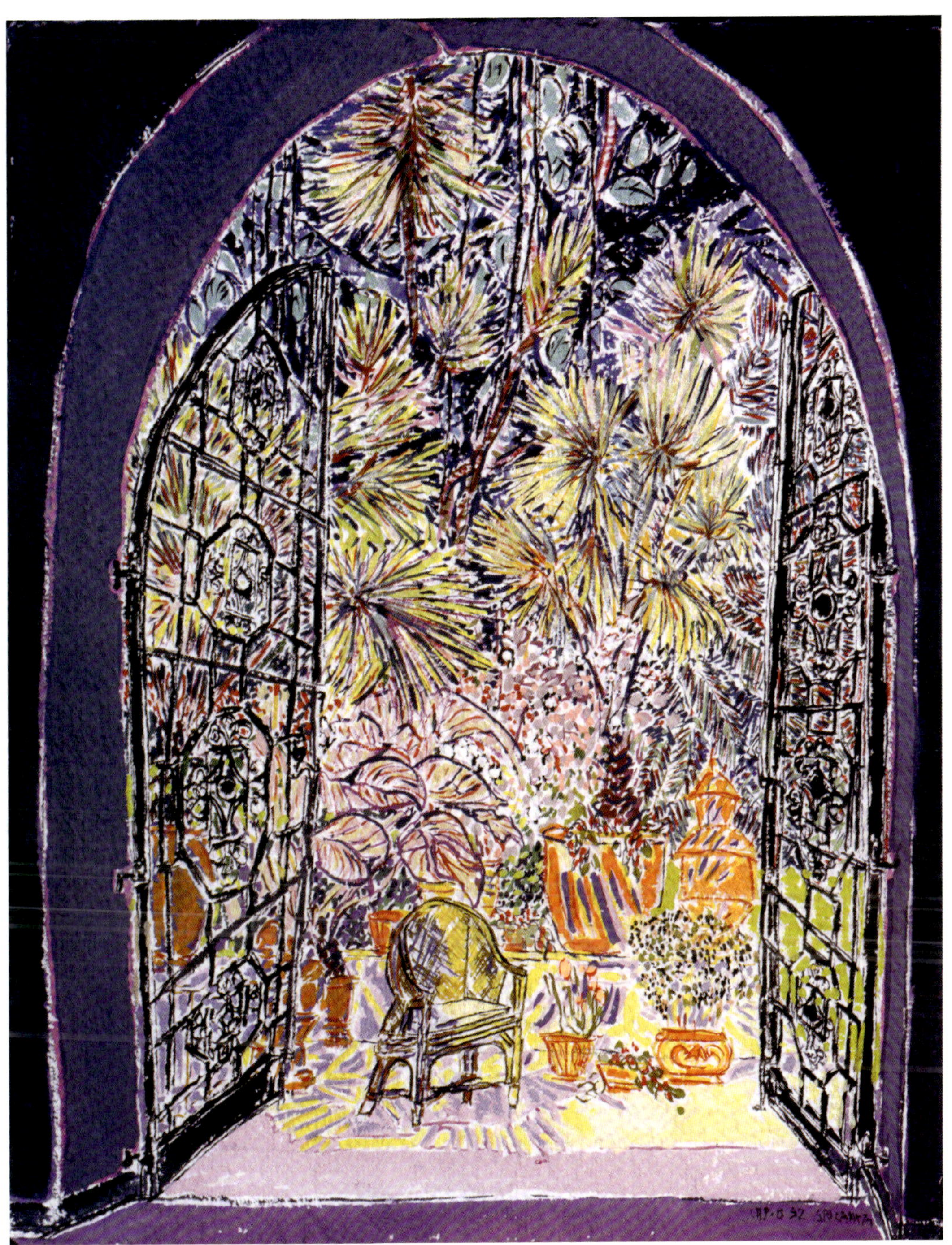

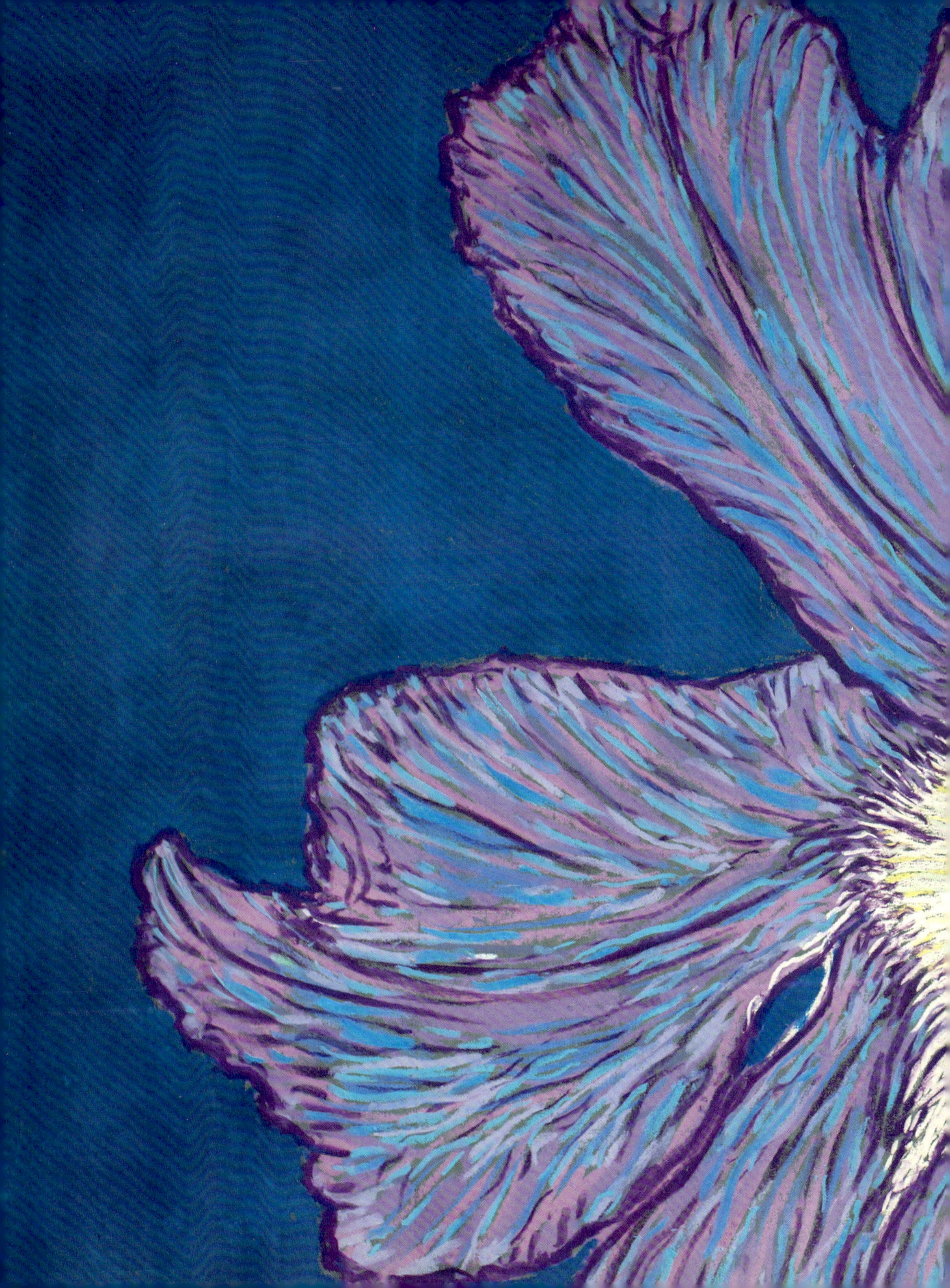

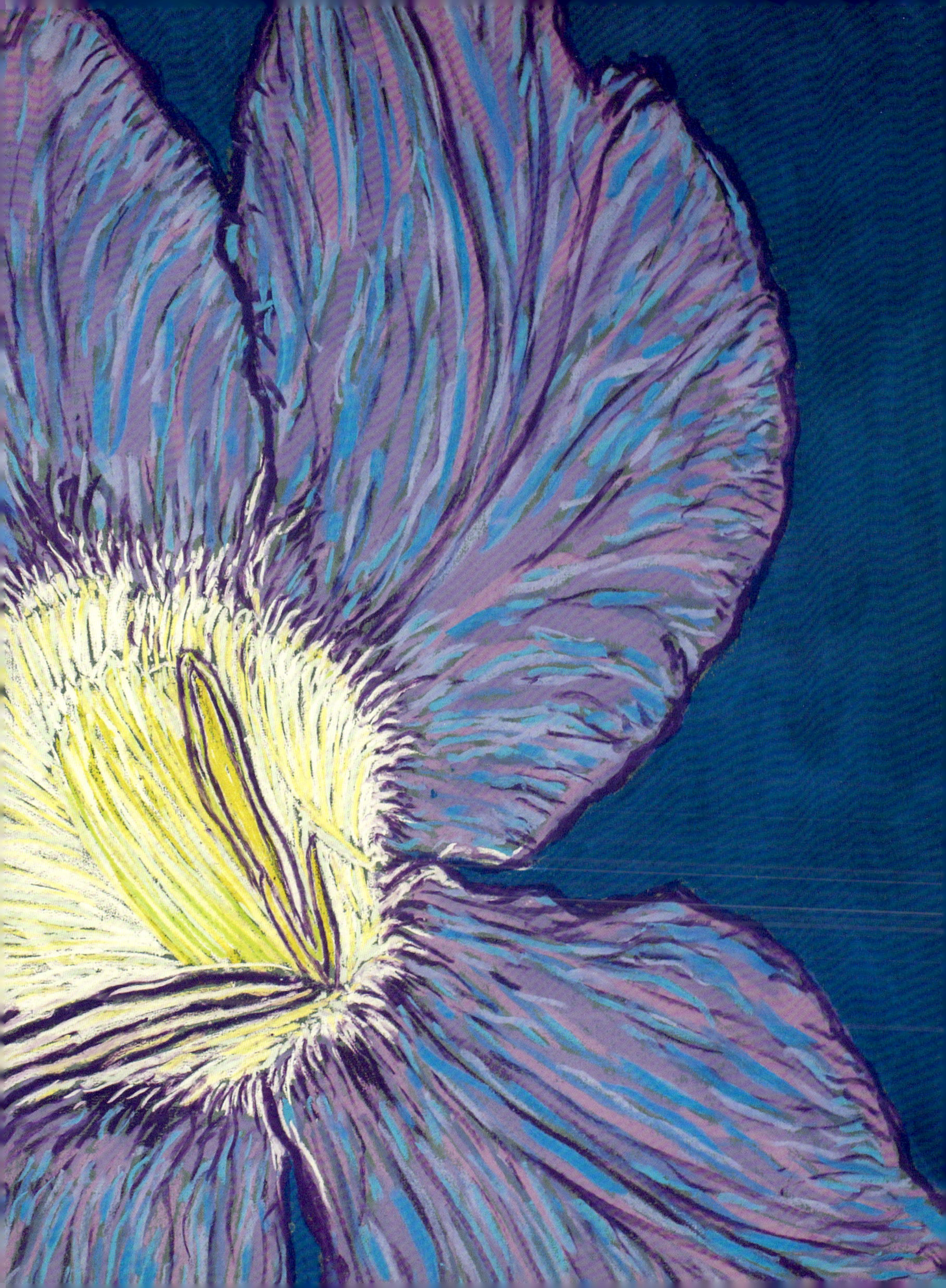

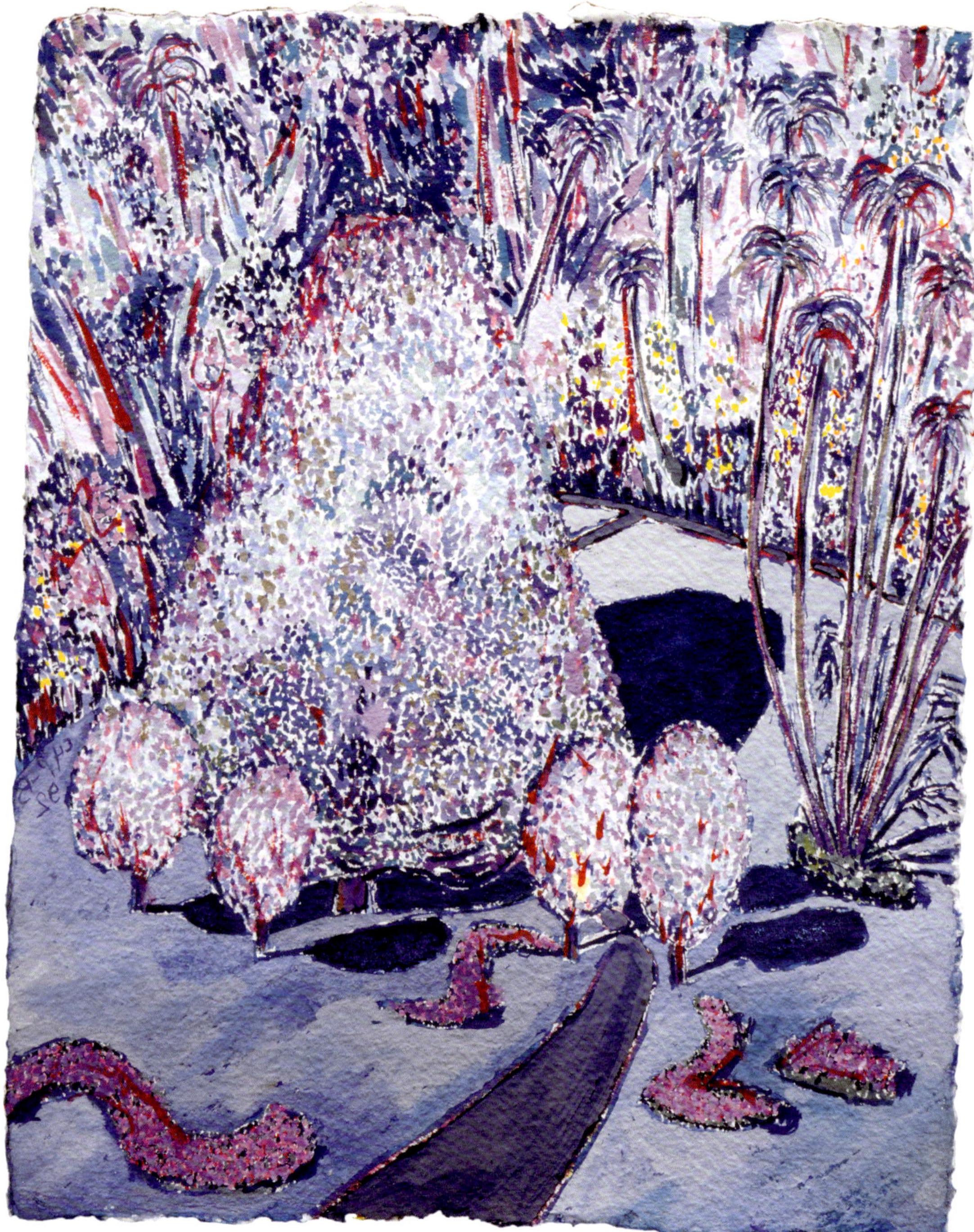

Kandy Botanical Gardens

Kandy, Sri Lanka

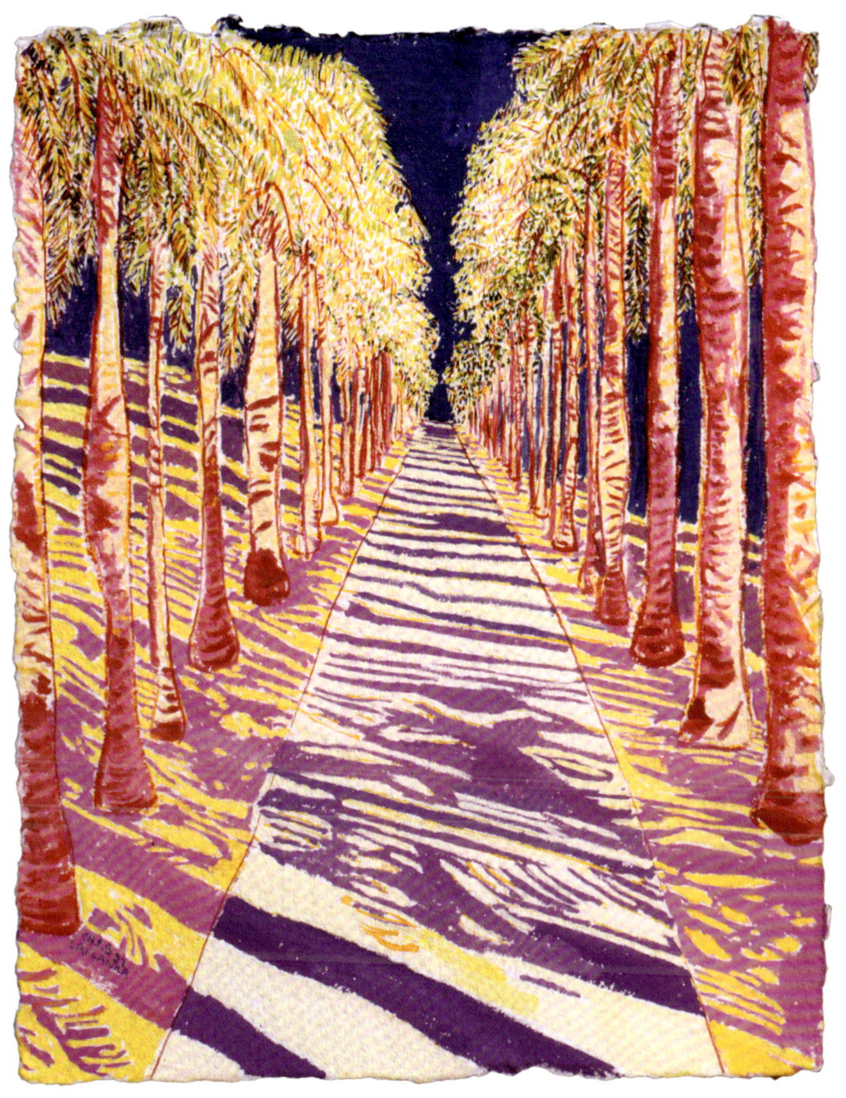

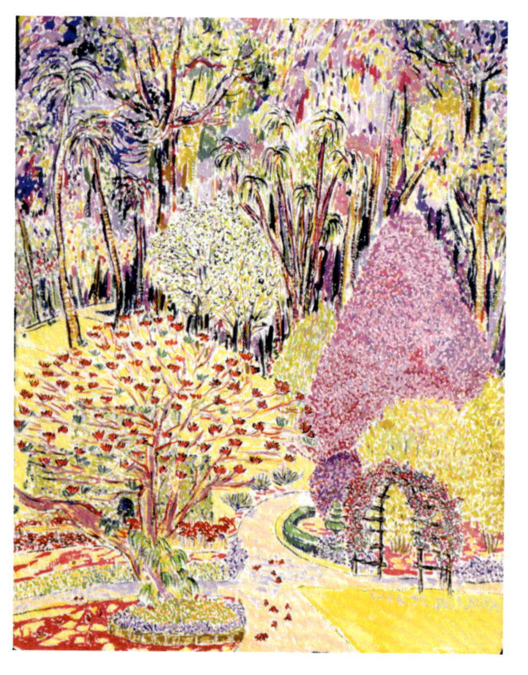

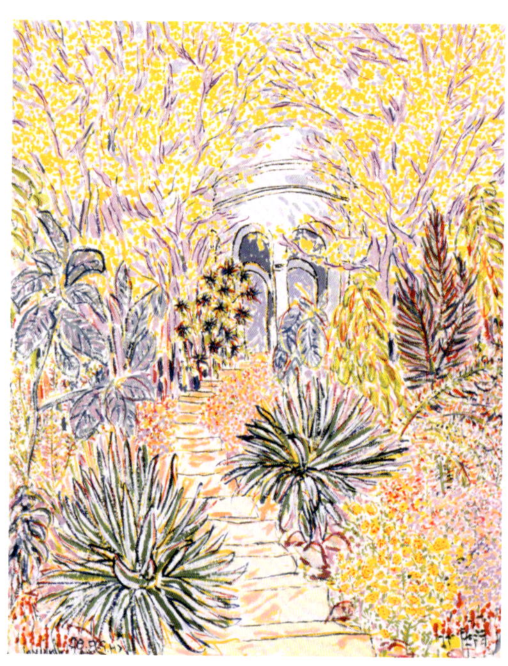

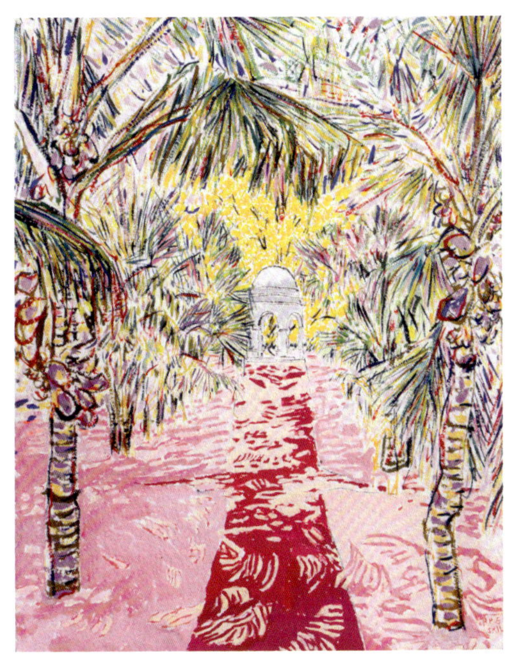

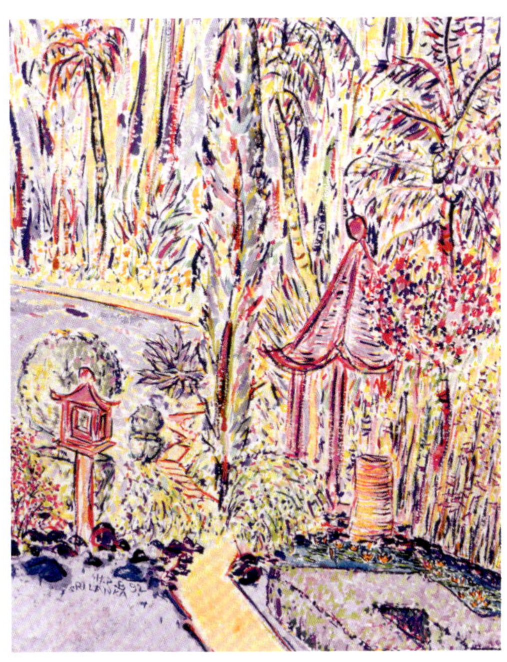

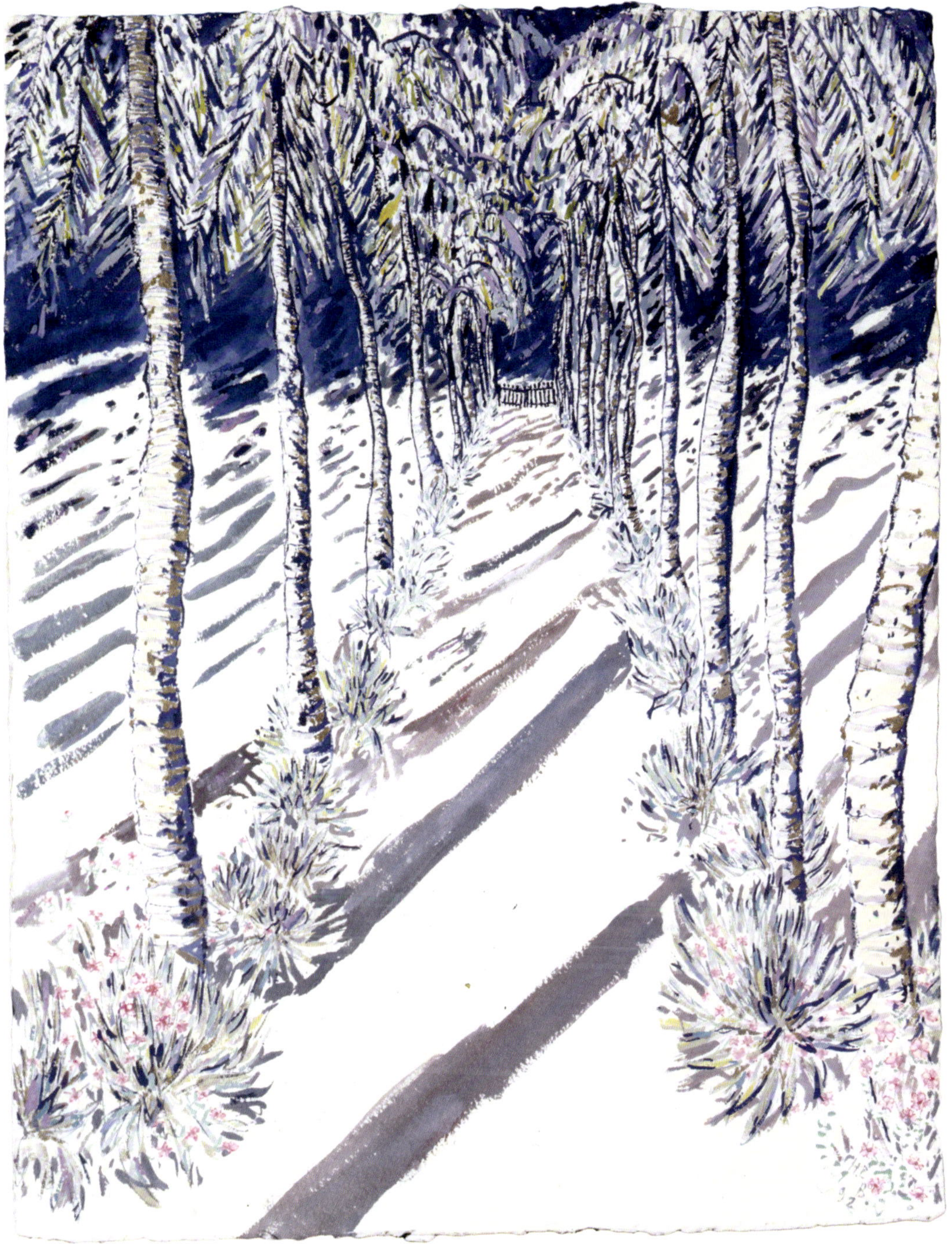

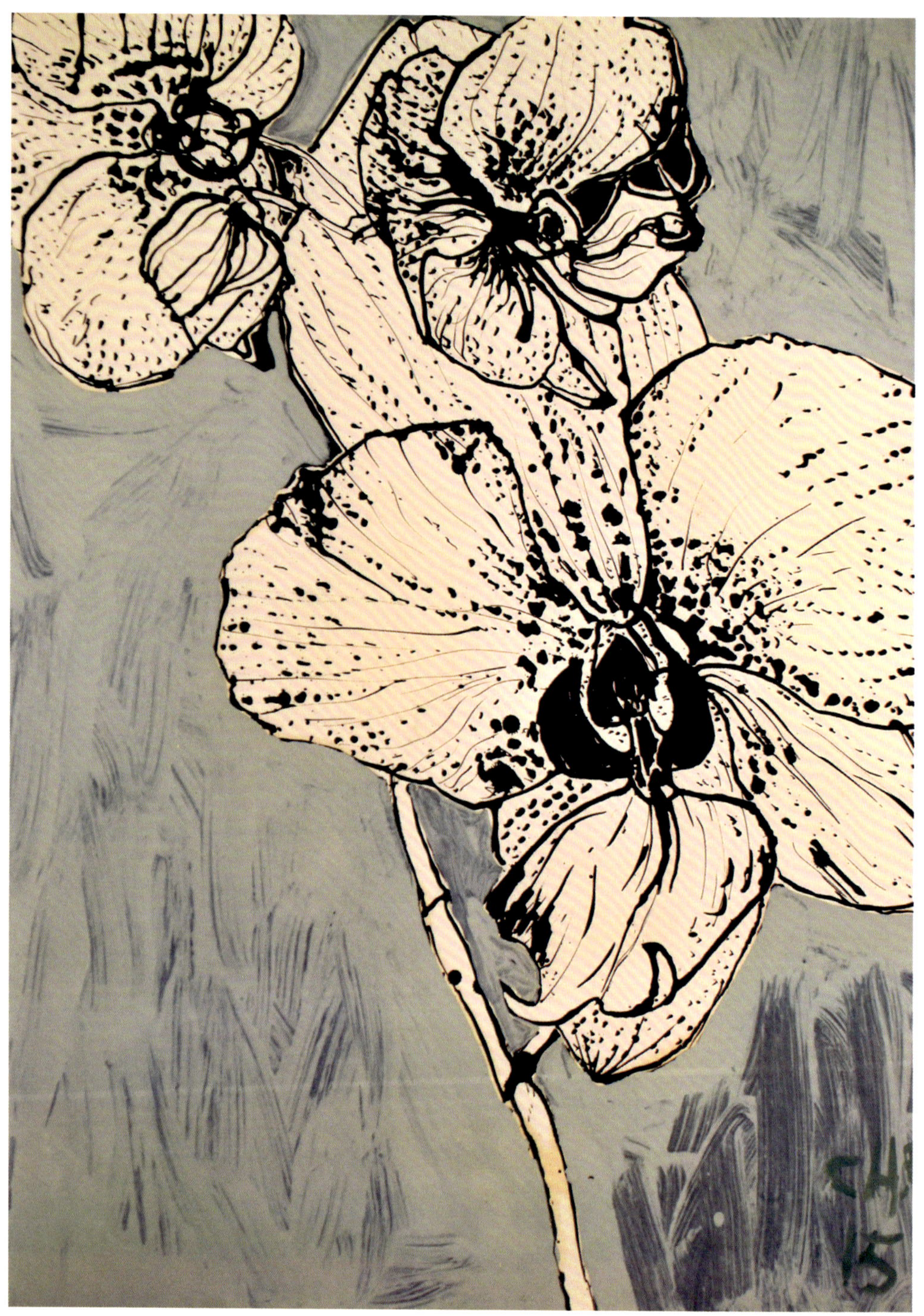

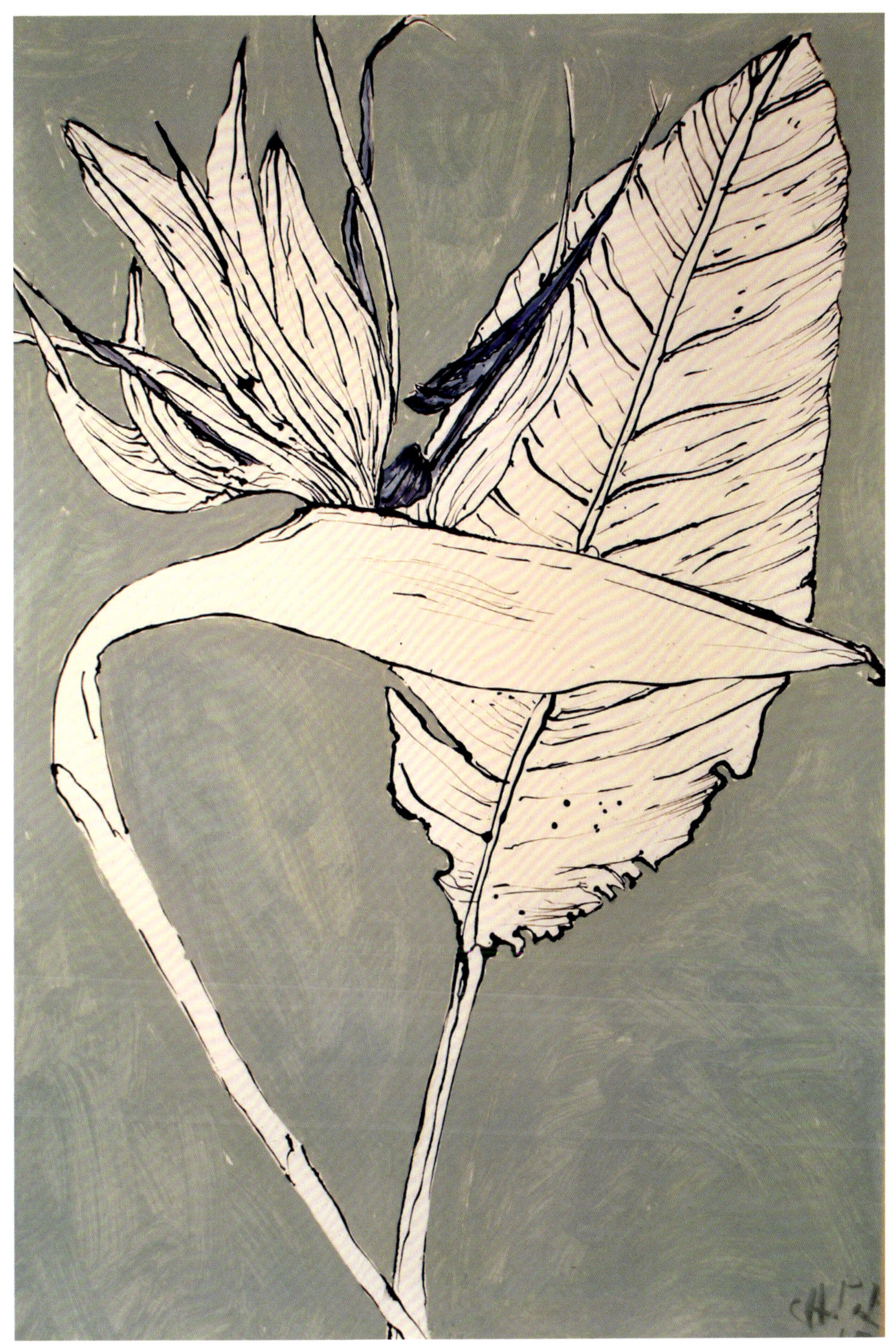

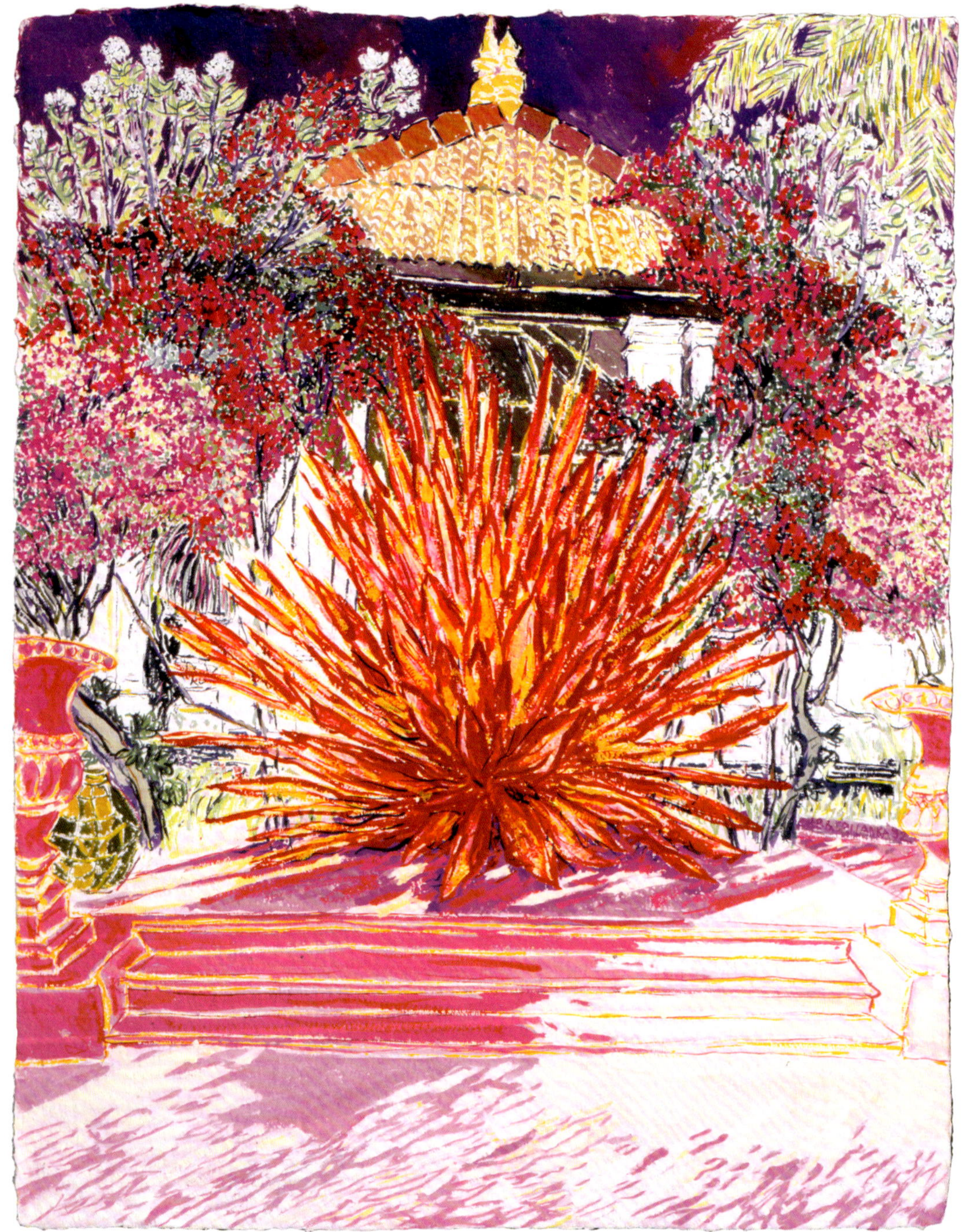

Dorawana

Bentota, Sri Lanka

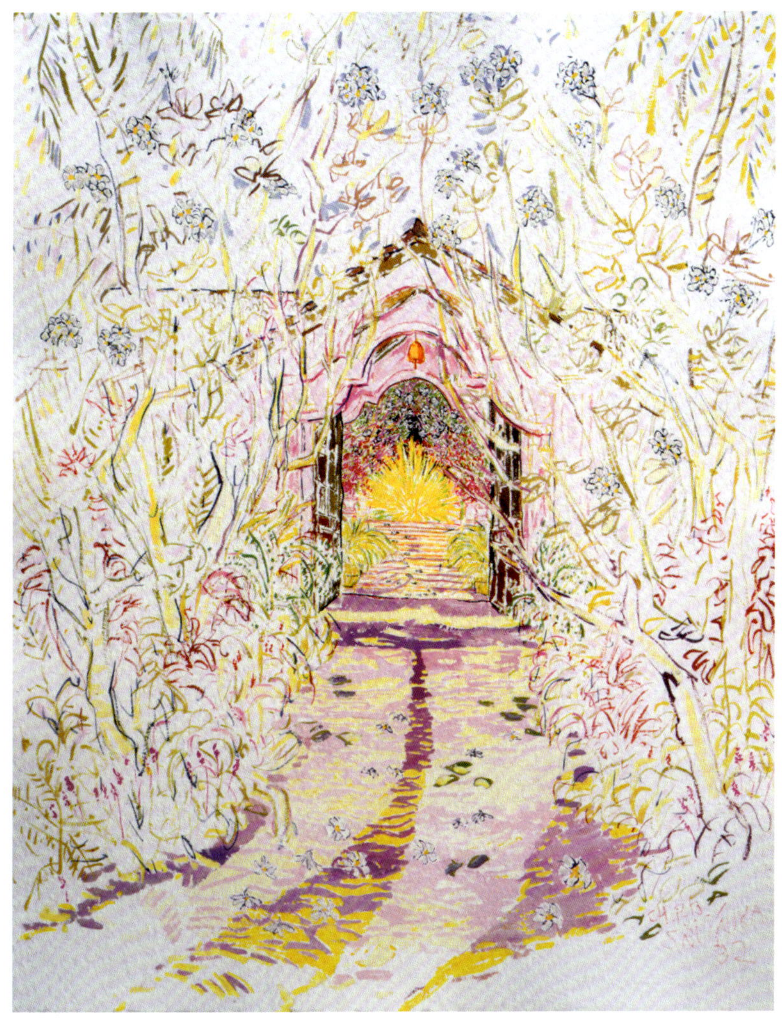

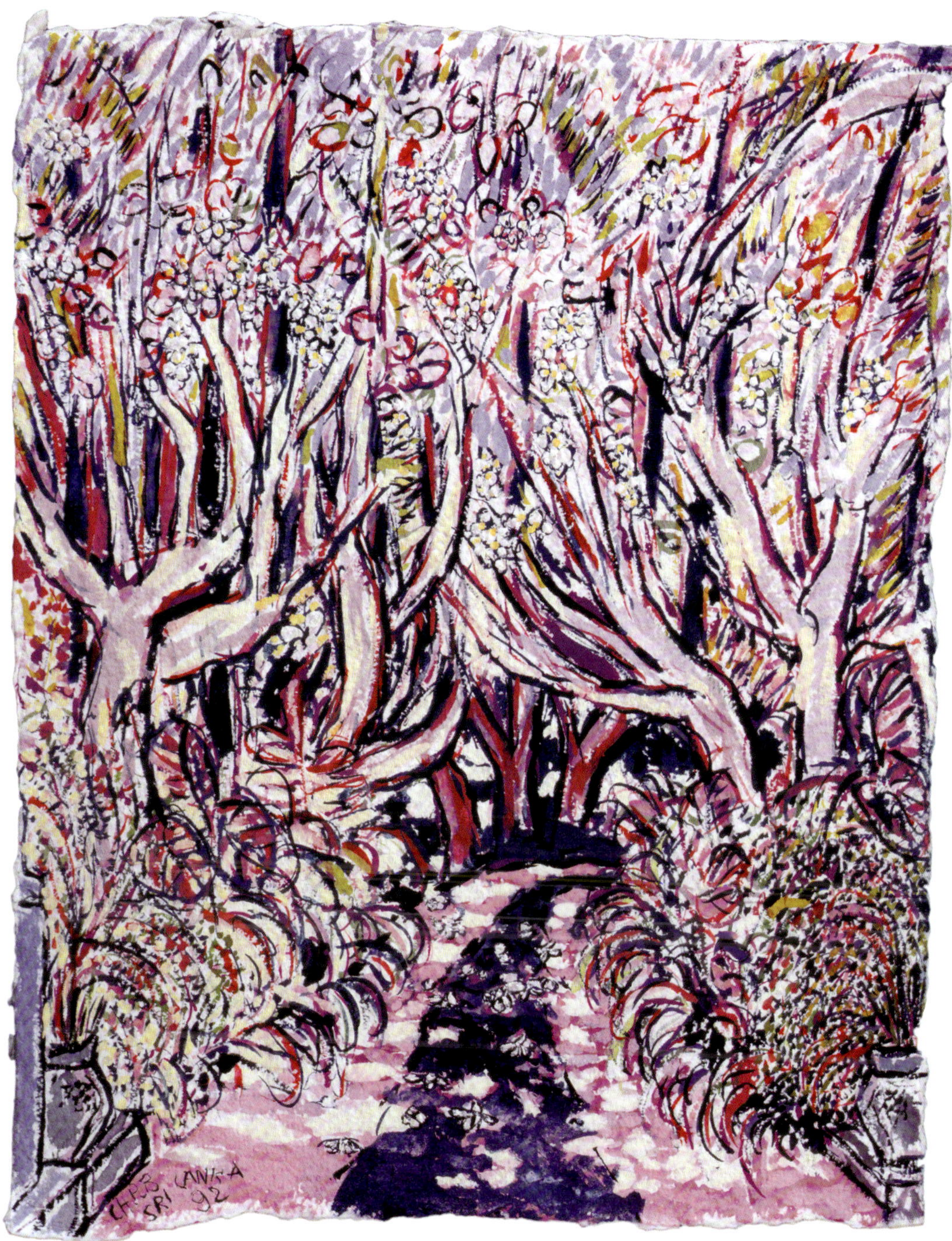
CHRIS
SRI LANKA
92

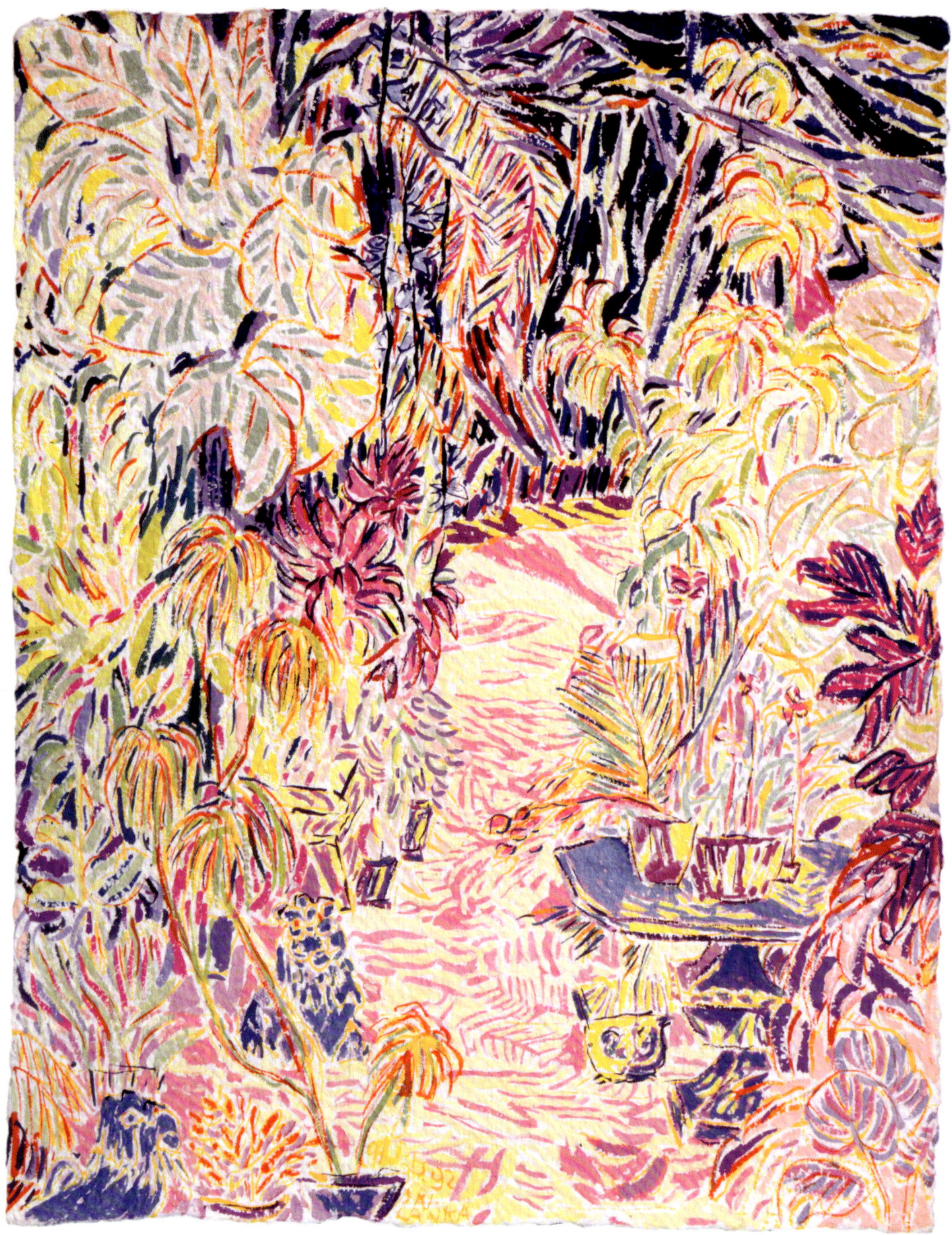

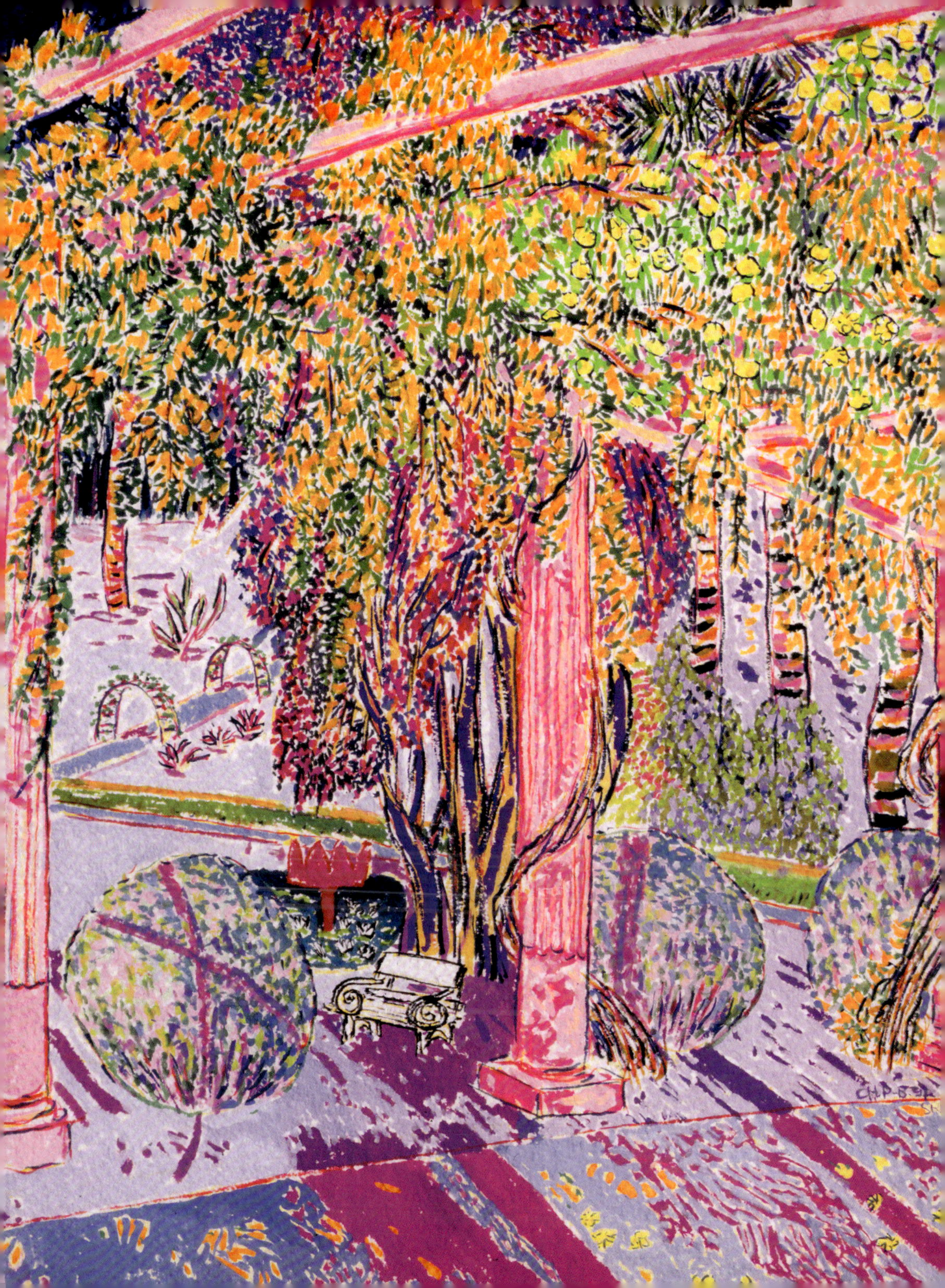

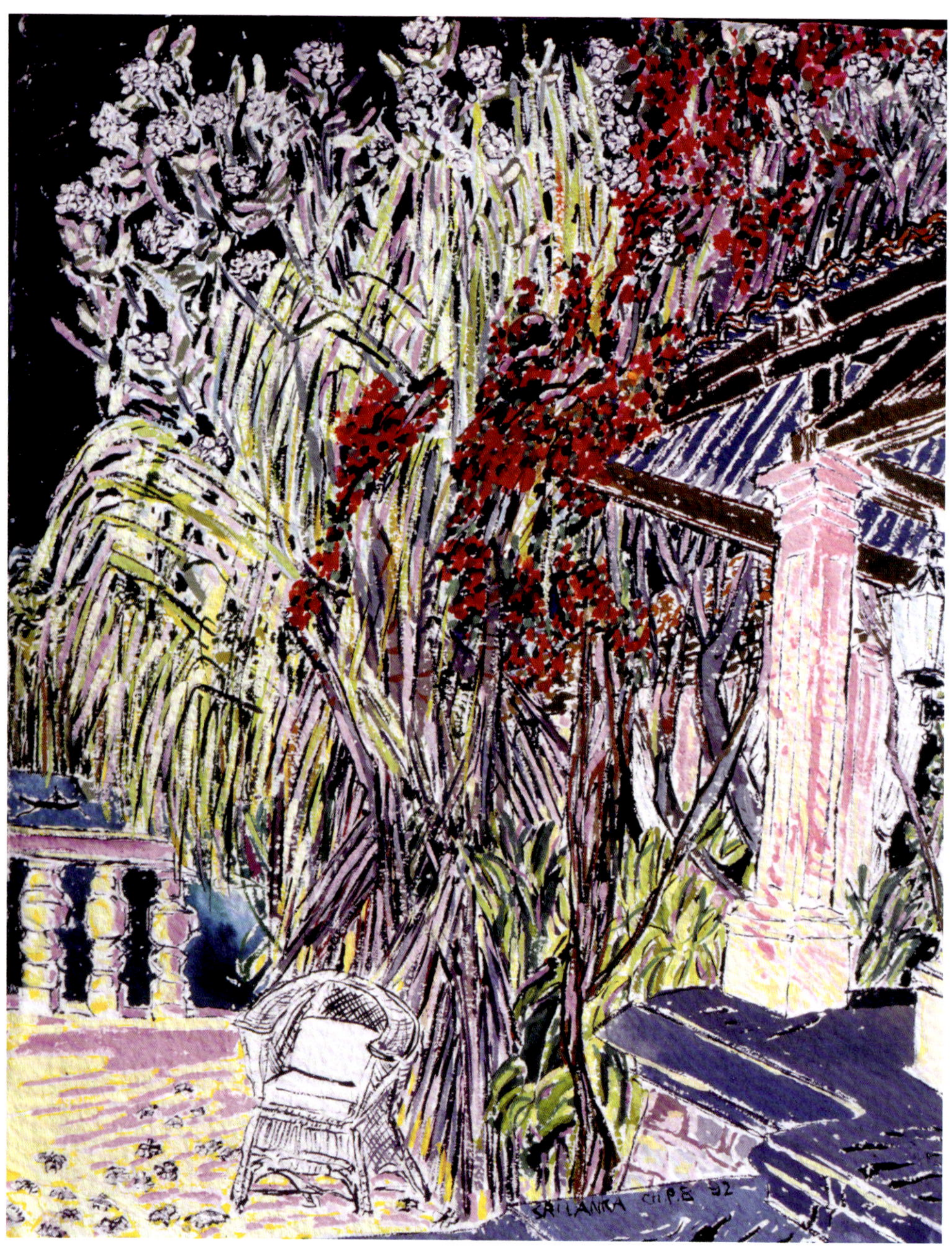
SRI LANKA CH.P.B 92

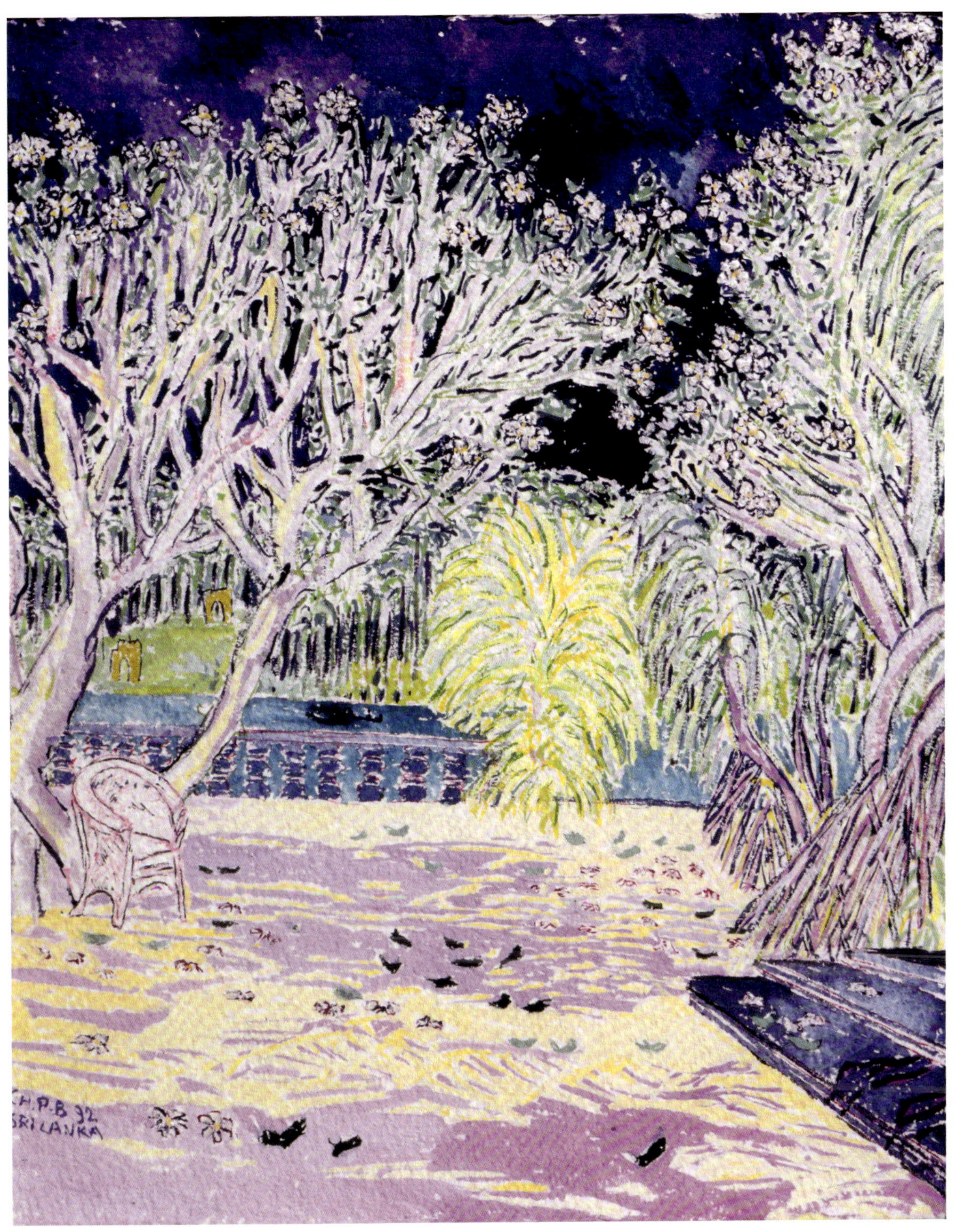
CH.P.B 92
SRILANKA

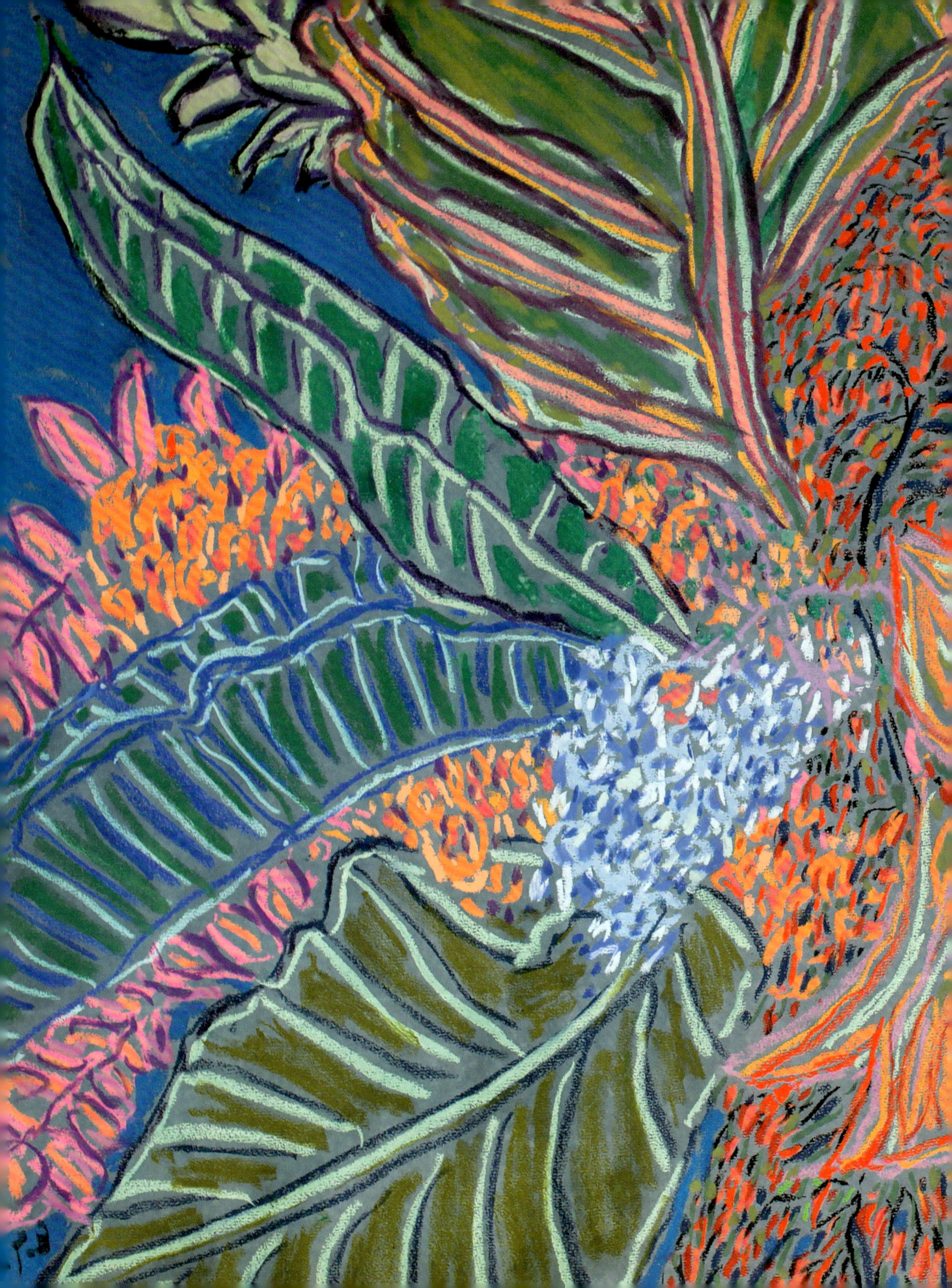

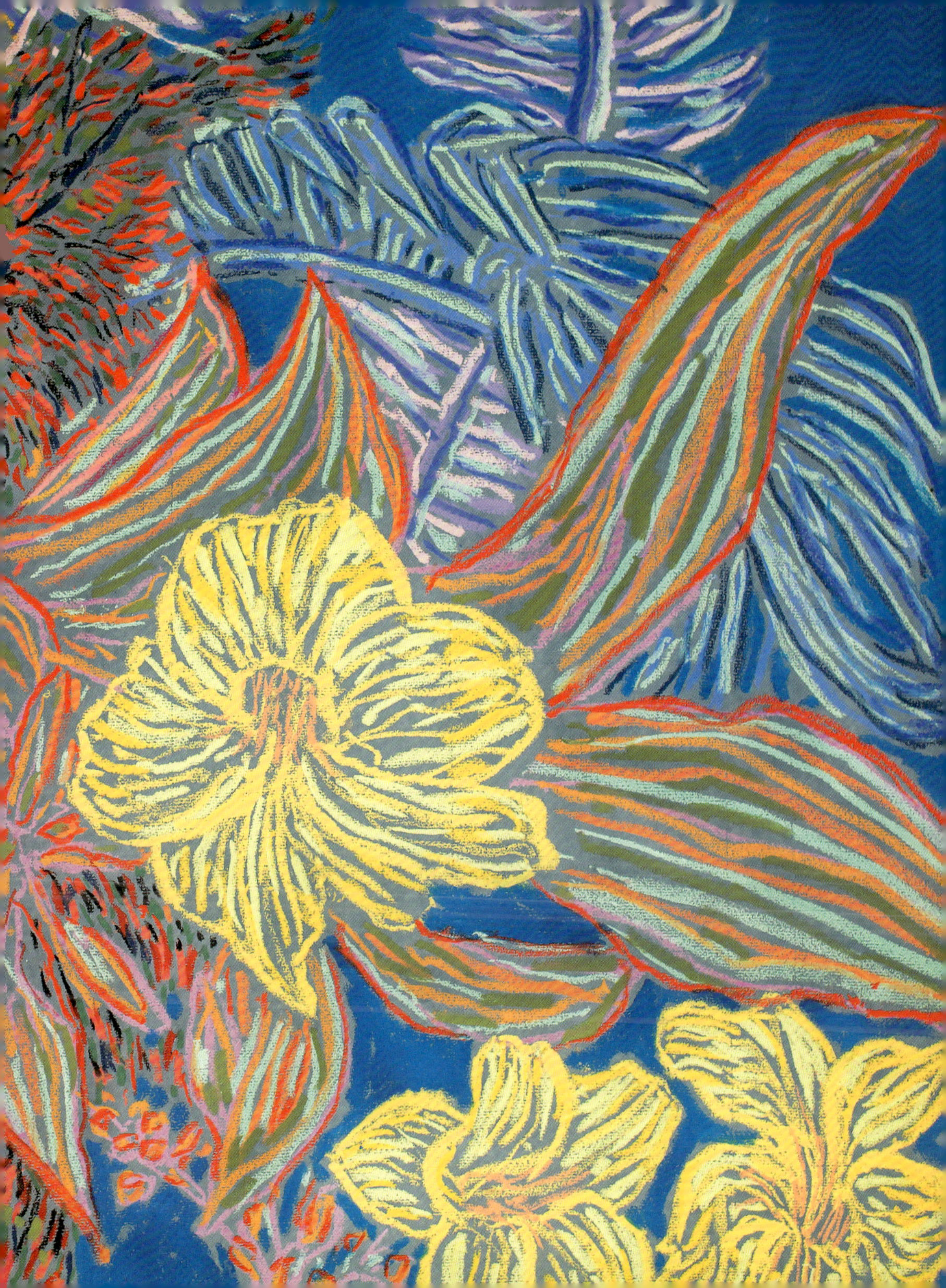

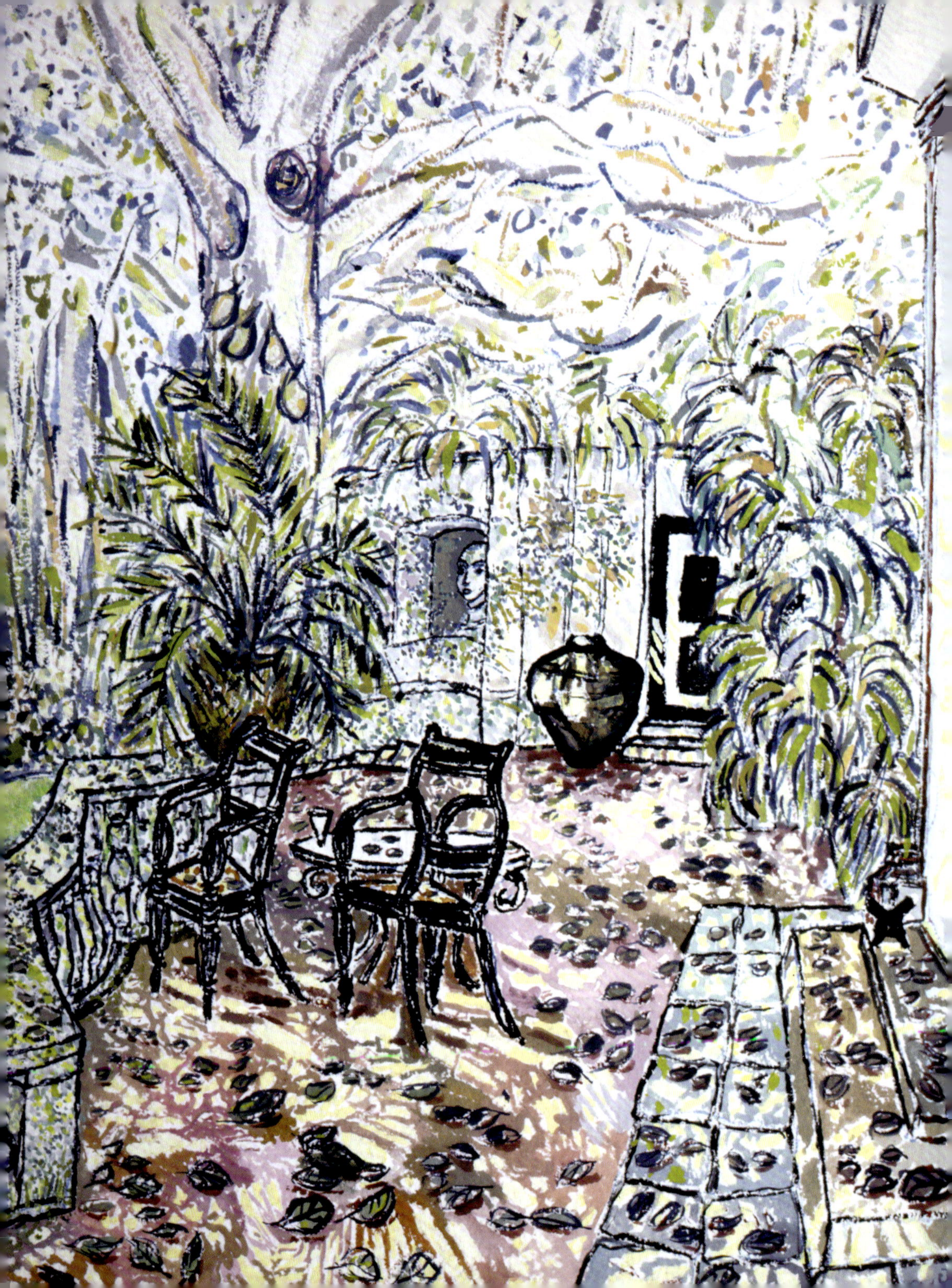

LUNUGANGA

Bentota, Sri Lanka

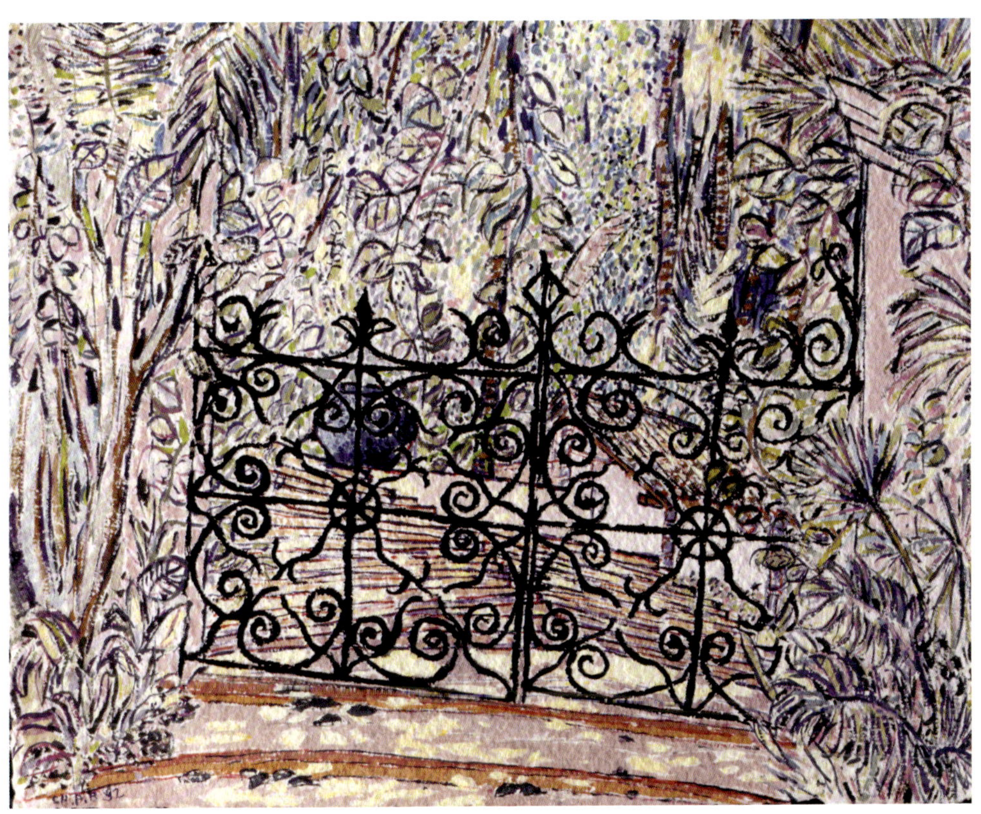

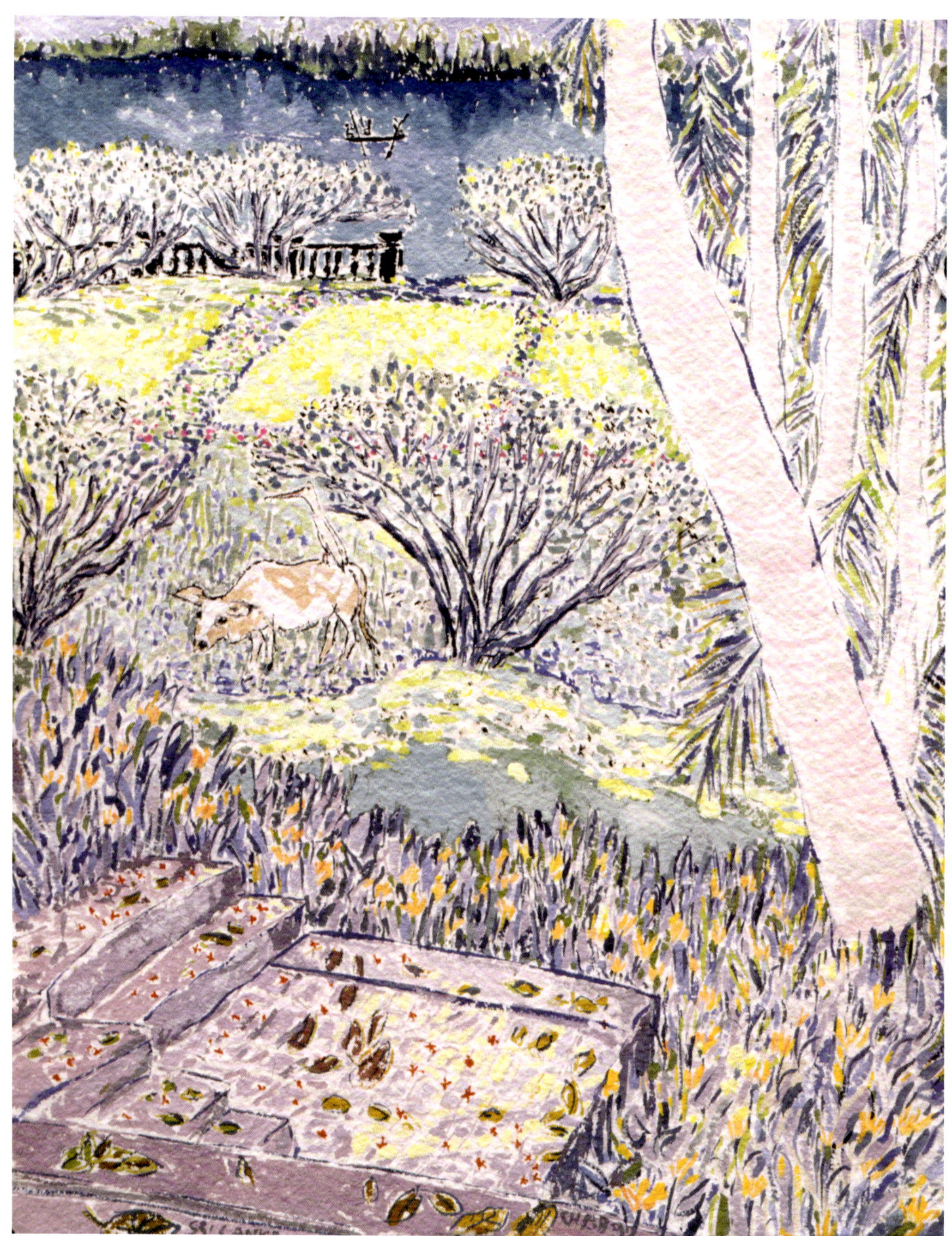

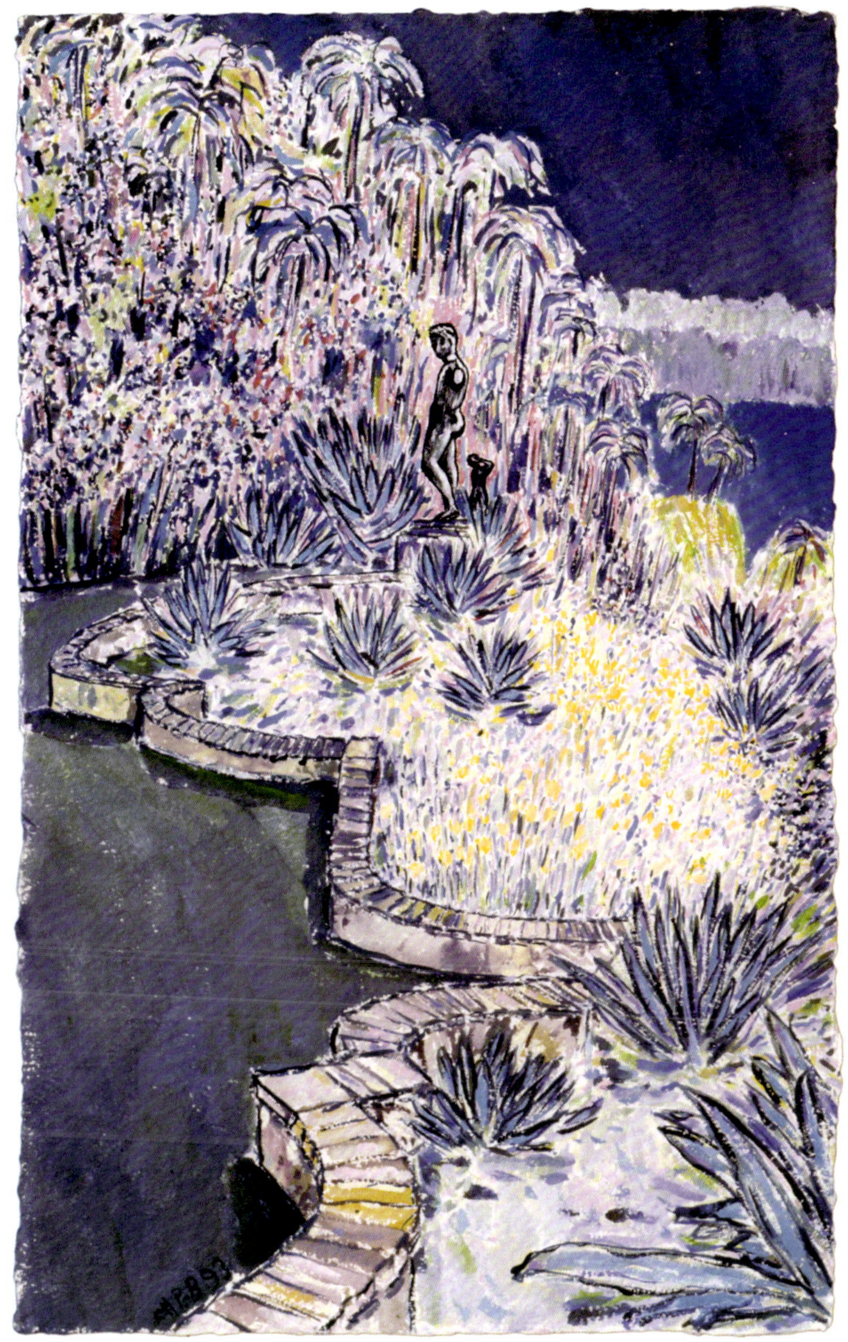

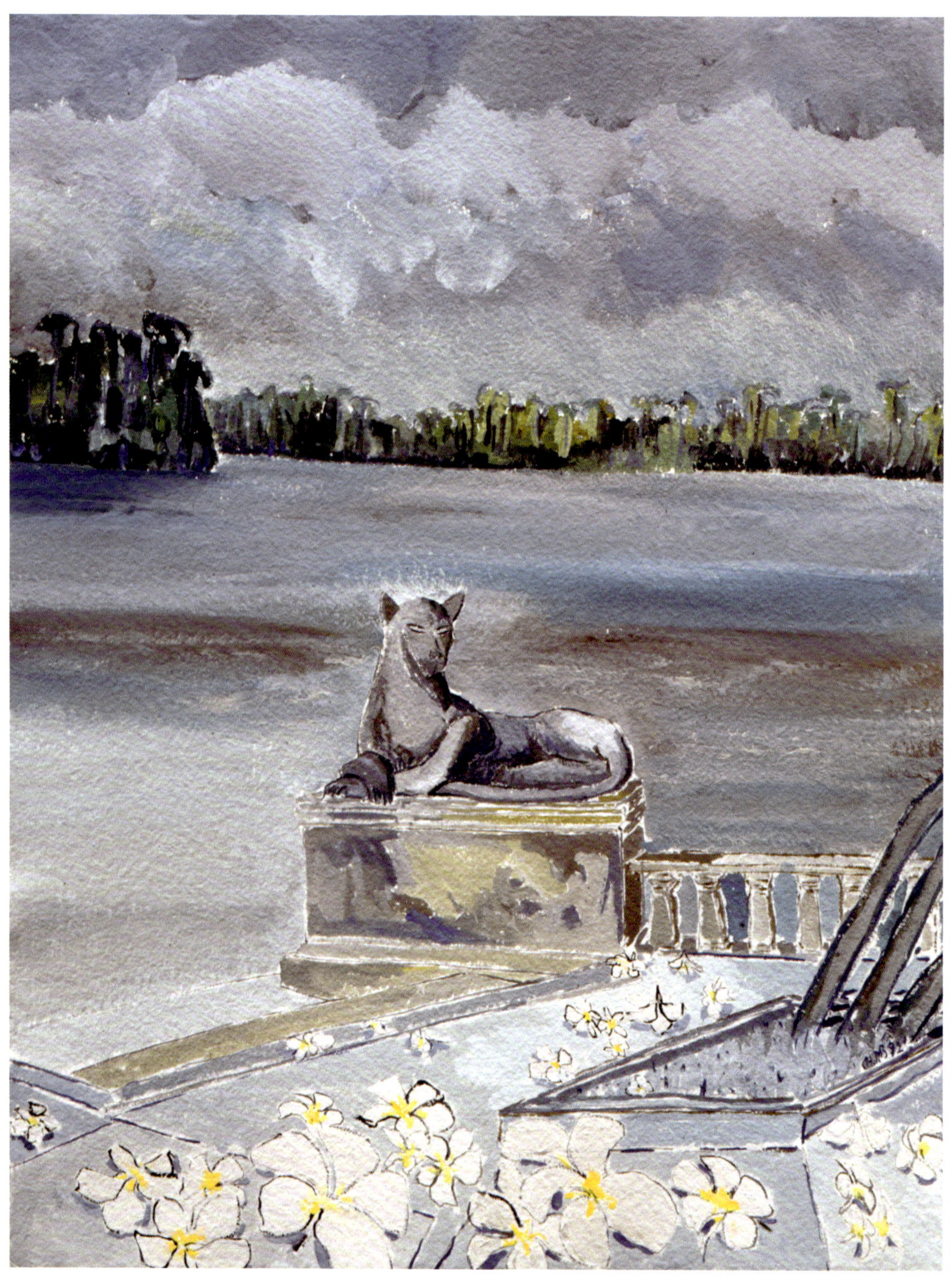

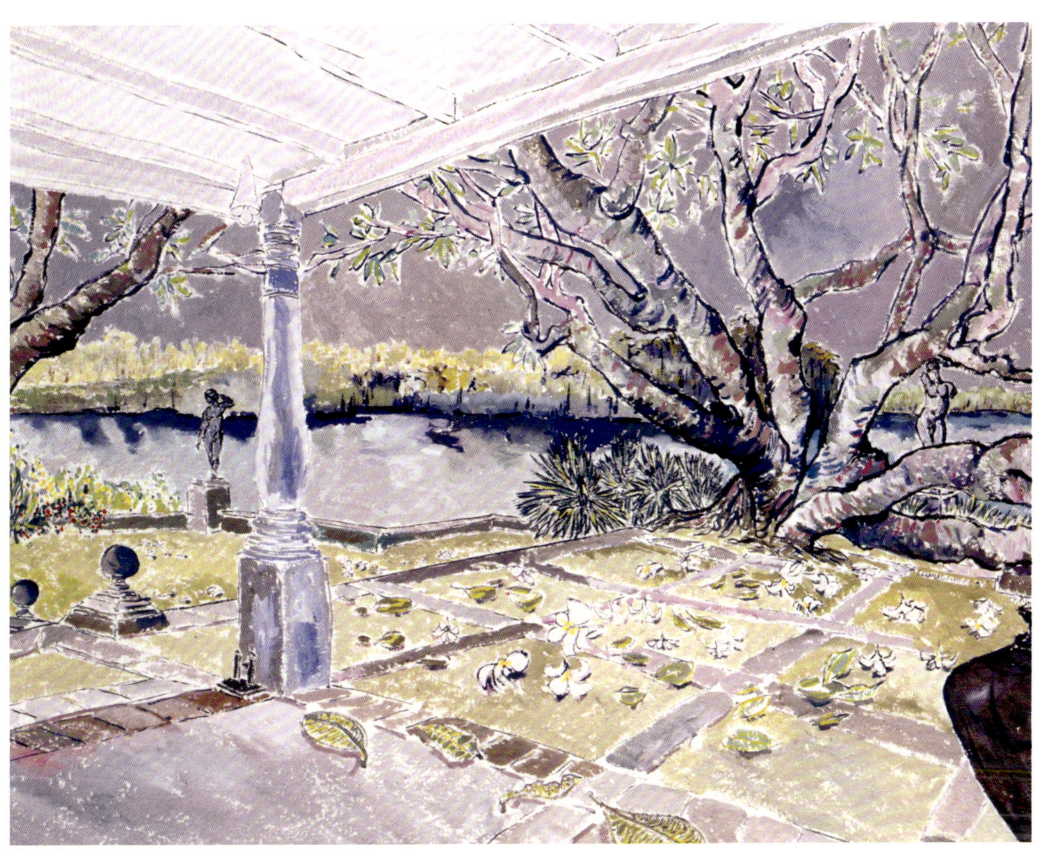

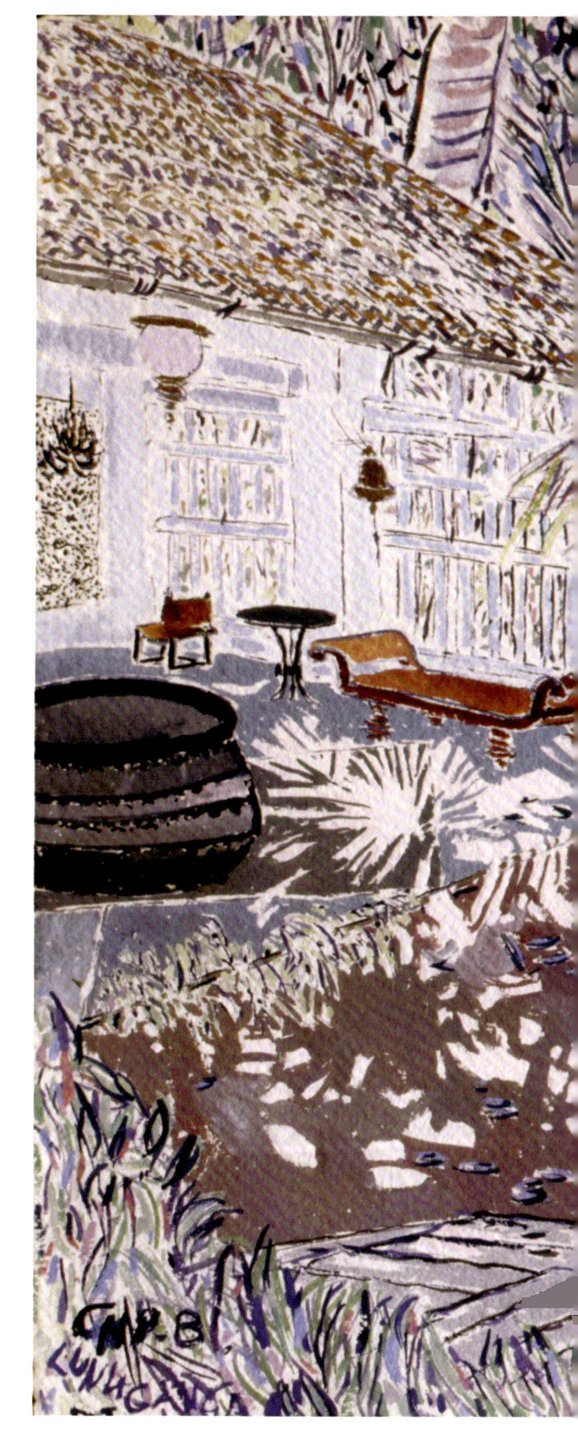
LUNUGANGA

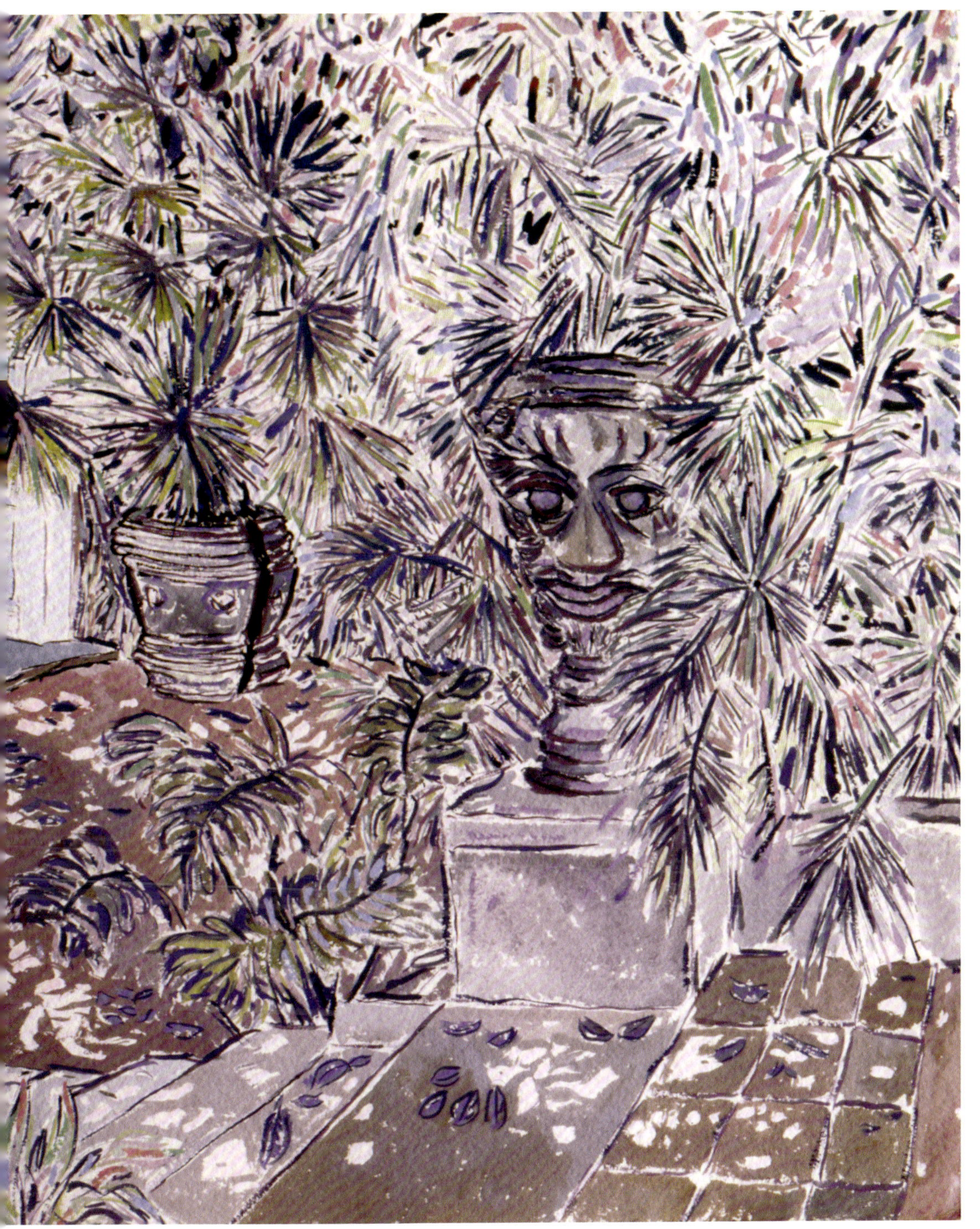

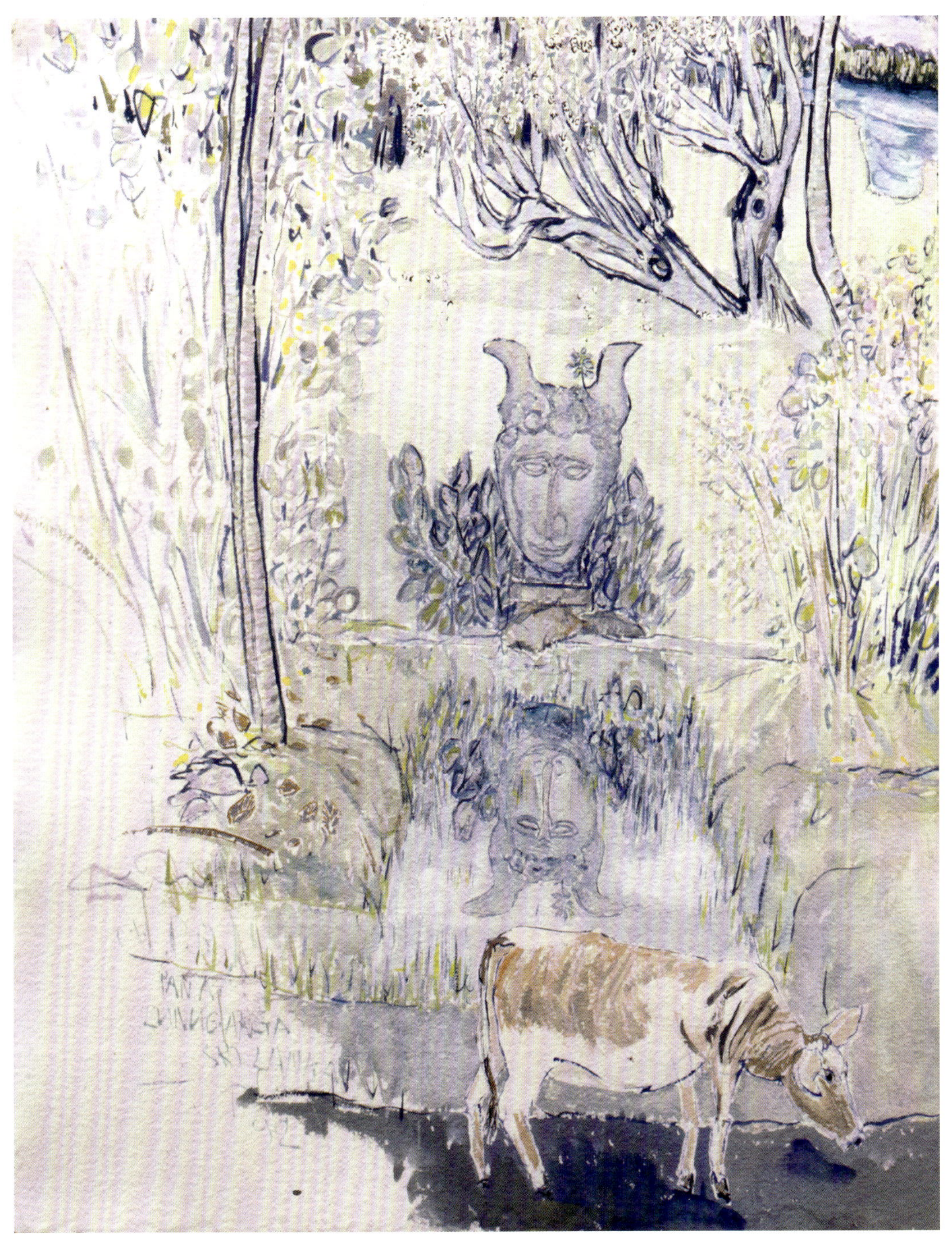

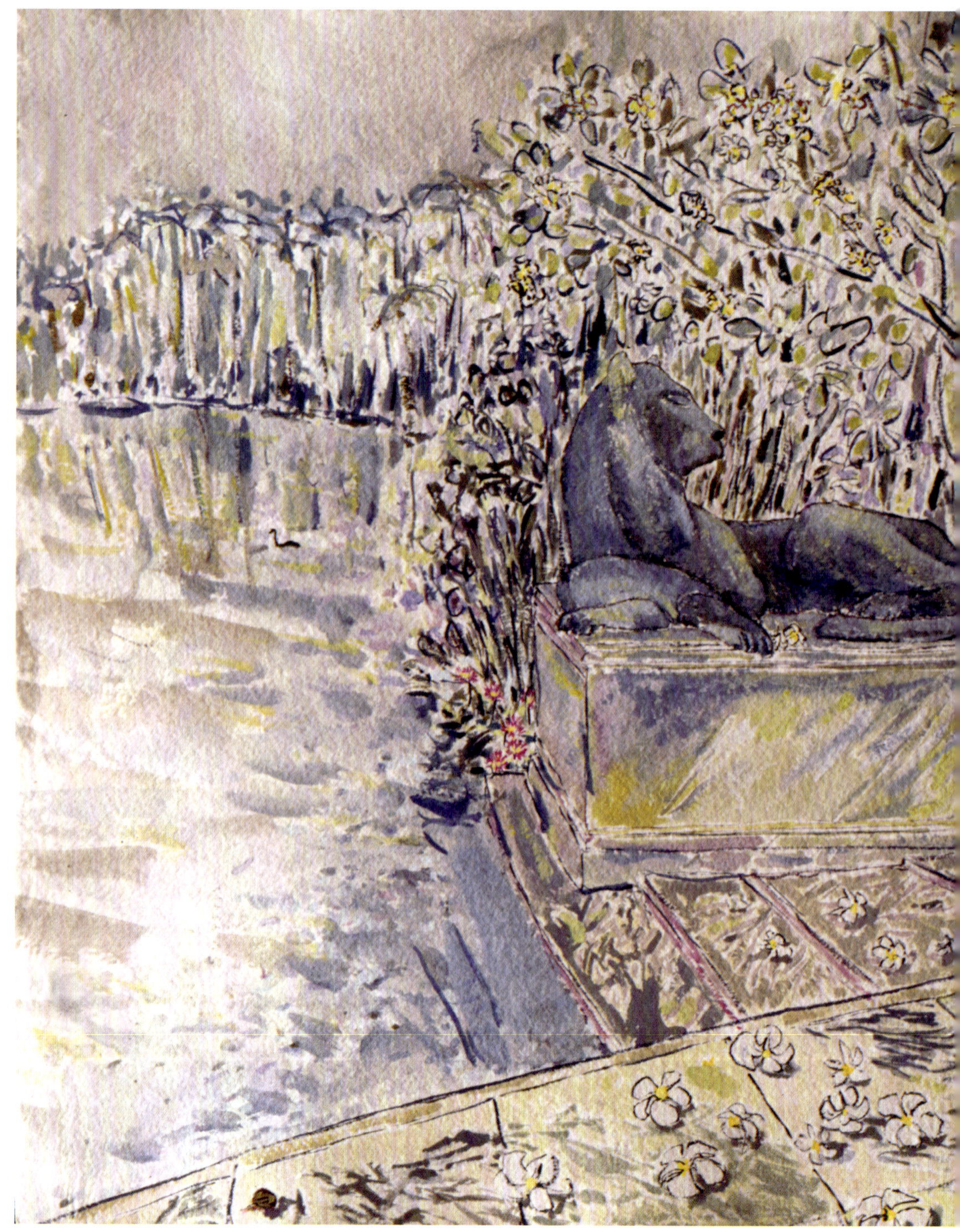

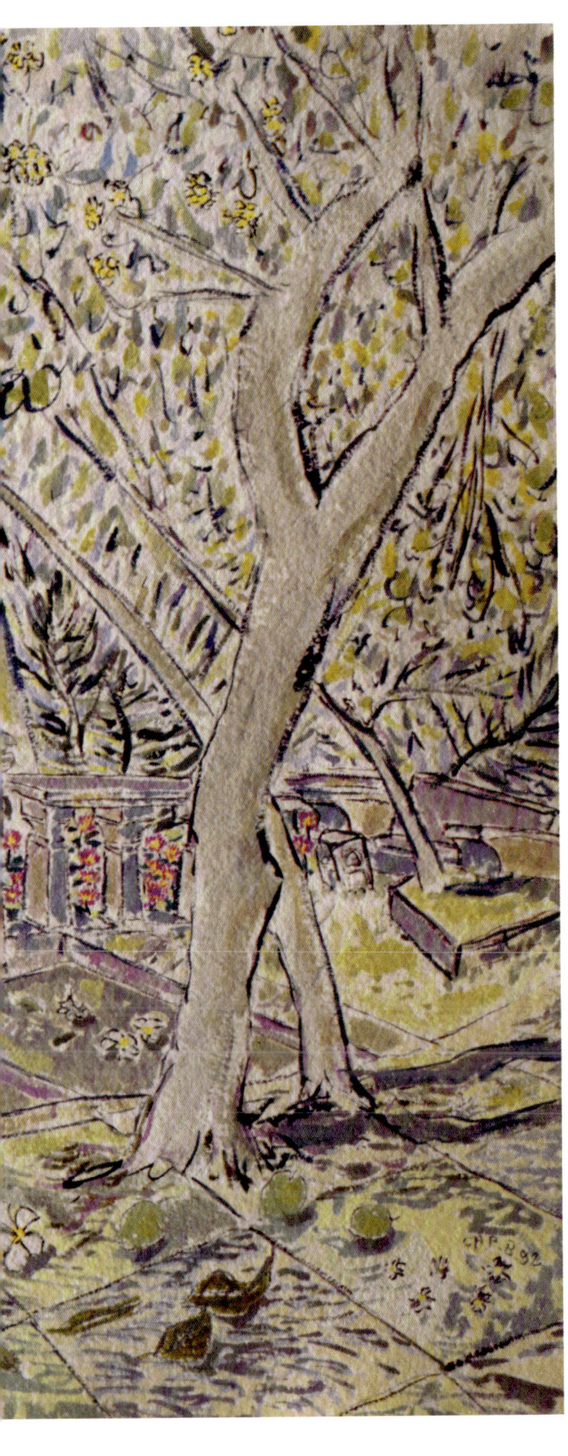

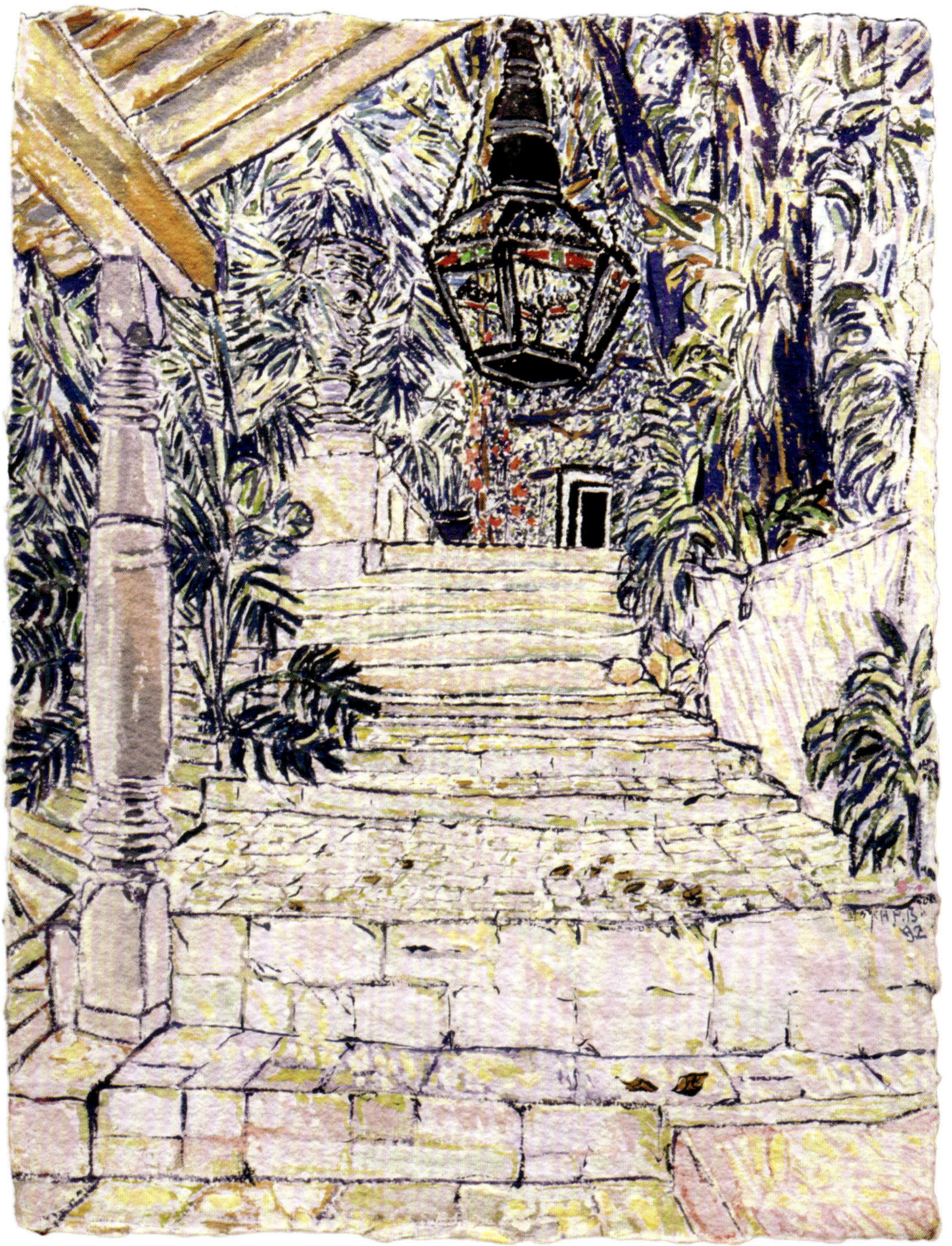

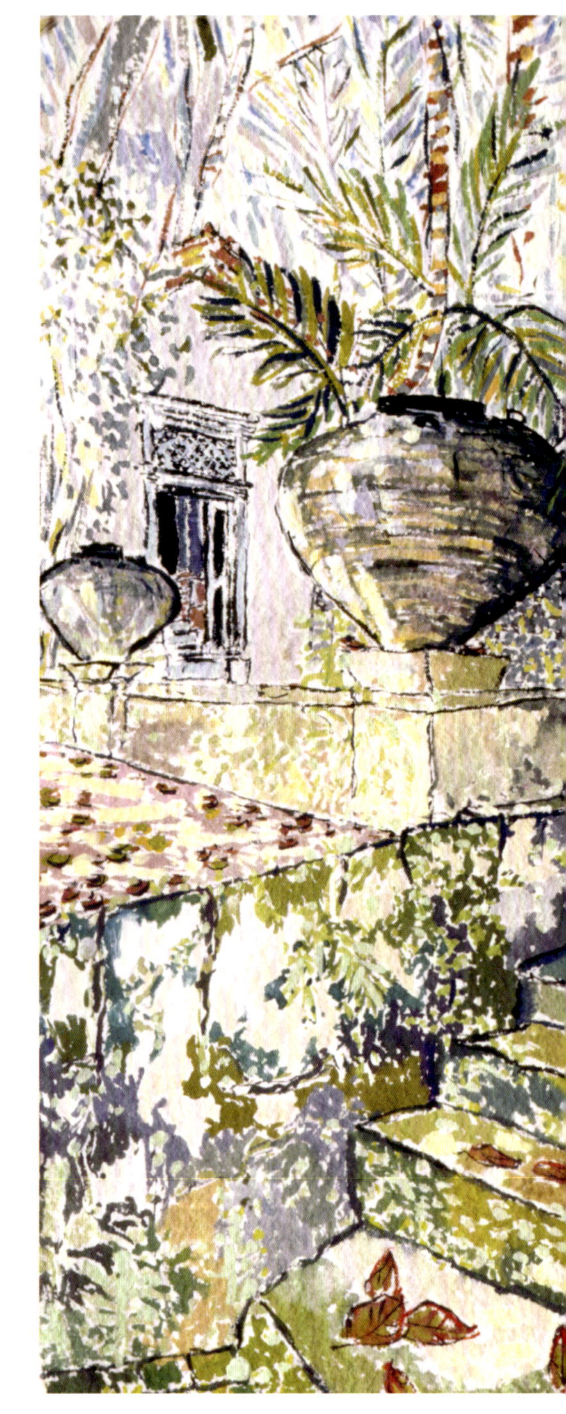

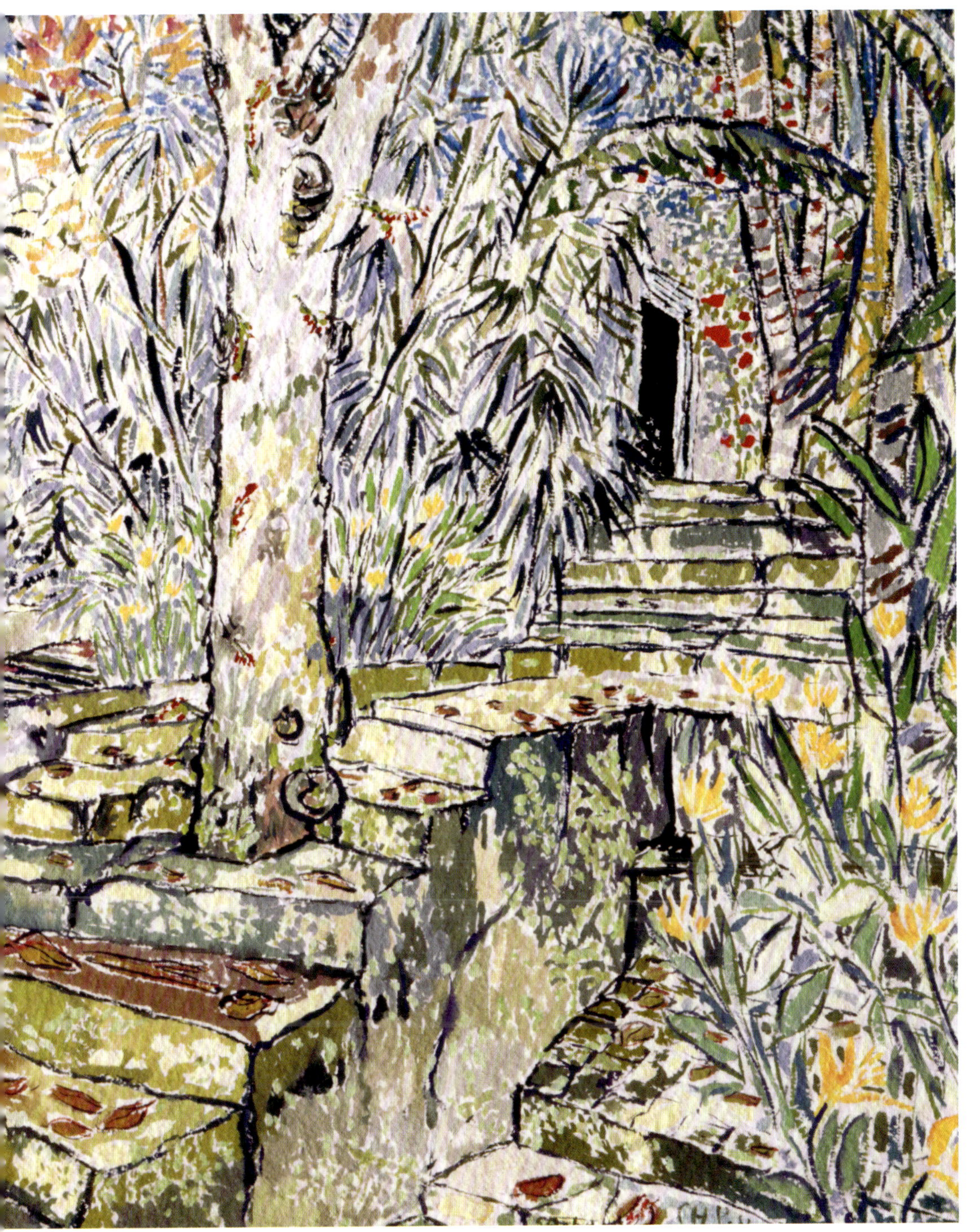

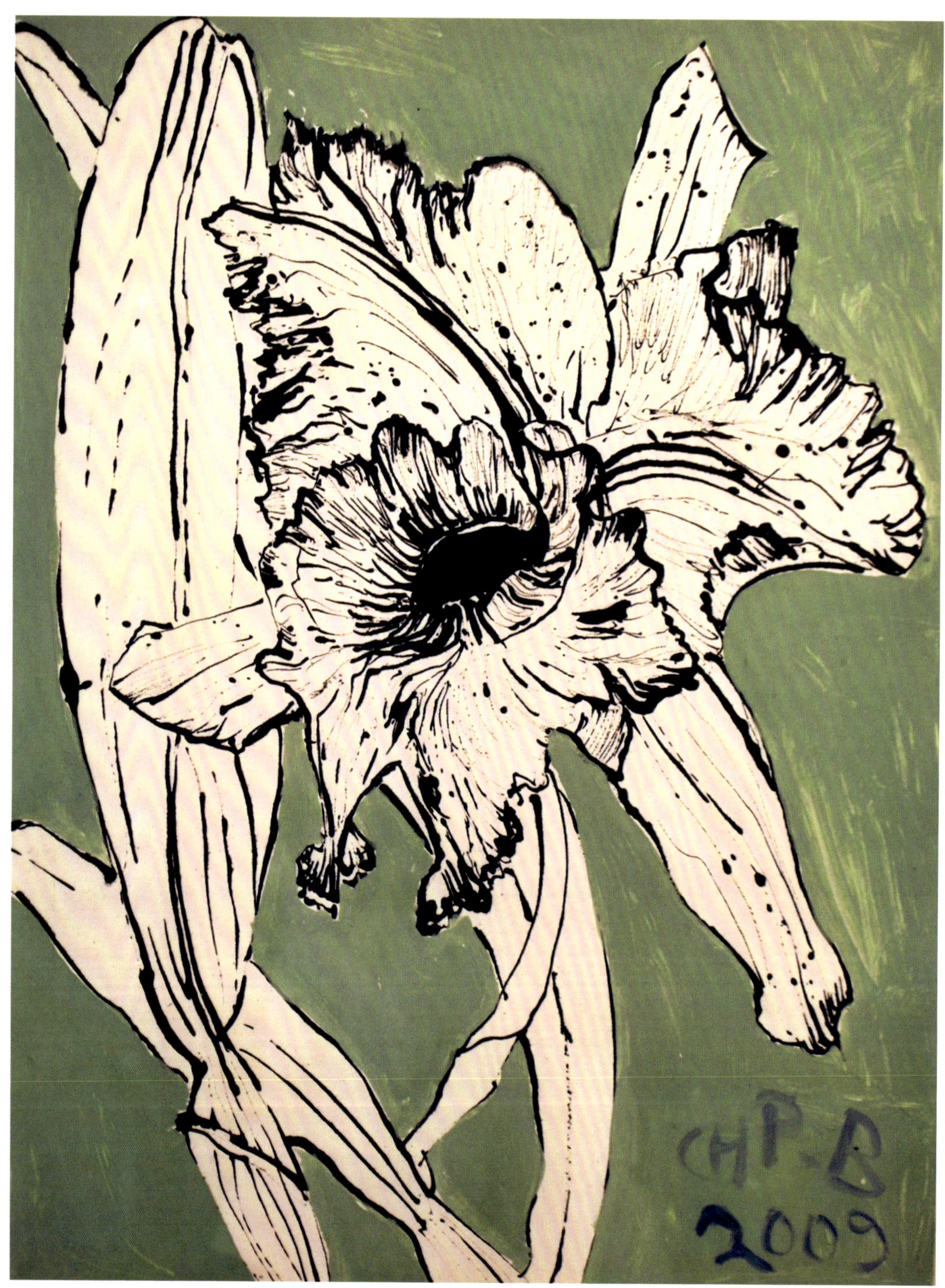
CHP.B
2009

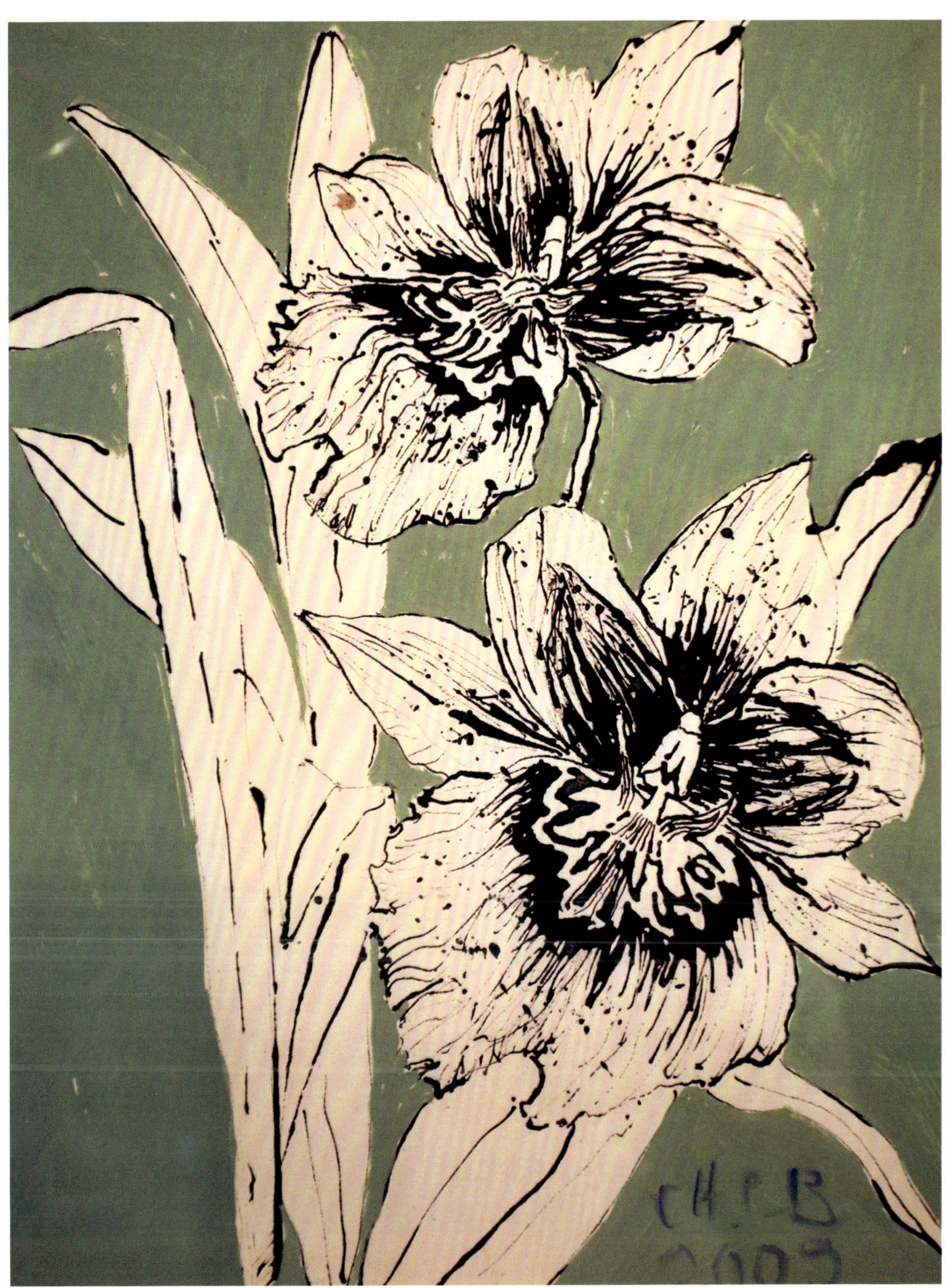

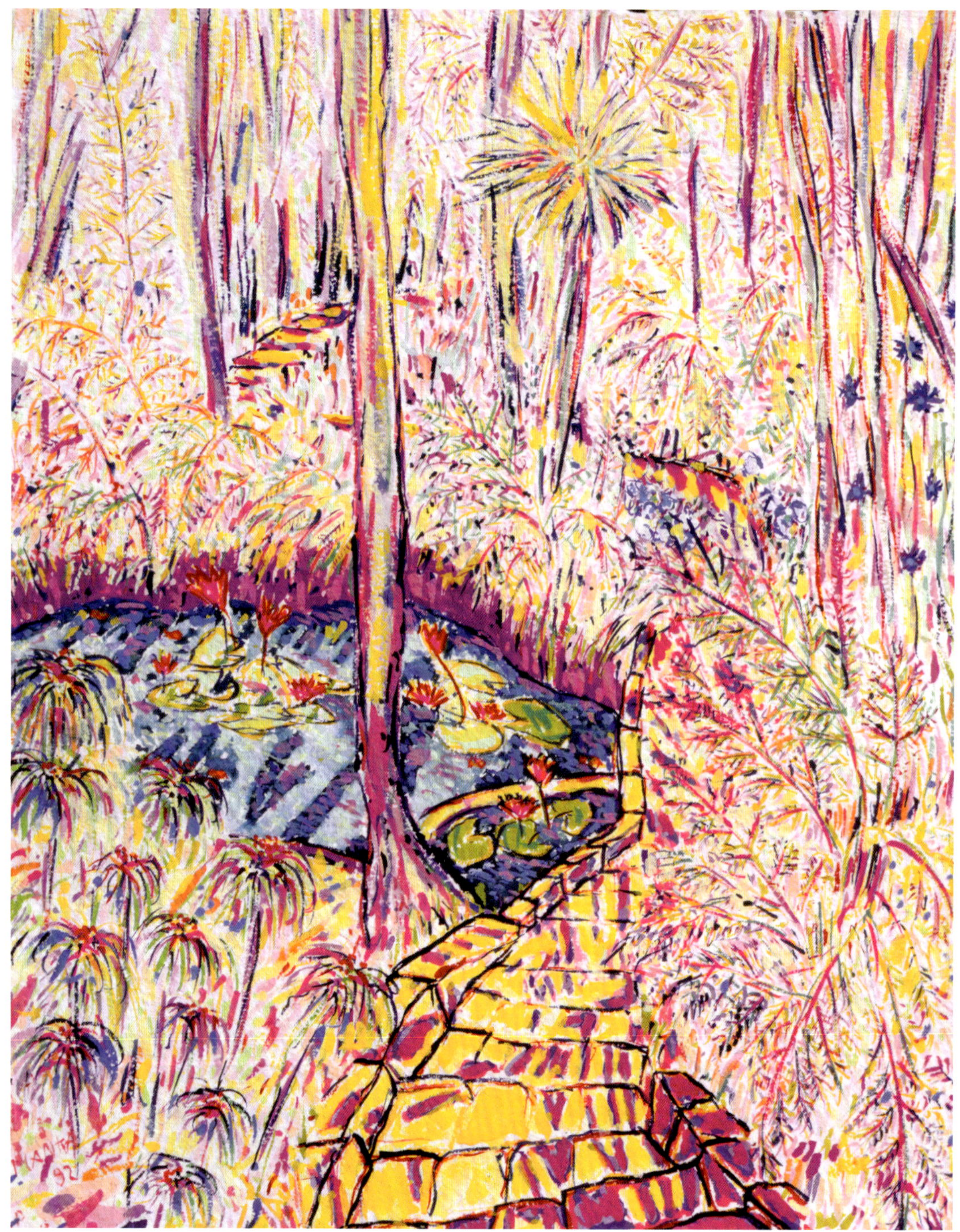

Hakgala Botanical Gardens

Nuwara Eliya, Sri Lanka

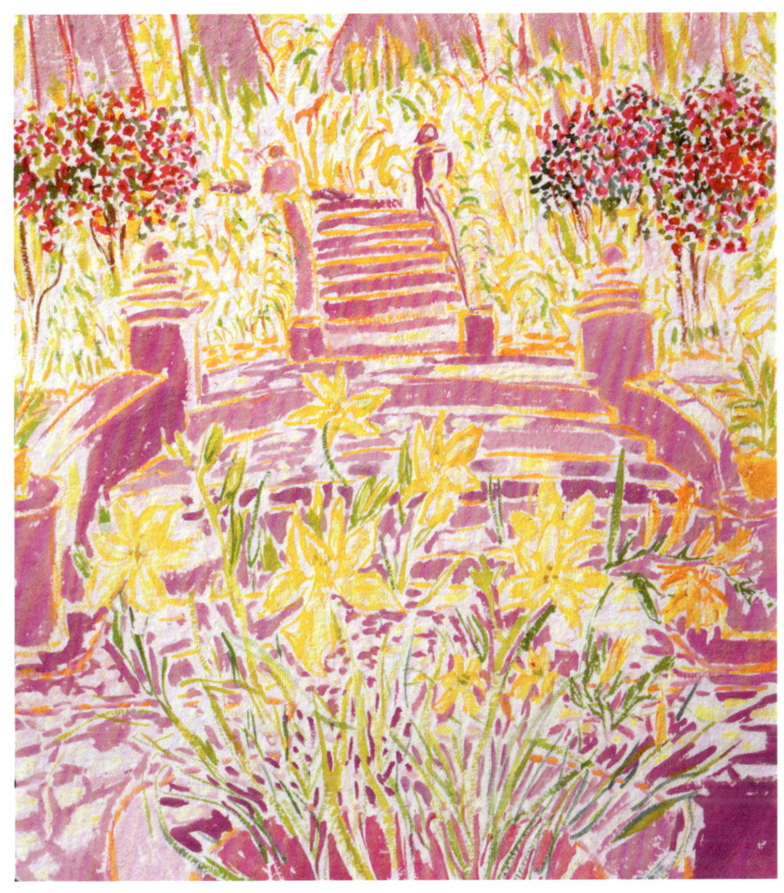

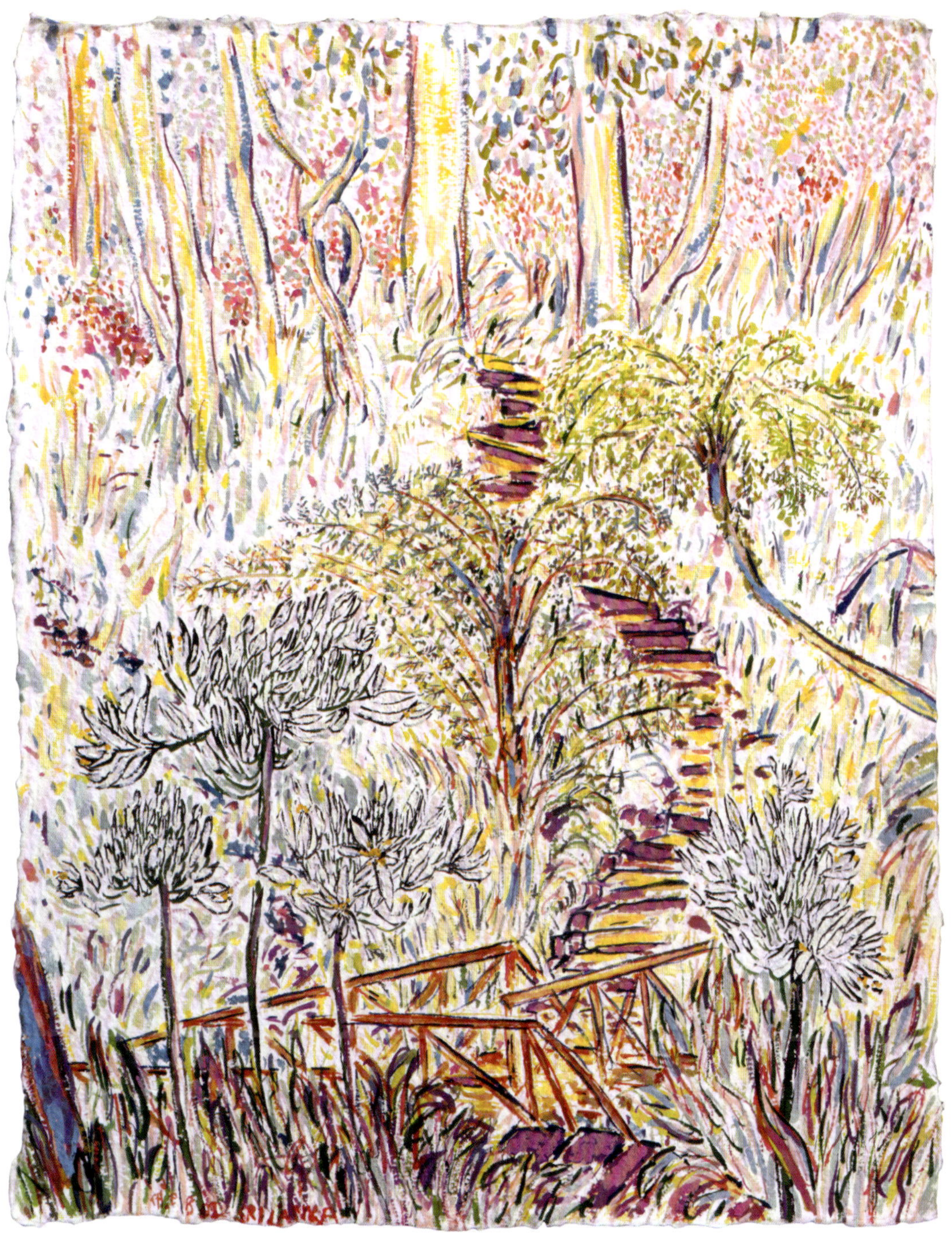

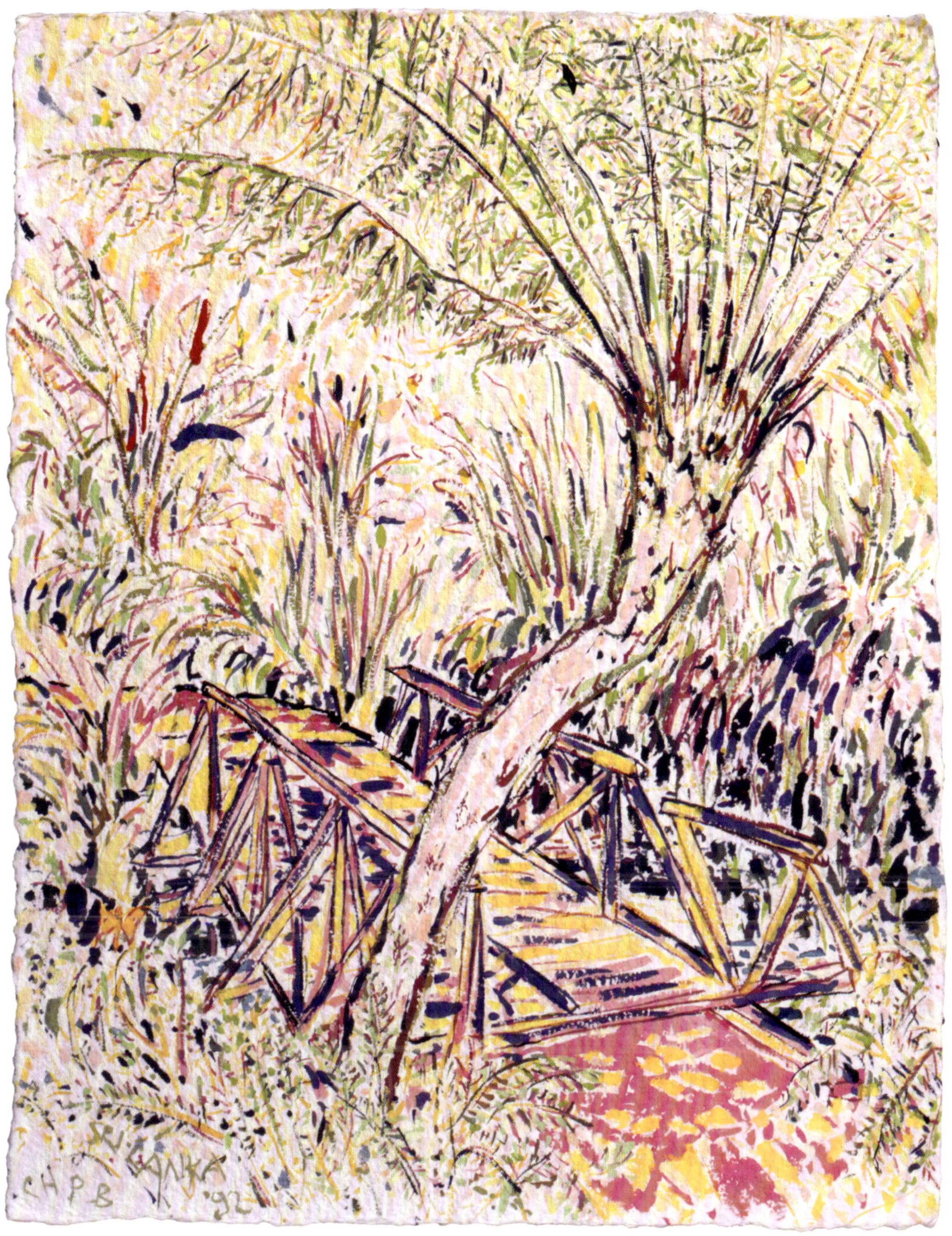

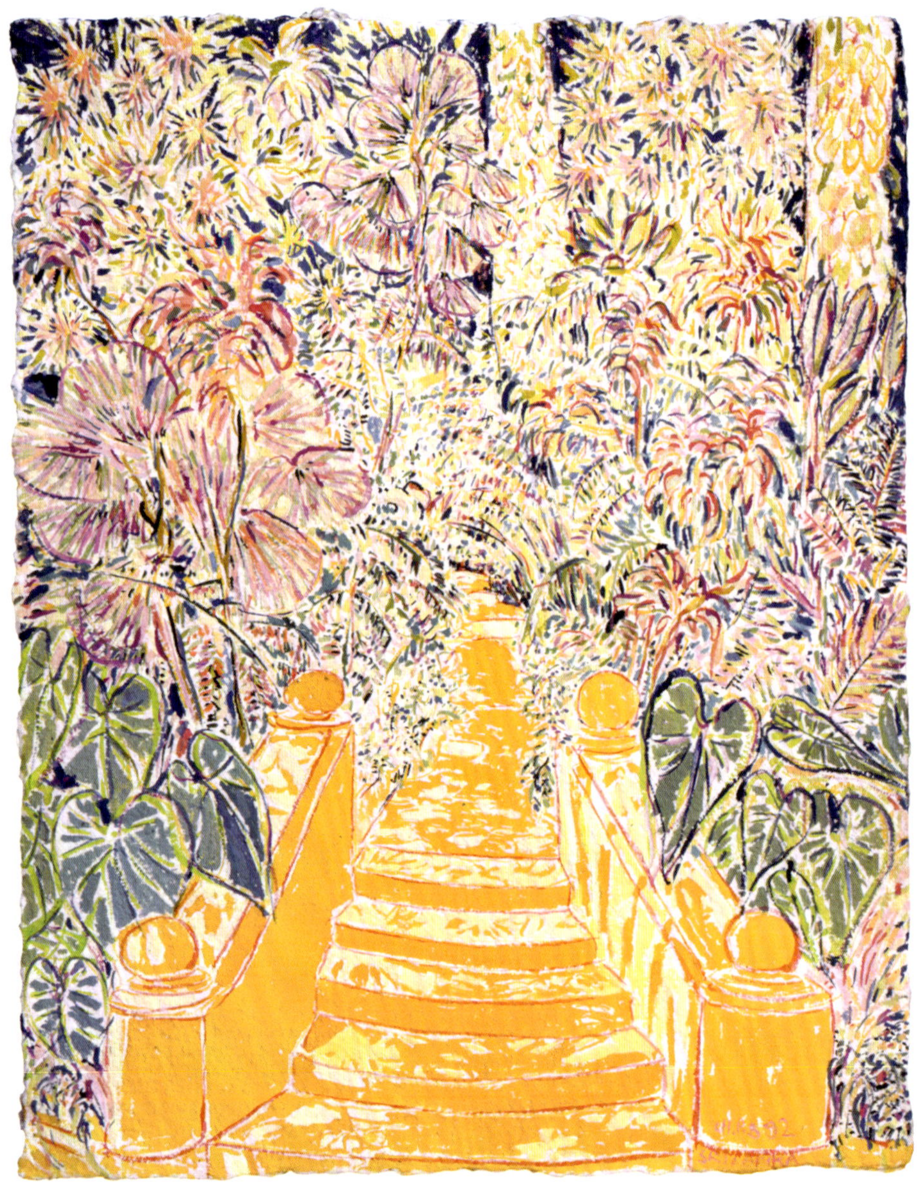

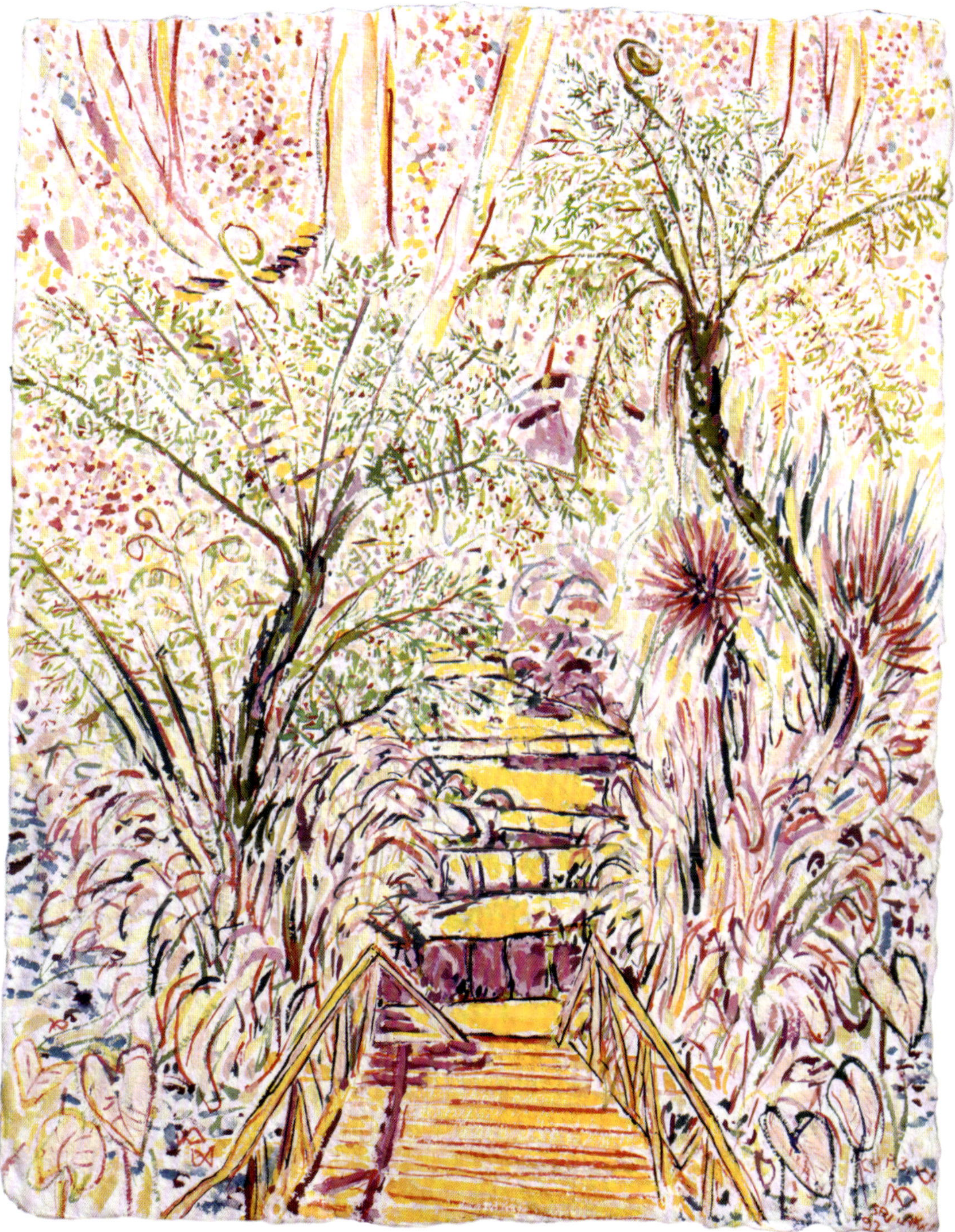

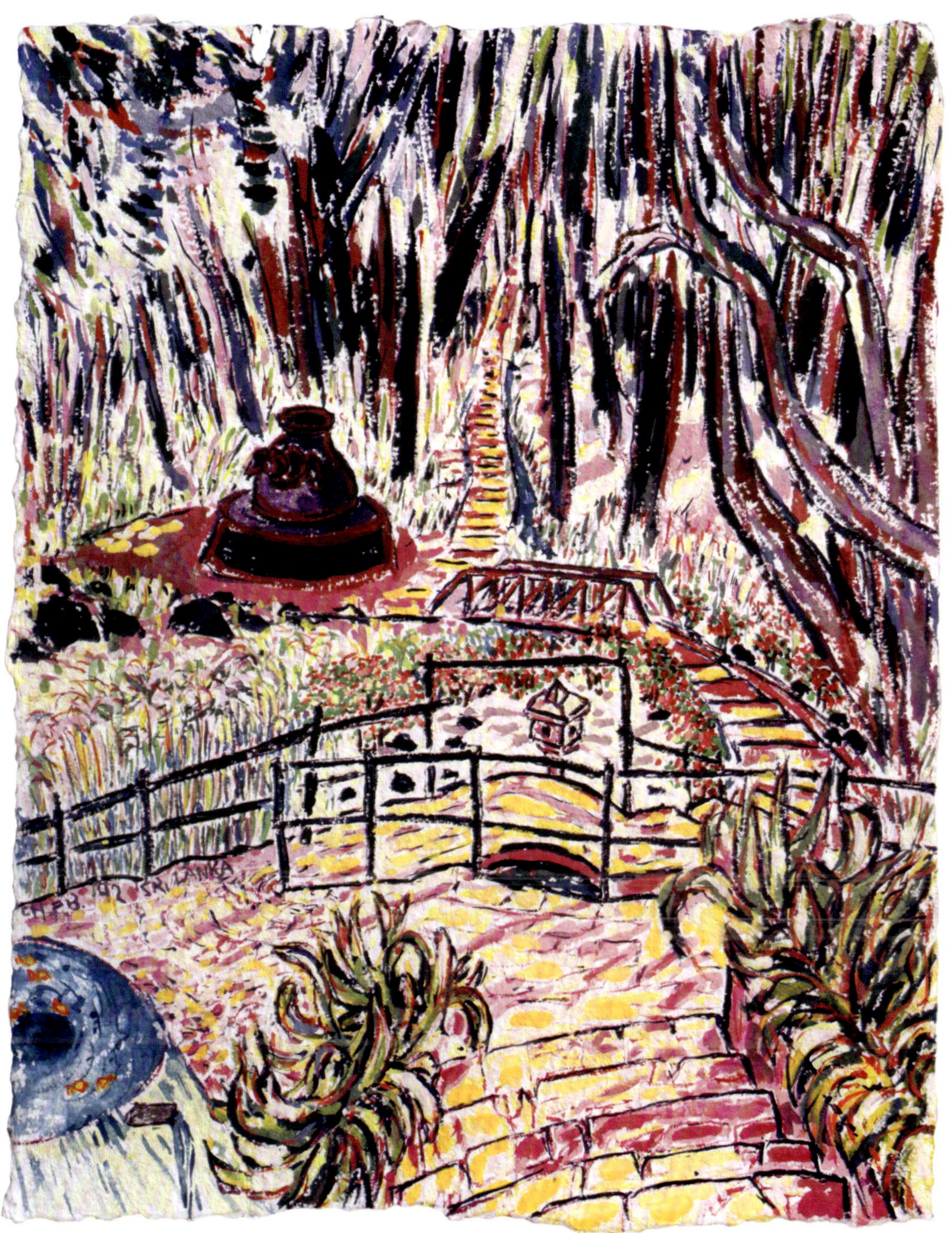
SRI LANKA

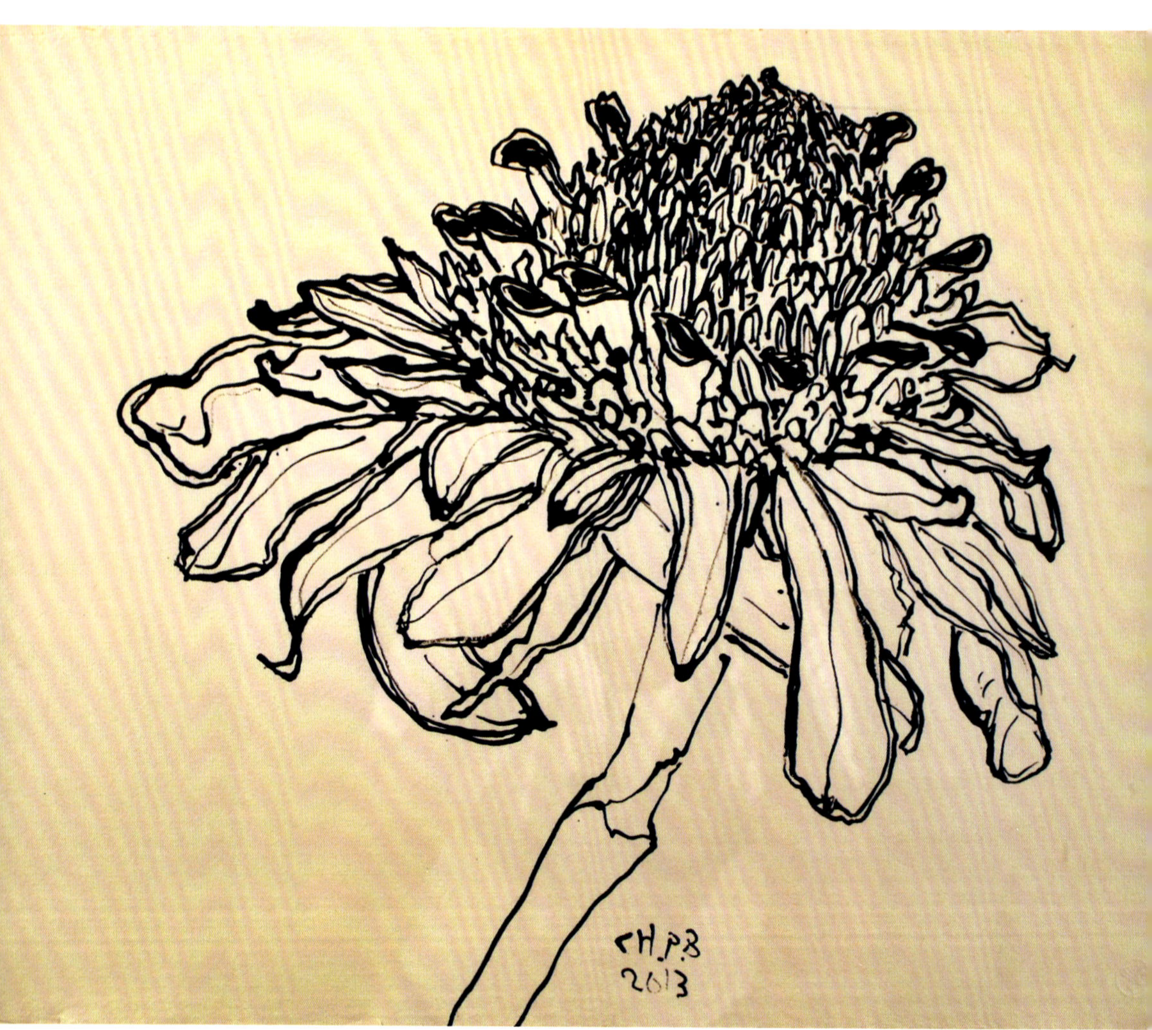
CH.P.B
2013

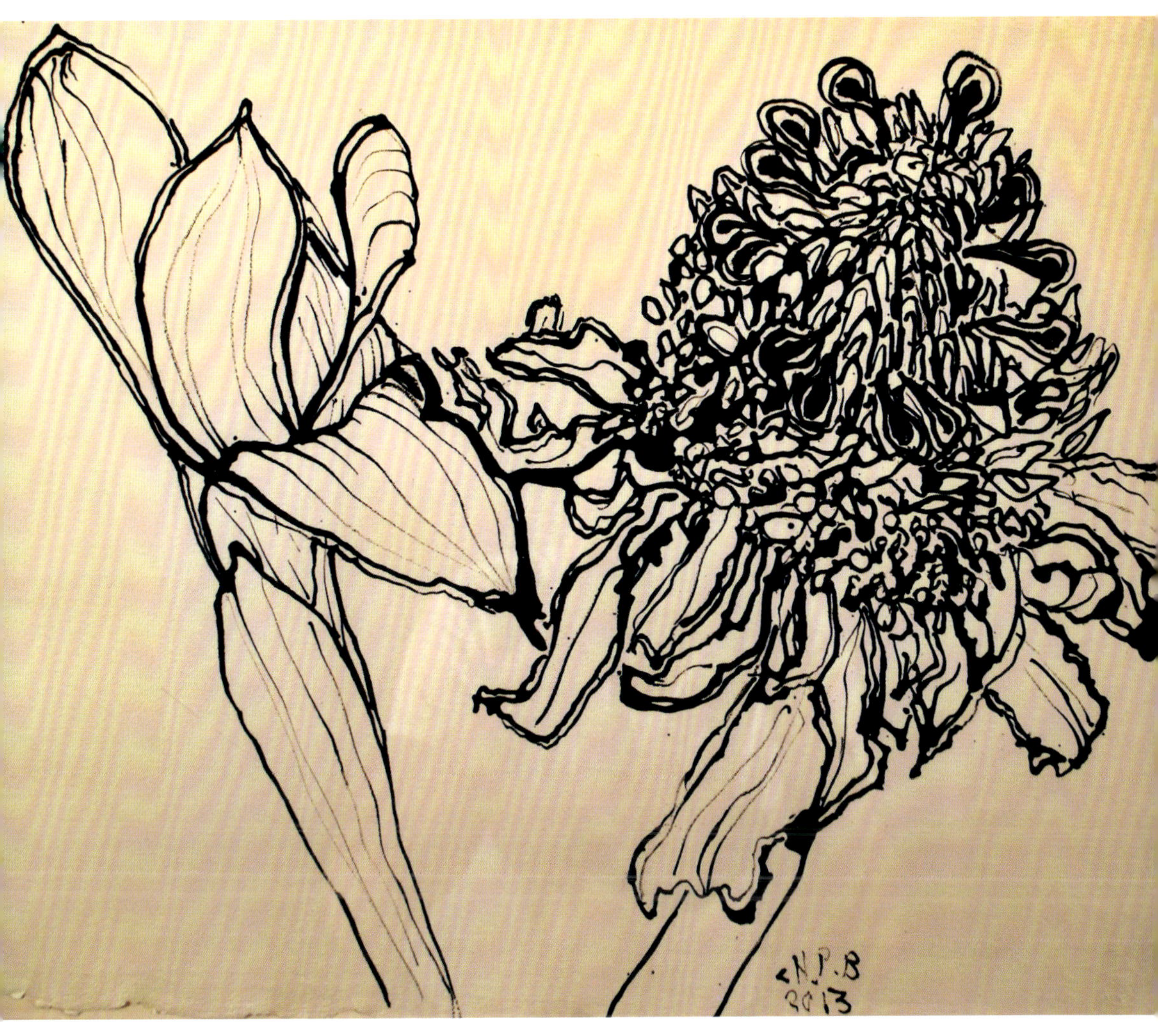
N.P.B
2013

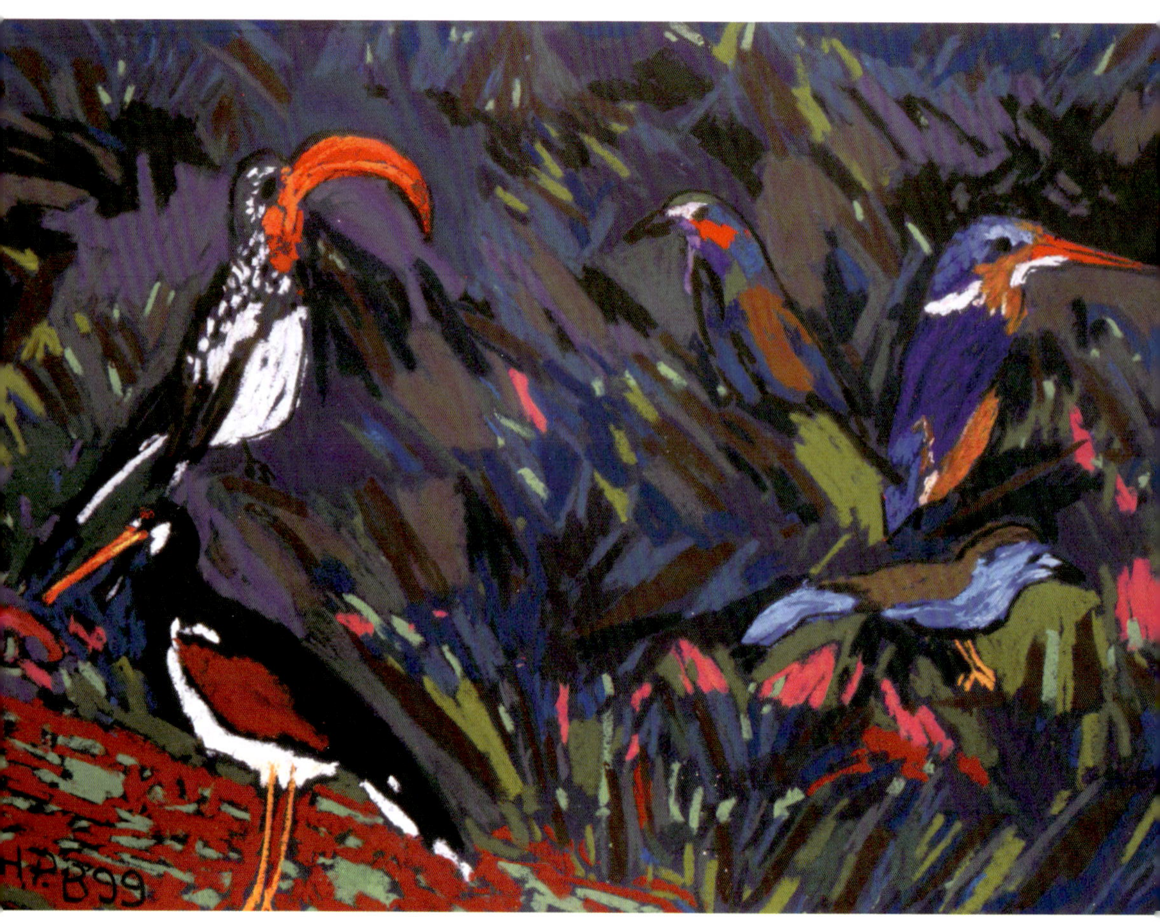
H.P.B99

Dune Garden

Rocktail Bay, South Africa

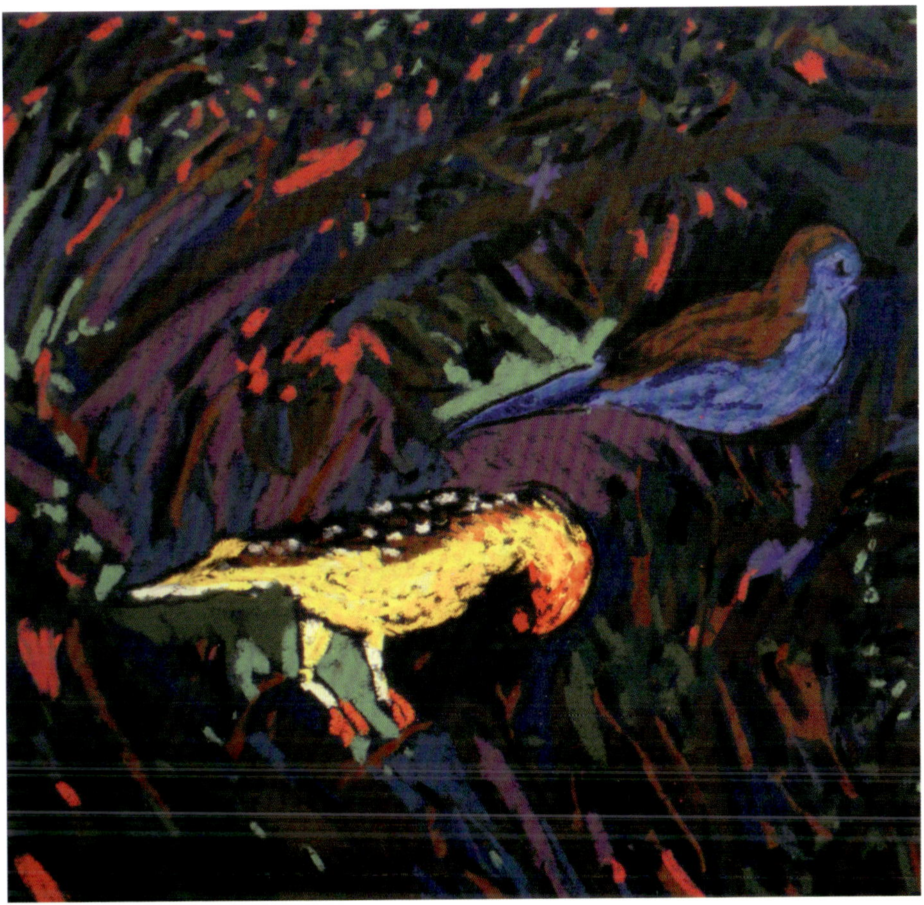

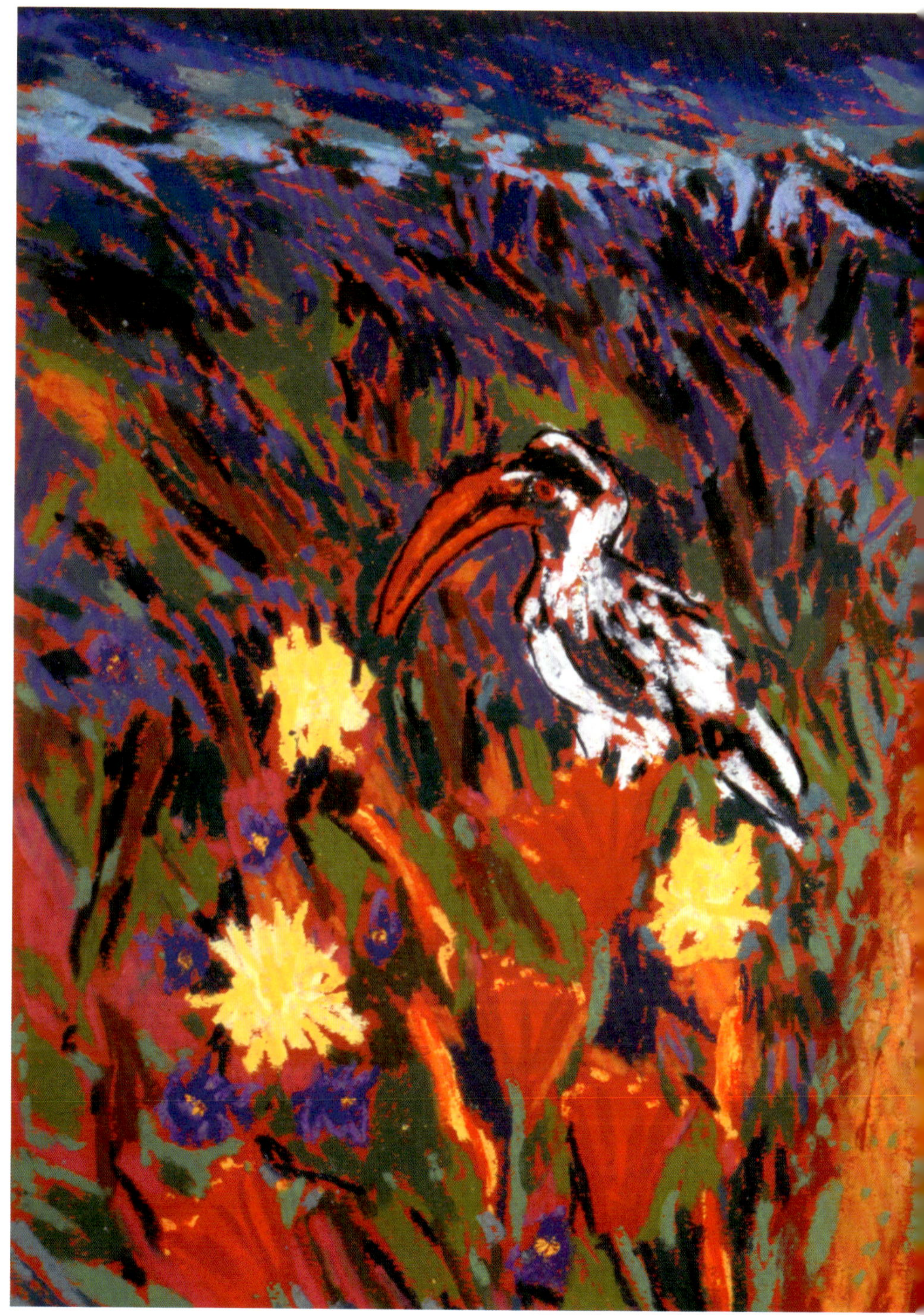

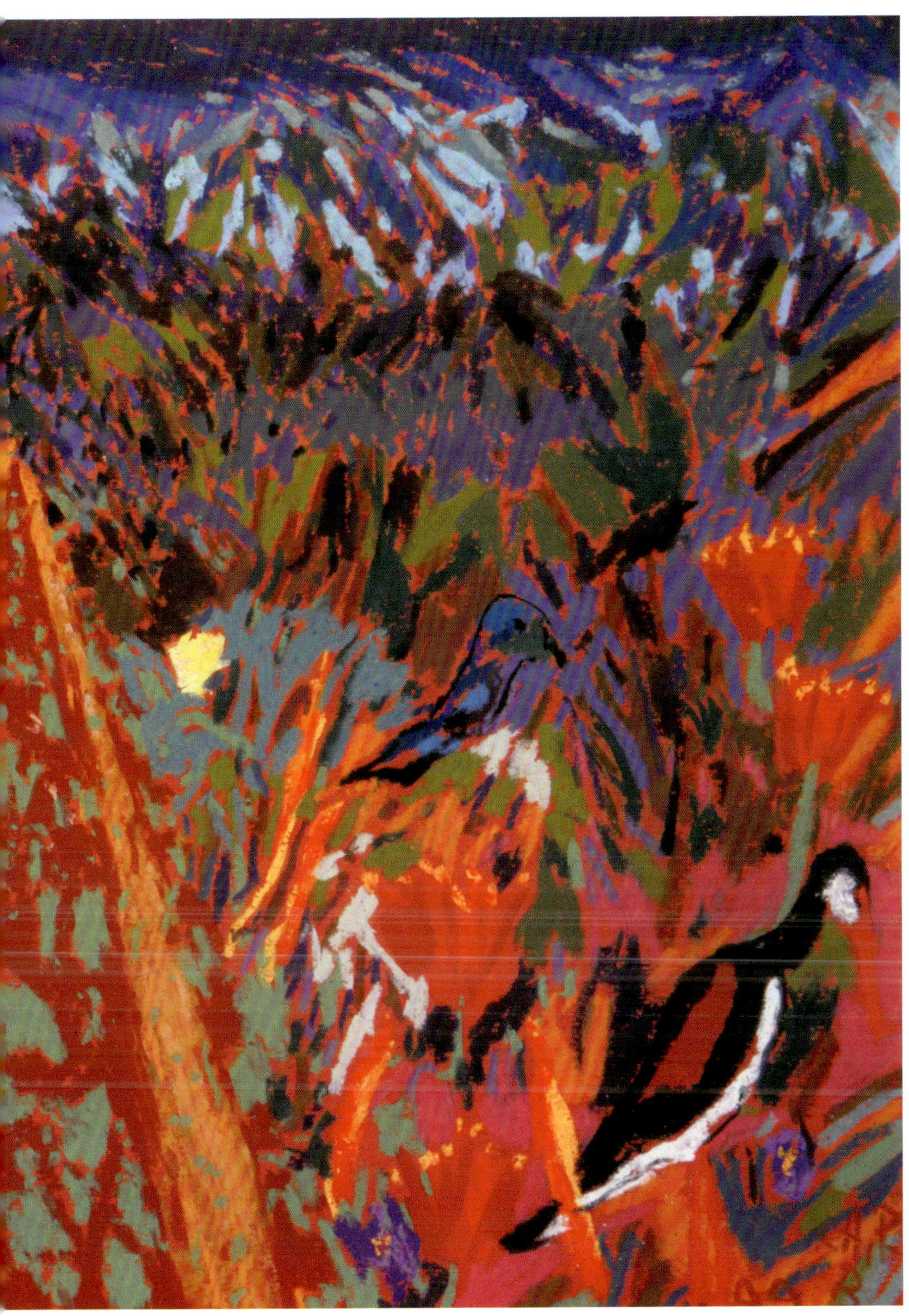

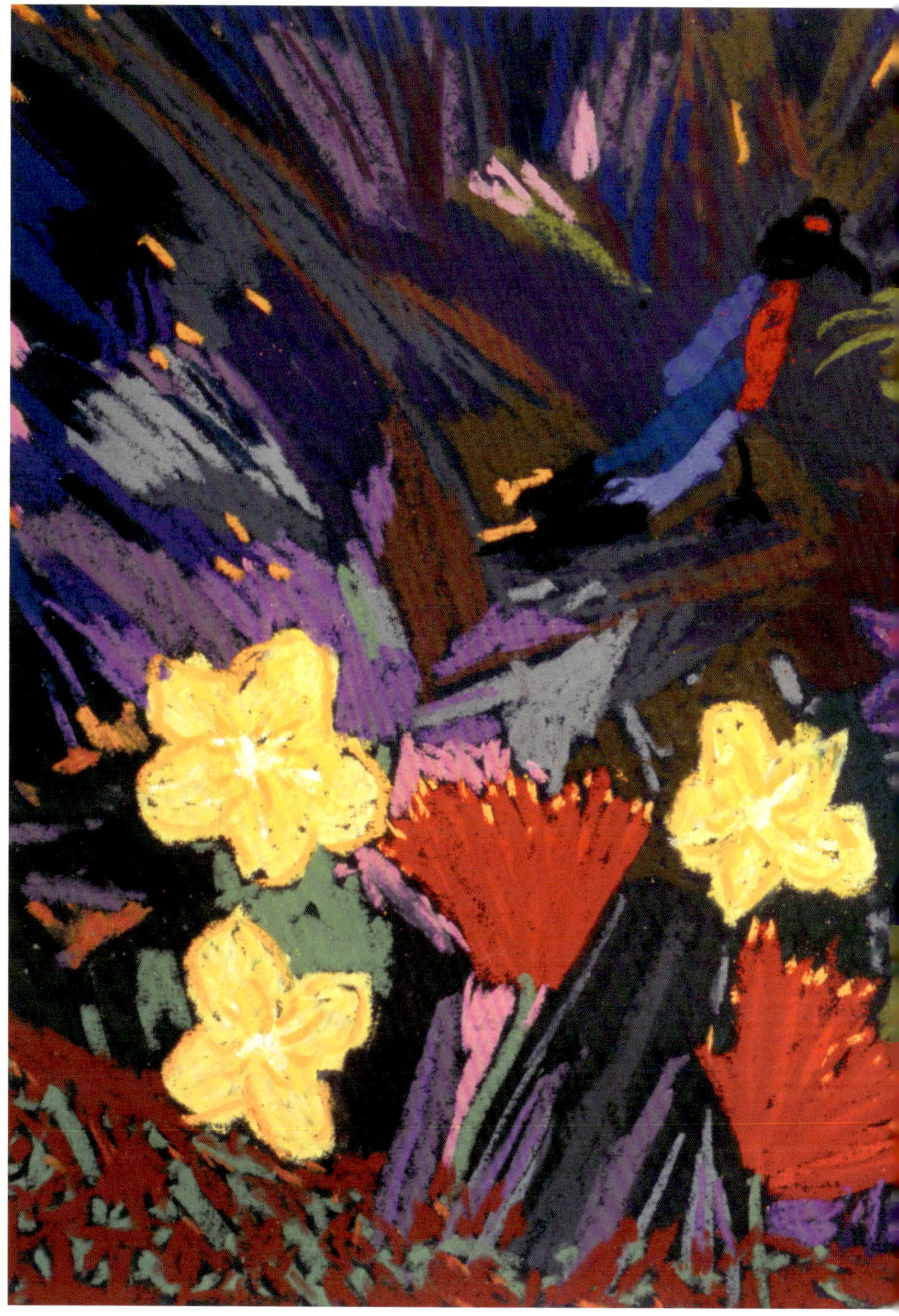

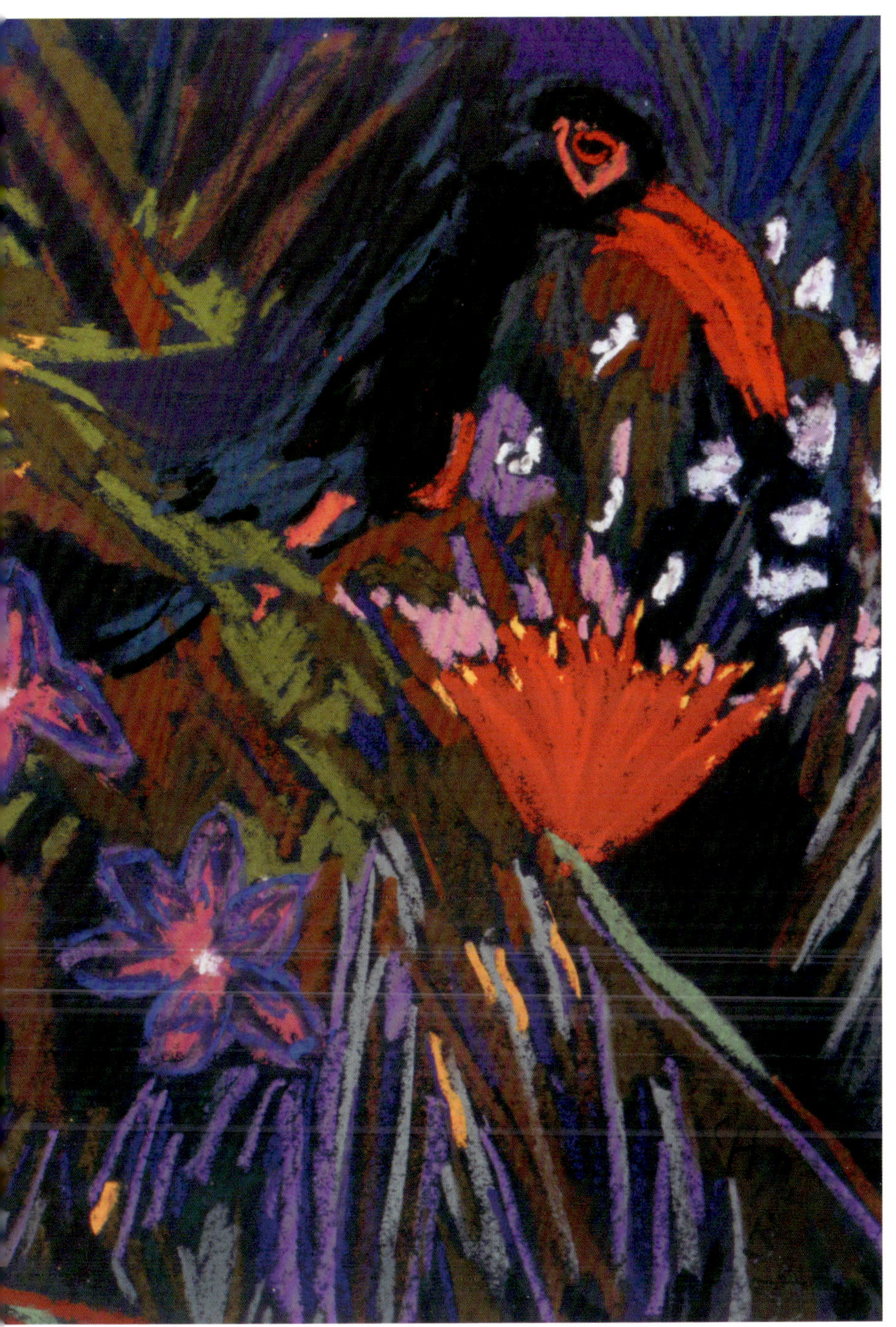

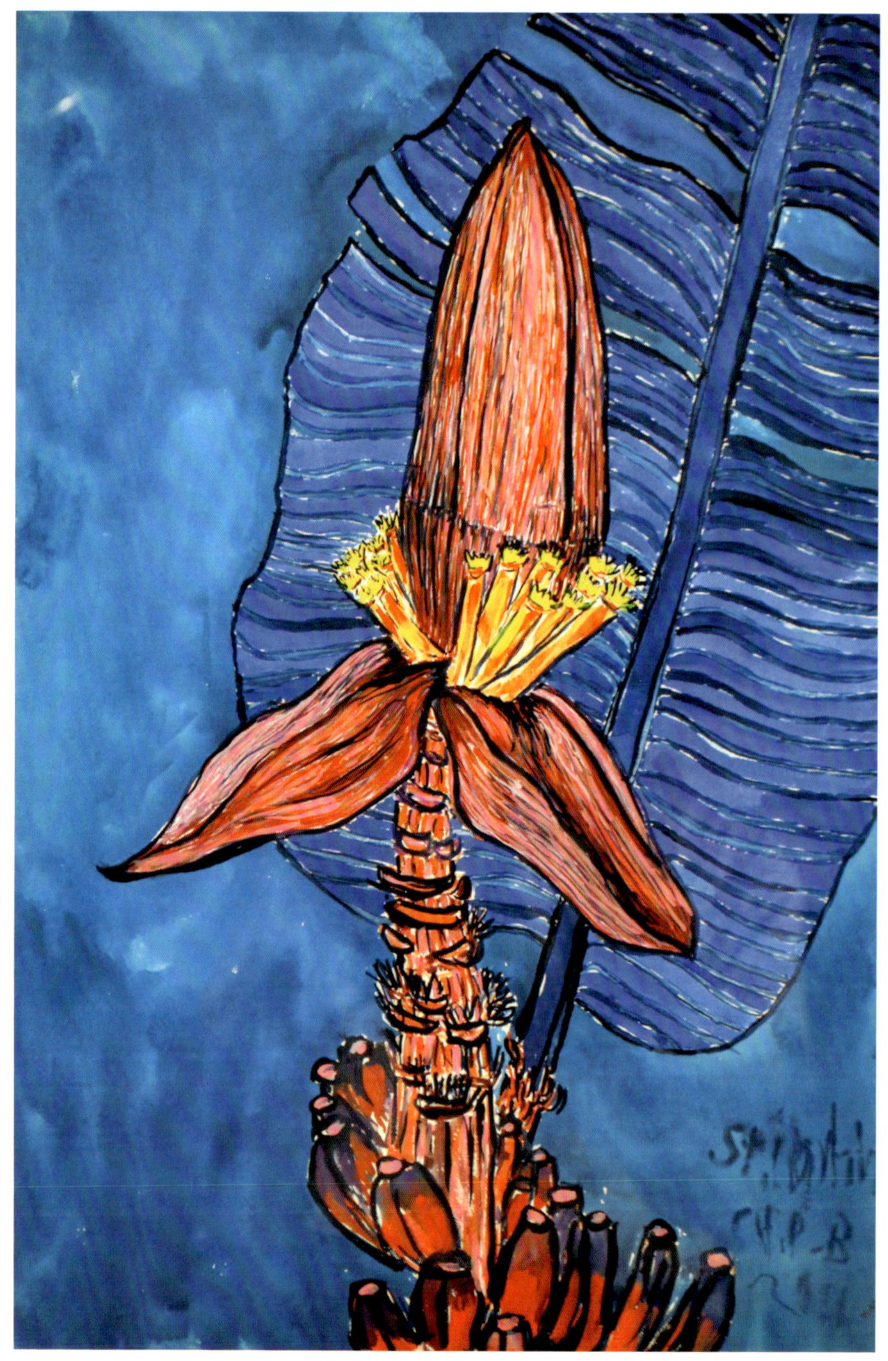

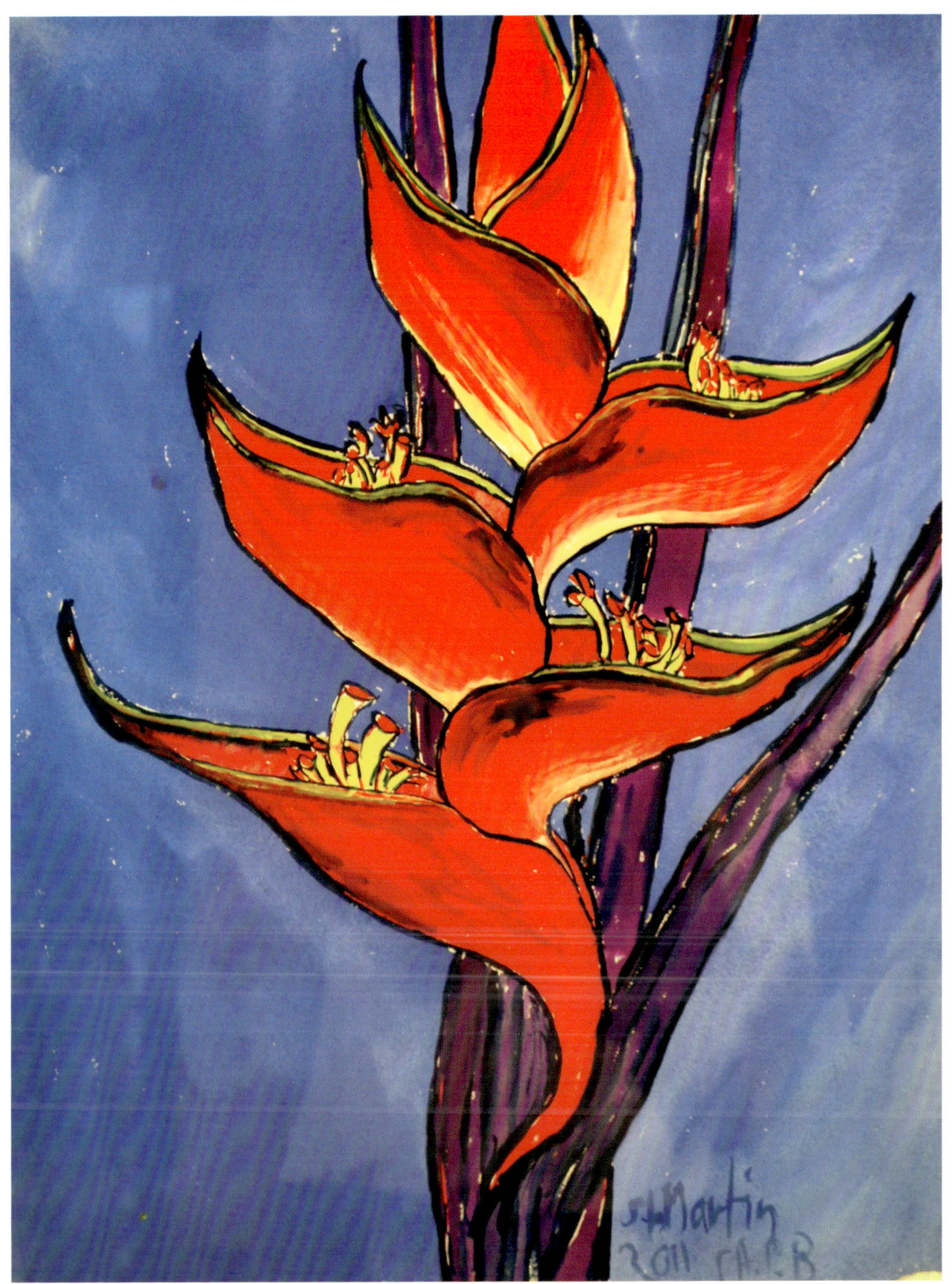

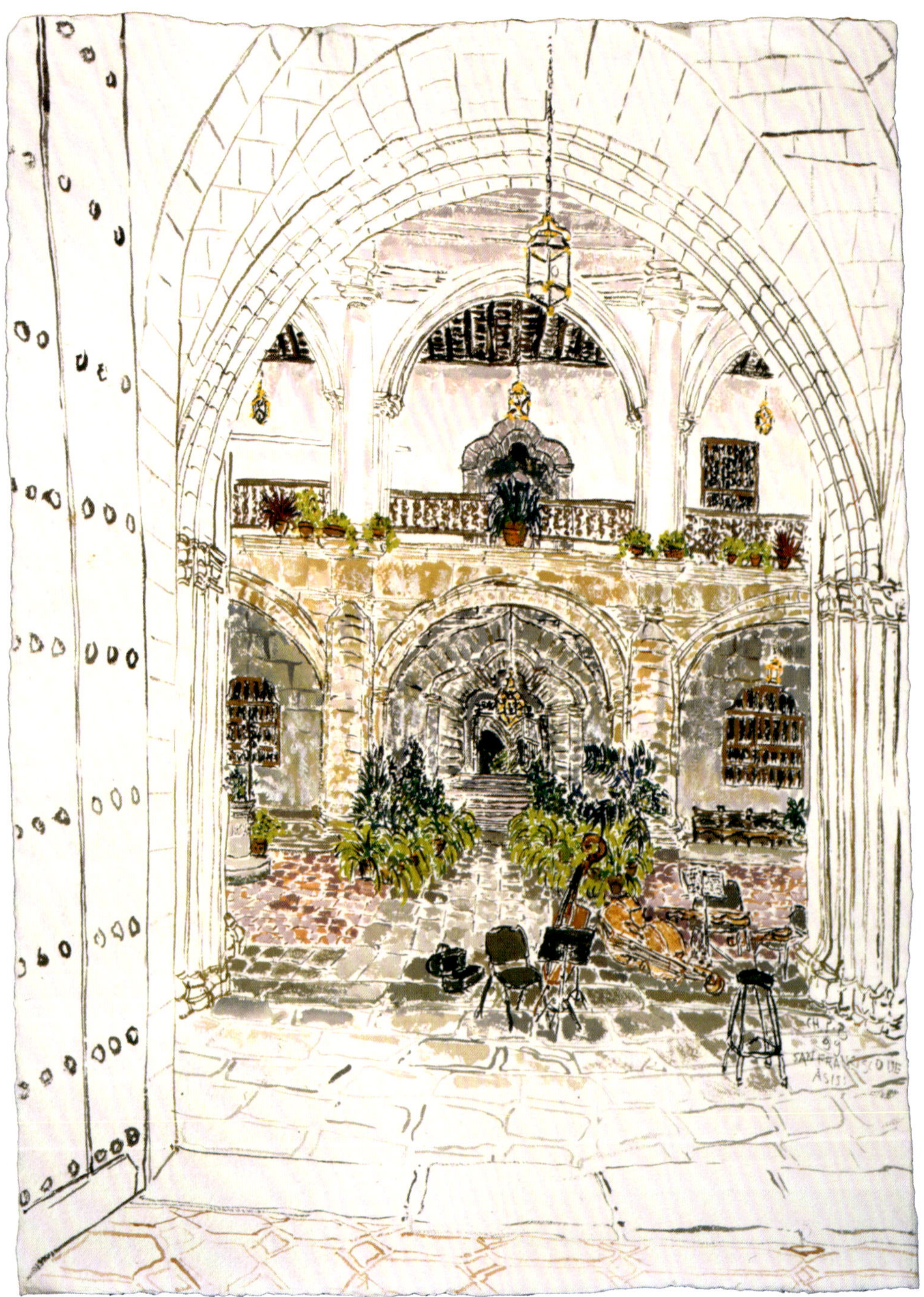
CH P B
99
SAN FRANCISCO DE
ASIS

Havana, Cuba

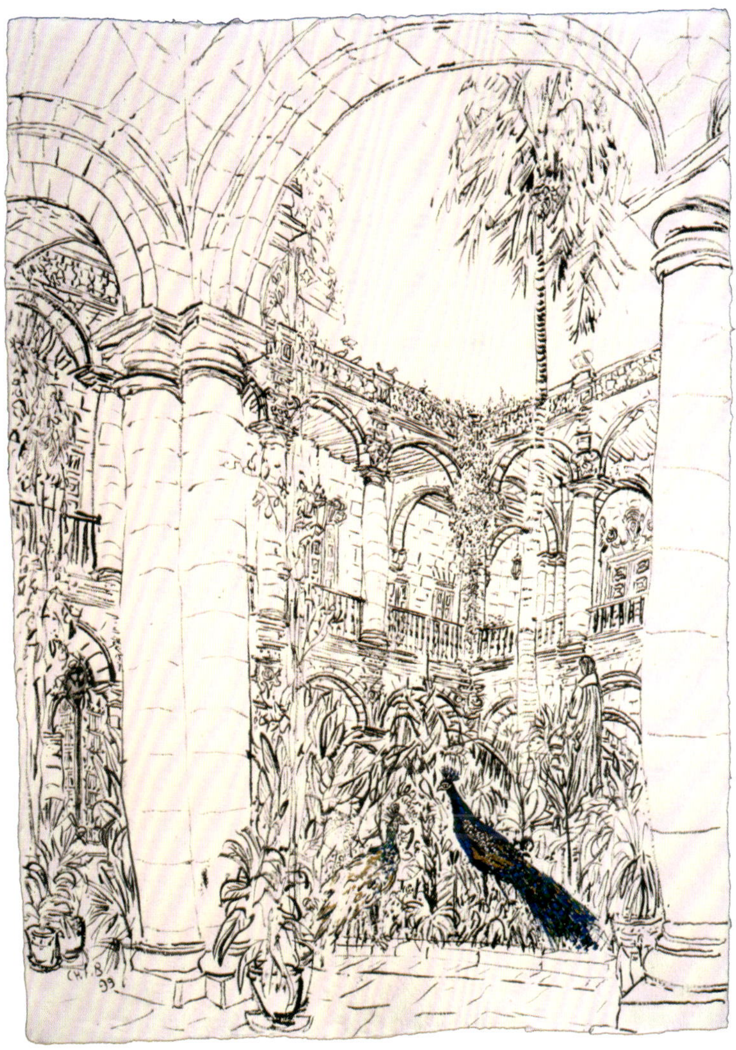

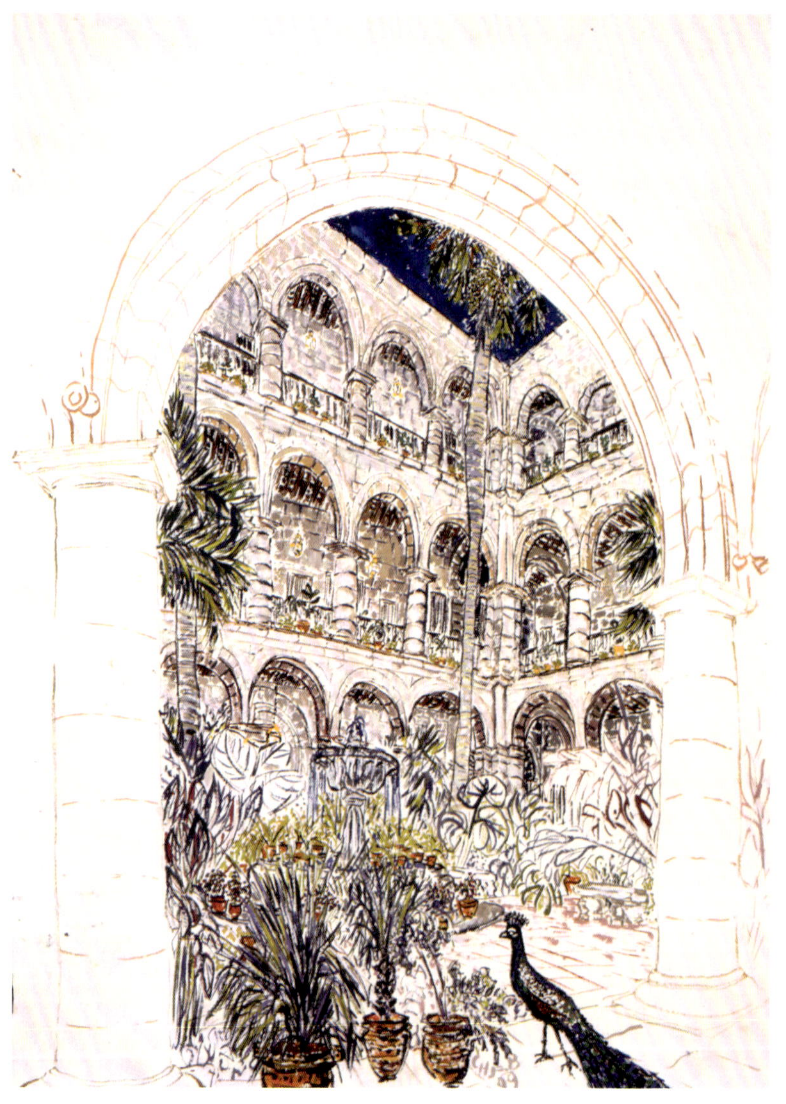

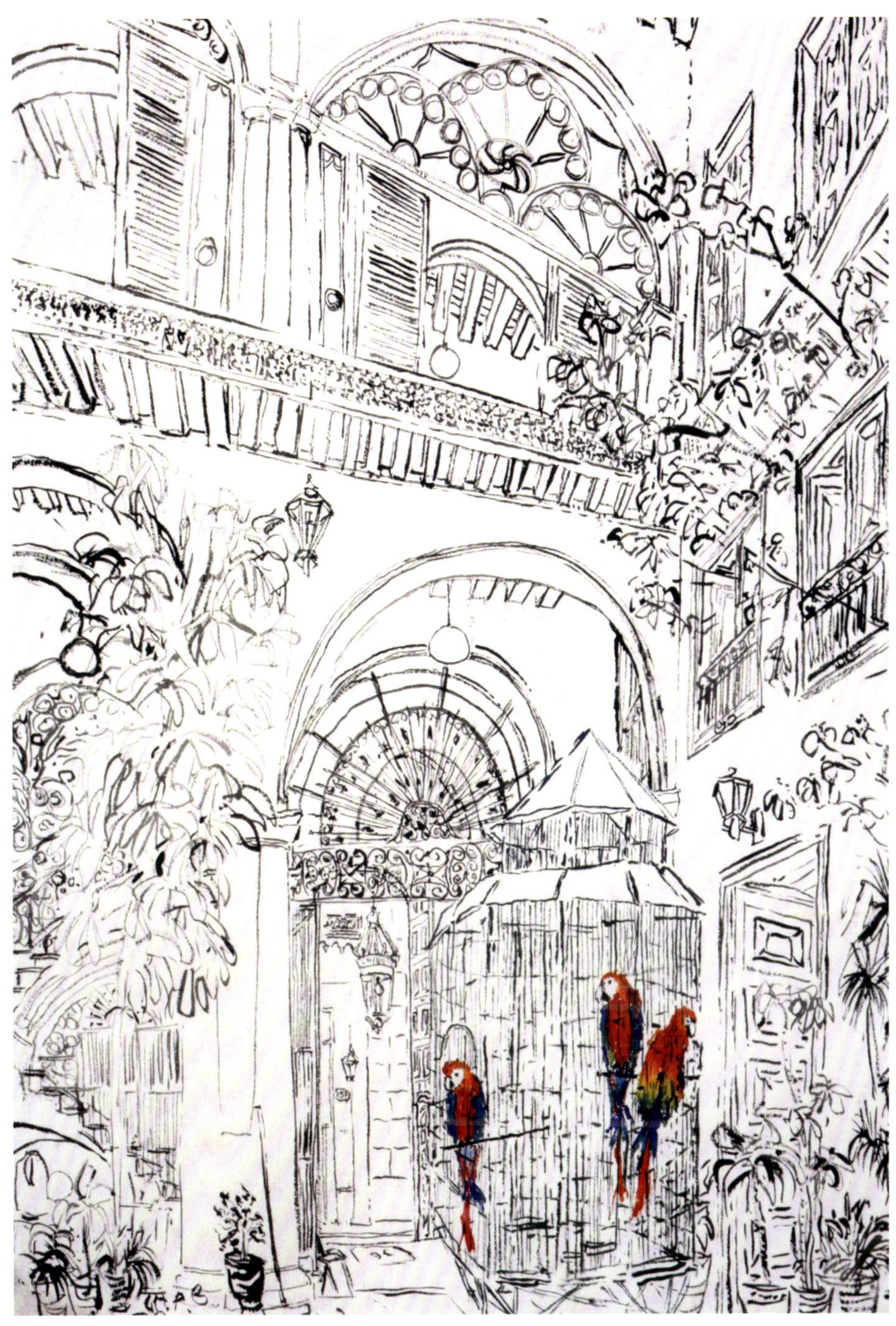

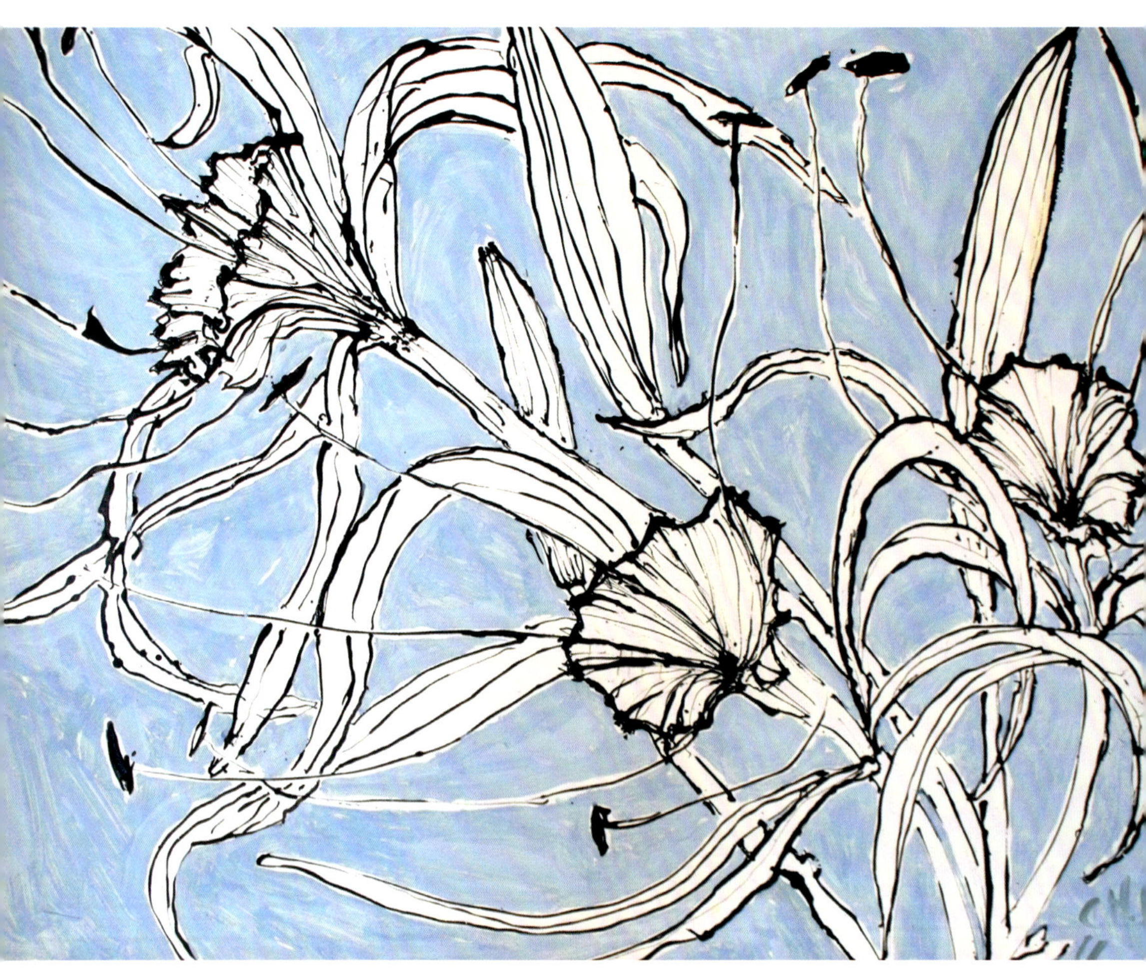

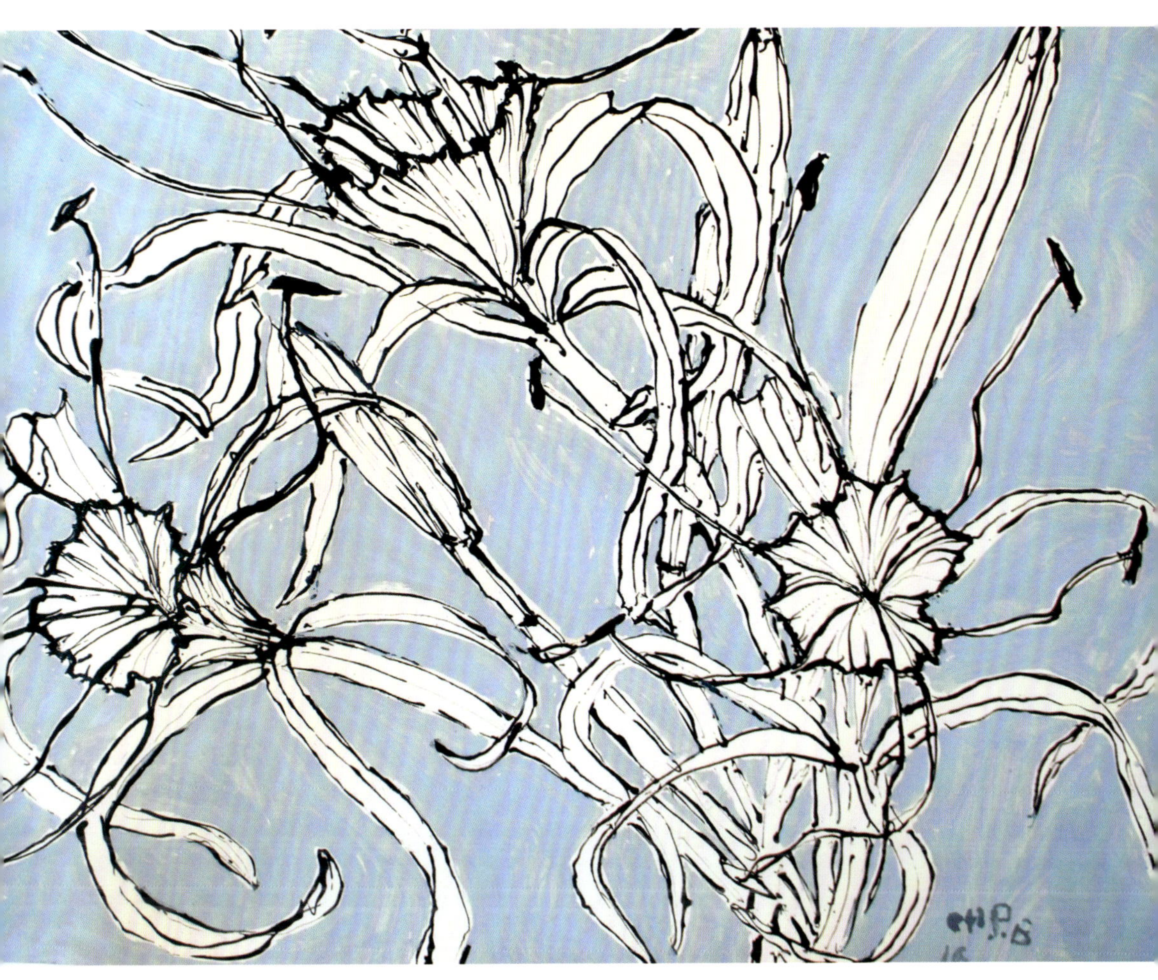

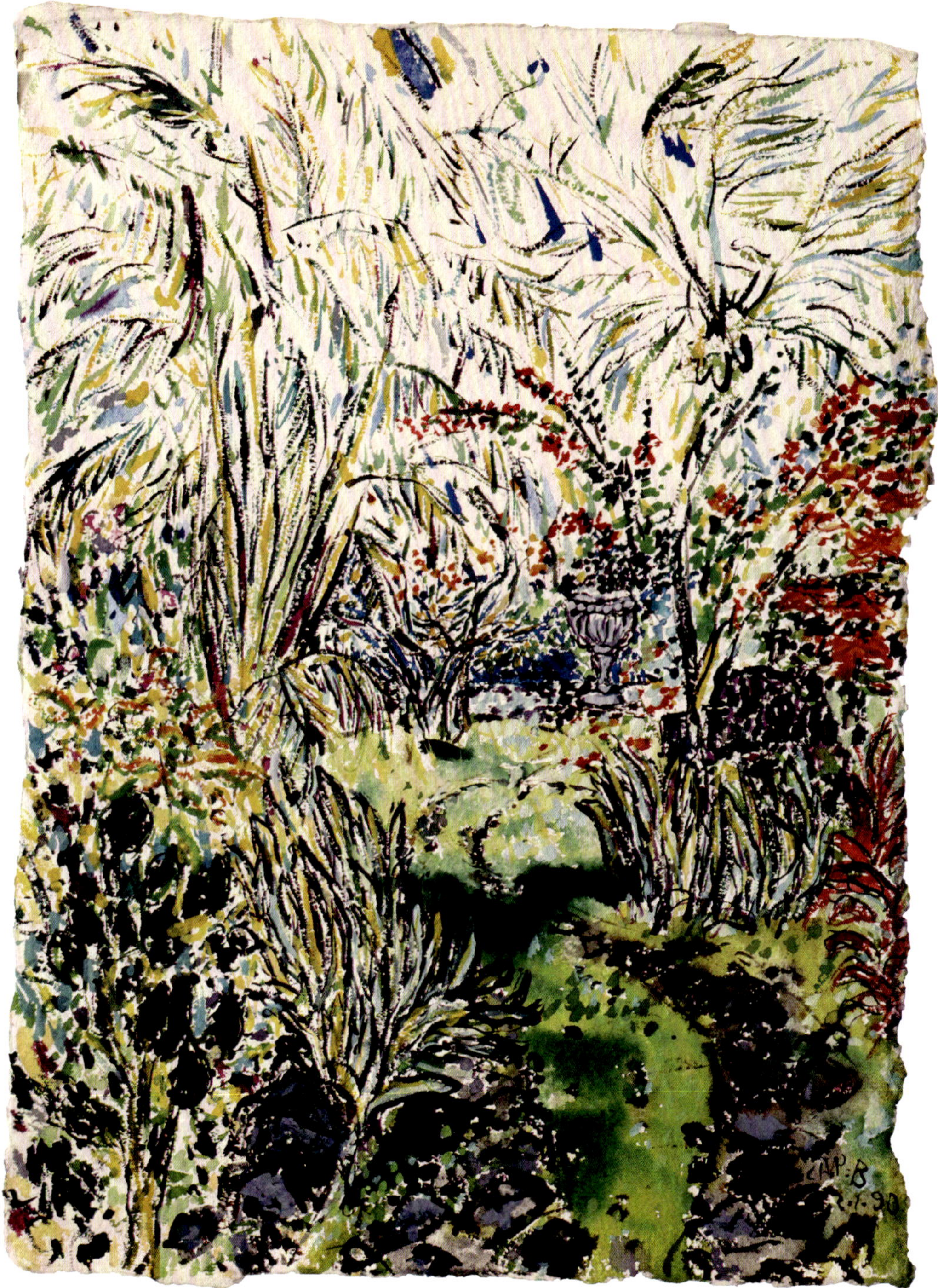

Morne Rouge, Angus and Will's Garden

Dominica, West Indies

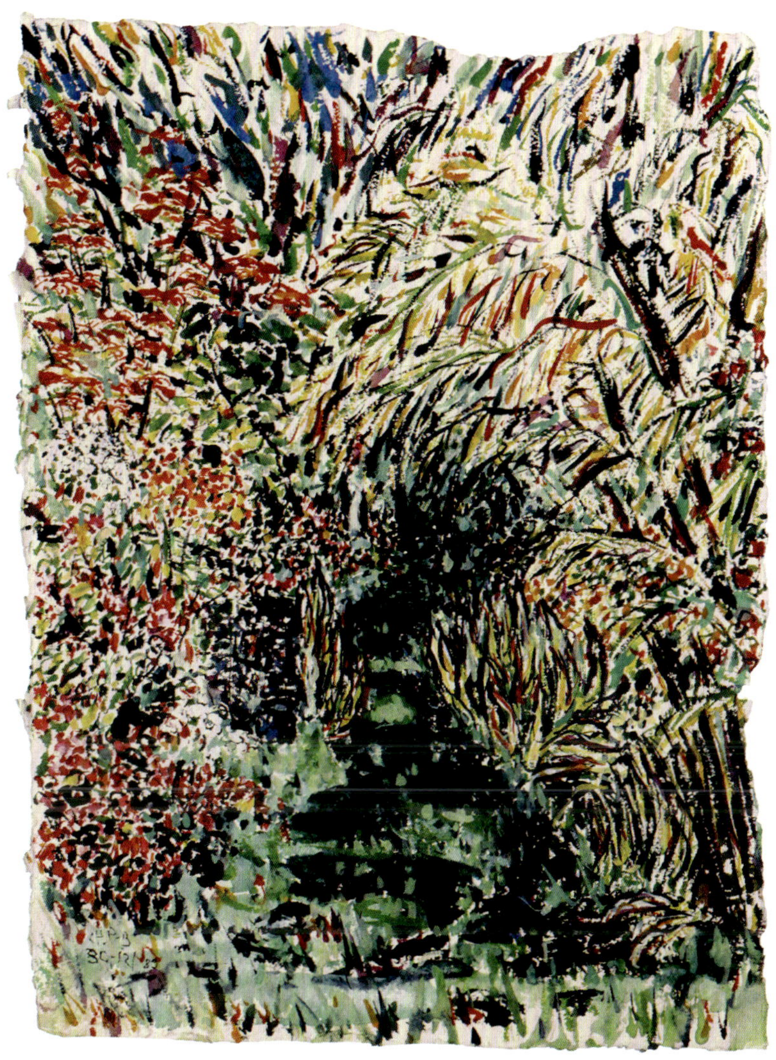

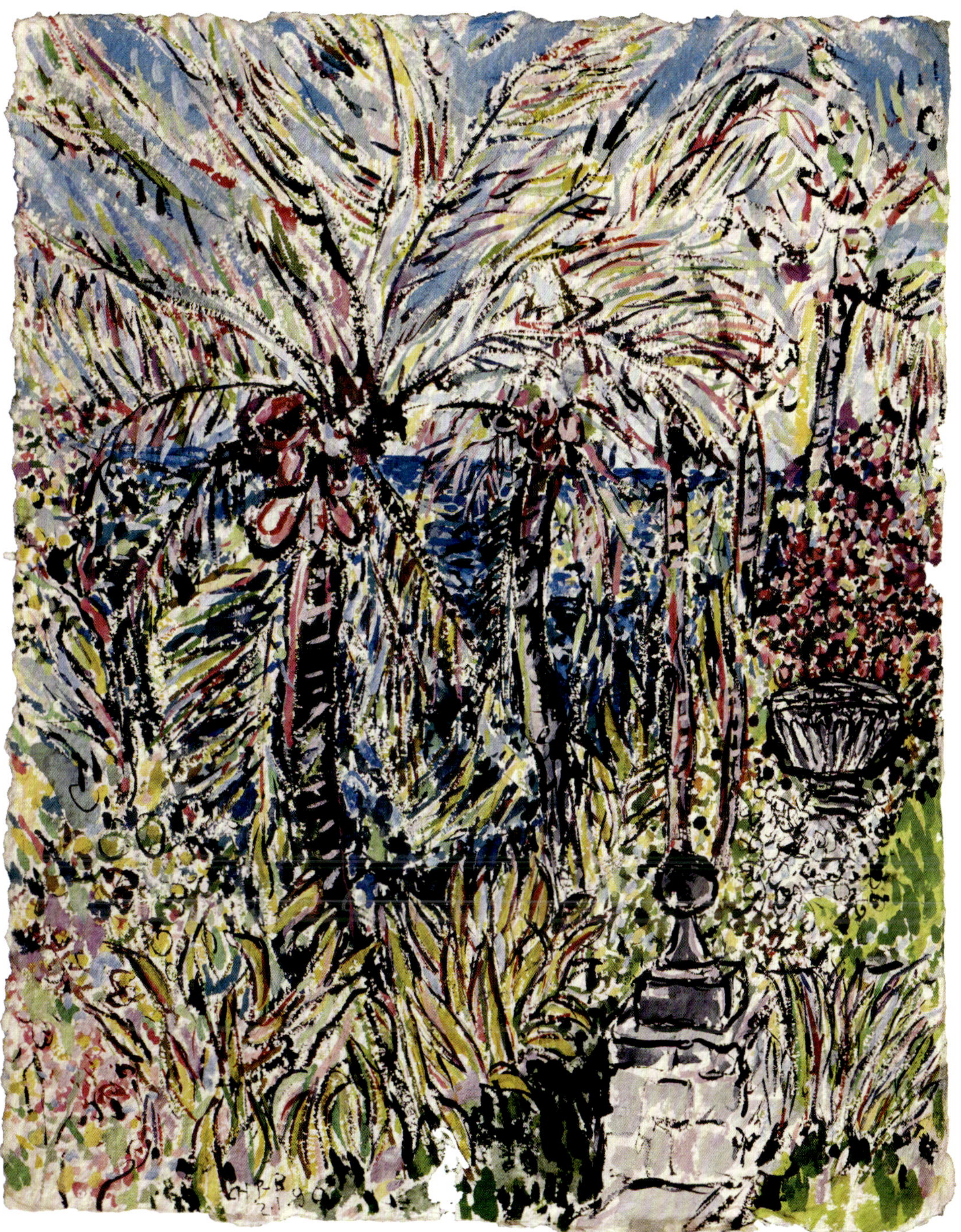

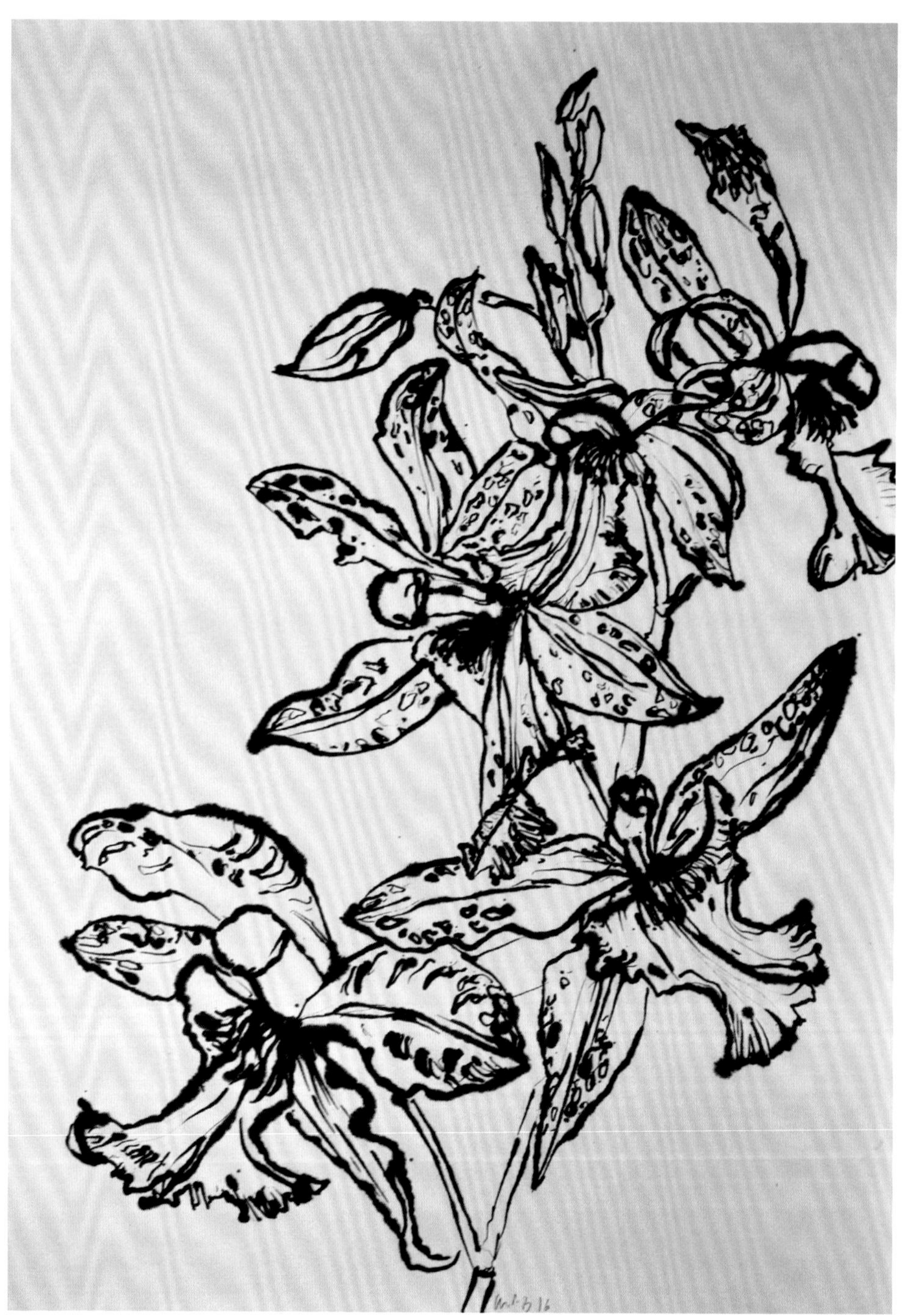

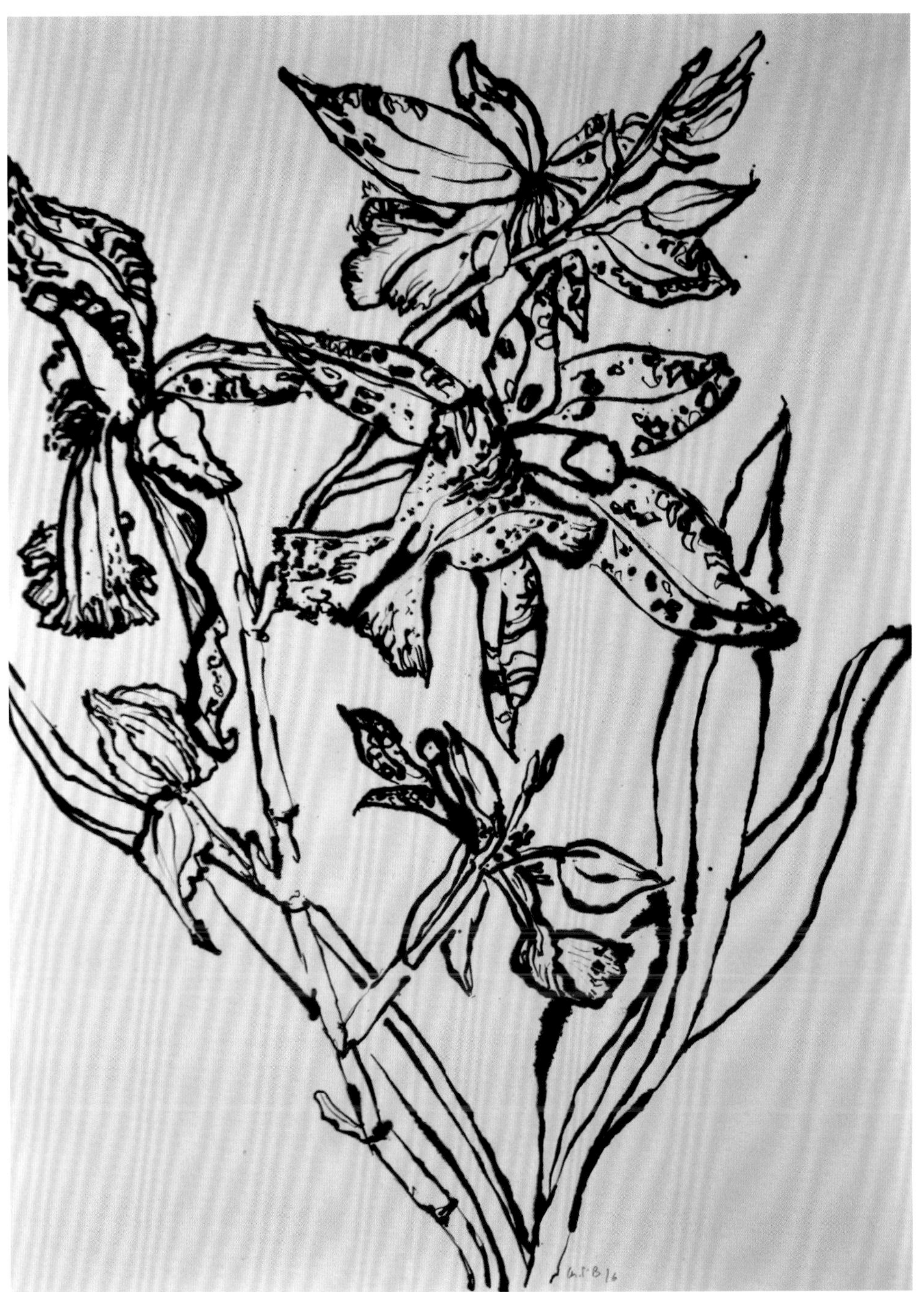

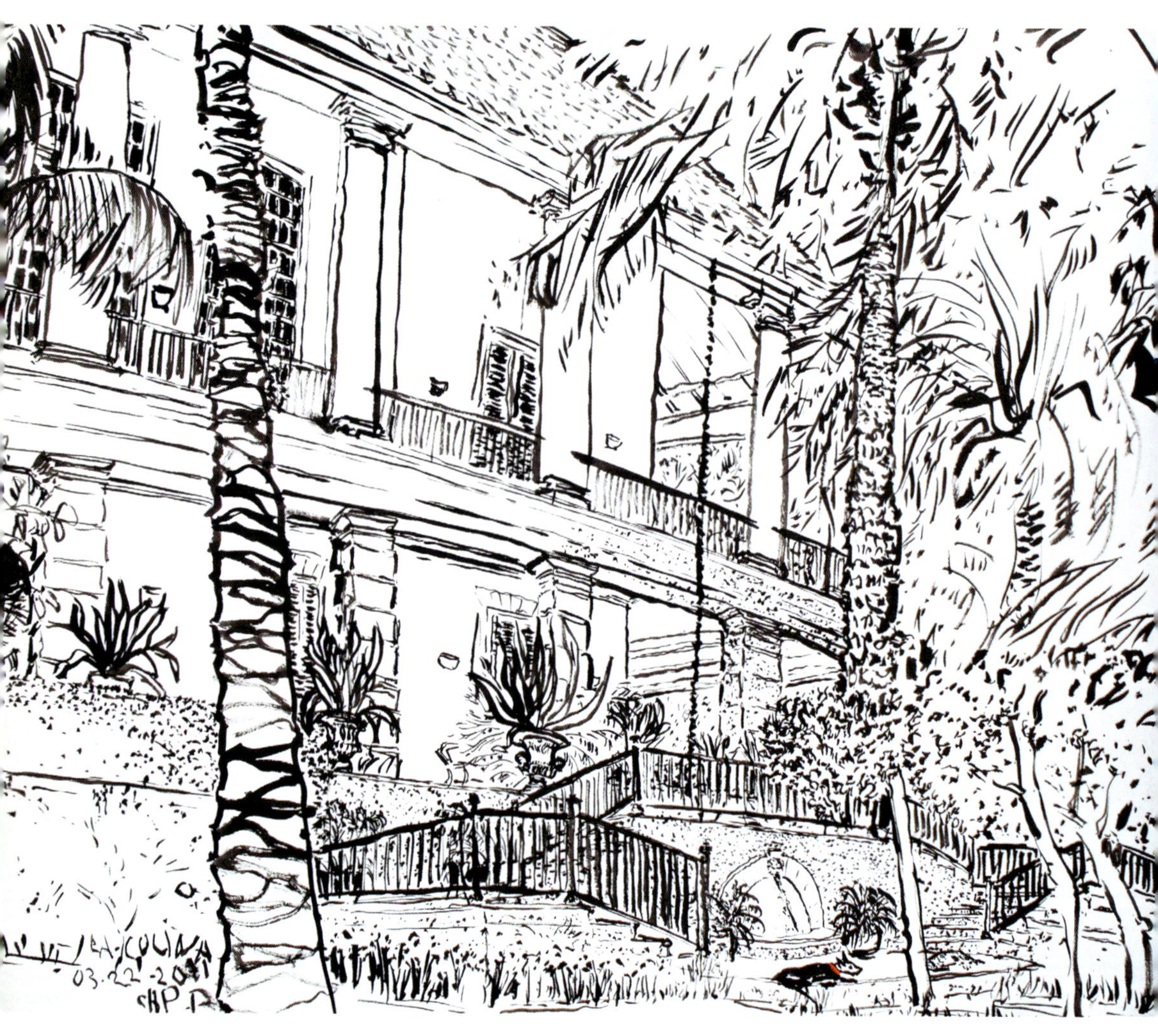
LA COLINA
03.22.2011

La Colina, Bunny and John's Garden

Punta Cana, Dominican Republic

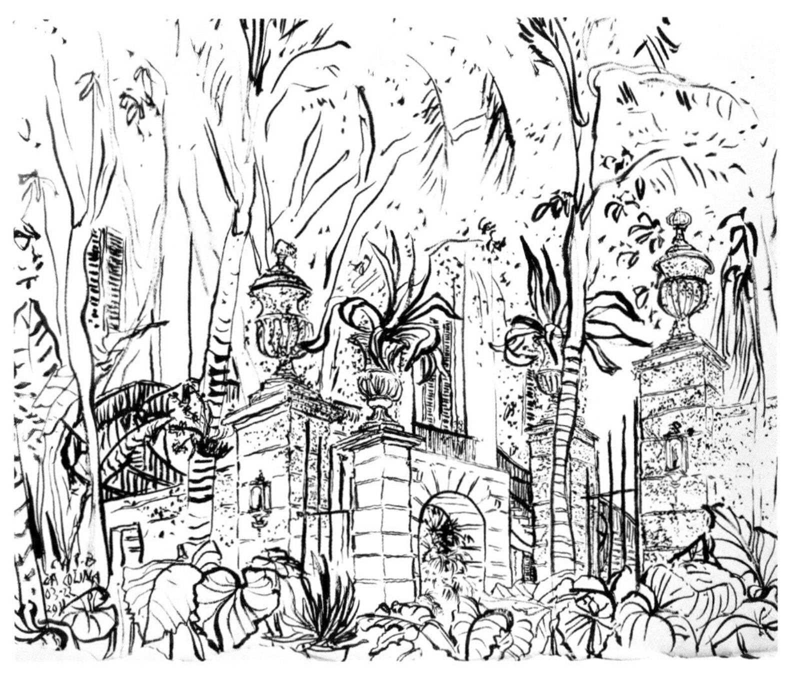

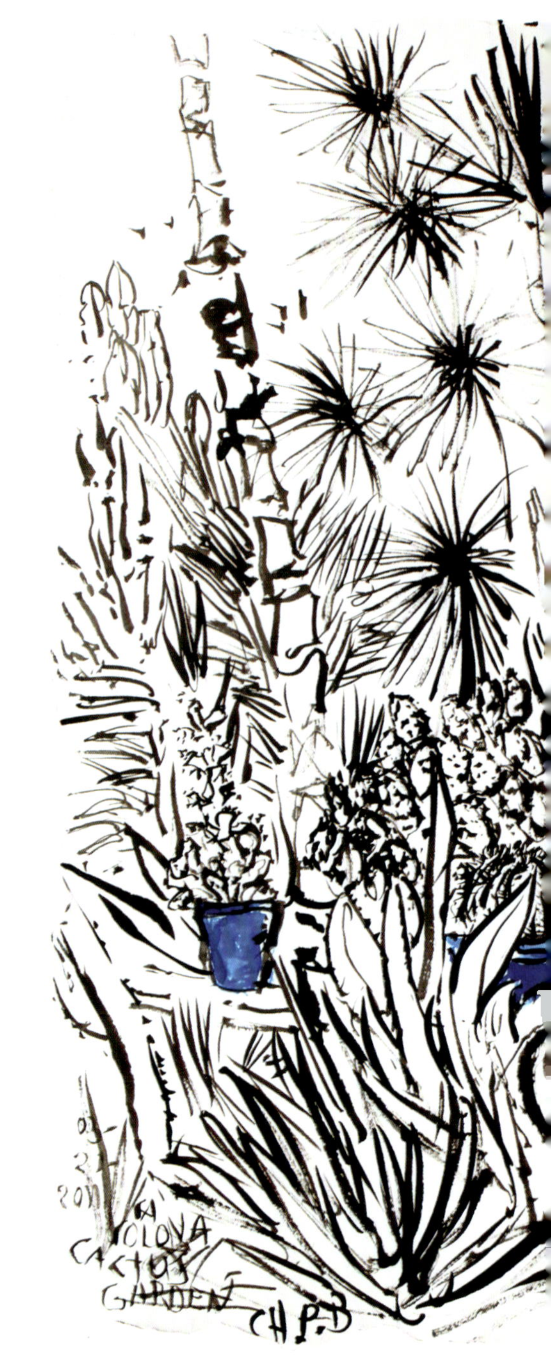
CACTUS
GARDEN
CH.P.B

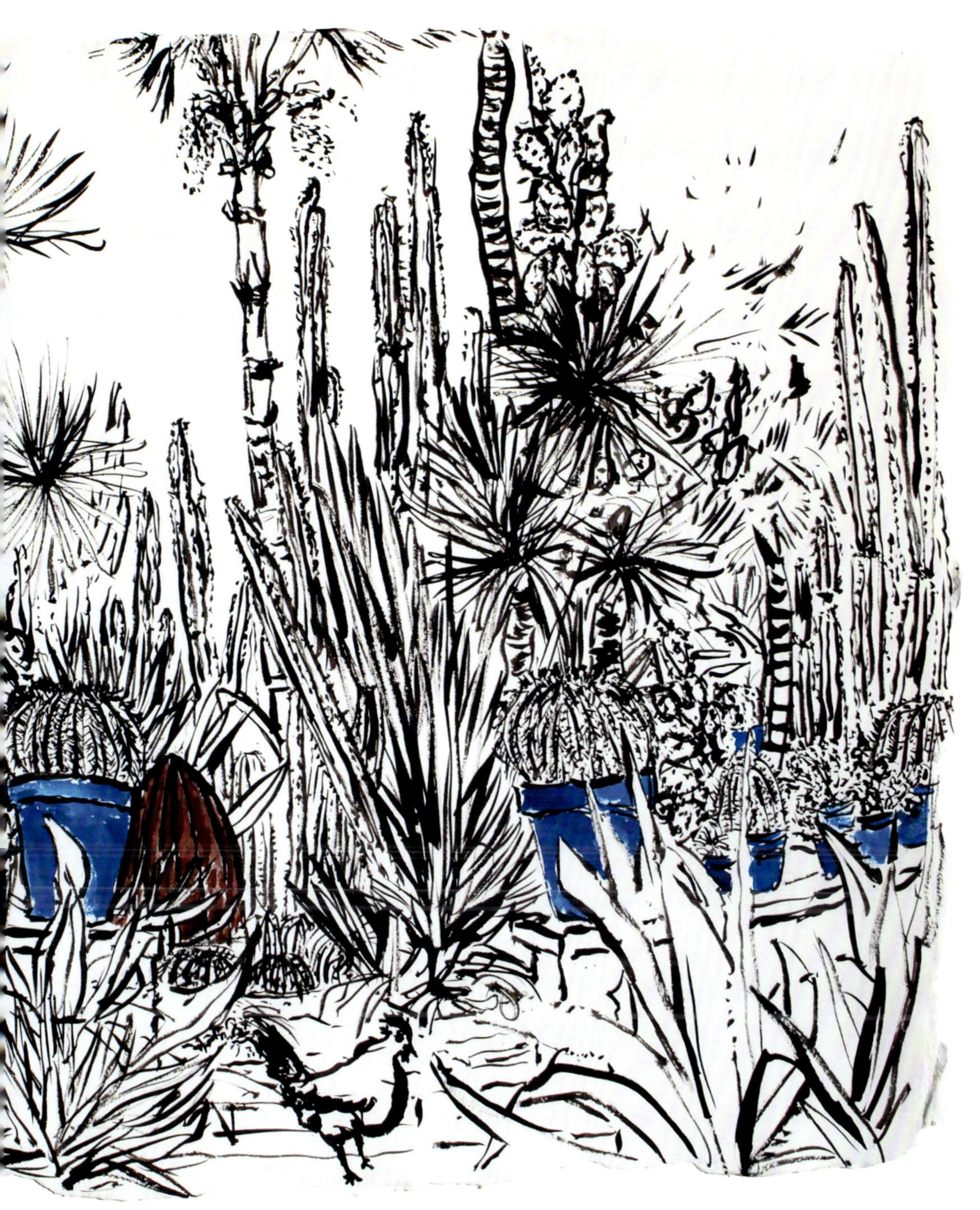

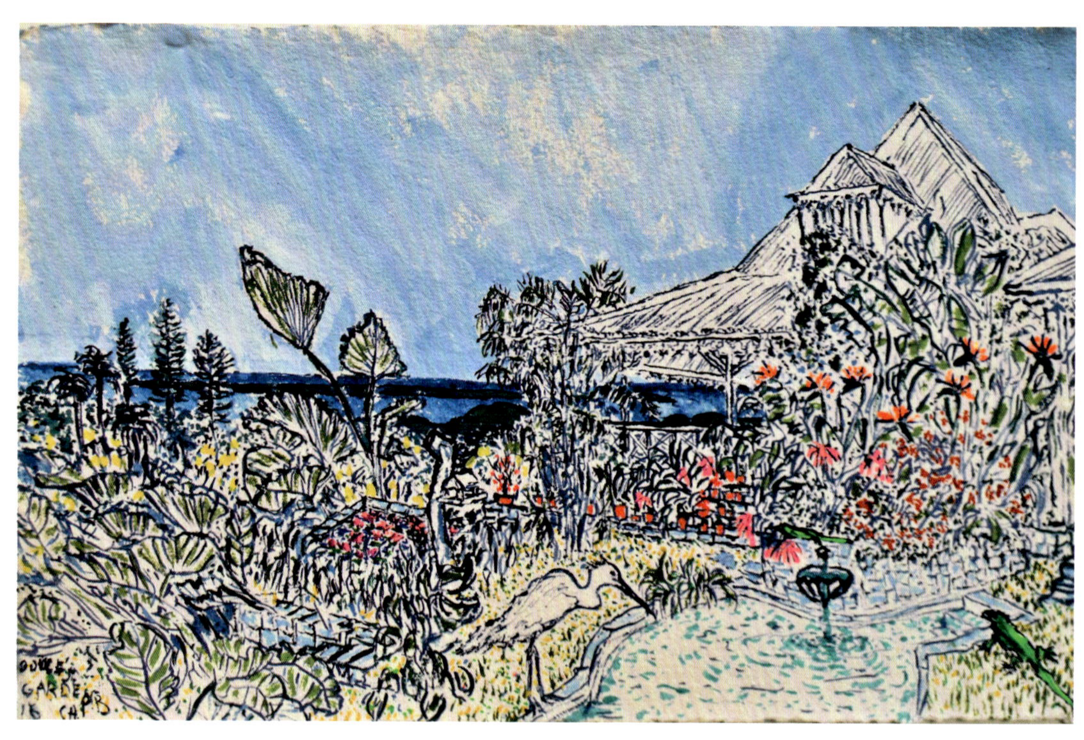

Odile's Garden

Pic Paradis, St. Martin

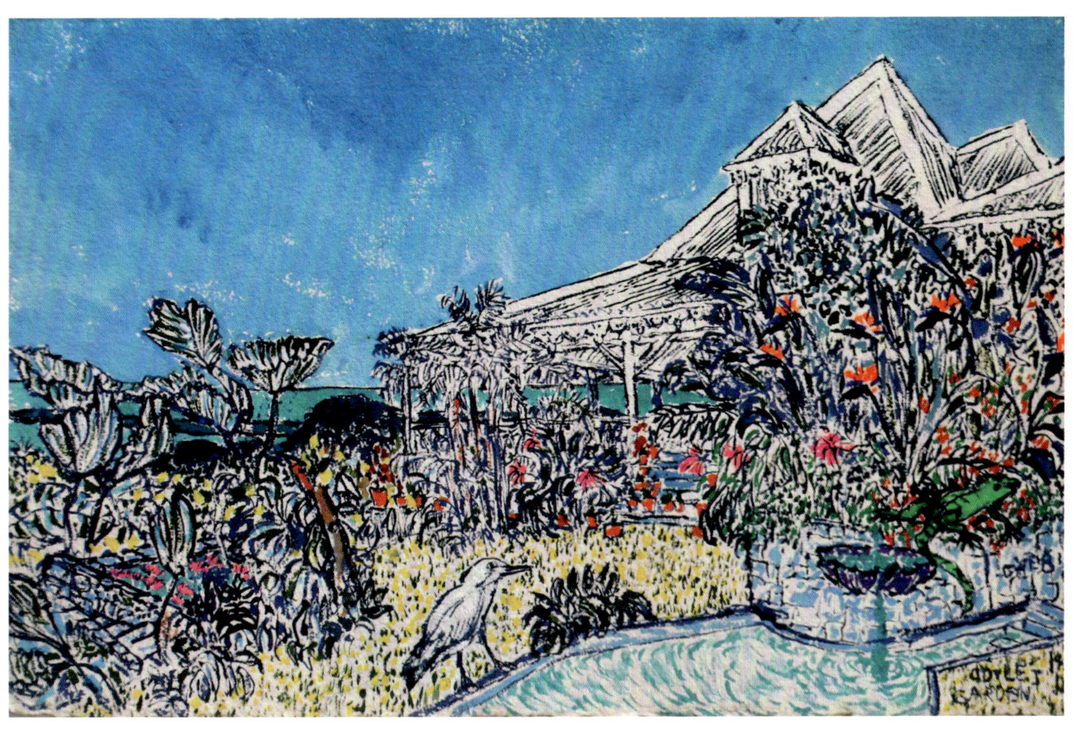

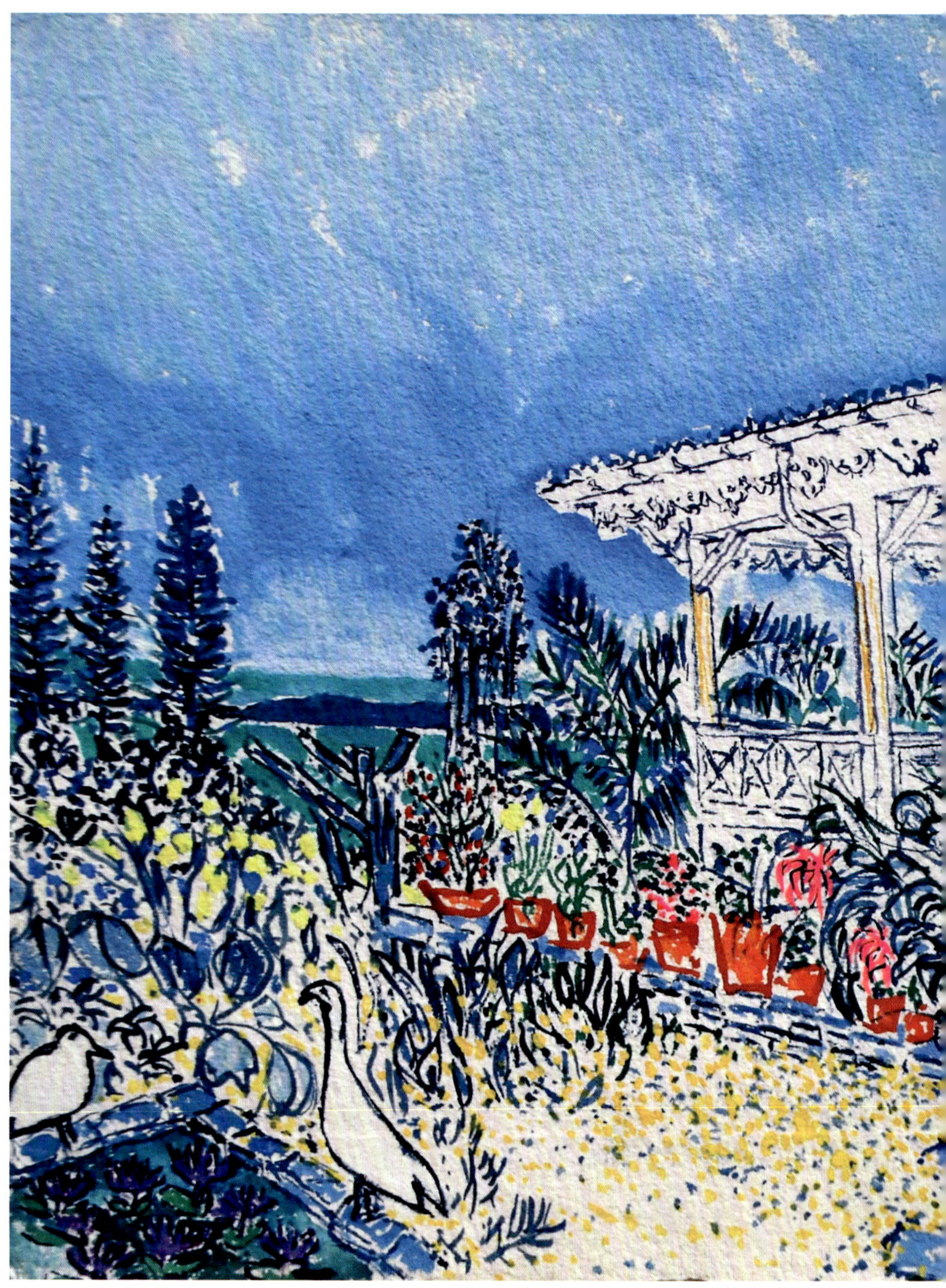

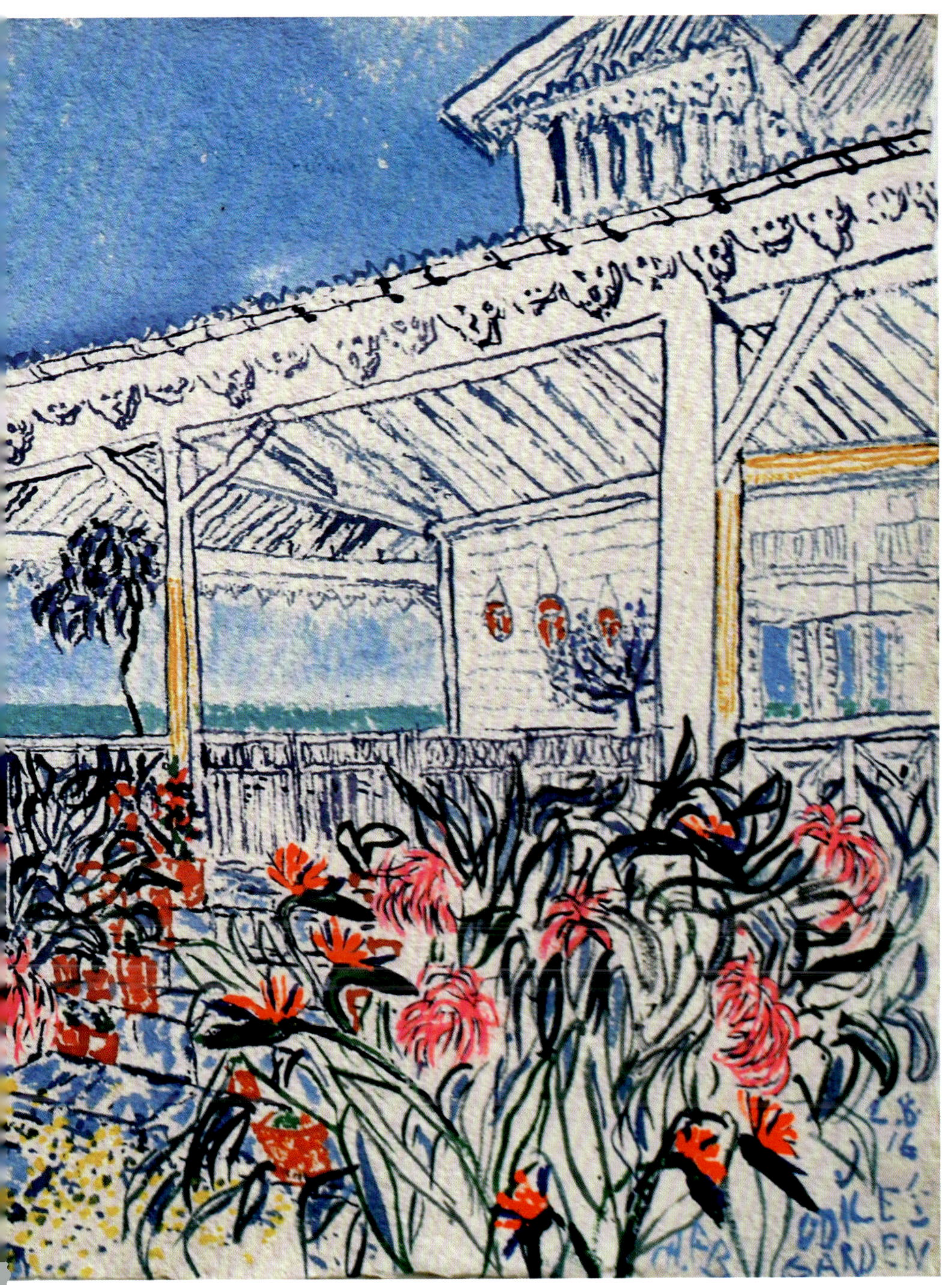
GARDEN

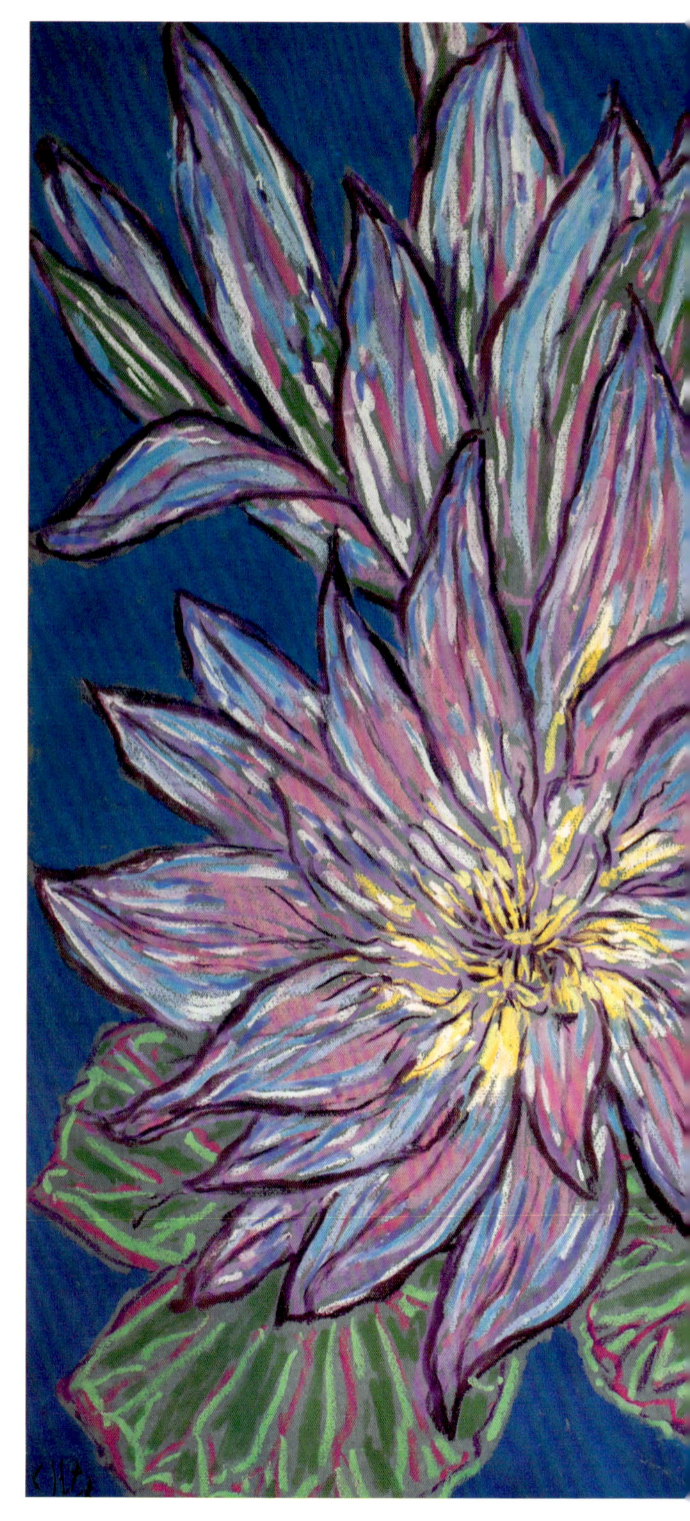

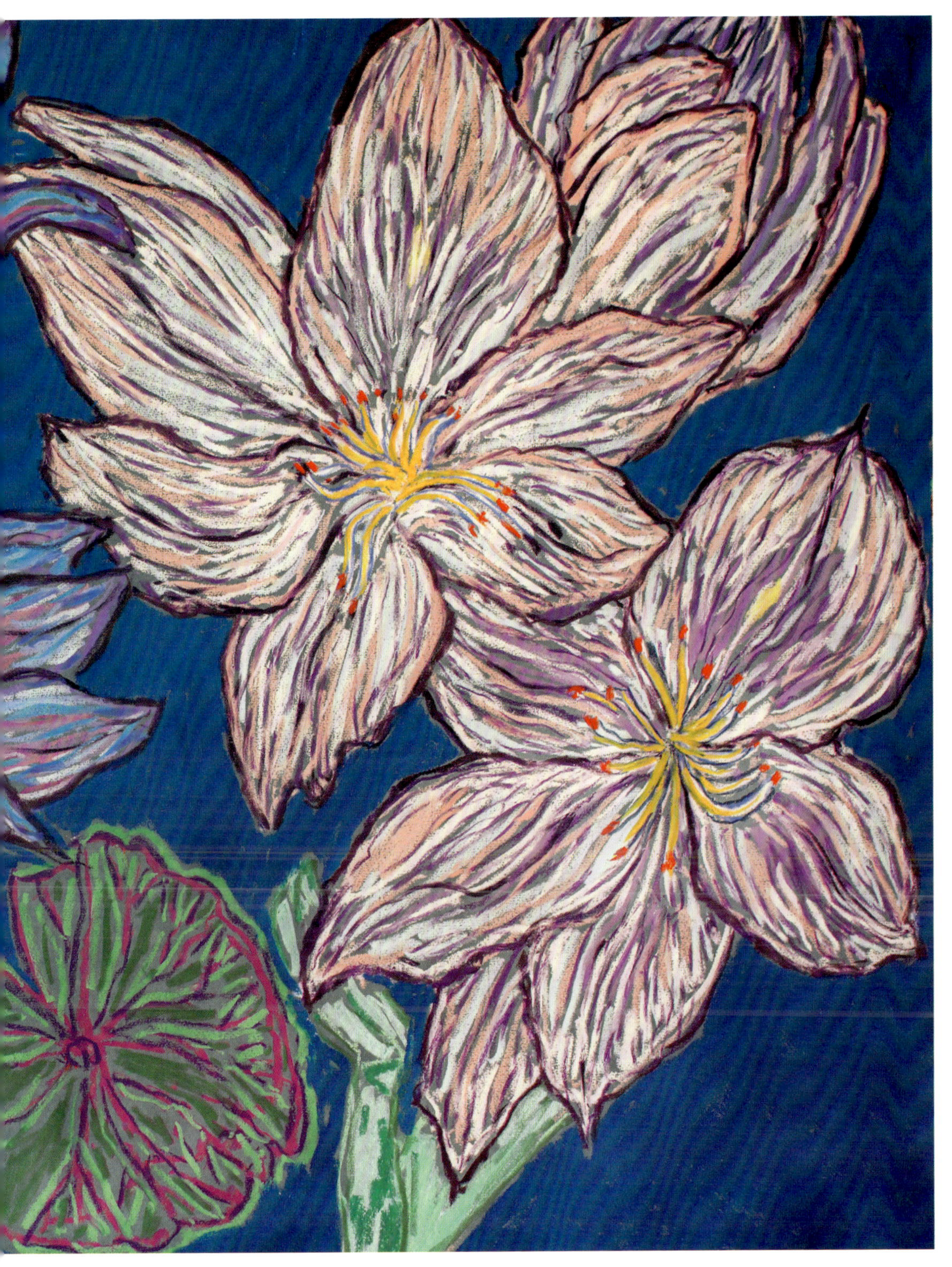

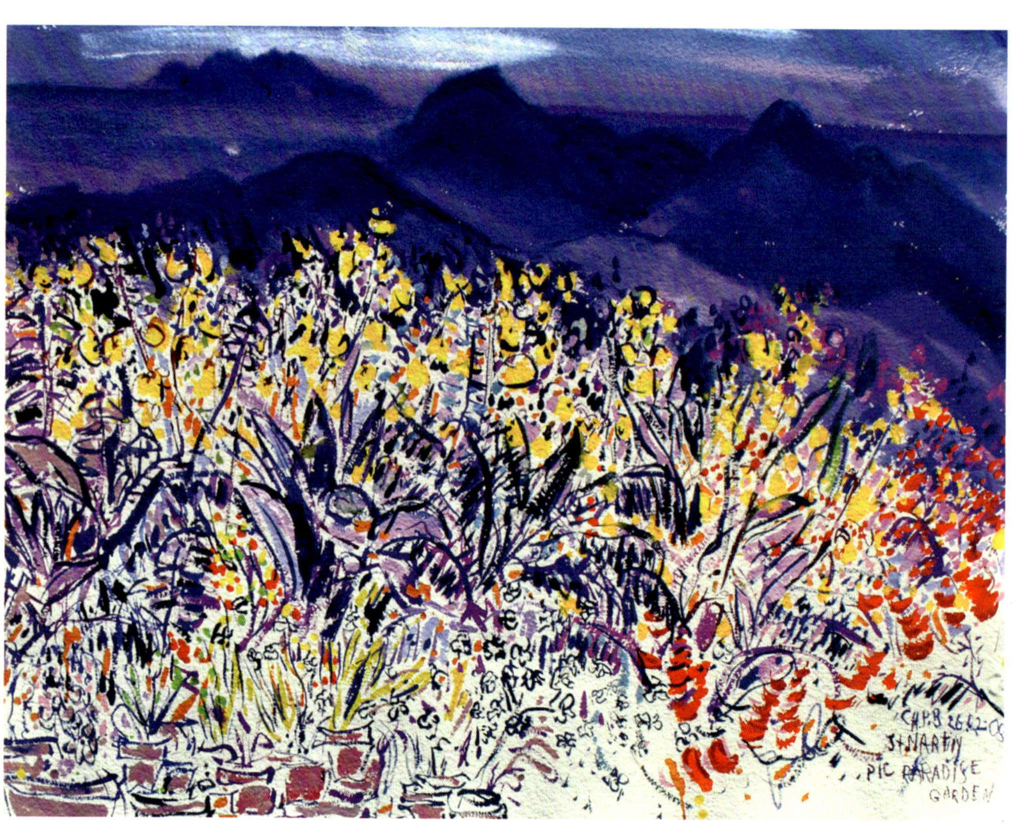
CH.P.B 26.02
St MARTIN
PIC PARADISE
GARDEN

Jean-Louis and Jean-Christophe's Garden

Pic Paradis, St. Martin

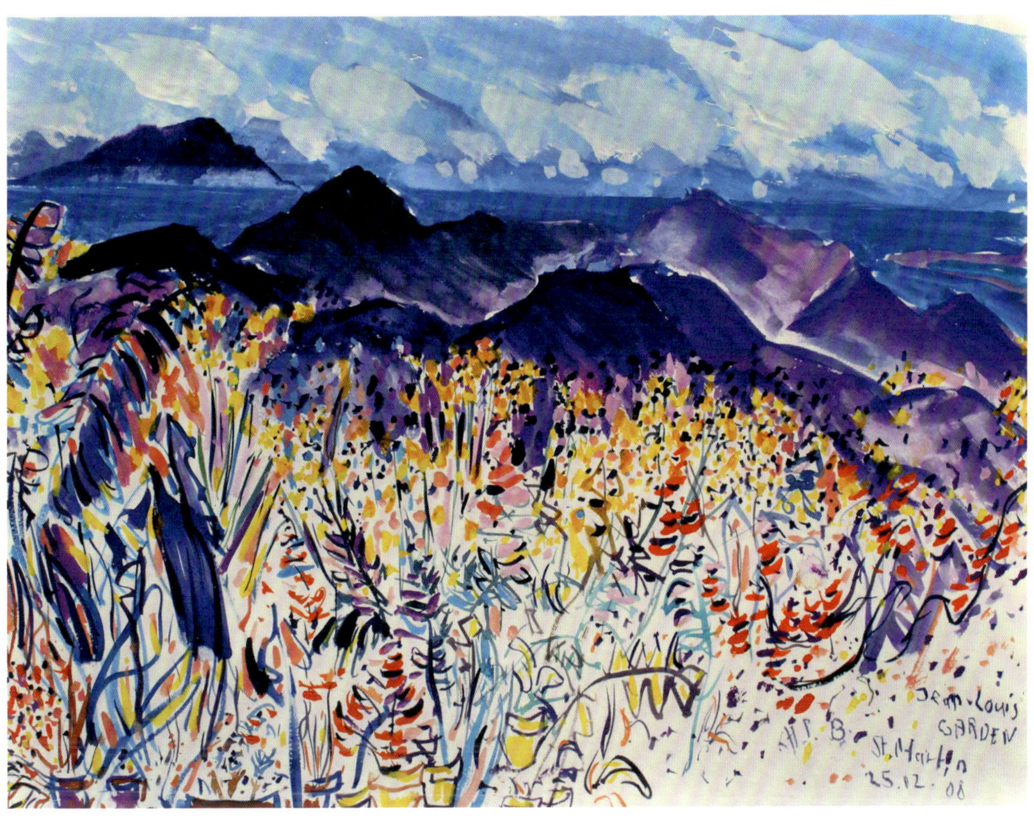

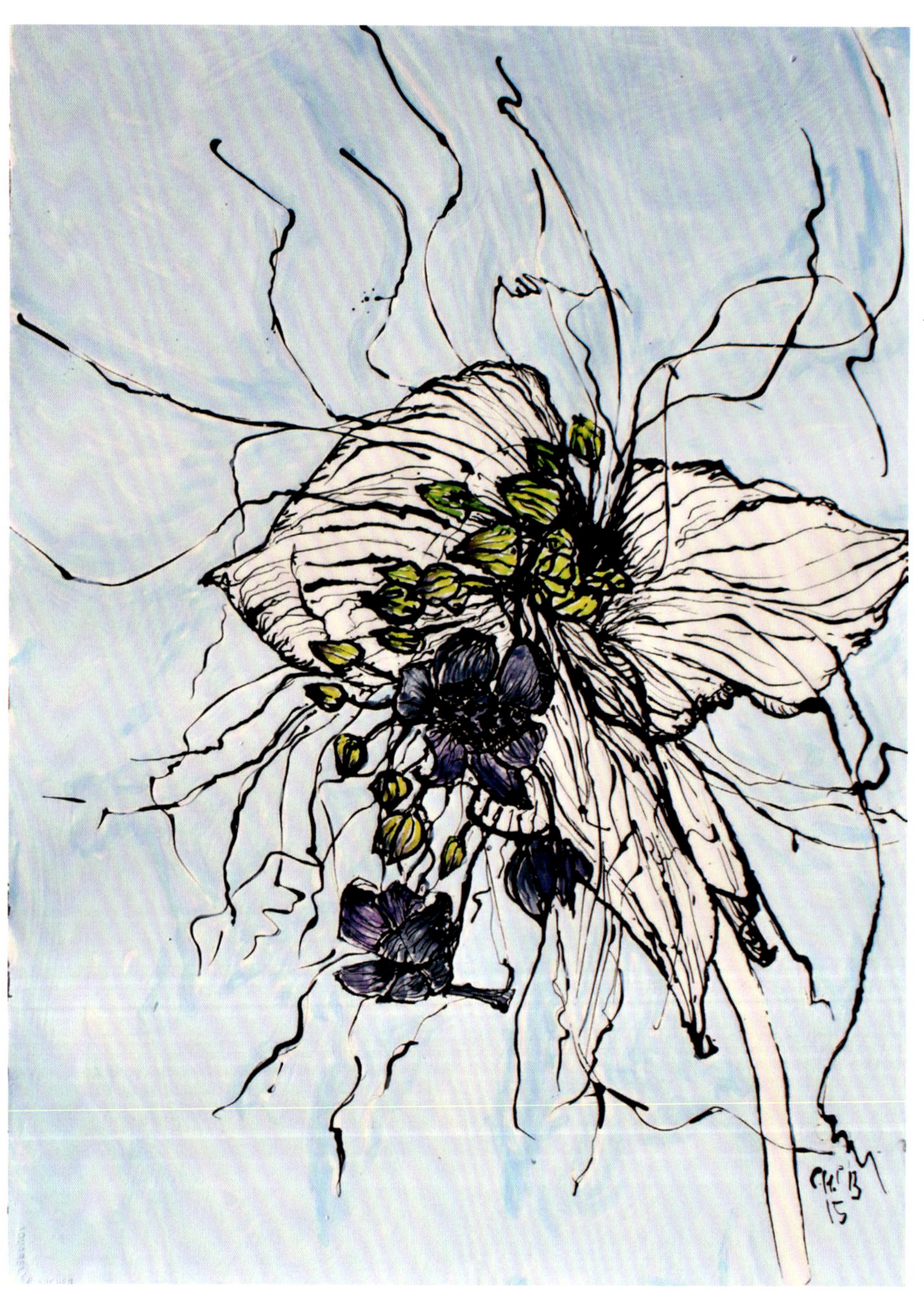

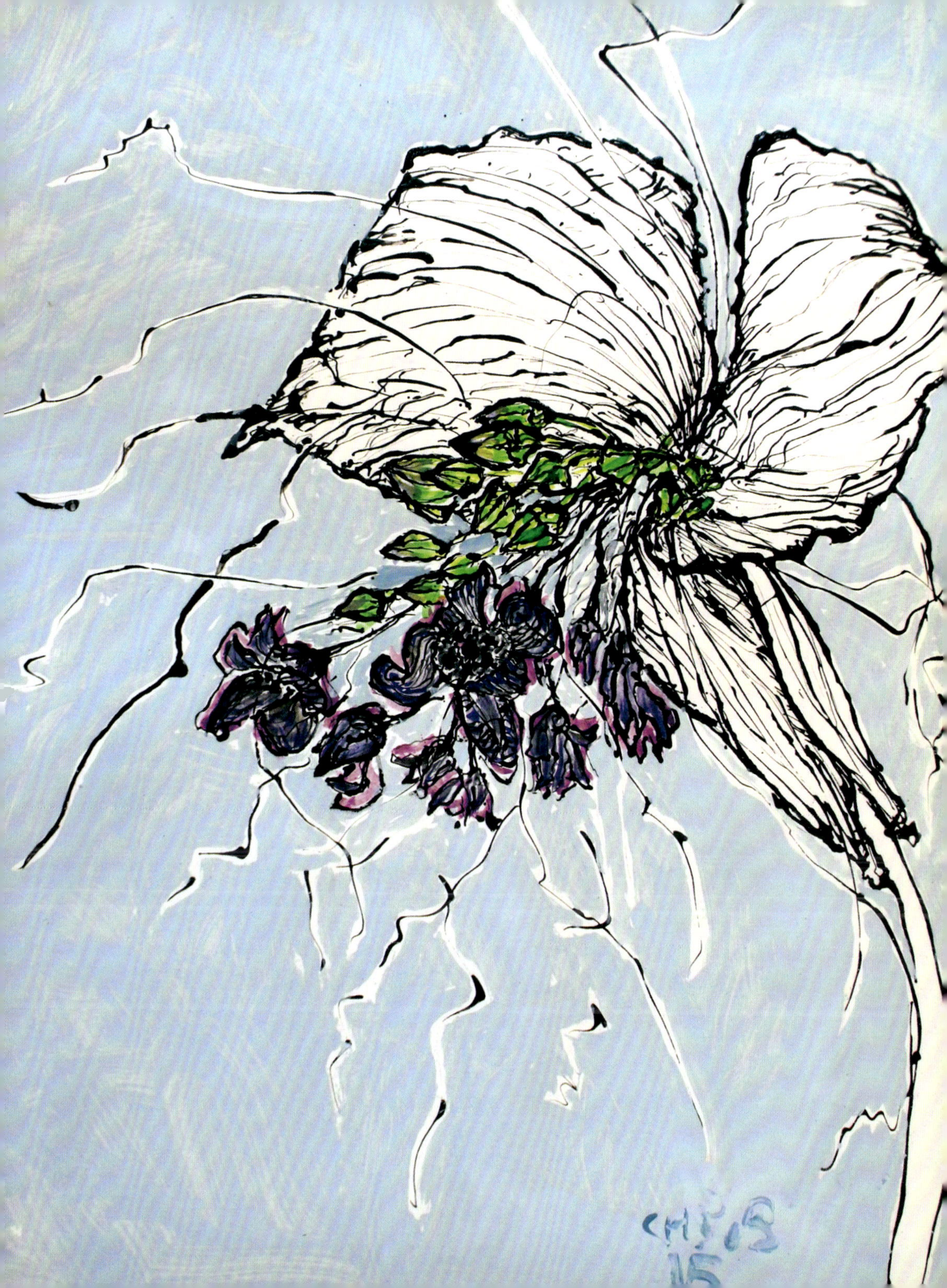

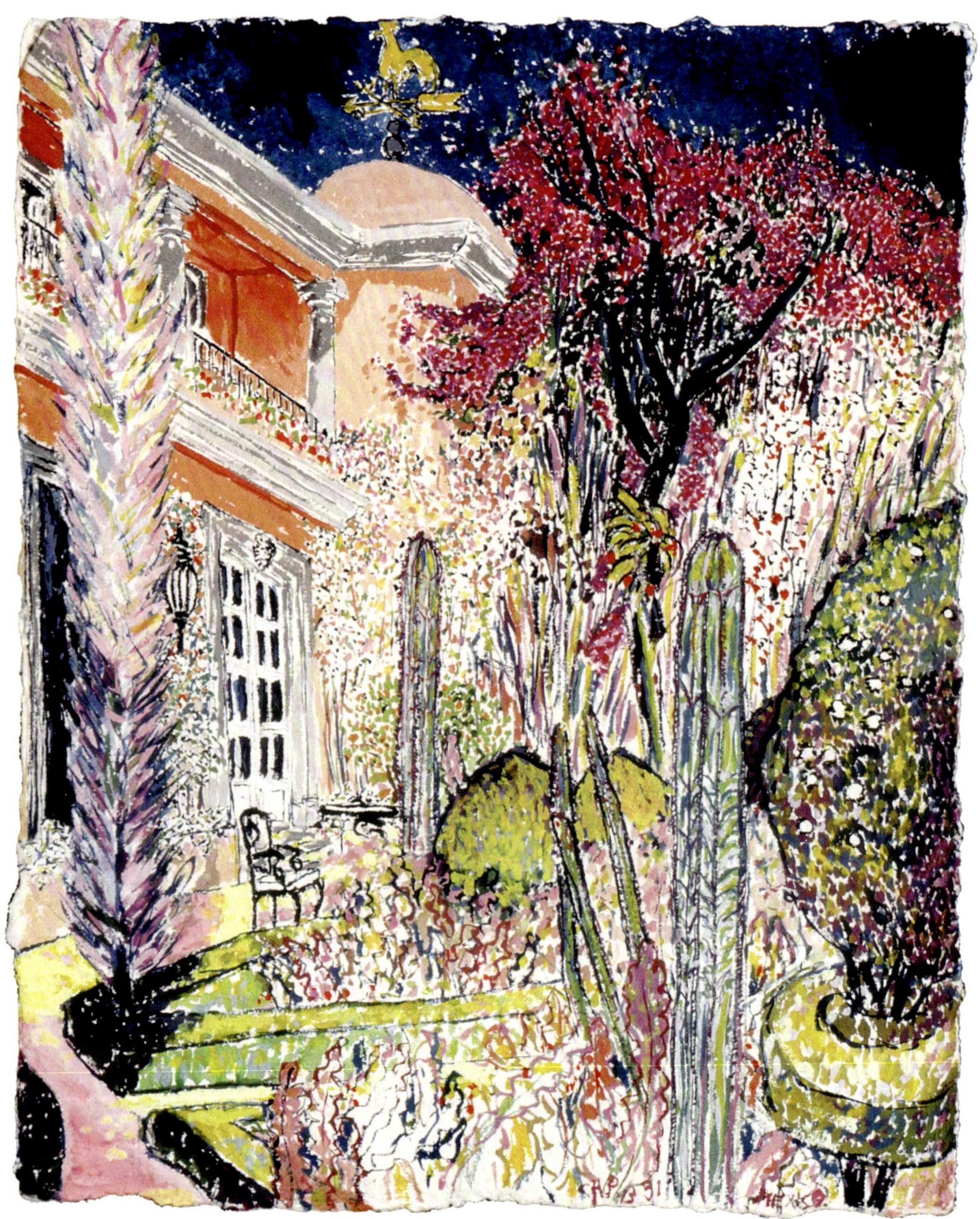

San Ángel, Mexico

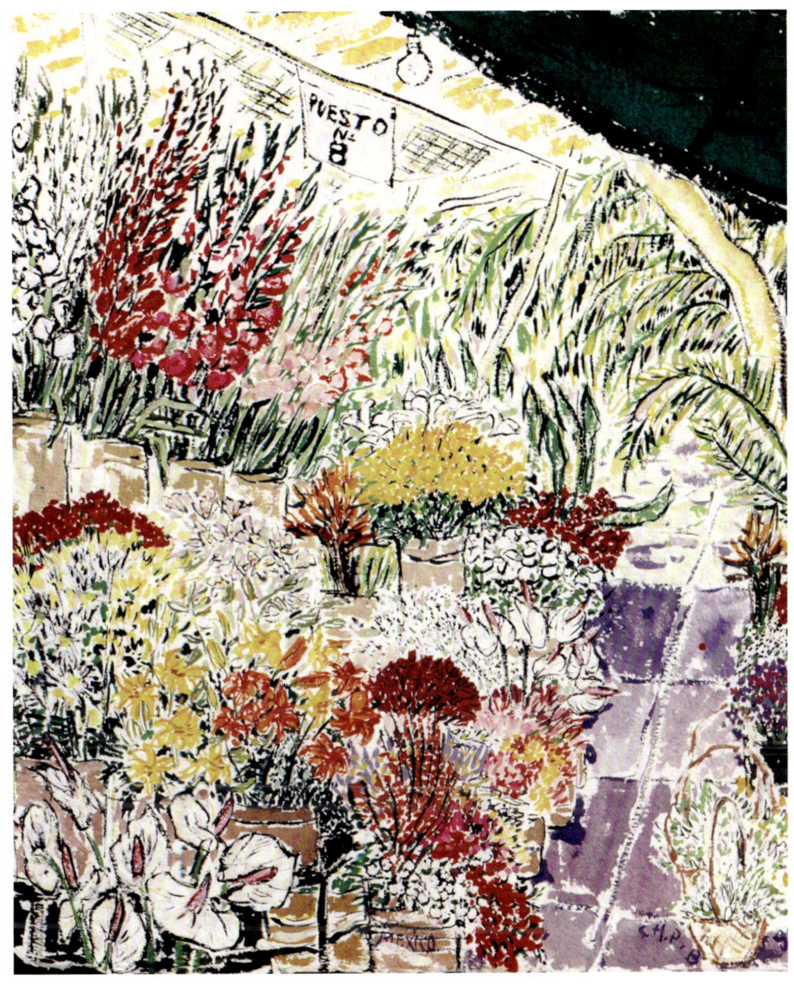

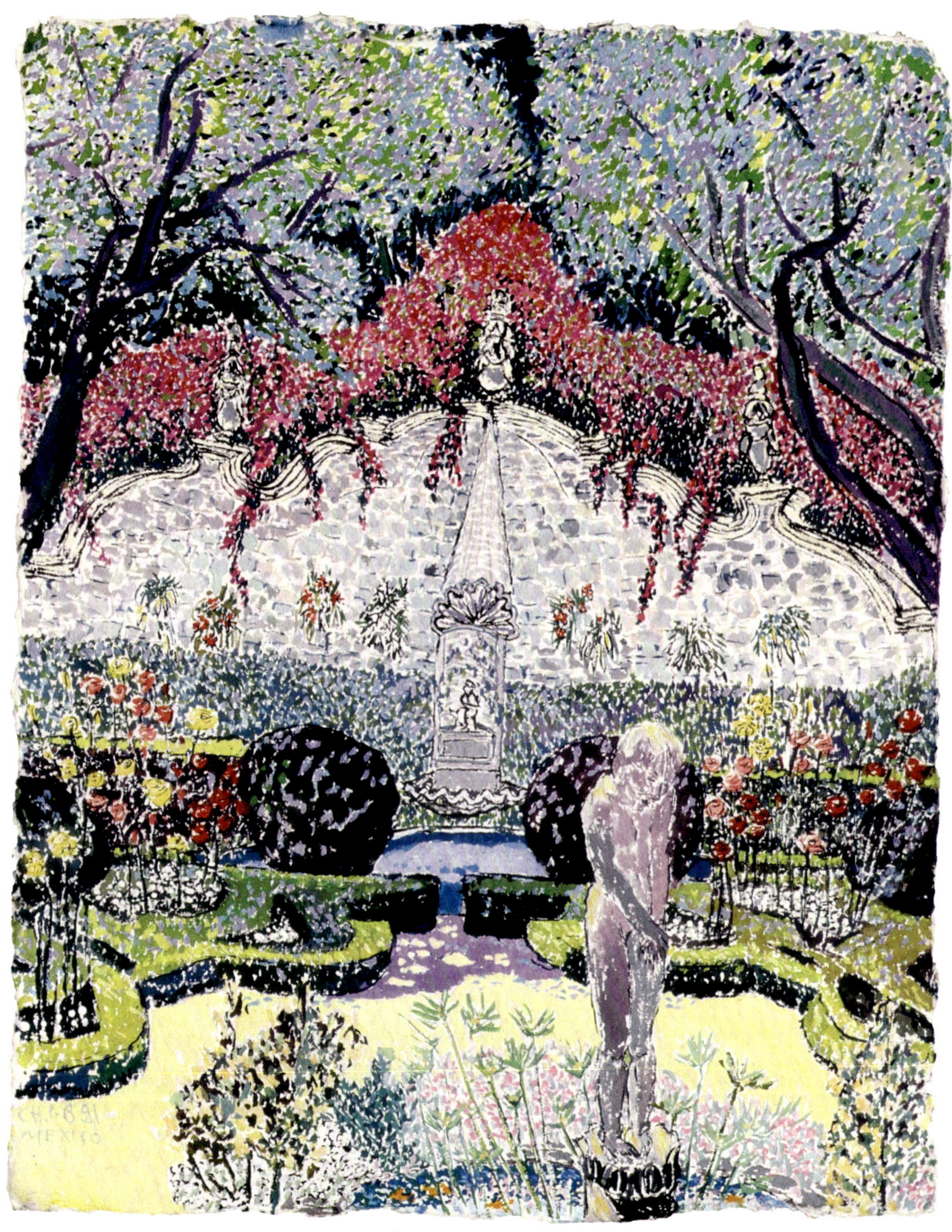

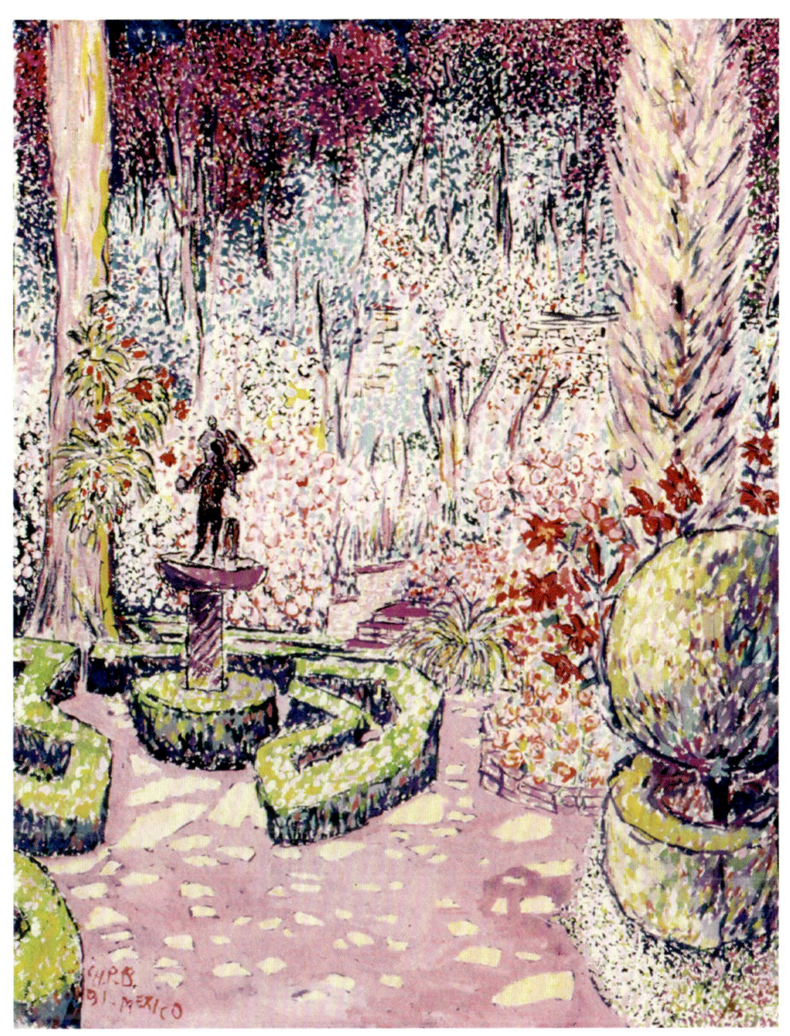
CHPB.
81 · MEXICO

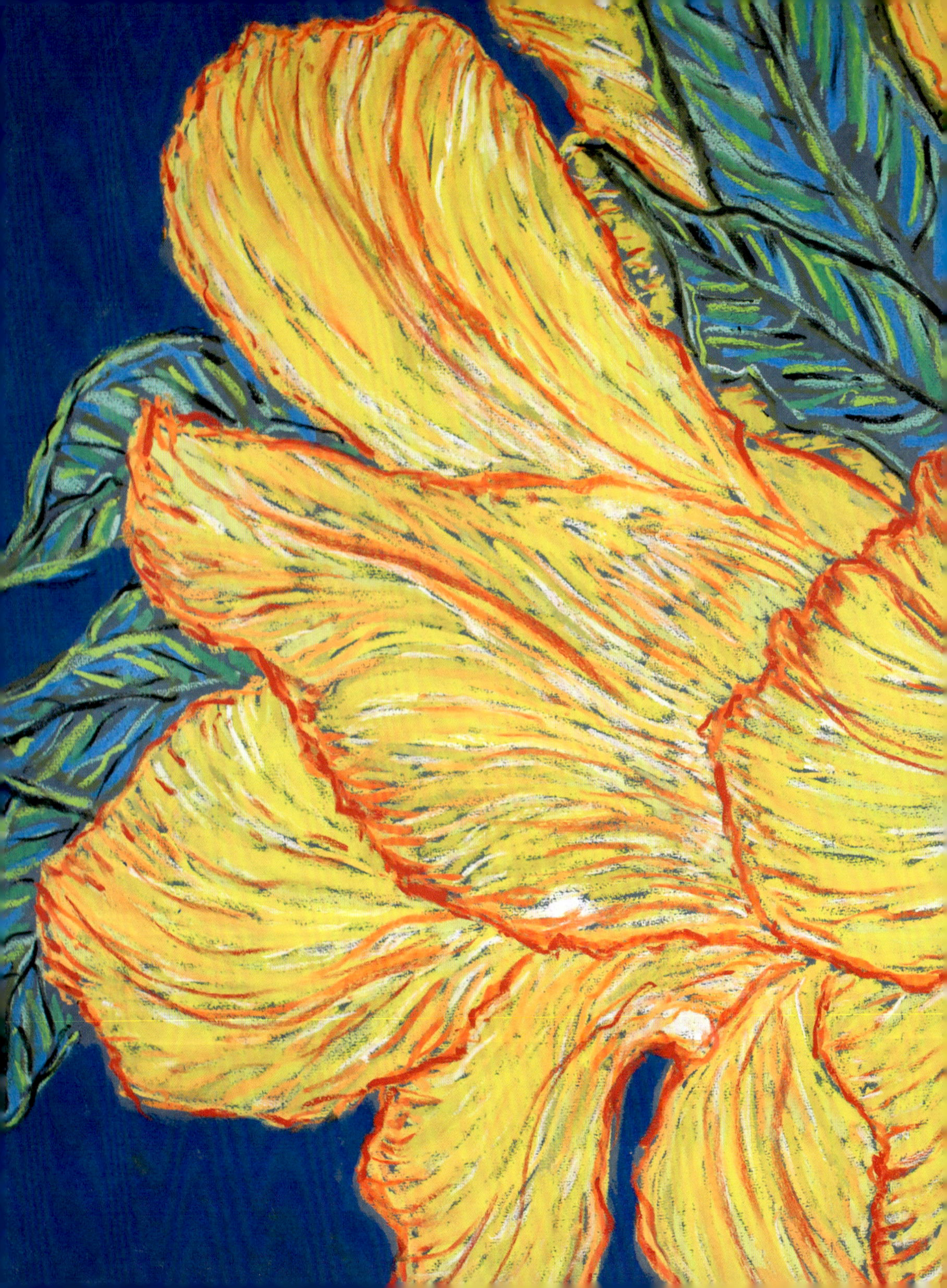

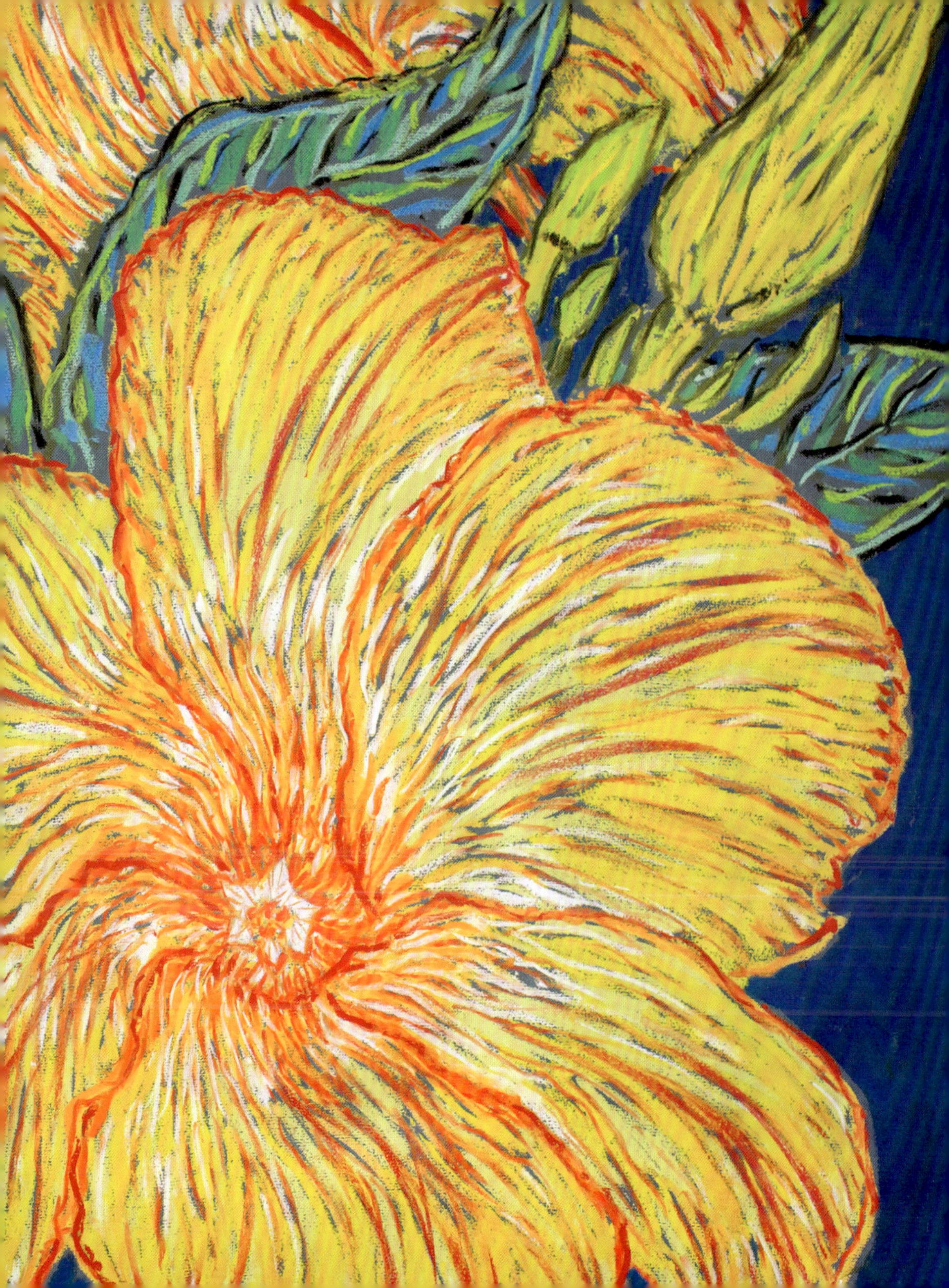

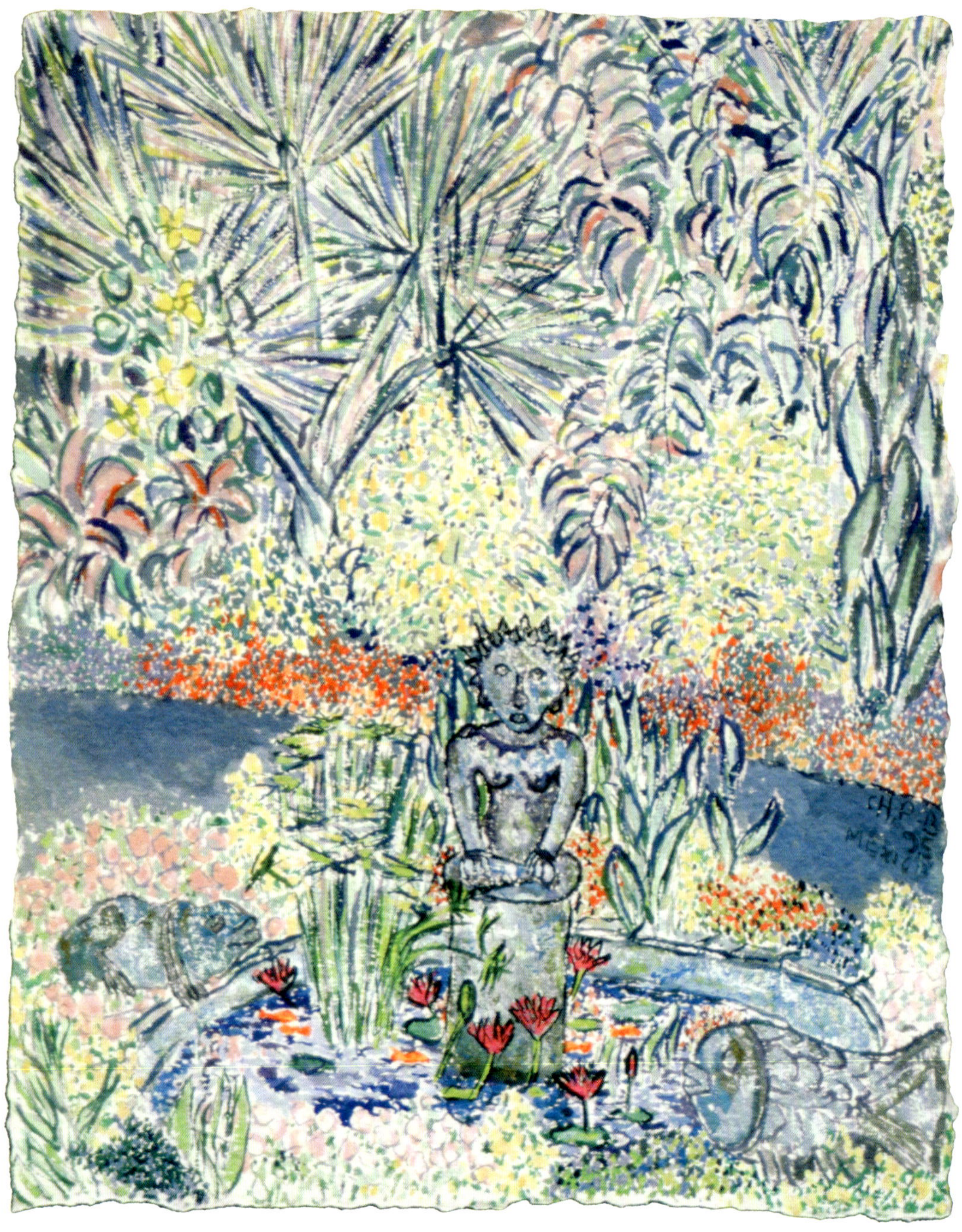

Sonia's Garden

Cuernavaca, Mexico

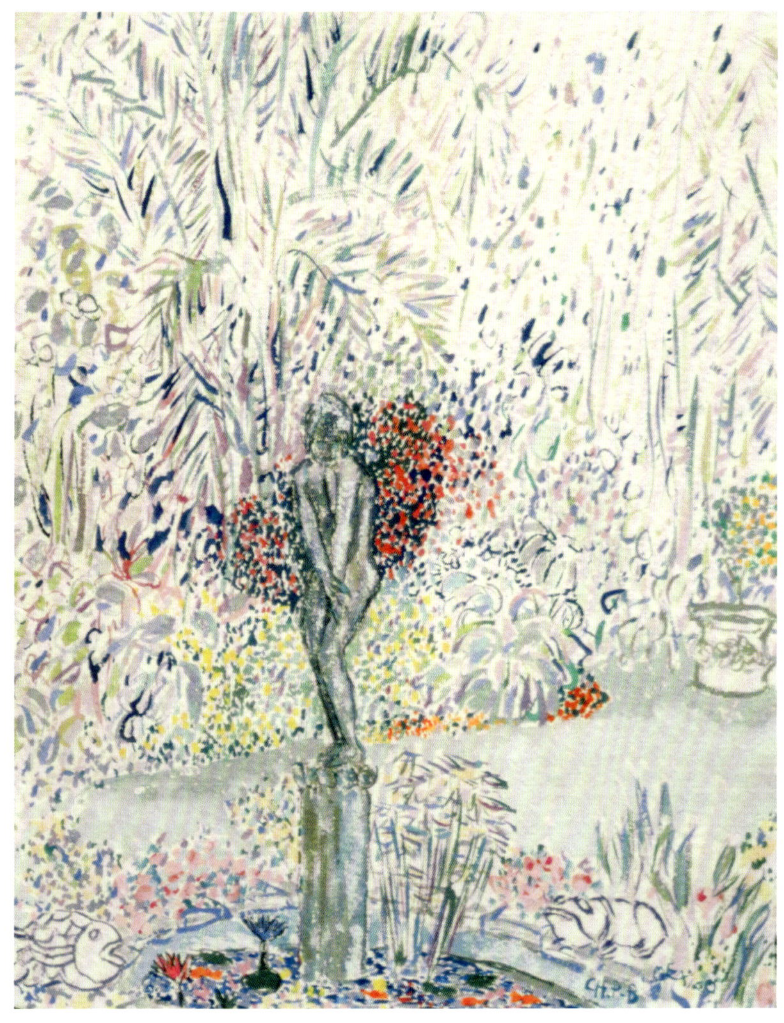

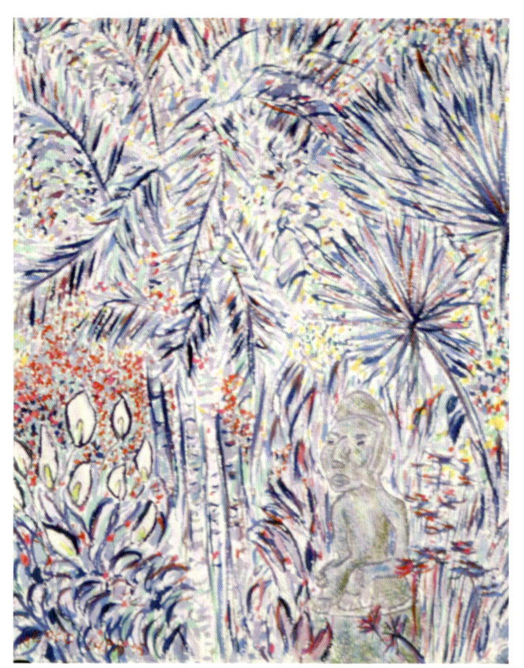

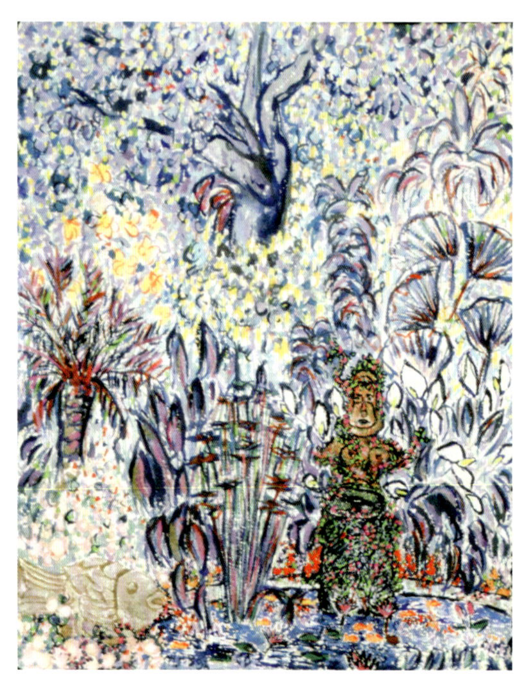

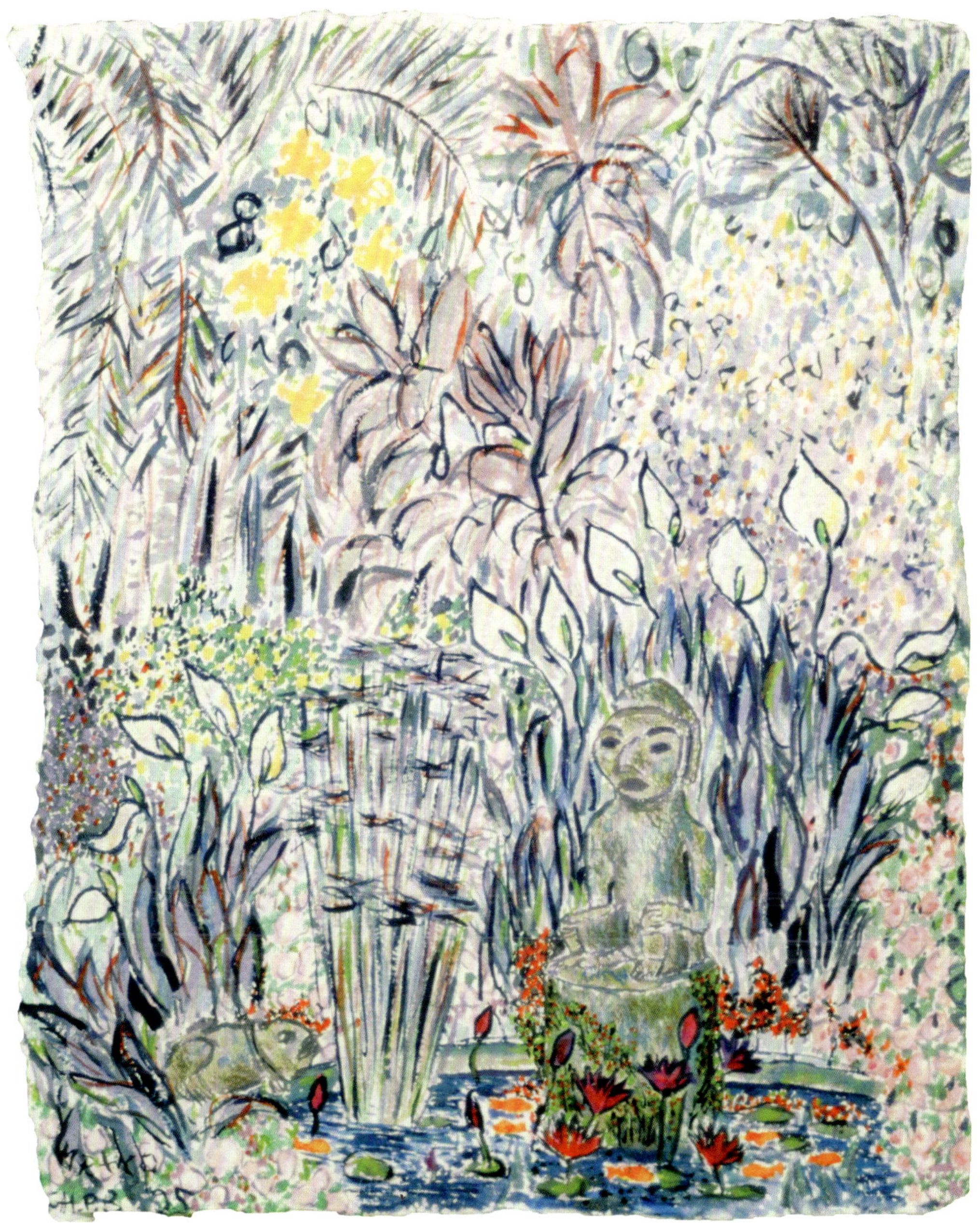

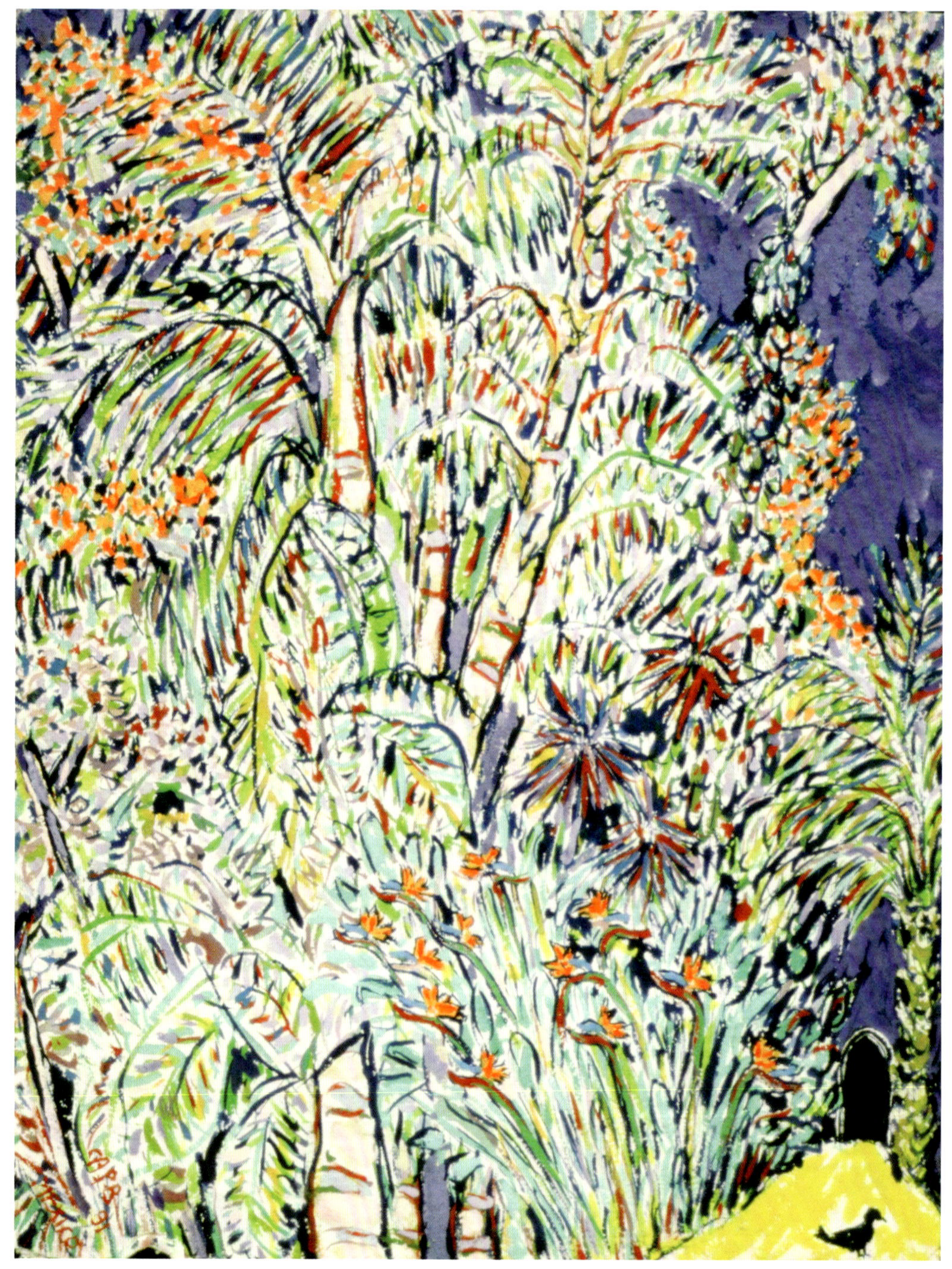

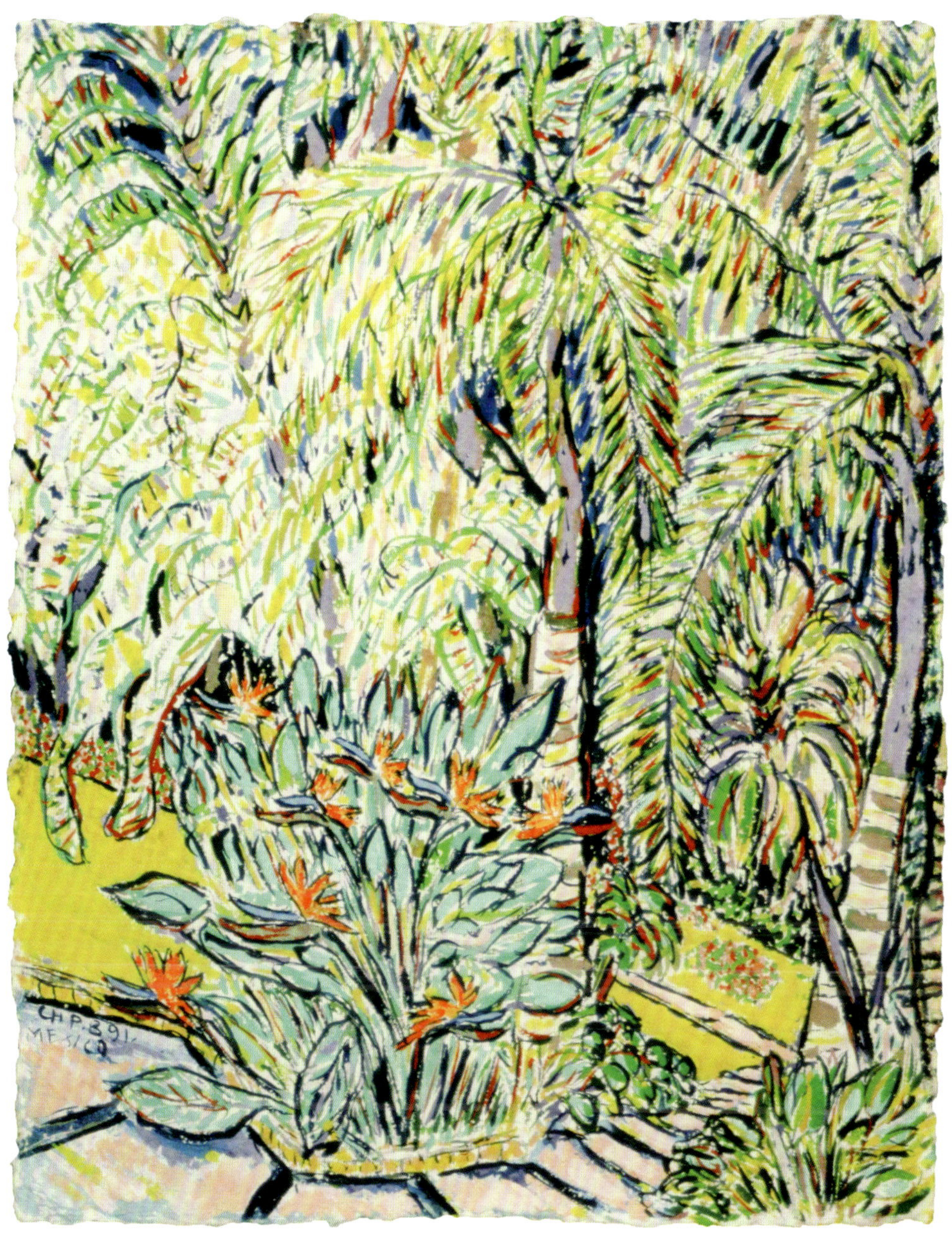
CH.P.891
MEXICO

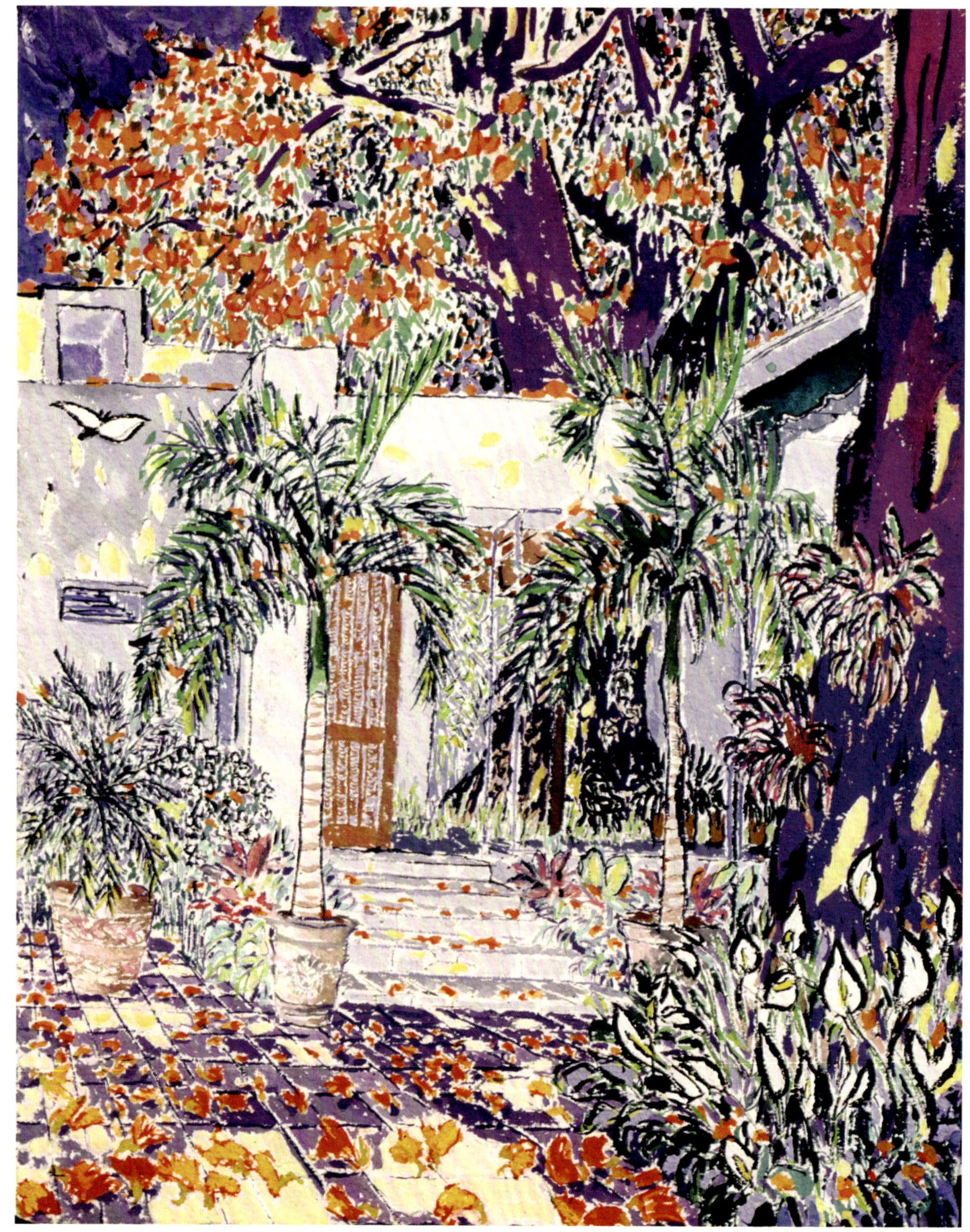

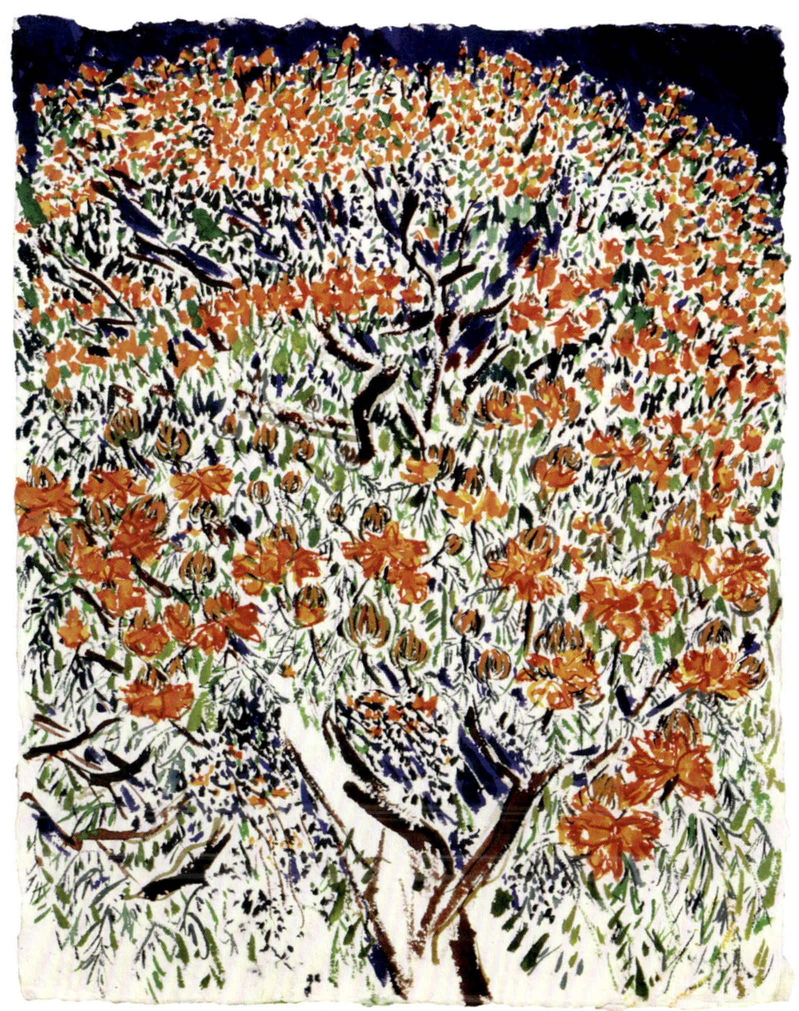

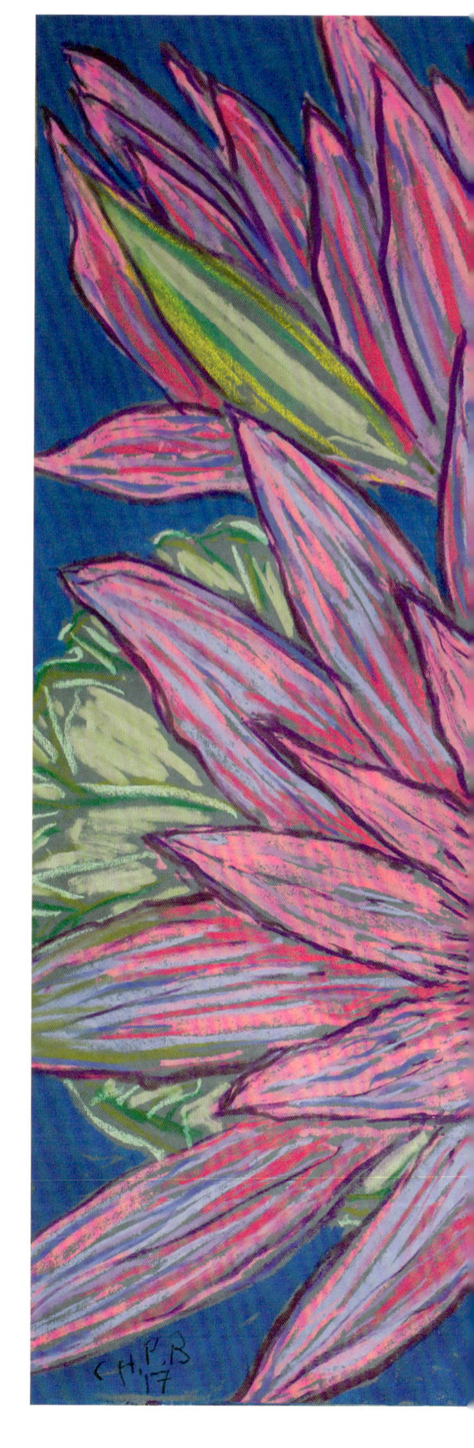

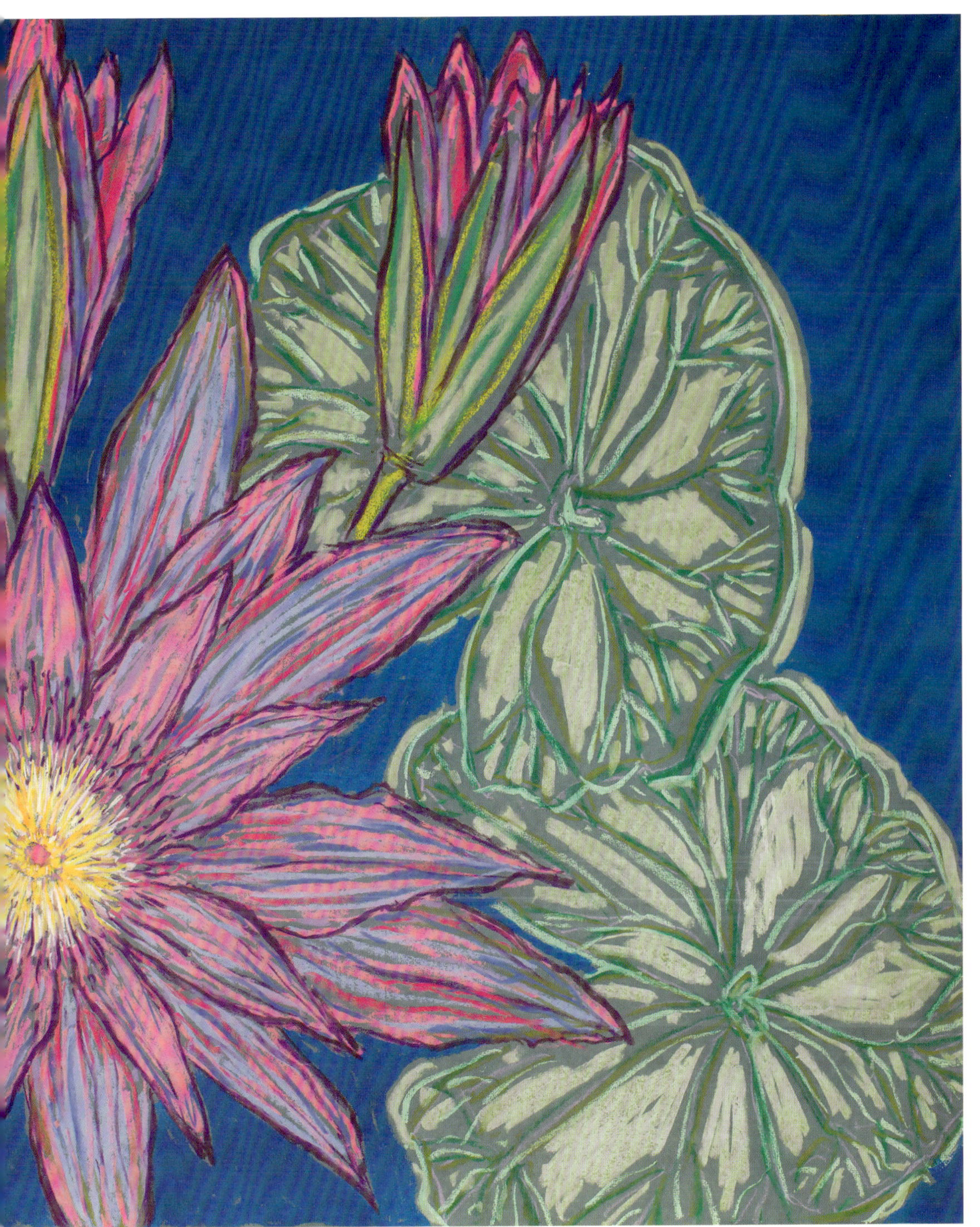

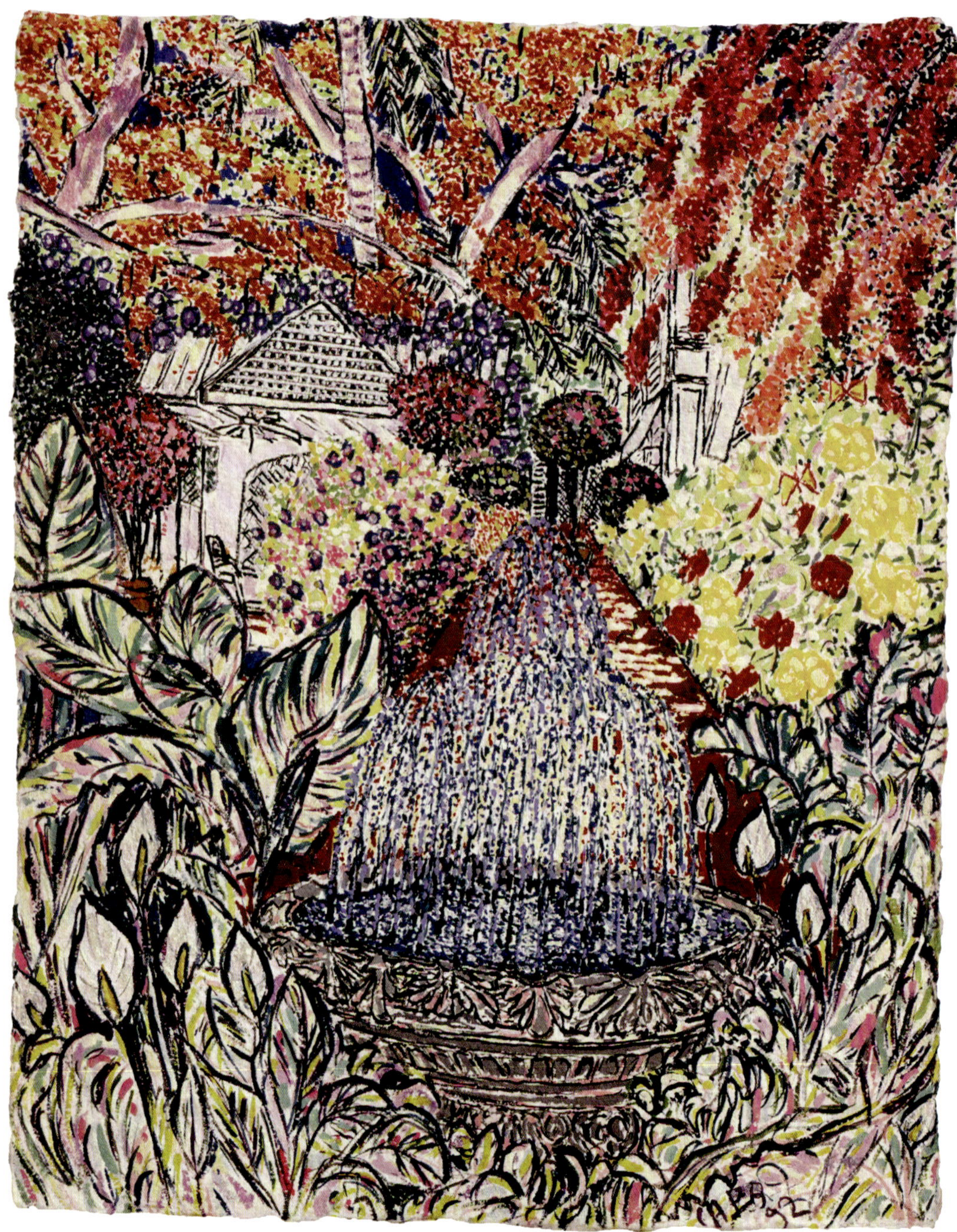

Ferdinand's Garden

Key West, Florida

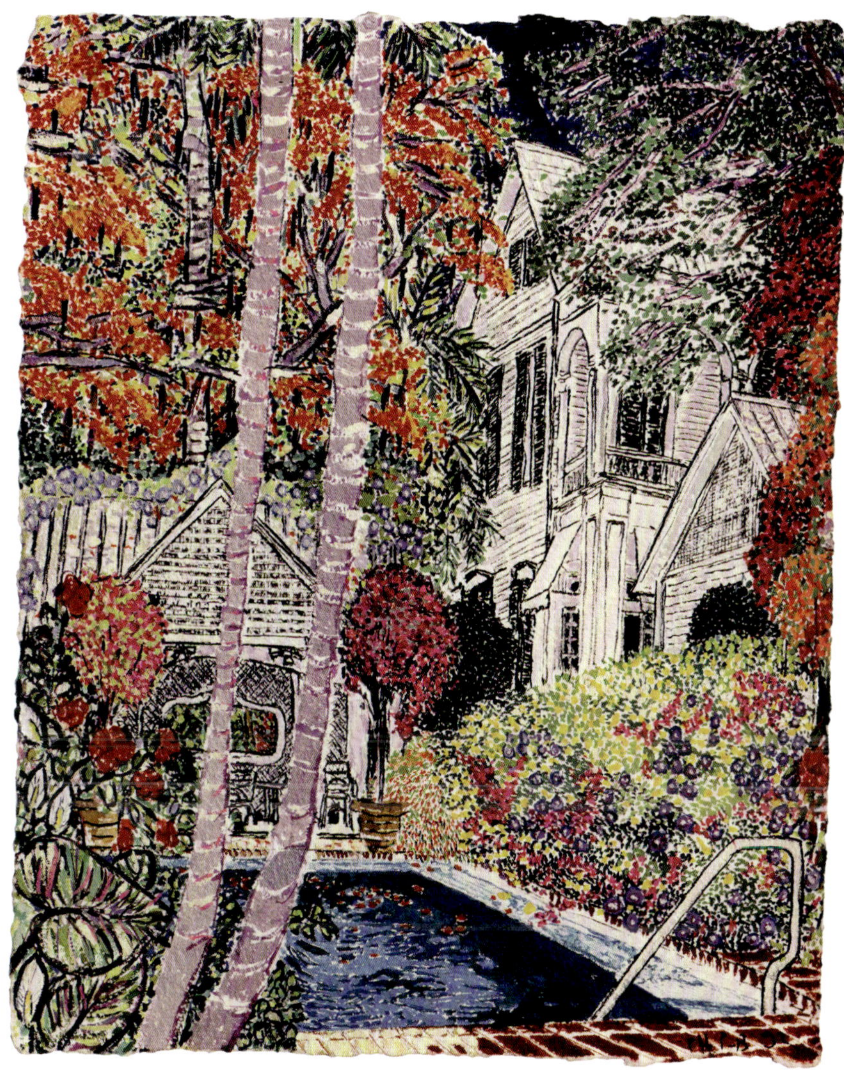

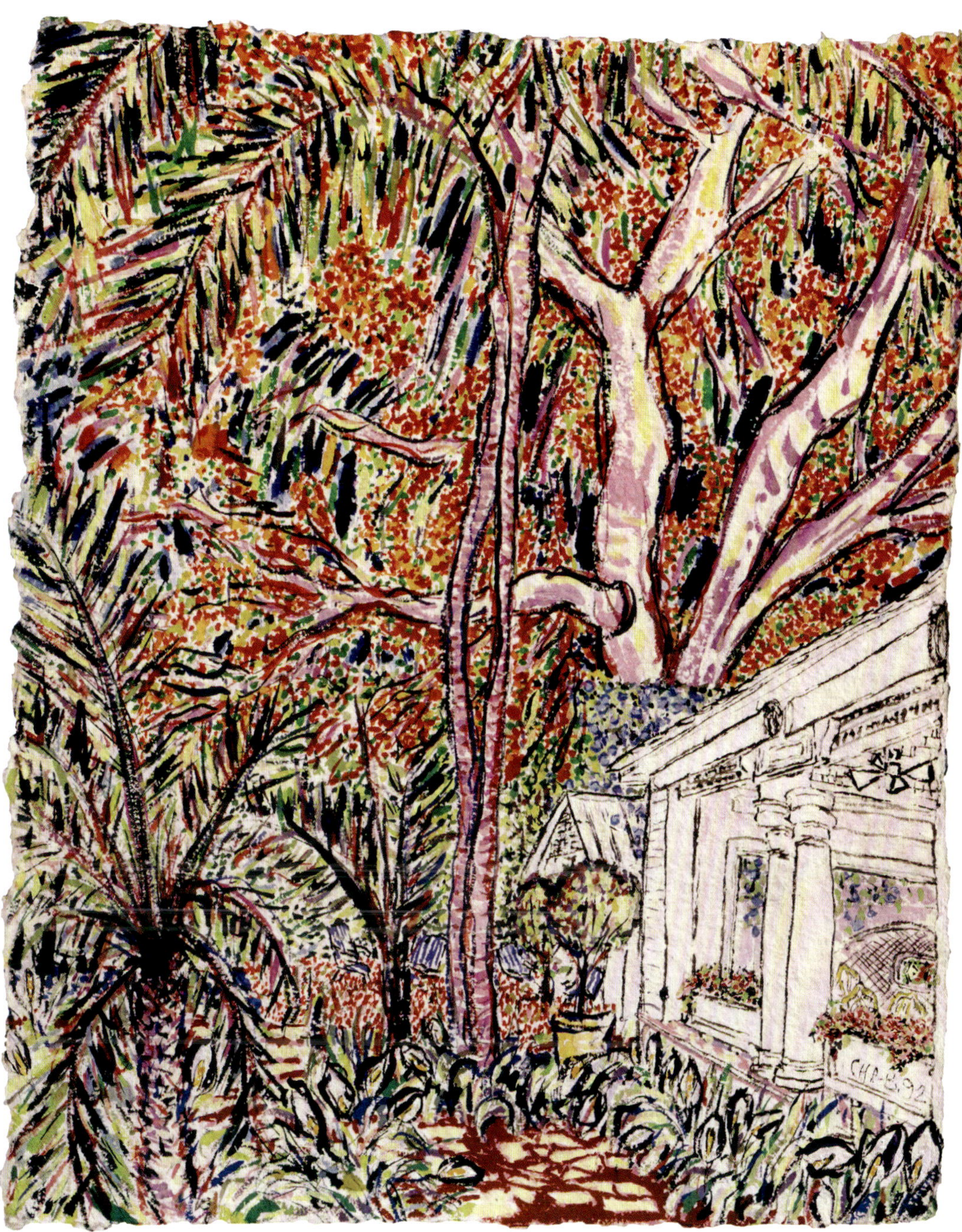

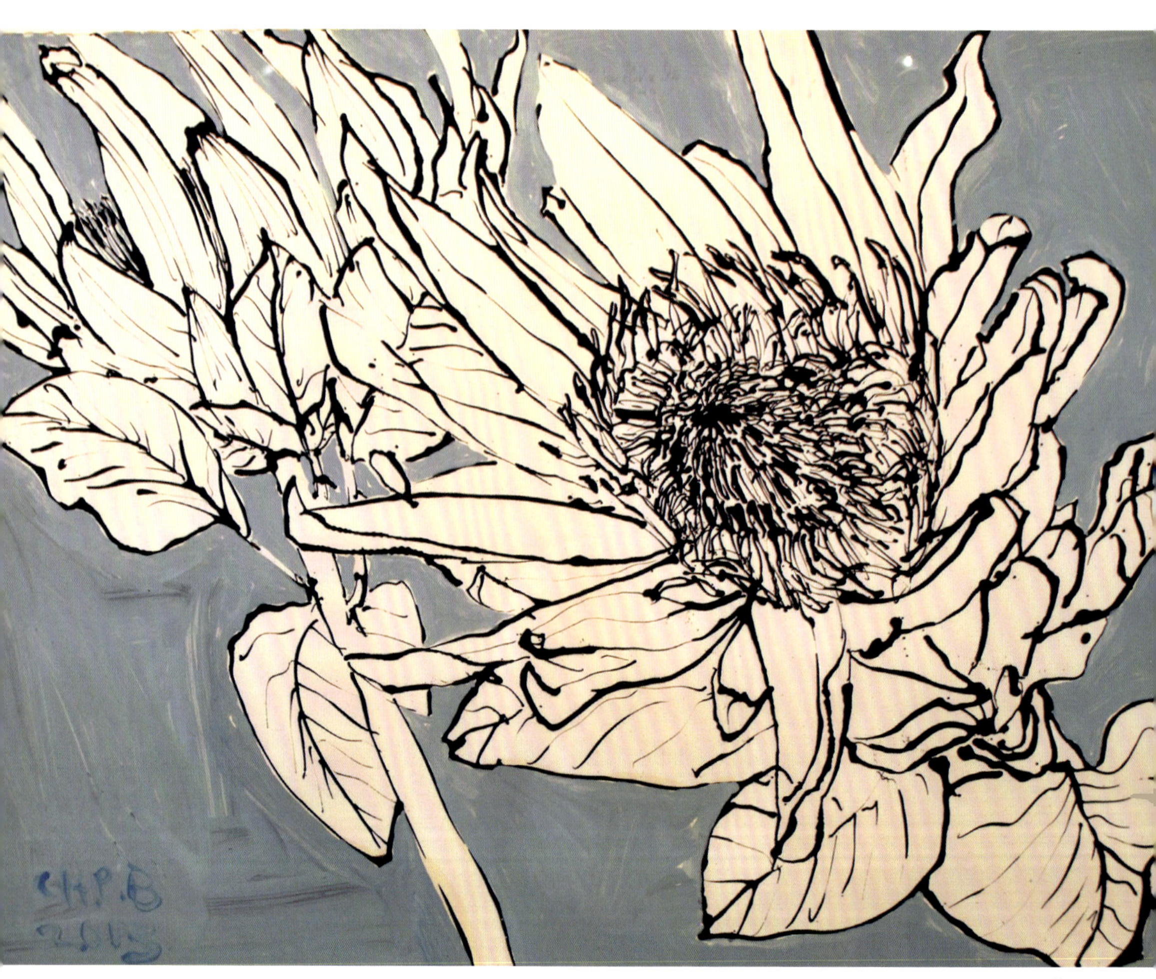

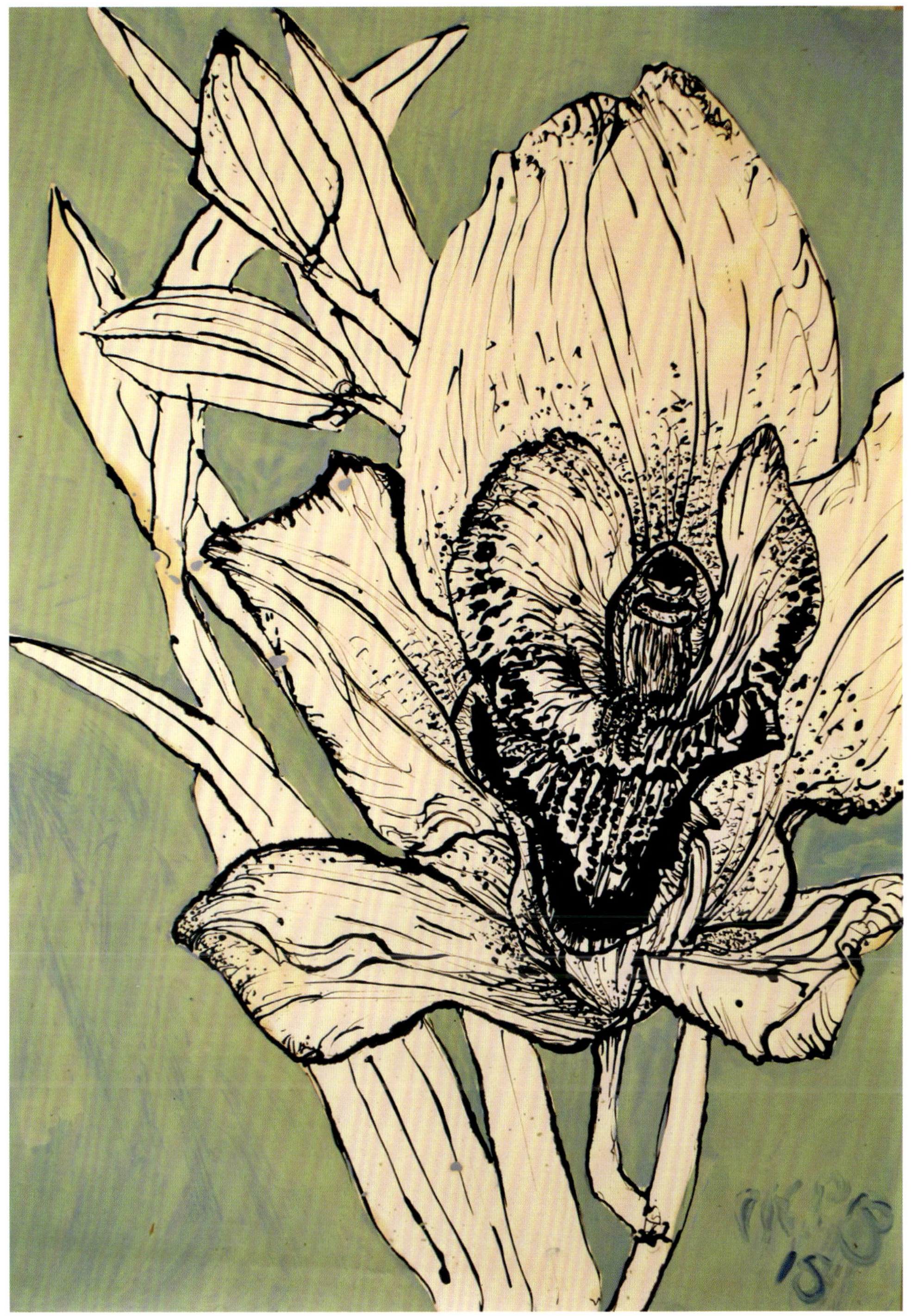

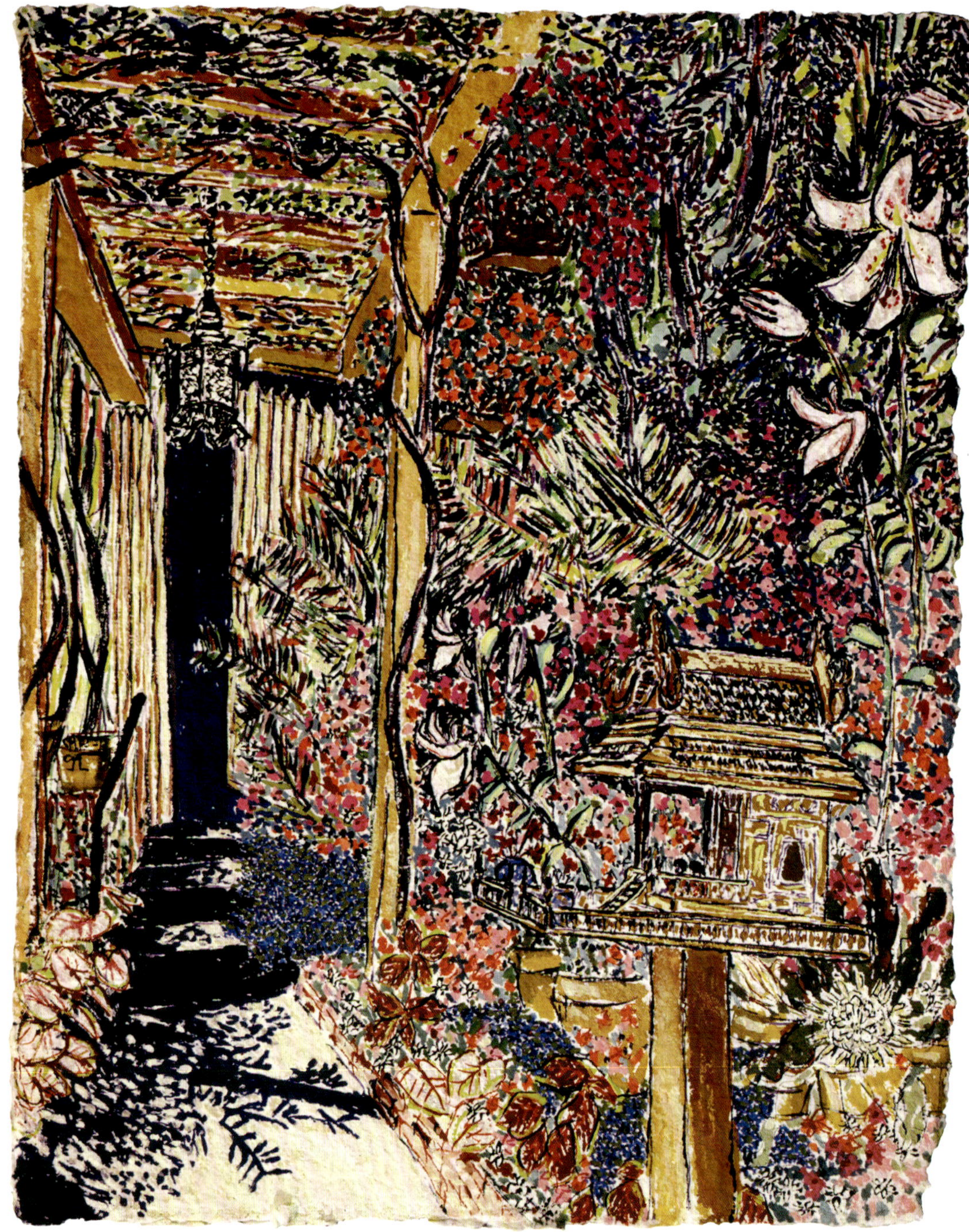

Jeff's Garden

Los Angeles, California

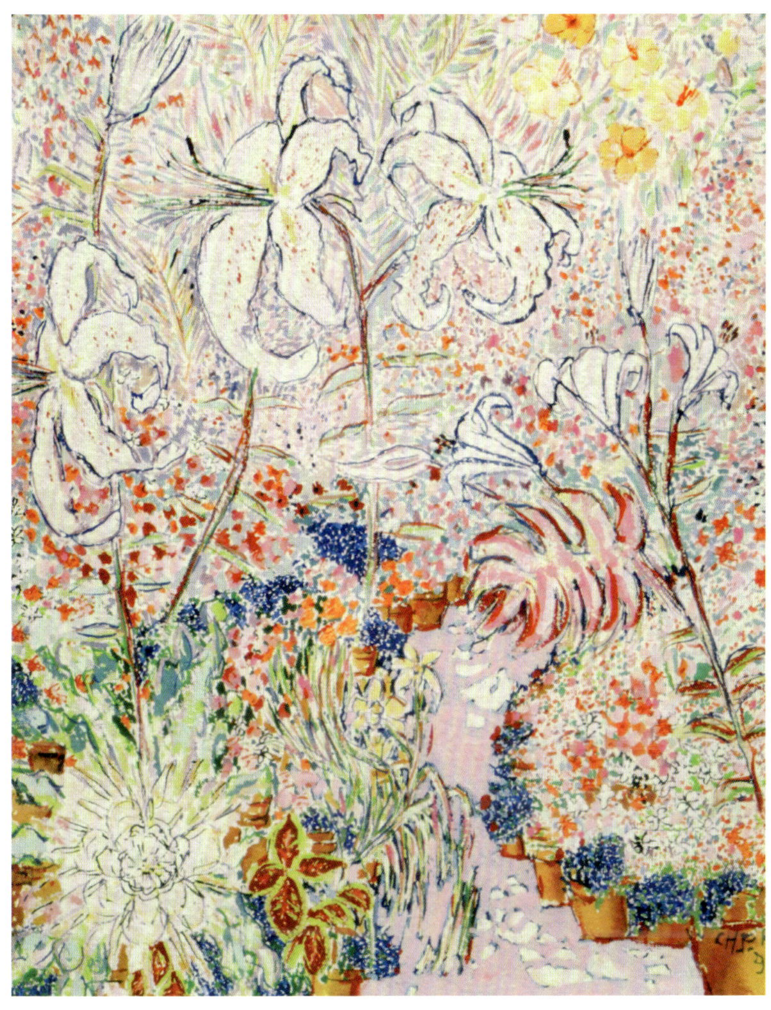

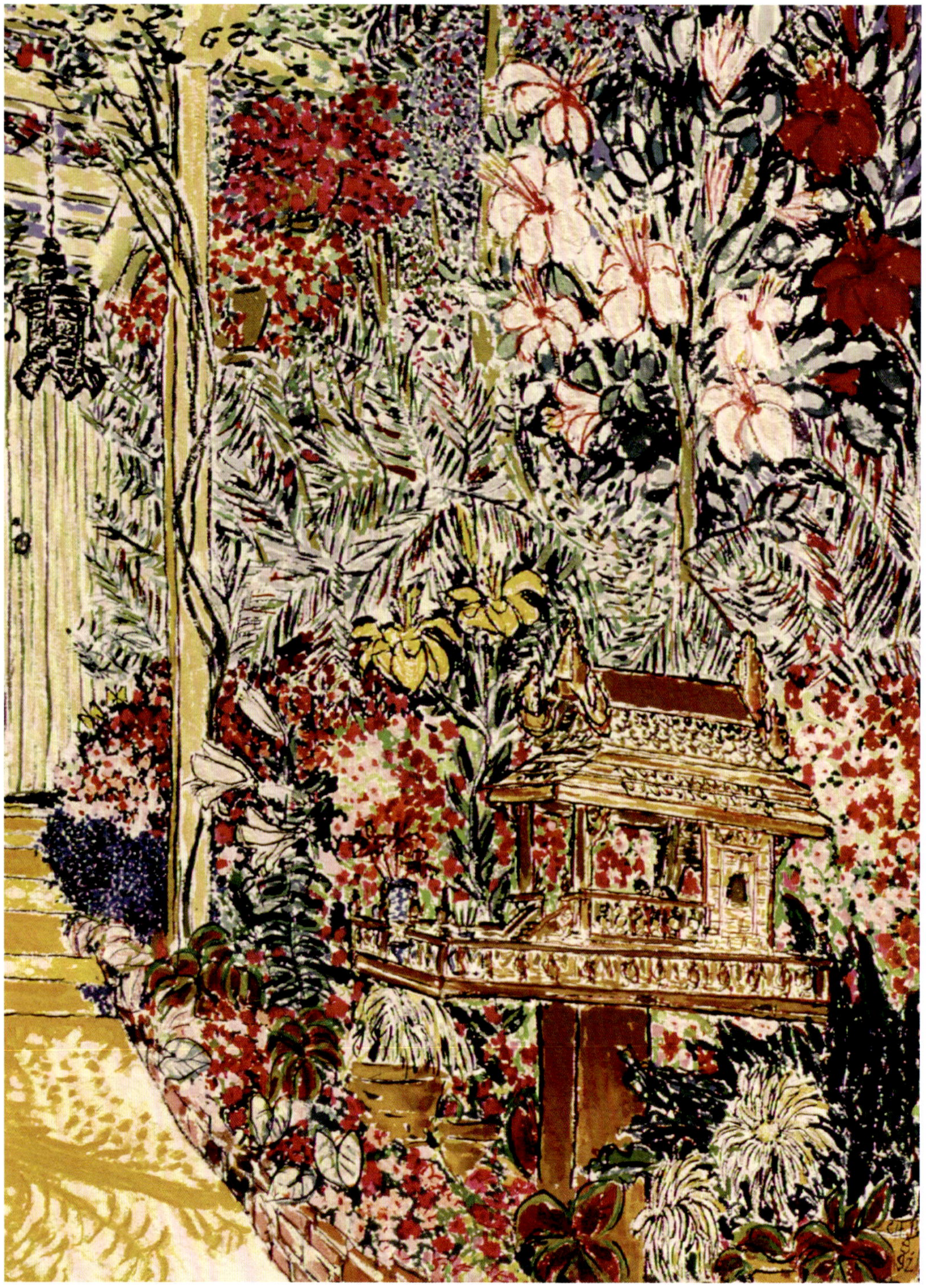

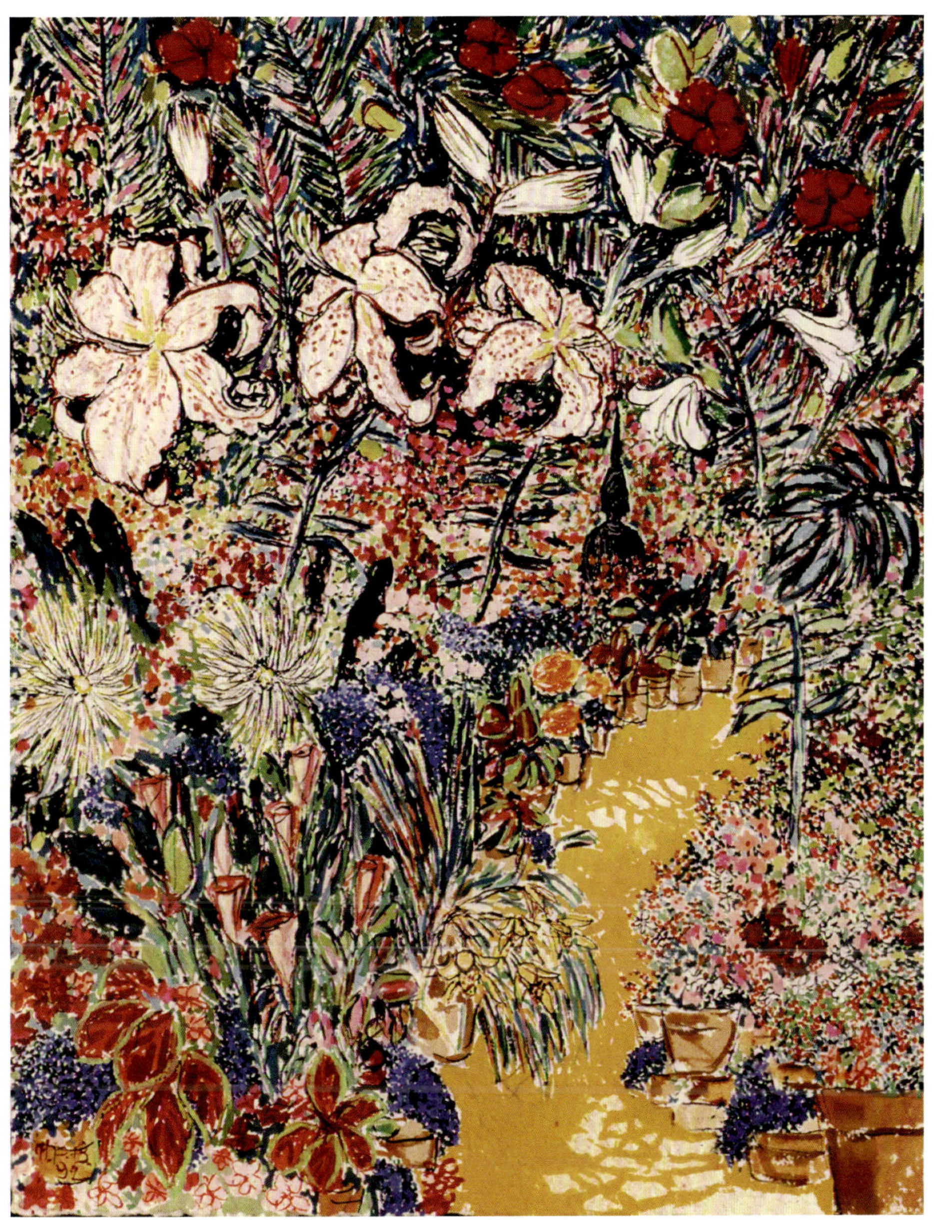

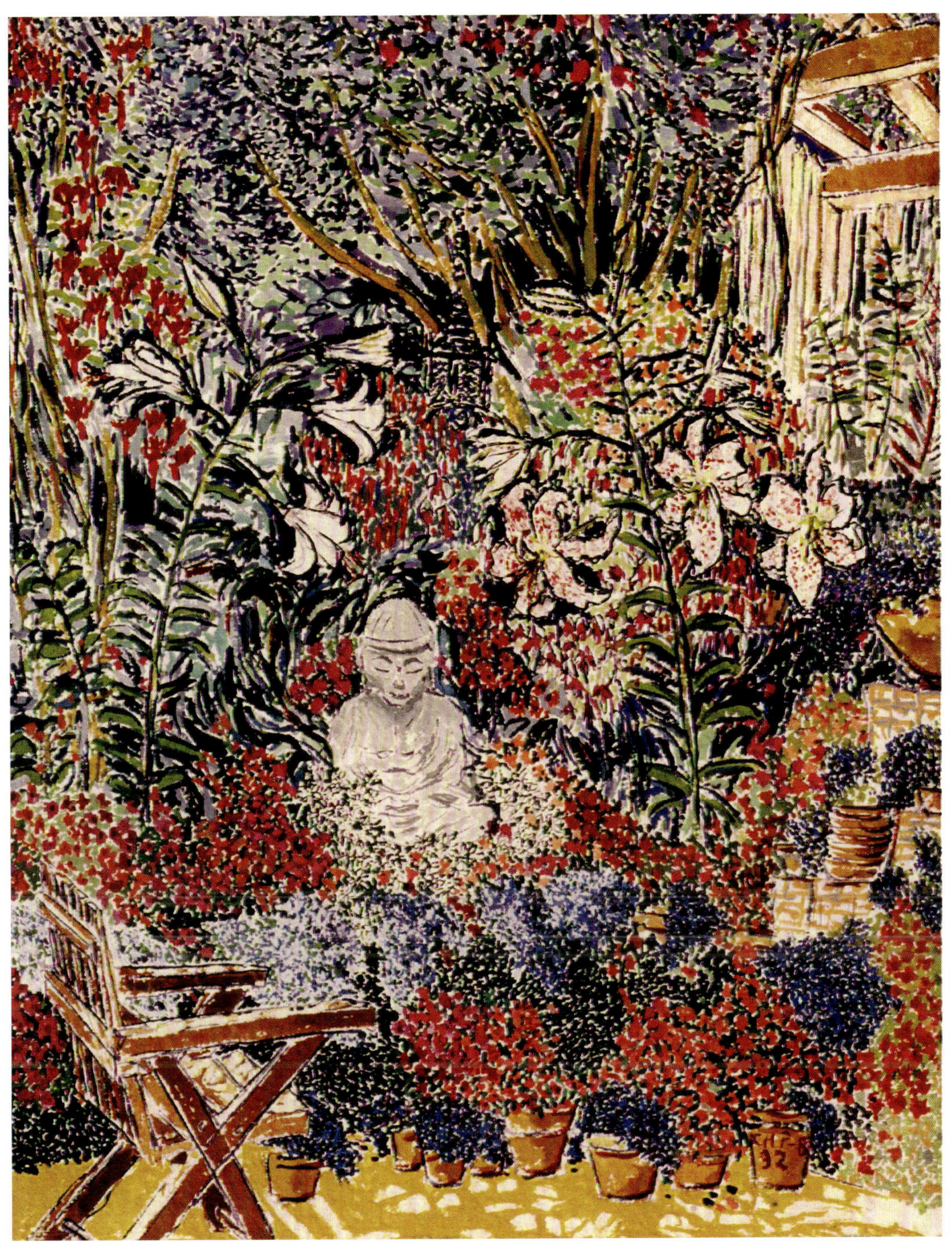

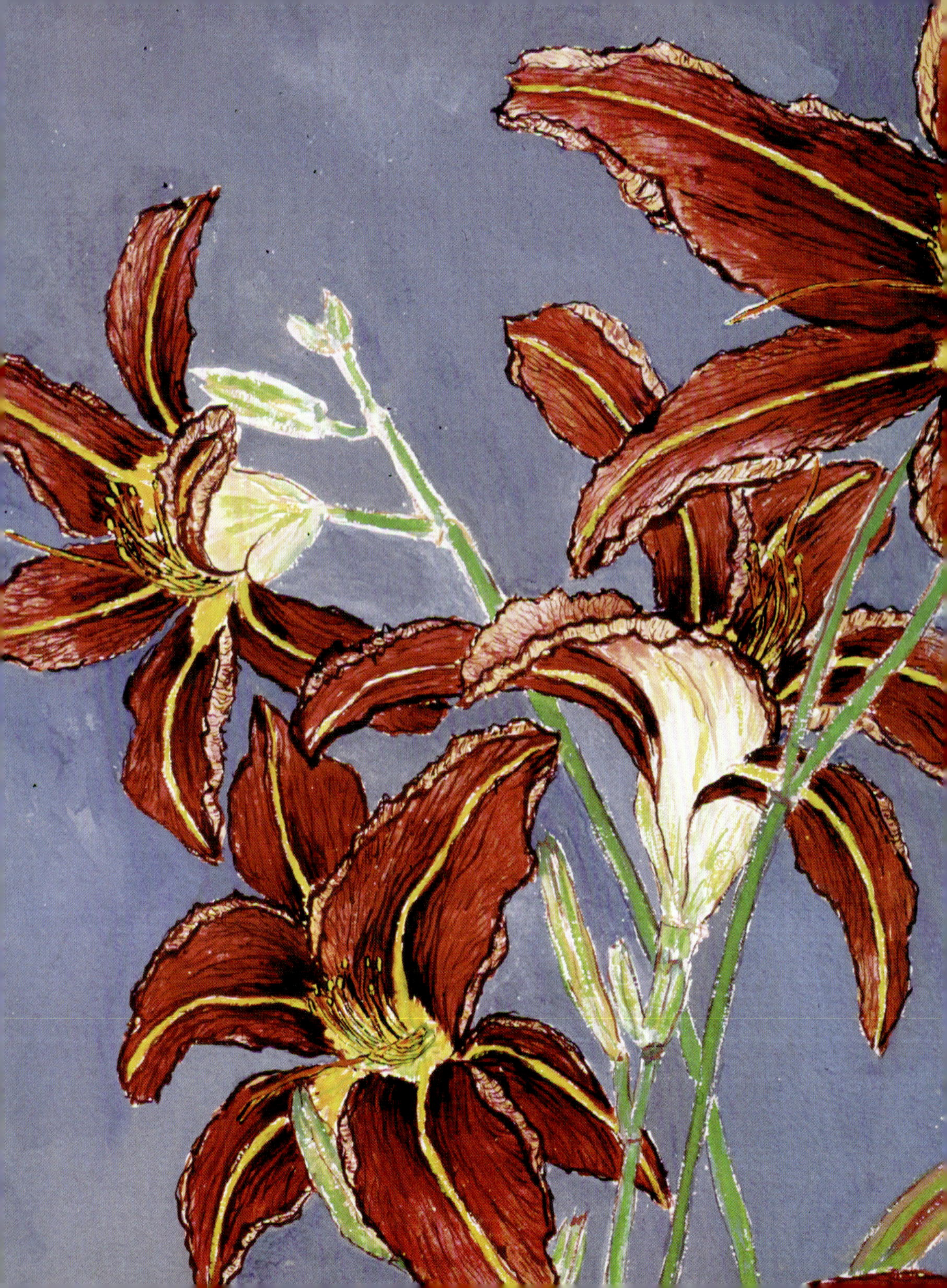

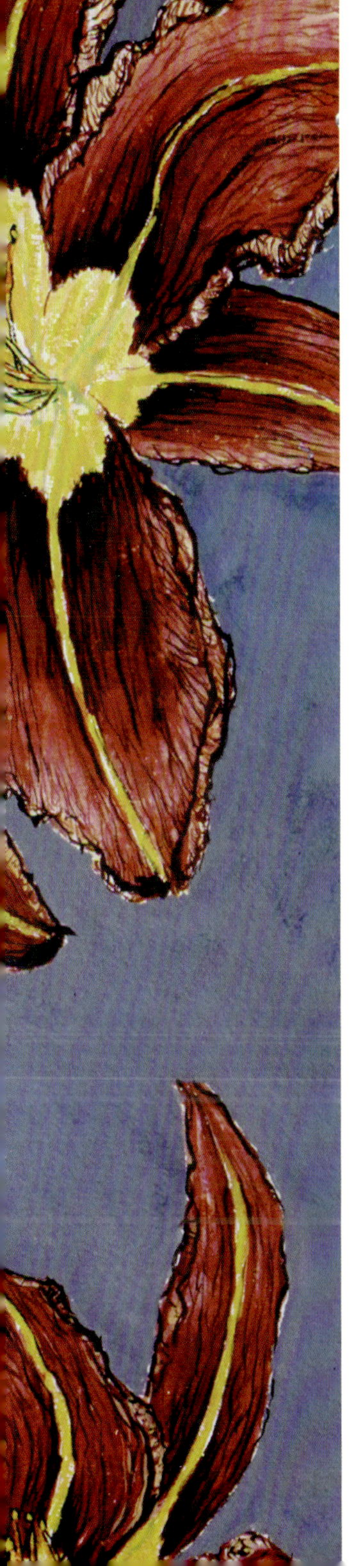

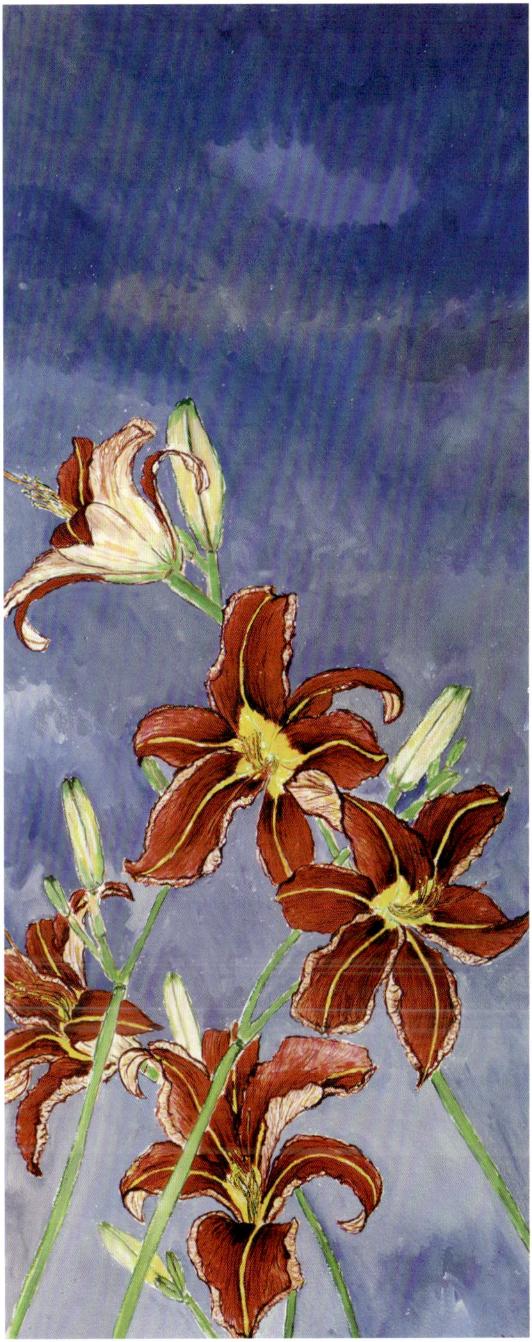

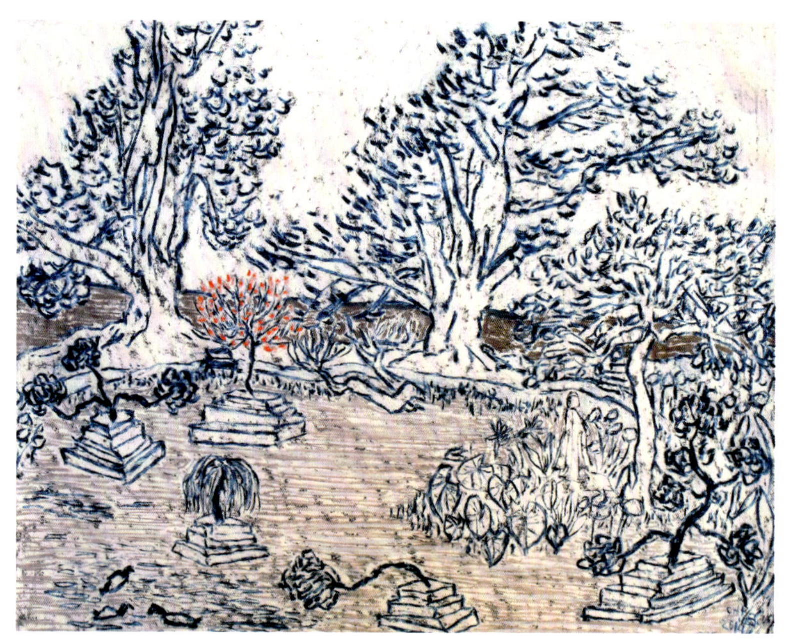

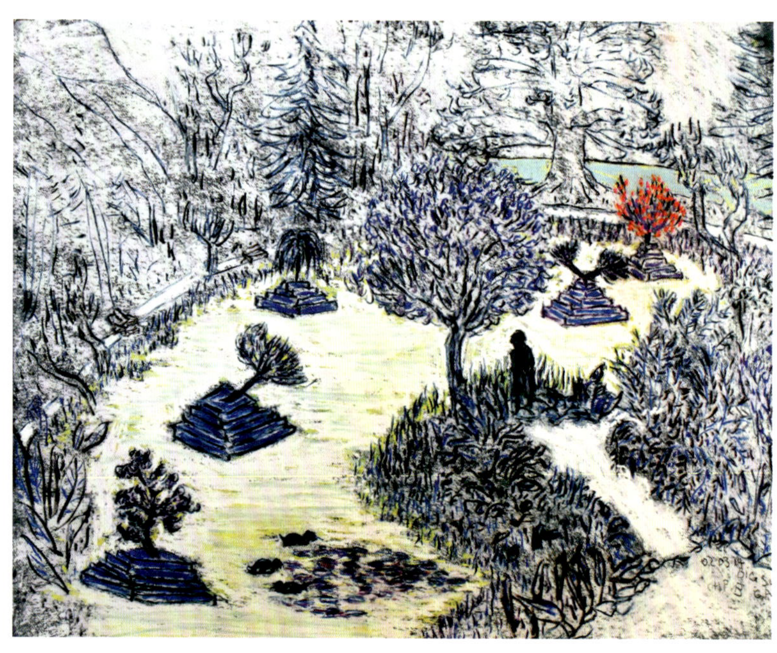

Bobo's Garden, Santa Lucia Ranch

Big Sur, California

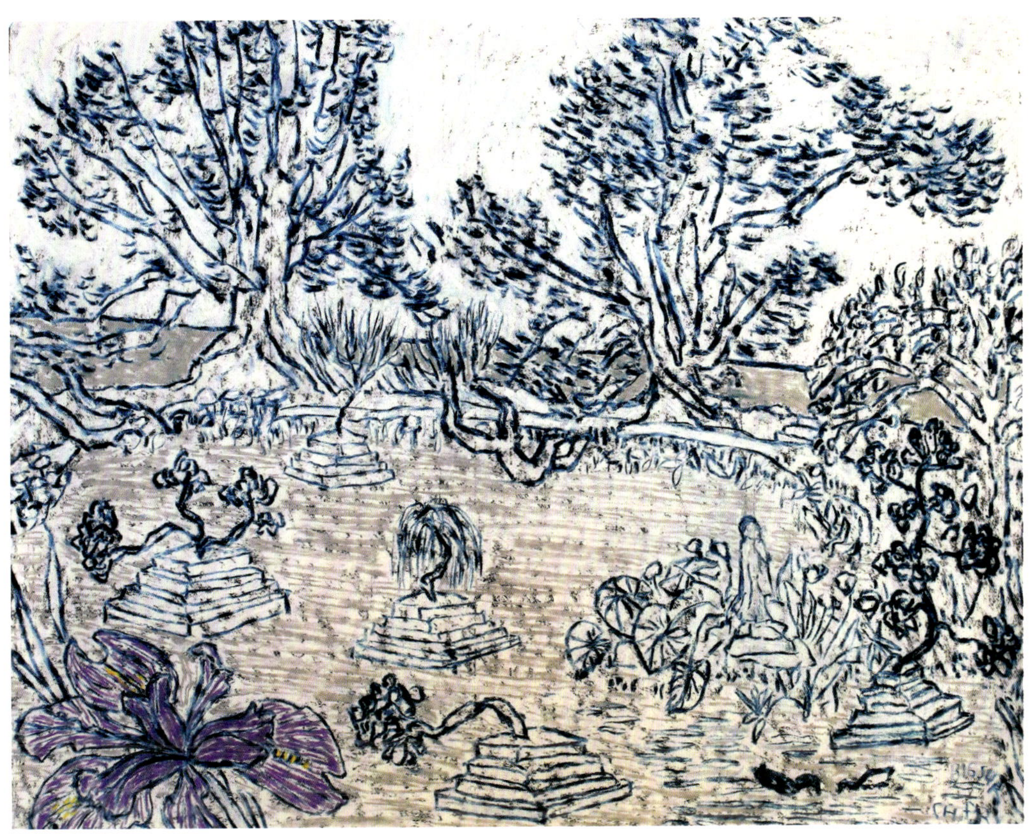

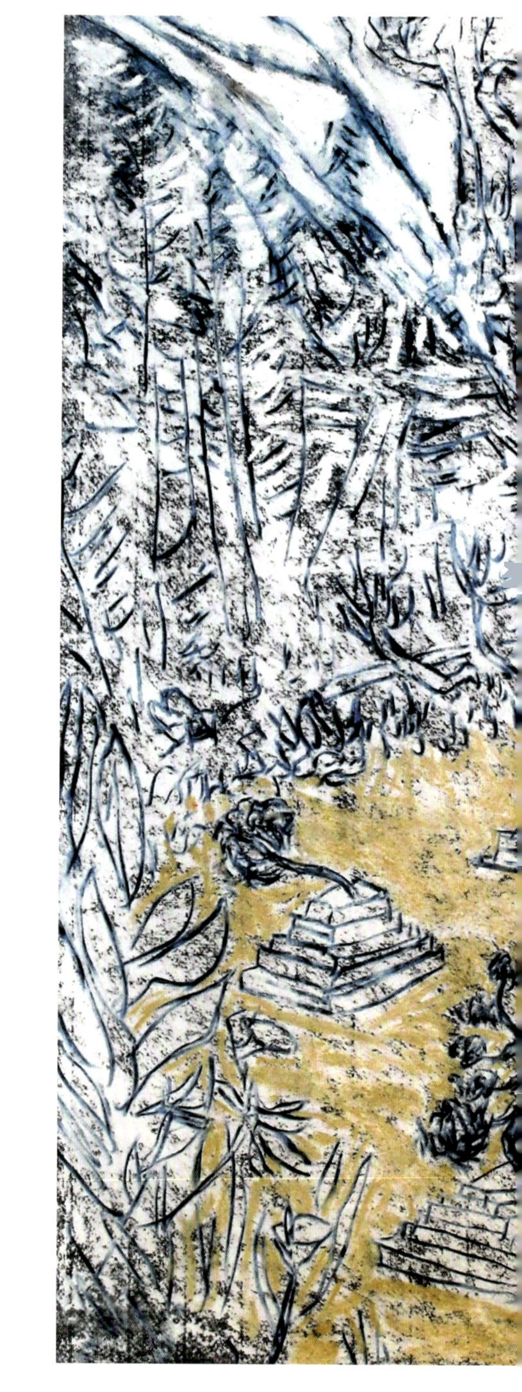

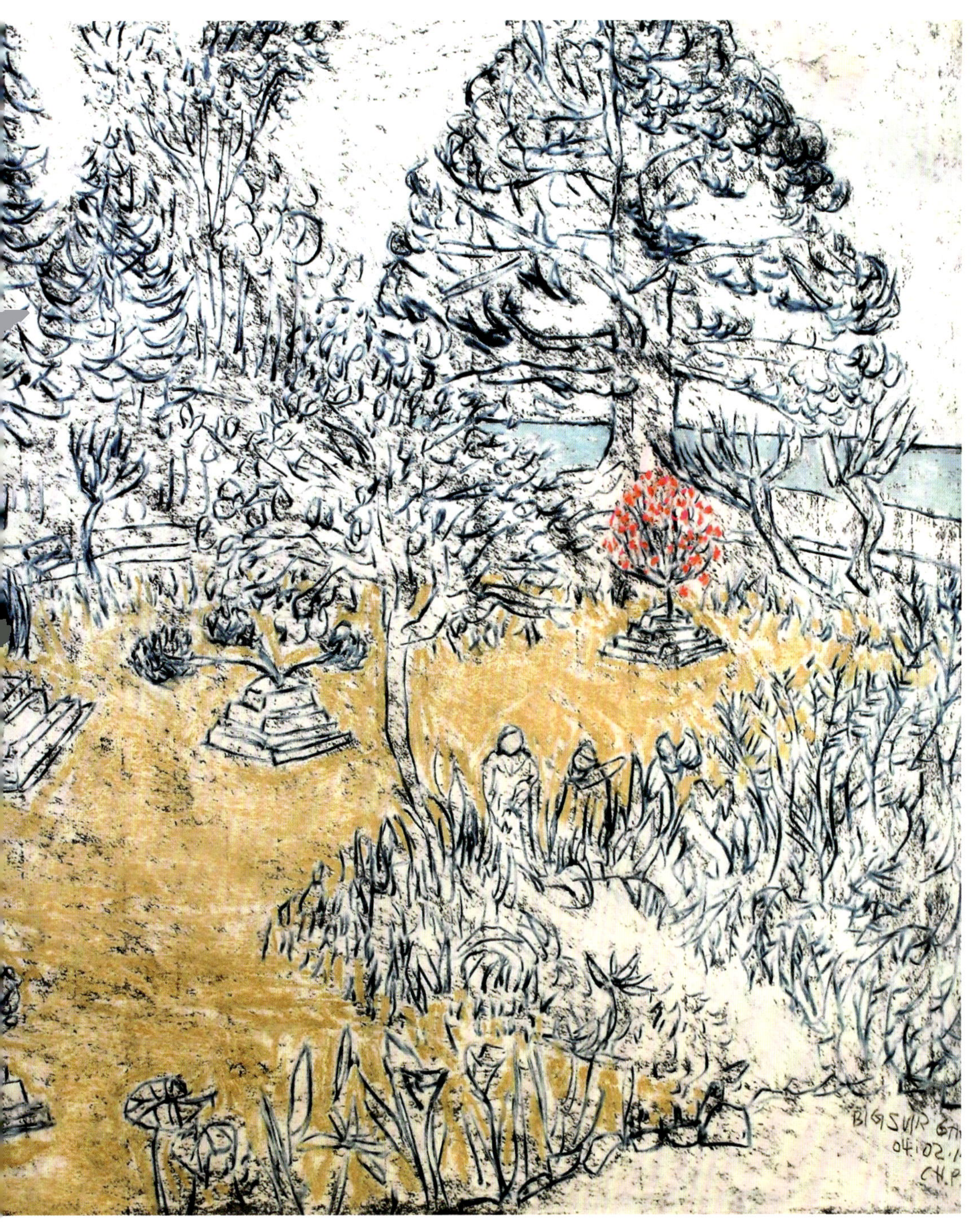

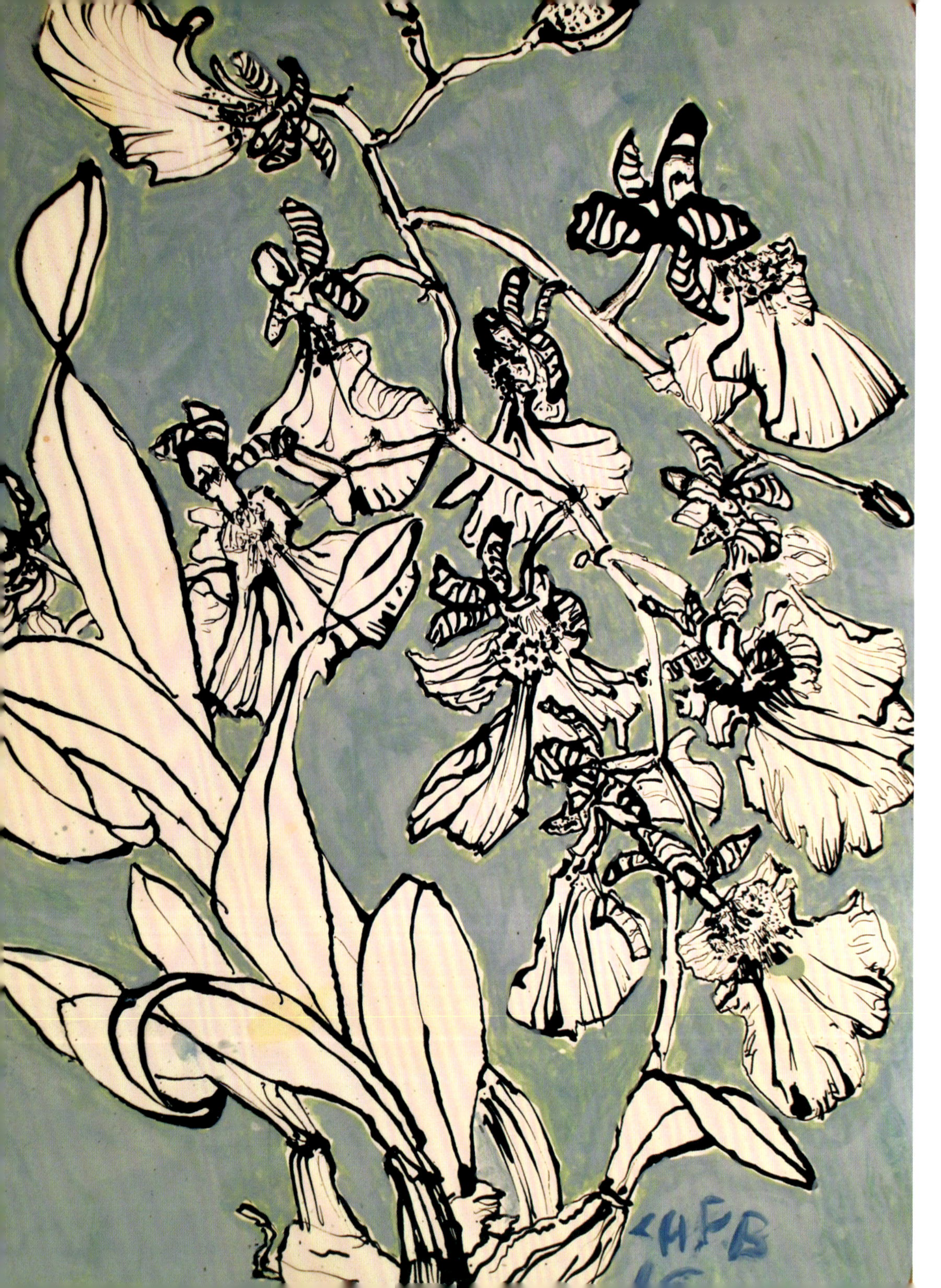

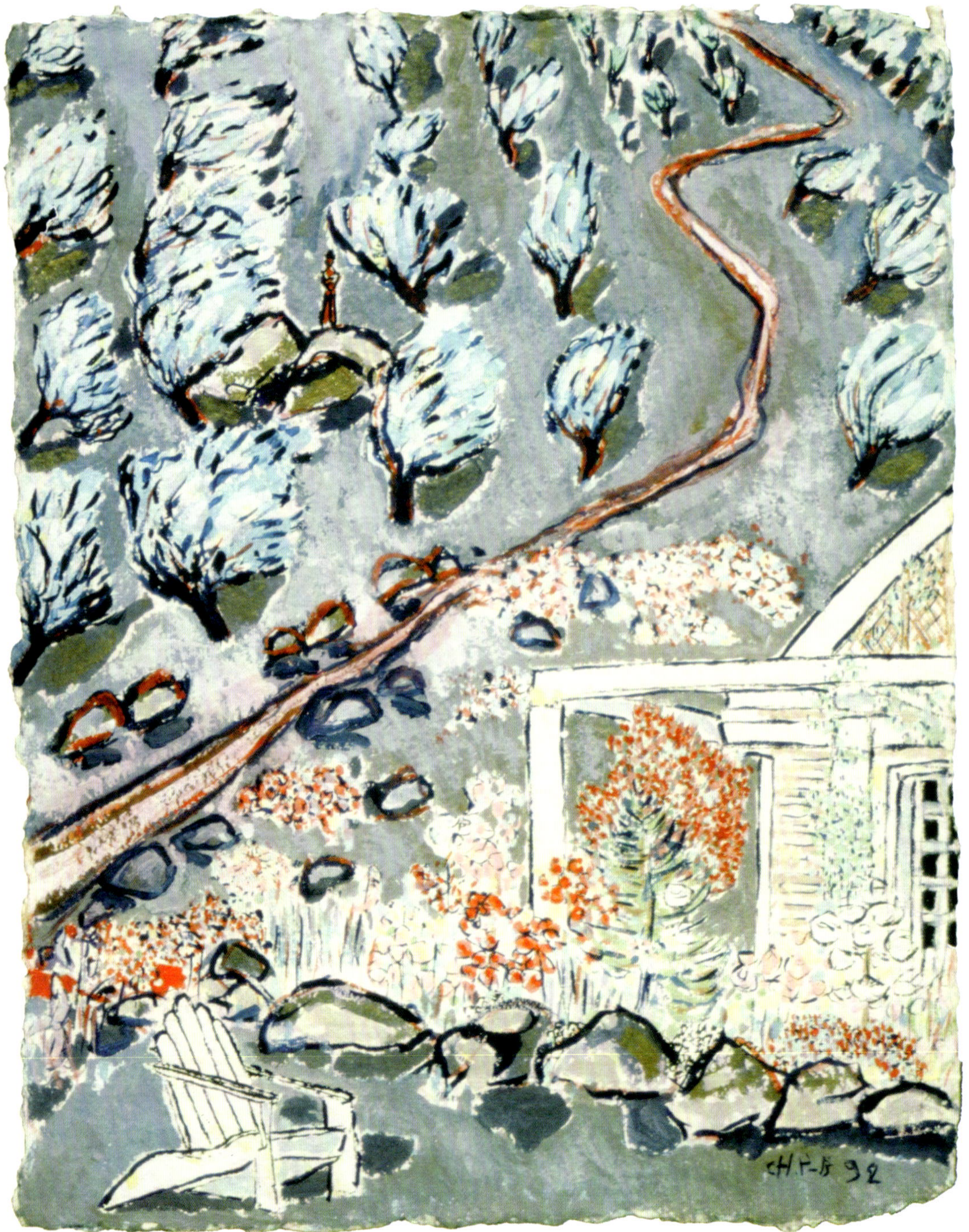

Healdsburg

Sonoma County, California

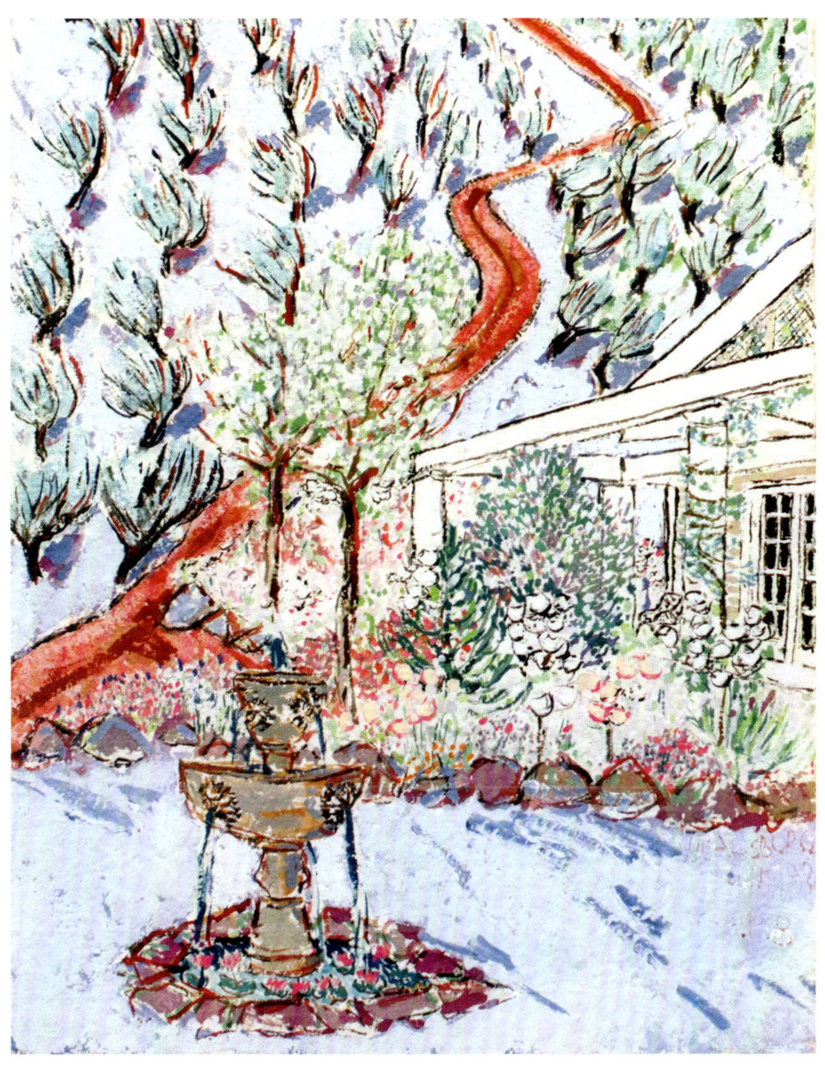

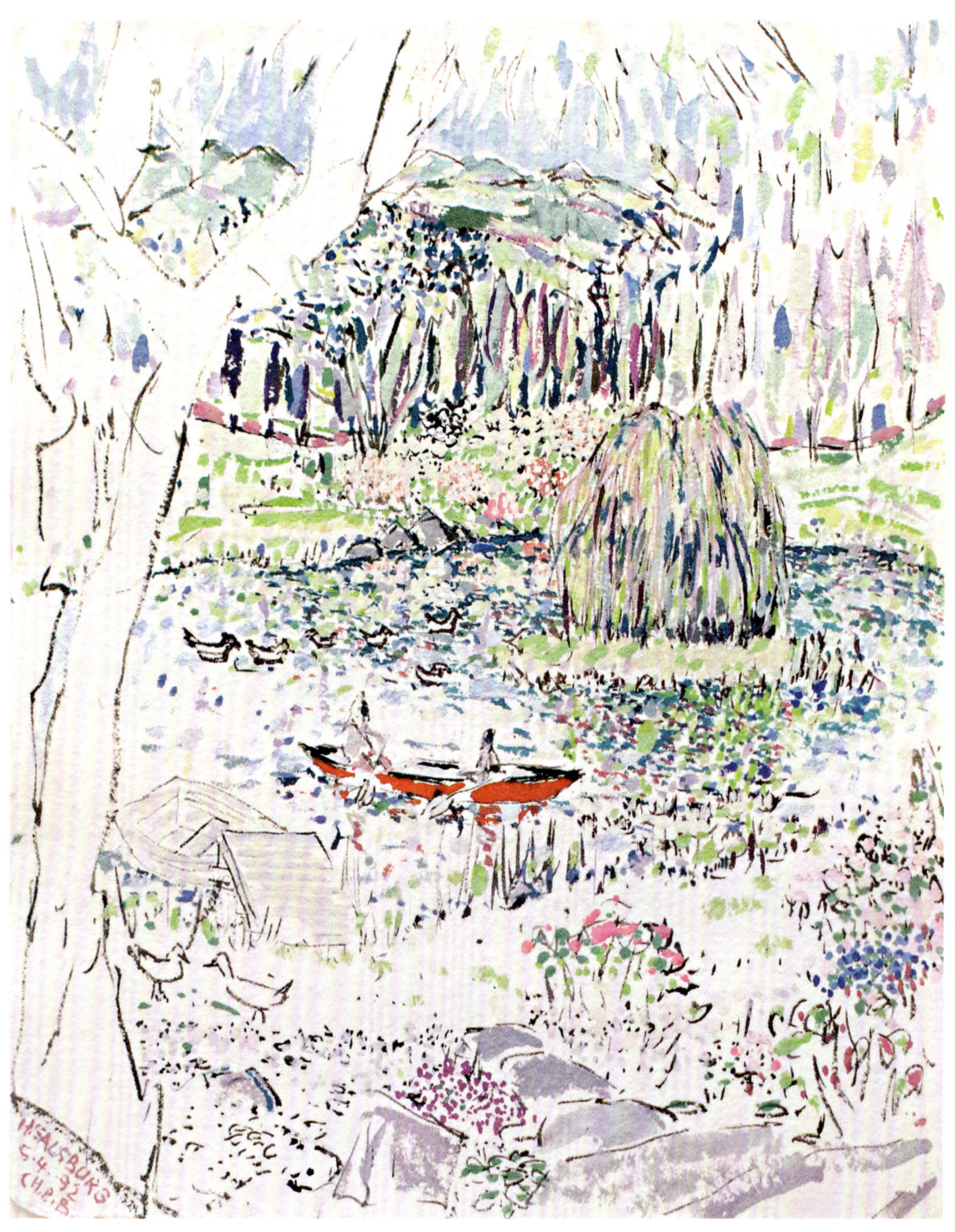
HEALSBURG
5.4.92
CH.P.B

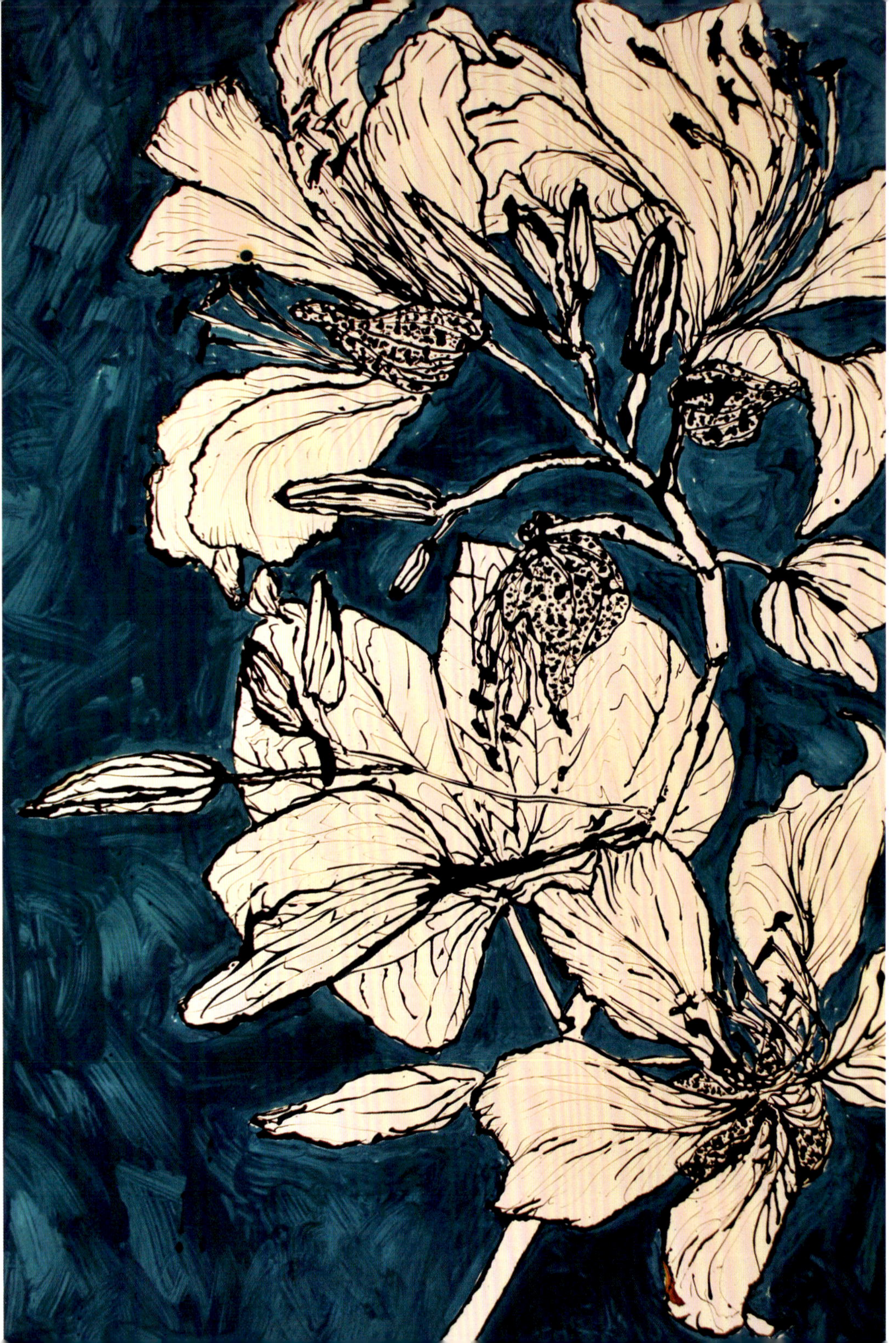

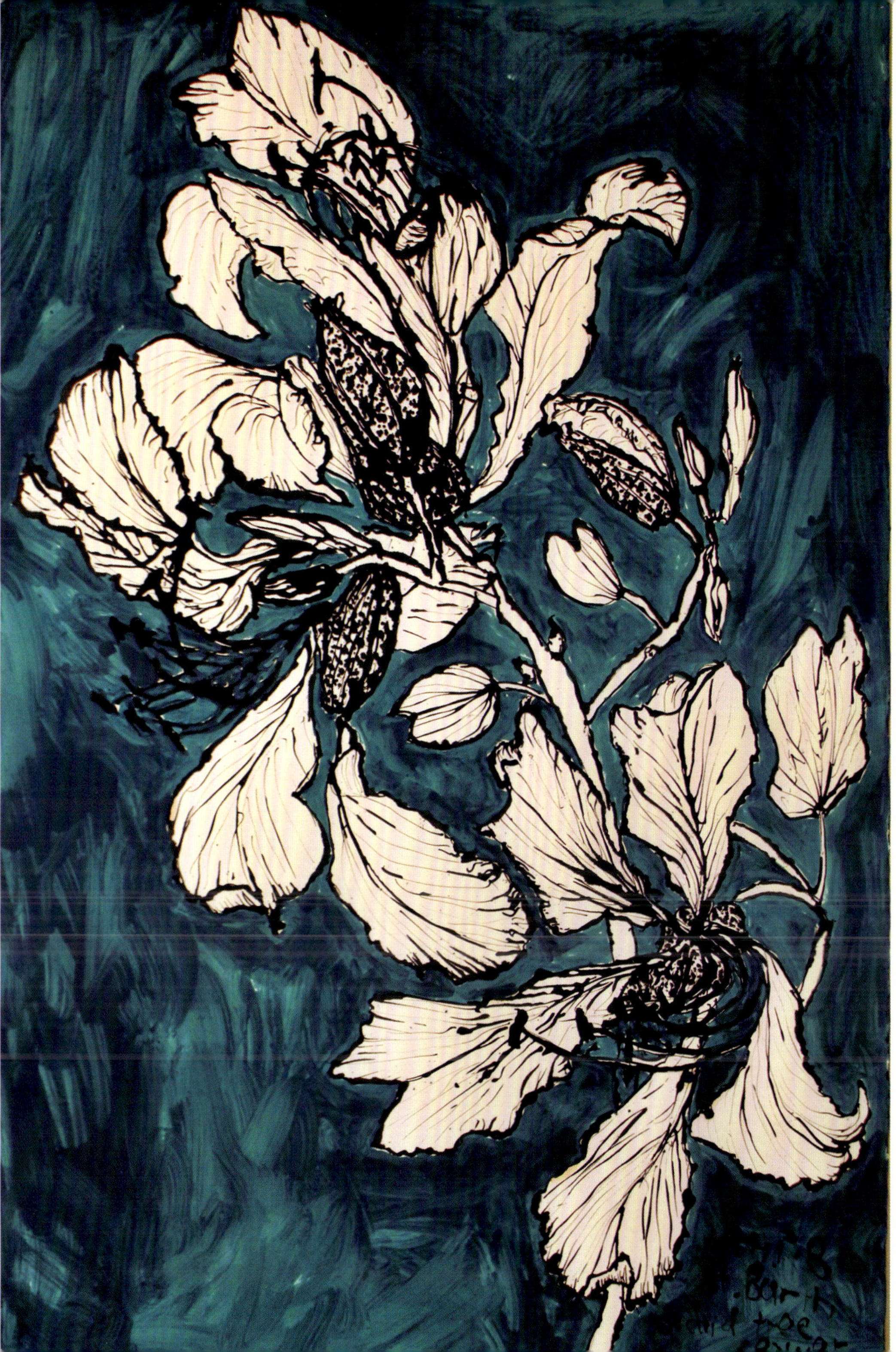

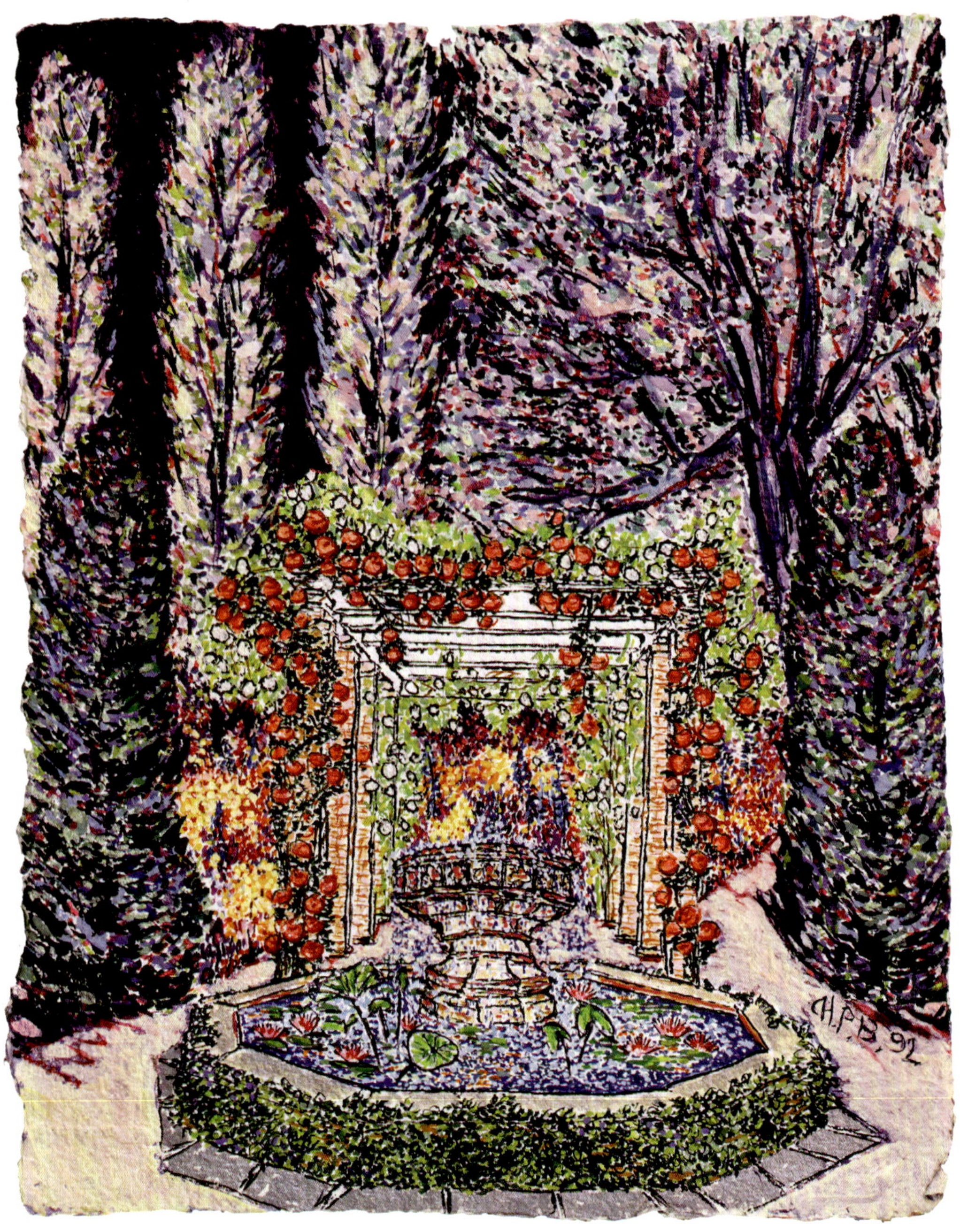
H.P.B. 92

Nashville Garden

Nashville, Tennessee

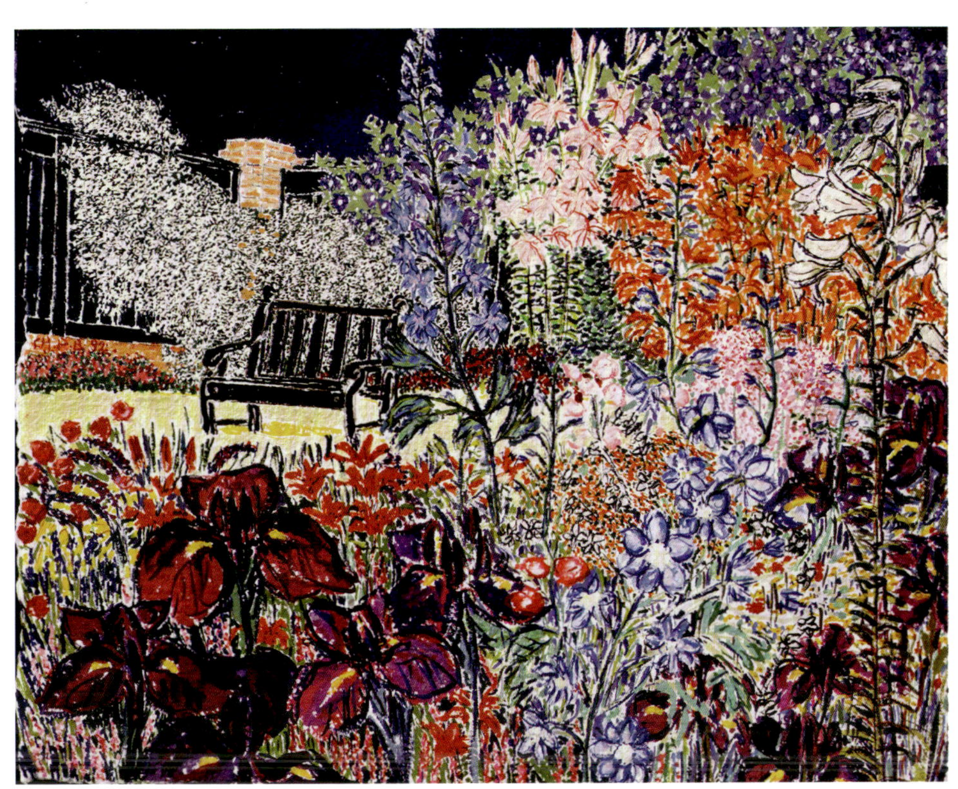

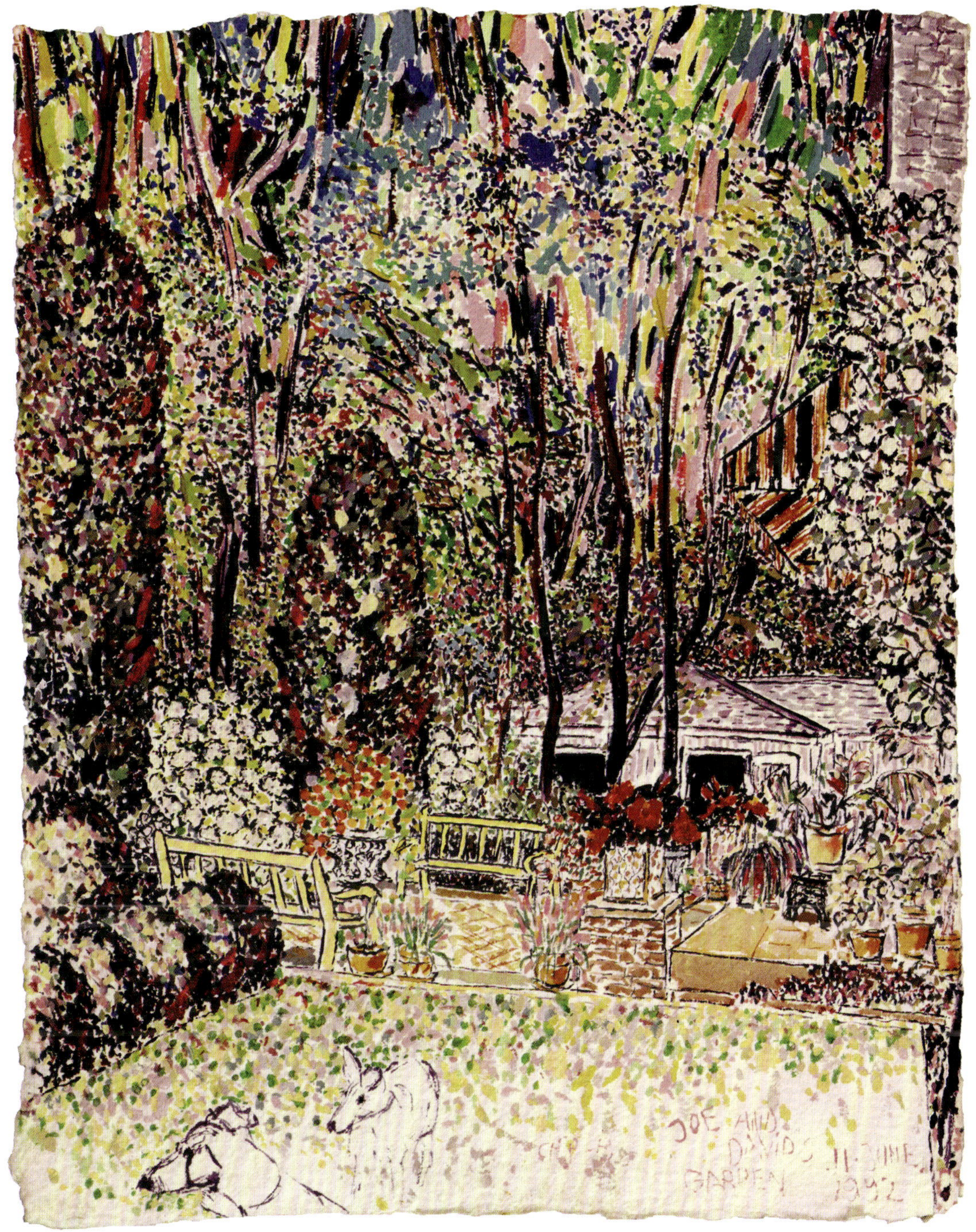

JOE AND DAVID'S GARDEN
11 JUNE 1992

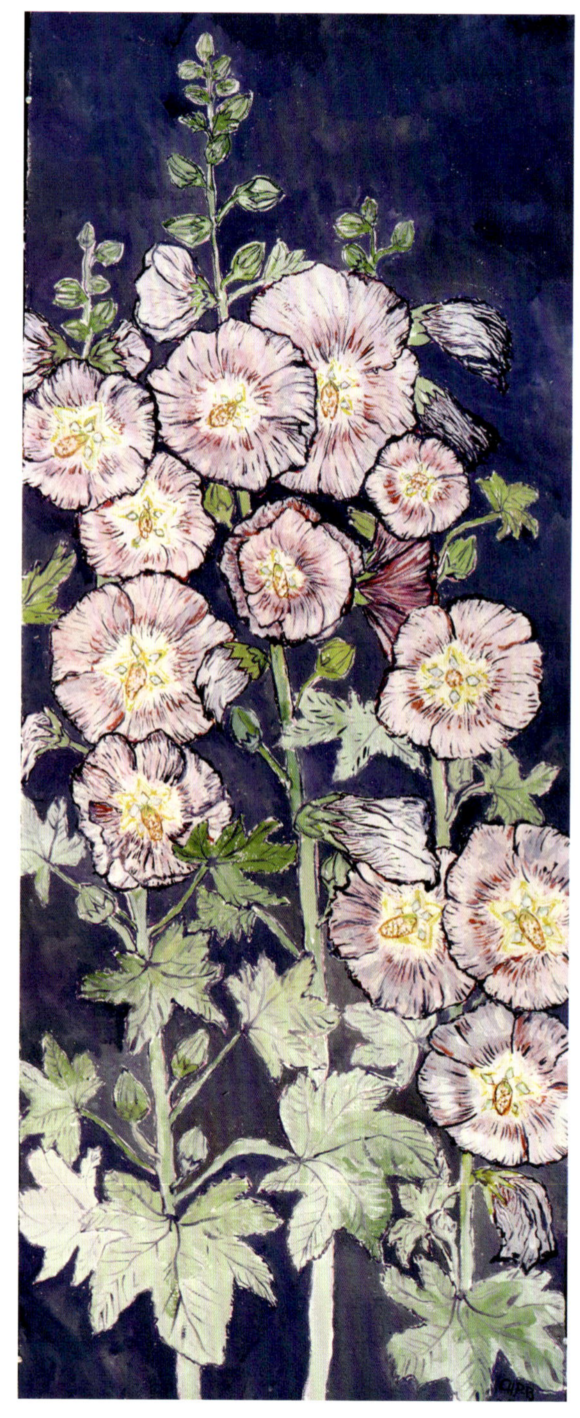

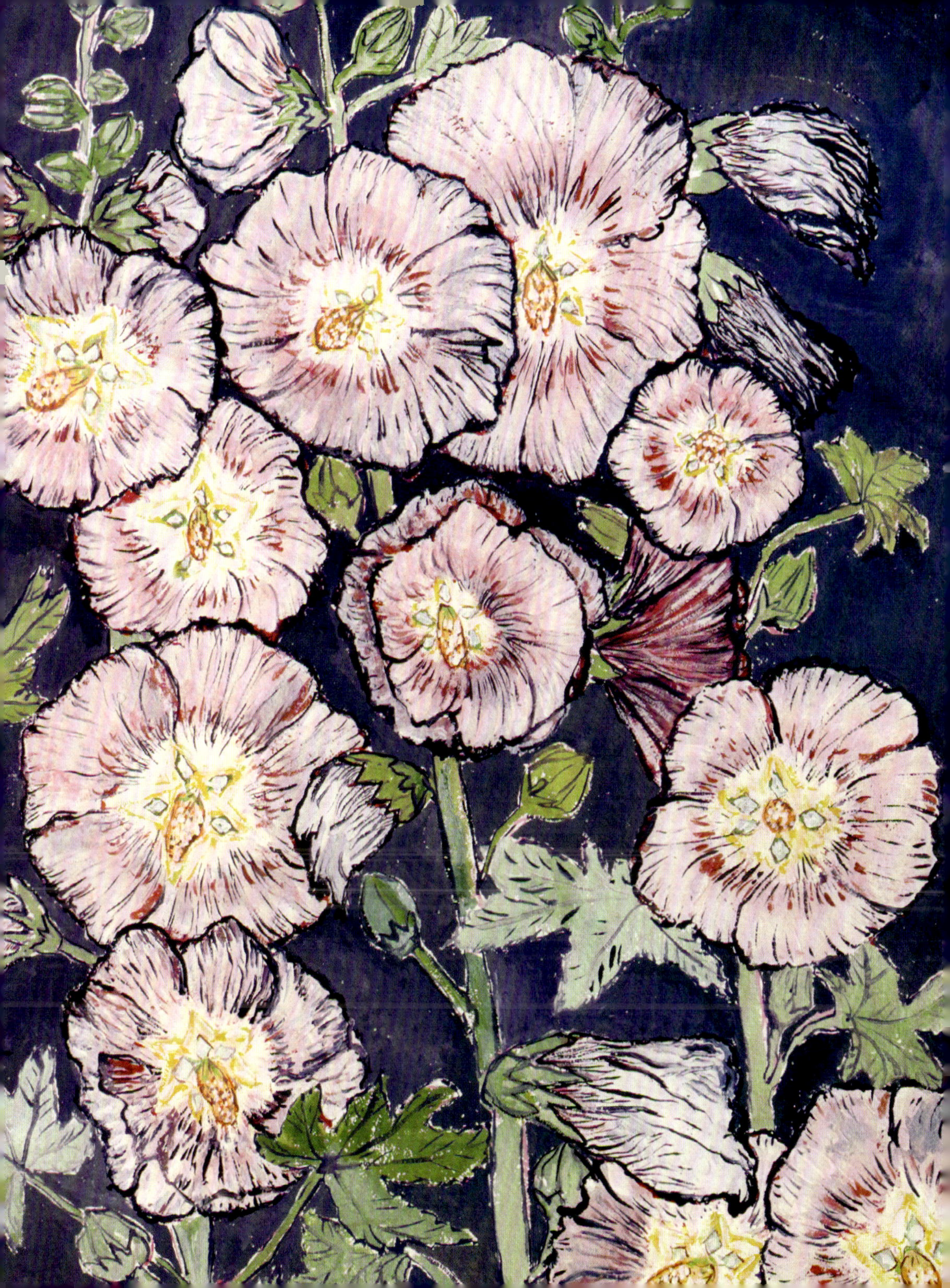

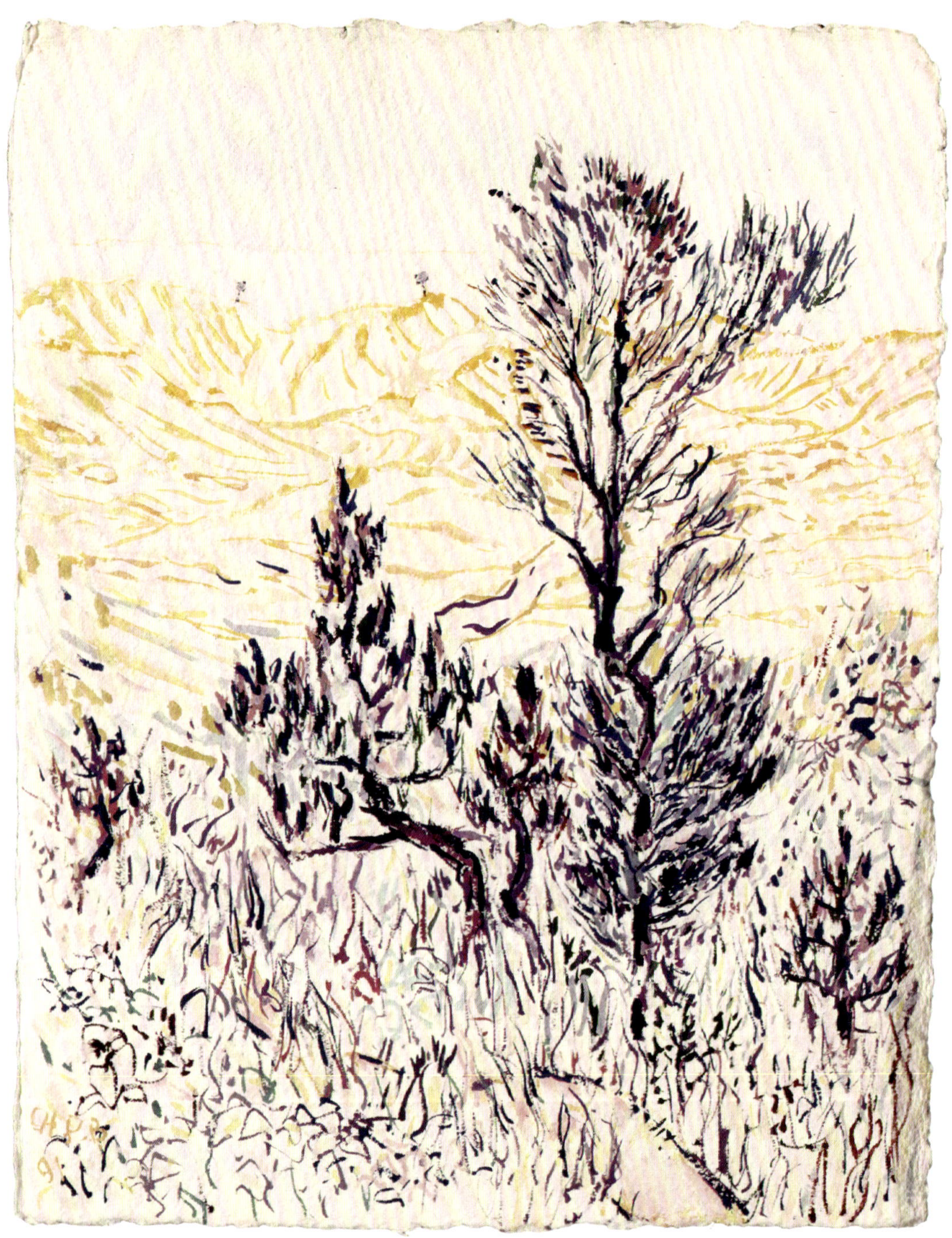

Dune Garden

East Hampton, New York

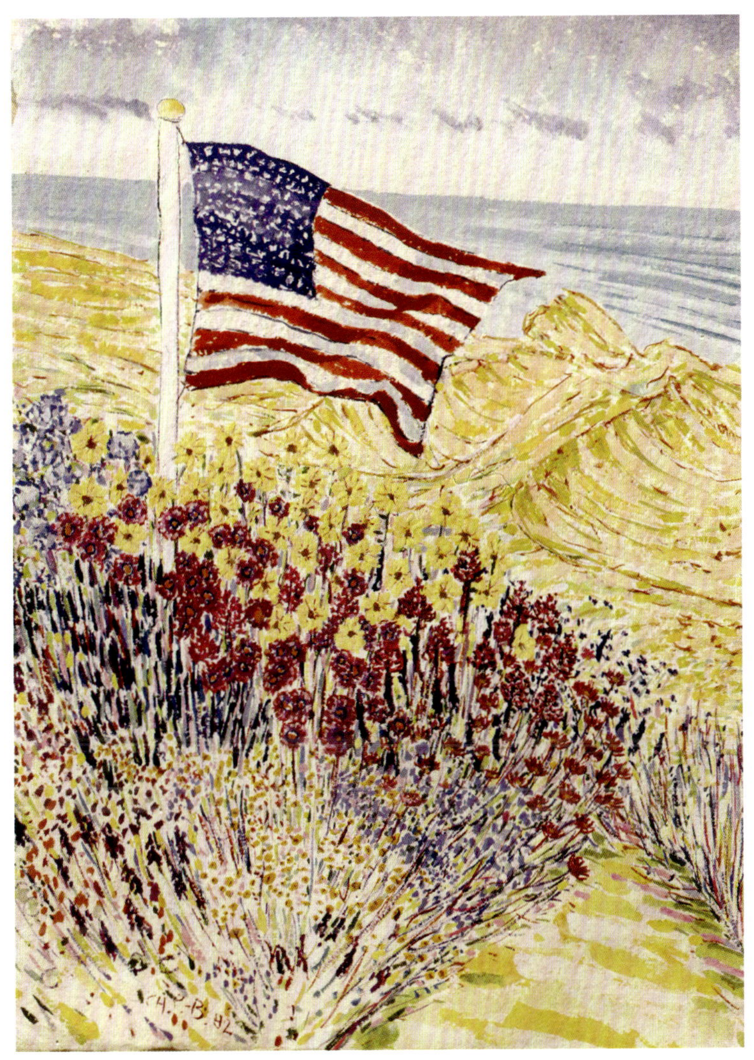

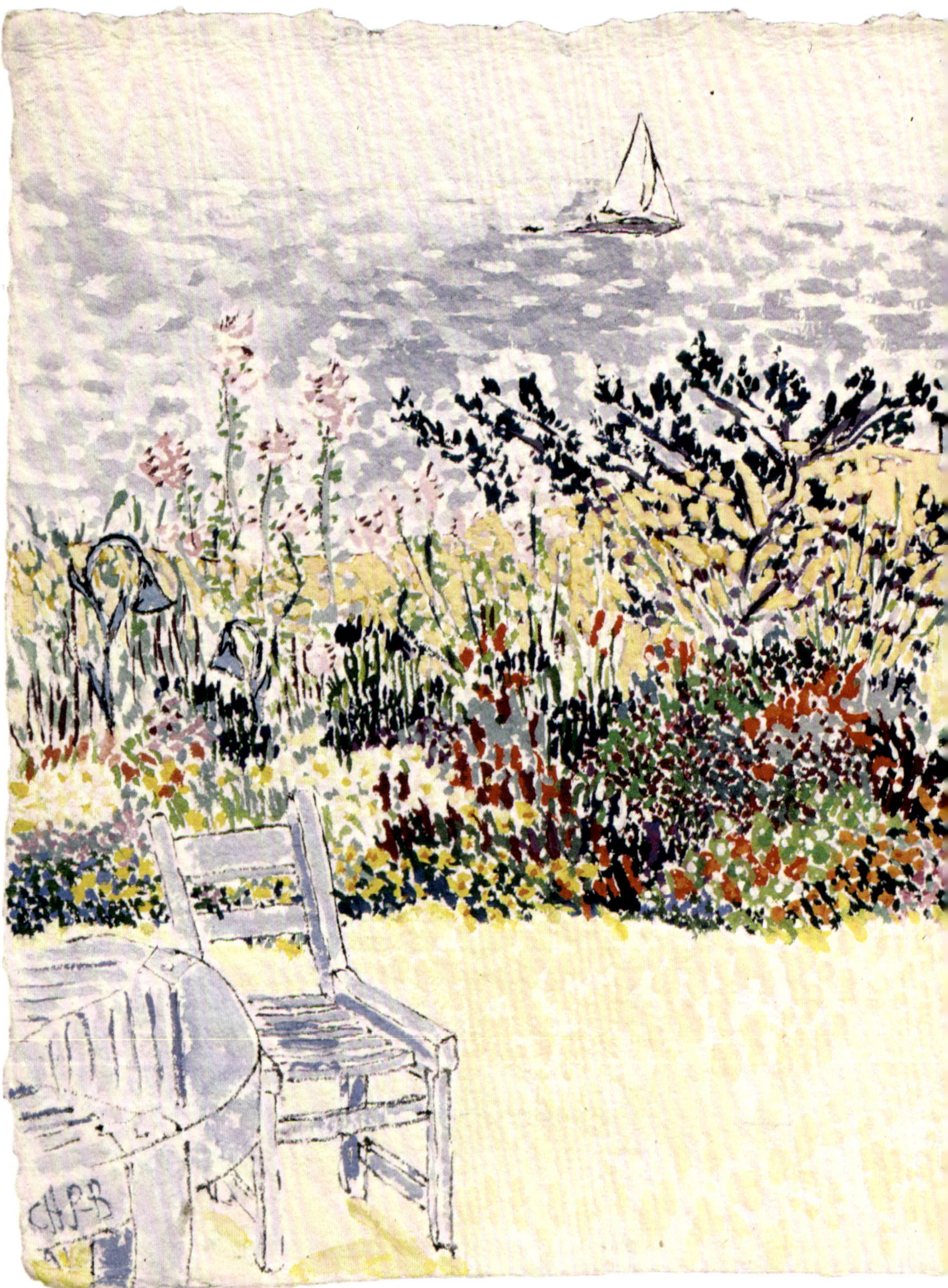
CHP-B

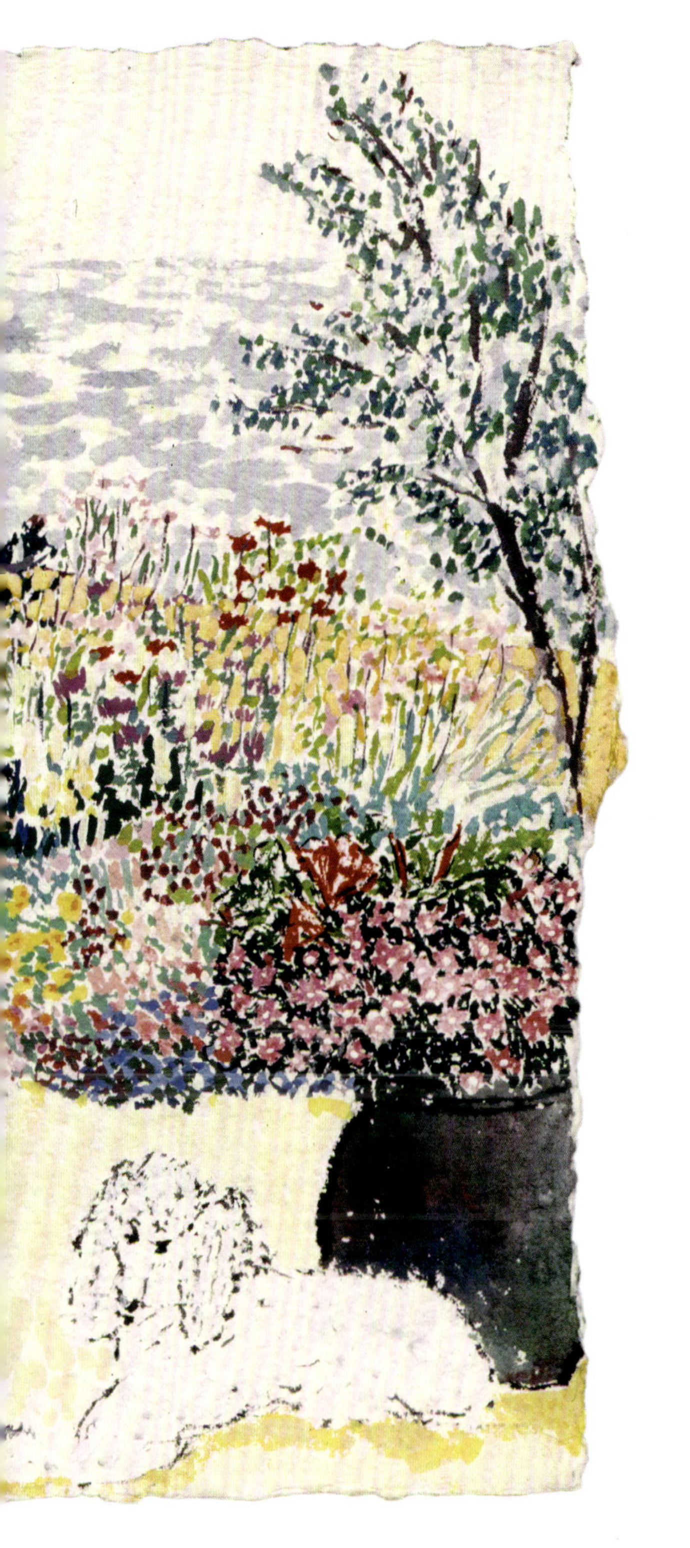

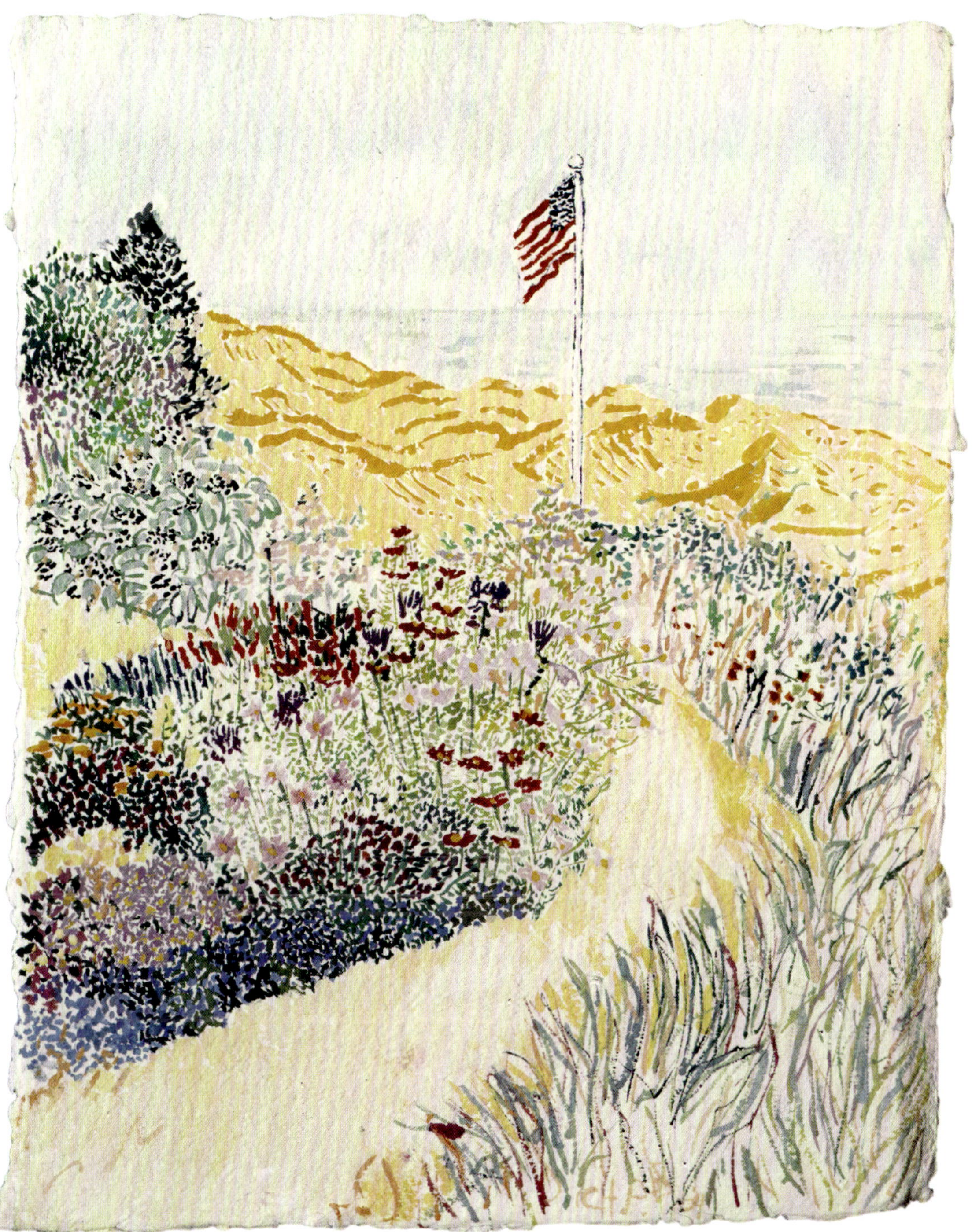

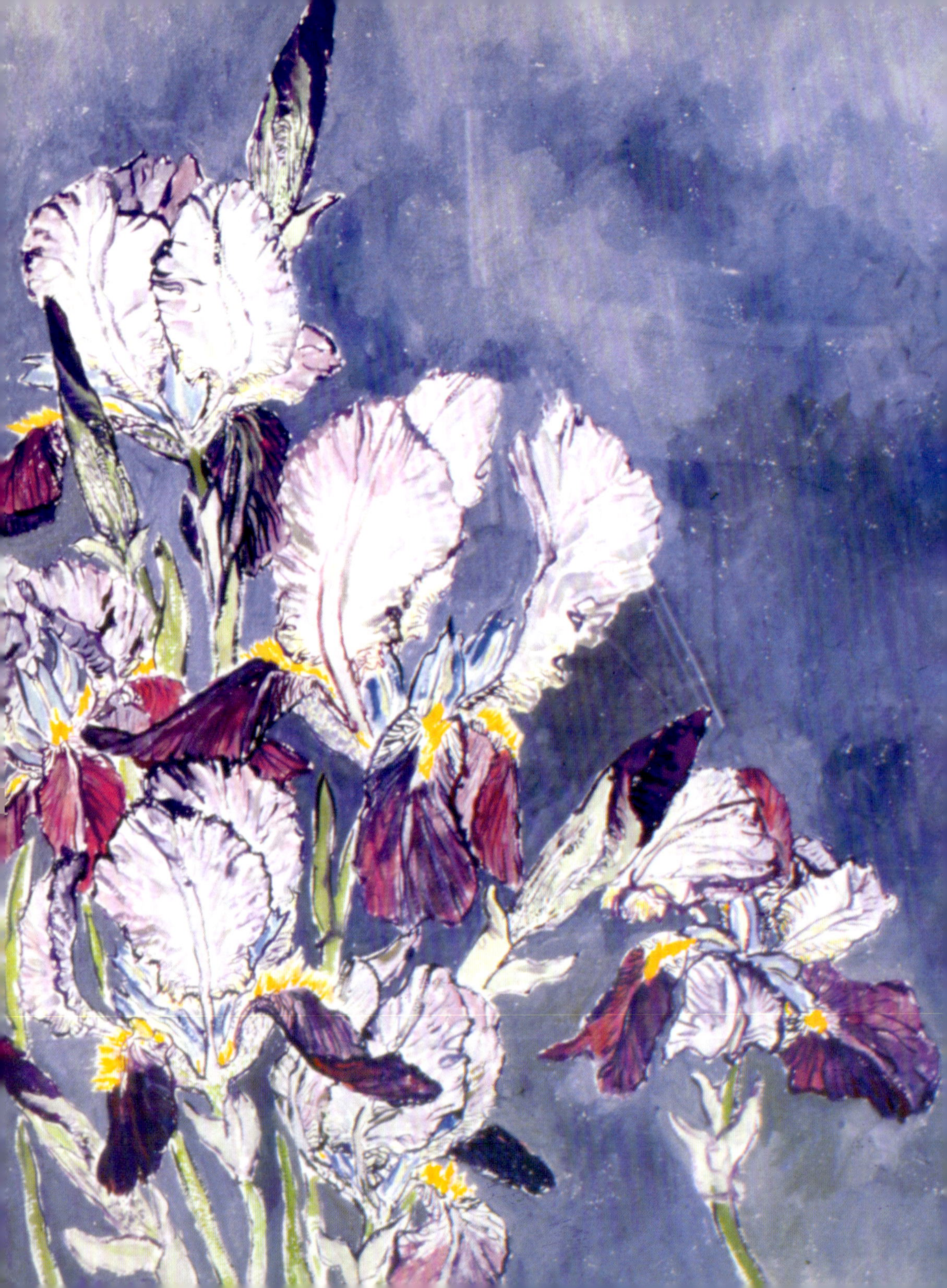

Index of Images

Cover: Woodyhouse, East Hampton, NY, 2015, gouache on paper, 21x16 inches, private collection.

Page 2: Detail, Flower (Hymenocallis) from Jean-Christophe and Jean-Louis's garden, St. Martin, 2016, ink and oil on paper, 30x44 inches.

Page 5: Orchid, St. Martin, 2016, ink and oil on paper, 30x44 inches.

Page 6: Detail, Bird of paradise flower, 2016, ink and oil on paper, 21x16 inches.

Pages 8-9: Orchid, St. Martin, 2016, ink and oil on paper, 23x26 inches.

Pages 10-11: Orchid, St. Martin, 2016, ink and oil on paper, 23x26 inches.

Page 12: Iris, 2006, oil on paper, 52x33 inches.

Page 14: Day lilies, 3 panels, 1999, gouache on paper, each 75x30 inches, private collection.

Page 18: Cactus flower in Odile's garden, 2017, ink and oil on paper, 32x26 inches.

Pages 22-23: Passion fruit flowers, 3 panels, 2014, oil on canvas, each 75x30 inches, collection of the artist.

Page 24: Tim and Christian's garden, Whalebone Cove, CT, 1992, gouache on paper, 14x11 inches, private collection.

Page 25: Tim and Christian's garden, Whalebone Cove, CT, 1992, gouache on paper, 14x11 inches, private collection.

Page 26: Tim and Christian's garden, Whalebone Cove, CT, 1989, gouache on paper, 14x11 inches, private collection.

Page 27: Tim and Christian's garden, Whalebone Cove, CT, 1991, gouache on paper, 11x14 inches, private collection.

Page 29: Tim and Christian's garden, Whalebone Cove, CT, 1992, gouache on paper, 14x11 inches, private collection.

Page 31: Tim and Christian's garden, Whalebone Cove, CT, 1992, gouache on paper, 14x11 inches, private collection.

Page 32: Tim and Christian's garden, Whalebone Cove, CT, 1992, gouache on paper, 14x11 inches, private collection.

Page 33: Tim and Christian's garden, Whalebone Cove, CT, 1992, gouache on paper, 14x11 inches, private collection.

Pages 34-35: Flower (Nenuphar) in Odile's garden, St. Martin, 2017, pastel on paper, 32x43 inches, private collection.

Page 36: Peter's garden, Roxbury, CT, 1991, gouache on paper, 14x11 inches, private collection.

Page 37: Peter's garden, Roxbury, CT, 1991, gouache on paper, 14x11 inches, private collection.

Page 39: Peter's garden, Roxbury, CT, 1991, gouache on paper, 14x11 inches, private collection.

Page 40: Peter's garden, Roxbury, CT, 1991, gouache on paper, 14x11 inches, private collection.

Page 41: Peter's garden, Roxbury, CT, 1991, gouache on paper, 14x11 inches, private collection.

Page 42: Hollyhock, 1999, gouache on paper, 75x30 inches, private collection.

Pages 42-43: Detail, Hollyhock, 1999, gouache on paper, 75x30 inches, private collection.

Page 44: Bunny and John's garden, Falls Village, CT, 2018, gouache on paper, 21x16 inches.

Page 45: Bunny and John's conservatory, Falls Village, CT, 2018, ink on paper, 21x16 inches.

Page 47: Bunny and John's garden, Falls Village, CT, 2018, gouache on paper, 21x16 inches.

Page 49: Bunny and John's garden, Falls Village, CT, 2018, gouache on paper, 21x16 inches.

Pages 50-51: Detail, Hollyhocks, 2017, gouache on paper, each 53x33 inches, private collections.

Page 52: Sylvester Manor, Shelter Island, NY, 1991, gouache on paper, 14x11 inches, private collection.

Page 53: Sylvester Manor, Shelter Island, NY, 1991, gouache on paper, 14x11 inches, private collection.

Page 55: Sylvester Manor, Shelter Island, NY, 1991, gouache on paper, 14x11 inches, private collection.

Page 57: Sylvester Manor, Shelter Island, NY, 1991, gouache on paper, 14x11 inches, private collection.

Pages 58-59: Lotus flowers in Odile's garden, St. Martin, 2017, pastel on paper, 32x43 inches.

Page 60: Madoo Conservancy, Bridgehampton, NY, 1991, gouache on paper, 14x11 inches, private collection.

Page 61: Madoo Conservancy, Bridgehampton, NY, 1991, gouache on paper, 14x11 inches.

Pages 62-63: Ginger flower, 2017, ink and oil on paper, 26x32 inches.

Page 64: Woodyhouse, East Hampton, NY, 2015, gouache on paper, 21x16 inches, private collection.

Page 65: Woodyhouse, East Hampton, NY, 2015, gouache on paper, 21x16 inches.

Page 67: Woodyhouse, East Hampton, NY, 2015, gouache on paper, 21x16 inches.

Page 69: Woodyhouse, East Hampton, NY, 2015, gouache on paper, 21x16 inches, private collection.

Page 70: Woodyhouse, East Hampton, NY, 2015, gouache on paper, 21x16 inches, private collection.

Page 71: Woodyhouse, East Hampton, NY, 2015, gouache on paper, 14x11 inches, private collection.

Page 73: Woodyhouse, East Hampton, NY, 2015, gouache on paper, 21x16 inches.

Pages 74-75: Flower in Odile's garden (Tulipier du Gabon), 2017, pastel on paper, 33x43 inches.

Page 76: Casetta Rossa, Venice, 1991, gouache on paper, 14x11 inches, private collection.

Page 77: Casetta Rossa, Venice, 1991, gouache on paper, 14x11 inches, private collection.

Page 79: Casetta Rossa, Venice, 1991, gouache on paper, 14x11 inches, private collection.

Page 80: Orchid, Paraty, Brazil, 2009, ink on paper, 24x19 inches.

Page 81: Passionfruit flower, 2009, ink on paper, 52x33 inches, private collection.

Page 82: Palazzo Albrizzi garden, Venice, gouache on paper, 14x11 inches, private collection.

Page 83: Palazzo Albrizzi garden, Venice, gouache on paper, 14x11 inches, private collection.

Page 85: Palazzo Albrizzi garden, Venice, gouache on paper, 14x11 inches, private collection.

Page 86: Detail, Orchid, St. Martin, 2016, ink and oil on paper, 32x26 inches.

Page 87: Orchid, St. Martin, 2016, ink and oil on paper, 30x44 inches.

Page 88: The dream house, Sifnos, 1995, gouache on paper, 14x11 inches, private collection.

Page 89: Gillian's garden, Sifnos, 1991, gouache on paper, 14x11 inches, private collection.

Page 90: Field of wild iris, Mangana, Sifnos, 1993, gouache on paper, 21x14 inches, private collection.

Page 91: Field of wild iris, Mangana, Sifnos, 1993, gouache on paper, 21x14 inches, private collection.

Page 92: Old Kaliopi's garden, Sifnos, 1991, gouache on paper, 14x11 inches, private collection.

Page 93: Halfway to heaven, Sifnos, 1993, gouache on paper, 75x30 inches, private collection.

Page 95: The dream house, Sifnos, 1992, gouache on paper, 14x11 inches, private collection.

Page 96: The dream house, Sifnos, 1991, gouache on paper, 14x11 inches, private collection.

Page 97: The dream house, Sifnos, 1992, gouache on paper, 14x11 inches, collection of the artist.

Pages 98-99: Lotus flowers in Odile's garden, 2017, pastel on paper, 32x43 inches.

Page 100: Into the garden, Colombo, Sri Lanka, 1992, gouache on paper, 27x21 inches, private collection.

Page 101: Into the garden, Colombo, Sri Lanka, 1992, gouache on paper, 27x21 inches.

Page 103: Into the garden, Colombo, Sri Lanka, 1992, gouache on paper, 27x21 inches, private collection.

Pages 104-105: Flower (Nenuphar) in Odile's garden, 2017, pastel on paper, 32x43 inches, private collection.

Page 106: Kandy botanical gardens, Sri Lanka, 1991, gouache on paper, 14x11 inches, private collection.

Page 107: Kandy botanical gardens, Sri Lanka, 1991, gouache on paper, 14x11 inches, private collection.

Page 108: Kandy botanical gardens, Sri Lanka, 1991, gouache on paper, each 14x11 inches, private collections.

Page 109: Kandy botanical gardens, Sri Lanka, 1991, gouache on paper, each 14x11 inches, private collections.

Page 111: Kandy botanical gardens, Sri Lanka, 1991, gouache on paper, 14x11 inches.

Page 112: Orchid, St. Martin, 2017, ink and oil on paper, 32x26 inches.

Page 113: Orchid, St. Martin, 2017, ink and oil on paper, 44x30 inches.

Page 114: Dorawana, Bentota, Sri Lanka, 1991, gouache on paper, 27x21 inches, private collection.

Page 115: Dorawana, Bentota, Sri Lanka, 1991, gouache on paper, 27x21 inches, private collection.

Page 117: Dorawana, Bentota, Sri Lanka, 1991, gouache on paper, 14x11 inches, private collection.

Page 118: Dorawana, Bentota, Sri Lanka, 1991, gouache on paper, 14x11 inches, private collection.

Page 119: Dorawana, Bentota, Sri Lanka, 1991, gouache on paper, 14x11 inches, private collection.

Page 120: Dorawana, Bentota, Sri Lanka, 1991, gouache on paper, 14x11 inches, private collection.

Page 121: Dorawana, Bentota, Sri Lanka, 1991, gouache on paper, 14x11 inches, private collection.

Pages 122-123: Flowers in Odile's garden, 2017, pastel on paper, 32x43 inches, private collection.

Page 124: Lunuganga, Bentota, Sri Lanka, 1992, gouache on paper, 14x11 inches, private collection.

Page 125: Lunuganga, Bentota, Sri Lanka, 1992, gouache on paper, 11x14 inches, private collection.

Page 126: Lunuganga, Bentota, Sri Lanka, 1992, gouache on paper, 14x11 inches, private collection.

Page 127: Lunuganga, Bentota, Sri Lanka, 1992, gouache on paper, 21x14 inches, private collection.

Page 128: Lunuganga, Bentota, Sri Lanka, 1992, gouache on paper, 27x21 inches, private collection.

Page 129: Lunuganga, Bentota, Sri Lanka, 1992, gouache on paper, 21x27 inches, private collection.

Pages 130-131: Lunuganga, Bentota, Sri Lanka, 1992, gouache on paper, 21x27 inches, private collection.

Page 133: Lunuganga, Bentota, Sri Lanka, 1992, gouache on paper, 27x21 inches, private collection.

Pages 134-135: Lunuganga, Bentota, Sri Lanka, 1992, gouache on paper, 21x27 inches, private collection.

Page 137: Lunuganga, Bentota, Sri Lanka, 1992, gouache on paper, 14x11 inches, collection of the artist.

Pages 138-139: Lunuganga, Bentota, Sri Lanka, 1992, gouache on paper, 11x14 inches, private collection.

Page 140: Orchid, Paraty, Brazil, 2009, ink and oil on paper, 24x19 inches.

Page 141: Orchid, Paraty, Brazil, 2009, ink and oil on paper, 24x19 inches.

Page 142: Hakgala botanical gardens, Nuwara Eliya, Sri Lanka, 1992, gouache on paper, 14x11 inches, private collection.

Page 143: Hakgala botanical gardens, Nuwara Eliya, Sri Lanka, 1992, gouache on paper, 14x11 inches, private collection.

Page 145: Hakgala botanical gardens, Nuwara Eliya, Sri Lanka, 1992, gouache on paper, 14x11 inches, private collection.

Page 147: Hakgala botanical gardens, Nuwara Eliya, Sri Lanka, 1992, gouache on paper, 14x11 inches, private collection.

Page 148: Hakgala botanical gardens, Nuwara Eliya, Sri Lanka, 1992, gouache on paper, 14x11 inches, private collection.

Page 149: Hakgala botanical gardens, Nuwara Eliya, Sri Lanka, 1992, gouache on paper, 14x11 inches, private collection.

Page 151: Hakgala botanical gardens, Nuwara Eliya, Sri Lanka, 1992, gouache on paper, 14x11 inches, private collection.

Page 152: Ginger flower, Punta Cana, 2013, ink on paper, 16x21 inches.

Page 153: Ginger flower, Punta Cana, 2013, ink on paper, 16x21 inches.

Page 154: Rocktail Bay dune garden, South Africa, 1999, pastel on paper, 15x22 inches, private collection.

Page 155: Detail, Rocktail Bay dune garden, South Africa, 1999, pastel on paper, 15x22 inches.

Pages 156-157: Rocktail Bay dune garden, South Africa, 1999, pastel on paper, 15x22 inches.

Pages 158-159: Rocktail Bay dune garden, South Africa, 1999, pastel on paper, 15x22 inches.

Page 160: St. Martin flower, 2011, gouache on paper, 21x16 inches.

Page 161: St. Martin flower, 2011, gouache on paper, 21x16 inches.

Page 162: Courtyard, Havana, Cuba, 1999, watercolor on paper, 27x21 inches, private collection.

Page 163: Courtyard, Havana, Cuba, 1999, watercolor on paper, 27x21 inches, private collection.

Page 164: Courtyard, Havana, Cuba, 1999, watercolor on paper, 27x21 inches.

Page 165: Courtyard, Havana, Cuba, 1999, watercolor on paper, 27x21 inches, private collection.

Pages 166-167: St. Martin flowers (Hymenocallis), 2016, ink and oil on paper, each 30x44 inches.

Page 168: Angus and the late Will Harmon's garden, Morne Rouge, Dominica, West Indies, 1989, gouache on paper, 14x11 inches, private collection.

Page 169: Angus and the late Will Harmon's garden, Morne Rouge, Dominica, West Indies, 1989, gouache on paper, 14x11 inches, private collection.

Page 171: Angus and the late Will Harmon's garden, Morne Rouge, Dominica, West Indies, 1990, gouache on paper, 14x11 inches, private collection.

Page 172: Orchid, St. Martin, 2016, ink on paper, 32x26 inches.

Page 173: Orchid, St. Martin, 2016, ink on paper, 32x26 inches.

Page 174: La Colina, Bunny Williams and John Rosselli's Garden, Punta Cana, Dominican Republic, 2011,ink and watercolor on handmade paper, 16X22 inches.

Page 175: La Colina, Bunny Williams and John Rosselli's Garden, Punta Cana, Dominican Republic, 2011,ink and watercolor on handmade paper, 16X22 inches.

Pages 176-177: The Cactus garden, La Colina, Bunny Williams and John Rosselli's Garden, Punta Cana, Dominican Republic, 2011, ink and watercolor on handmade paper, 16X22 inches.

Page 178: Odile's garden, Pic Paradis, St. Martin, 2016, gouache on paper, 14x21 inches.

Page 179: Odile's garden, Pic Paradis, St. Martin, 2016, gouache on paper, 14x21 inches.

Pages 180-181: Odile's garden, Pic Paradis, St. Martin, 2016, gouache on paper, 14x21 inches, private collection.

Pages 182-183: Lotus flowers in Odile's garden, 2017, pastel on paper, 32x43 inches.

Page 184: Jean-Christophe and Jean-Louis's garden, St. Martin, 2006, watercolor on paper, 19x24 inches.

Page 185: Jean-Christophe and Jean-Louis's garden, St. Martin, 2006, watercolor on paper, 19x24 inches.

Page 186: Tacca (bat) flower, St. Martin, 2015, ink, oil, and watercolor on paper, 32x26 inches.

Page 187: Tacca (bat) flower, St. Martin, 2015, ink, oil, and watercolor on paper, 32x26 inches.

Page 188: Sonia's garden, San Ángel, Mexico, 1991, gouache on paper, 14x11 inches, private collection.

Page 189: Street flower market, Mexico City, 1991, gouache on paper, 14x11 inches, private collection.

Page 190: Sonia's garden, San Ángel, Mexico, 1991, gouache on paper, 14x11 inches, private collection.

Page 191: Sonia's garden, San Ángel, Mexico, 1991, gouache on paper, 14x11 inches, private collection.

Pages 192-193: Flower (Allamanda) in Odile's garden, 2017, pastel on paper, 32x43 inches.

Page 194: Sonia's garden, Cuernavaca, Mexico, 1995, gouache on paper, 14x11 inches.

Page 195: Sonia's garden, Cuernavaca, Mexico, 1995, gouache on paper, 14x11 inches.

Page 196: Sonia's garden, Cuernavaca, Mexico, 1995, gouache on paper, each 14x11 inches.

Page 197: Sonia's garden, Cuernavaca, Mexico, 1995, gouache on paper, 14x11 inches.

Page 198: The Davidoff garden, Cuernavaca, Mexico, 1991, 14x11 inches, private collection.

Page 199: The Davidoff garden, Cuernavaca, Mexico, 1991, 14x11 inches, private collection.

Page 200: Sonia's garden, Cuernavaca, Mexico, 1991, gouache on paper, 14x11 inches, private collection.

Page 201: Sonia's garden, Cuernavaca, Mexico, 1991, gouache on paper, 14x11 inches, private collection.

Pages 202-203: Lotus flower in Odile's garden, 2017, pastel on paper, 32x43 inches.

Page 204: The late Ferdinand Coudert's garden, Key West, FL, 1992, gouache on paper, 14x11 inches, private collection.

Page 205: The late Ferdinand Coudert's garden, Key West, FL, 1992, gouache on paper, 14x11 inches, private collection.

Page 207: The late Ferdinand Coudert's garden, Key West, FL, 1992, gouache on paper, 14x11 inches, private collection.

Page 208: Ginger flower, Punta Cana, 2013, ink and oil on paper, 26x32 inches.

Page 209: Orchid, St. Martin, 2015, ink and oil on paper, 32x26 inches, private collection.

Page 210: The late Jeff Williams and his wife Hsing Mei's garden, Los Angeles, CA, 1992, gouache on paper, 14x11 inches, private collection.

Page 211: The late Jeff Williams and his wife Hsing Mei's garden, Los Angeles, CA, 1992, gouache on paper, 14x11 inches, private collection.

Page 212: The late Jeff Williams and his wife Hsing Mei's garden, Los Angeles, CA, 1992, gouache on paper, 14x11 inches, private collection.

Page 213: The late Jeff Williams and his wife Hsing Mei's garden, Los Angeles, CA, 1992, gouache on paper, 14x11 inches, private collection.

Page 215: The late Jeff Williams and his wife Hsing Mei's garden, Los Angeles, CA, 1992, gouache on paper, 14x11 inches, private collection.

Pages 216-217: Detail and one panel, Day lilies, 1999, gouache on paper, 75x30 inches, private collection.

Page 218: Bobo's garden, Big Sur, Santa Lucia Ranch, CA, 2014, pastel on paper, each 34x43 inches.

Page 219: Bobo's gardens, Big Sur, Santa Lucia Ranch, CA, 2014, pastel on paper, 34x43 inches.

Pages 220-221: Bobo's garden, Big Sur, Santa Lucia Ranch, CA, 2014, pastel on paper, 34x43 inches.

Page 222: Orchid, St. Martin, 2016, ink and oil on paper, 21x16 inches.

Page 223: Orchid, St. Martin, 2016, ink and oil on paper, 21x16 inches.

Page 224: Healdsburg garden, Sonoma, CA, 1992, gouache on paper, 14x11 inches, private collection.

Page 225: Healdsburg garden, Sonoma, CA, 1992, gouache on paper, 14x11 inches, private collection.

Page 227: Healdsburg garden, Sonoma, CA, 1992, gouache on paper, 14x11 inches, private collection.

Page 228: Orchid tree, St. Barth, 2013, ink and oil on paper, 30x44 inches.

Page 229: Orchid tree, St. Barth, 2013, ink and oil on paper, 30x44 inches.

Page 230: David and the late Joe Erwin's garden, Nashville, TN, 1992, gouache on paper, 14x11 inches, private collection.

Page 231: David and the late Joe Erwin's garden, Nashville, TN, 1992, gouache on paper, 14x11 inches, private collection.

Page 233: David and the late Joe Erwin's garden, Nashville, TN, 1992, gouache on paper, 14x11 inches, private collection.

Page 234: Hollyhocks, 1999, gouache on paper, 75x30 inches, private collection.

Page 235: Detail, Hollyhocks, 1999, gouache on paper, 75x30 inches, private collection.

Page 236: Dune garden, East Hampton, NY, 1991, gouache on paper, 14x11 inches, private collection.

Page 237: Dune garden, East Hampton, NY, 1991, gouache on paper, 14x11 inches, private collection.

Pages 238-239: Dune garden, East Hampton, NY, 1991, gouache on paper, 11x14 inches, private collection.

Page 241: Dune garden, East Hampton, NY, 1991, gouache on paper, 14x11 inches, private collection.

Page 242: Detail, Iris, 1999, gouache on paper, 75x30 inches, private collection.

Page 250: Hollyhocks, 1999, gouache on paper, 75x30 inches.

Back cover: Tacca (bat) flower, St. Martin, 2015, ink, oil, and watercolor on paper, 32x26 inches, private collection.

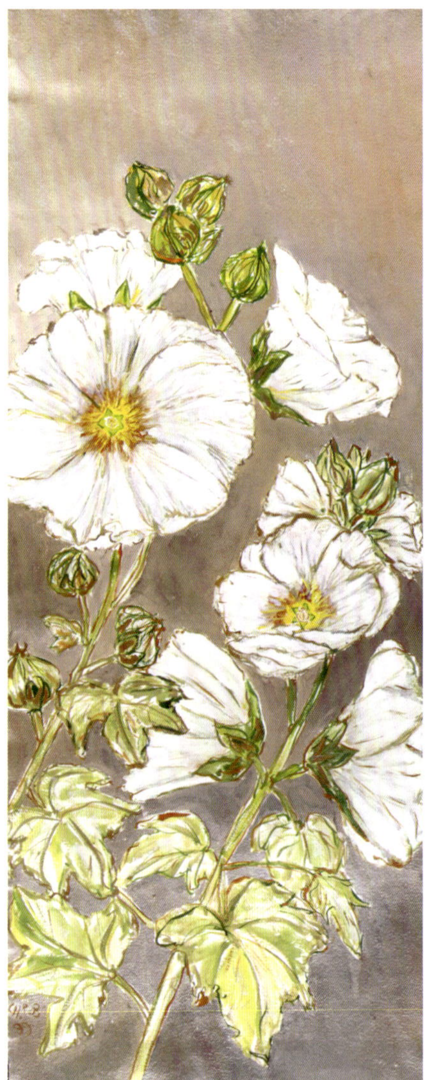

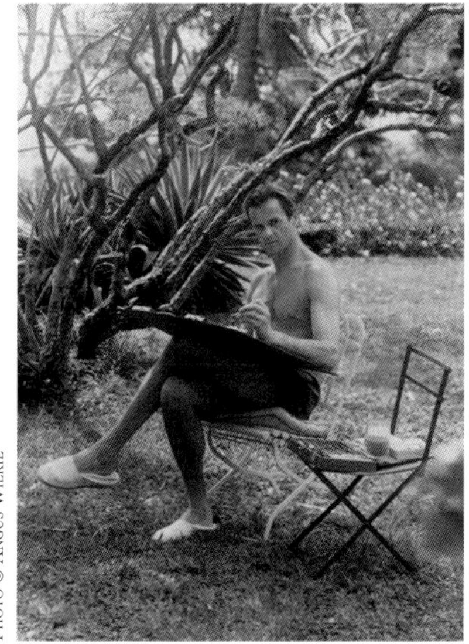
Photo © Angus Wilkie

Born in the former Belgian Congo, artist **Christian Peltenburg-Brechneff** has exhibited his drawings and paintings in numerous galleries across Europe and the United States. Unlike many of his contemporaries, he often draws and paints outdoors, and this can involve traveling to remote terrain and hiring sherpas to accompany him with his supplies and canvases so that he can paint in living environments.

Educated in Switzerland, England, and the United States, Peltenburg-Brechneff received his master of art degree in 1975 from the Royal College of Art in London. In addition to winning prestigious awards, such as the Swiss Federal Government Scholarship, his paintings appear in distinguished public and private collections worldwide, including the Metropolitan Museum of Art. Furthermore, he is the author of two previous books, *Homage: Encounters with the East* (Glitterati) and *The Greek House* (Farrar, Straus and Giroux) and the subject of the 2016 documentary film, *Like Notes of Music* by Michael Magee. He currently divides his time between Hadlyme, CT, New York City, and St. Martin.

Personal Data

Born in Belgian Congo (Democratic Republic of the Congo)

1975 Master of Art, Royal College of Art

Selected Exhibitions

2018 Daniel Blaise Thorens Fine Art Gallery, Basel, Switzerland

2017 Galerie Curtins, St. Moritz, Switzerland
WBB Gallery, Zürich, Switzerland

2016 Sifnos School Gallery Artemonas, Sifnos, Greece
Galerie Karouzou, Zürich, Switzerland
Cooley Gallery, Old Lyme, CT

2015 Planetarium Gallery Eugenides Foundation, Athens, Greece
Barr & Ochsner Gallery, Zürich, Switzerland
Swifty's Back Room Gallery, New York, NY

2014 Daniel Blaise Thorens Fine Art Gallery, Basel, Switzerland

2013 Cooley Gallery, Old Lyme, CT
Montgomery Gallery, San Francisco, CA

2012 Indar Pasricha Fine Arts, London, UK
Projektraum M54, Basel, Switzerland
Daniel Blaise Thorens Fine Art Gallery, Basel, Switzerland

2011 Galerie Curtins, St. Moritz, Switzerland
Treillage Gallery, New York, NY
Hollyhock Gallery, Los Angeles, CA

2010 Galerie Esther Hufschmid, Zürich, Switzerland
Daniel BlaiseThorens Fine Art Gallery, Basel, Switzerland

2008 Lyme Academy, Old Lyme, CT

2007 Daniel Blaise Thorens Fine Art Gallery, Basel, Switzerland
Projektraum M54, Basel, Switzerland
Treillage Gallery, New York, NY
Galerie Esther Hufschmid, Zürich, Switzerland
Anderson Galleries, Beverly Hills, CA

2006 Treillage Gallery, New York, NY
Galerie Curtins, St. Moritz, Switzerland
Galerie Reygers, München, Germany
Kleine Galerie, Regensburg, Germany
Galerie Trittligasse, Zürich, Switzerland

2005 Alva Gallery, New London, CT
Daniel Blaise Thorens Fine Art Gallery, Basel, Switzerland

2004 Galerie Trittligasse, Zürich, Switzerland

2003 Galerie Curtins, St. Moritz, Switzerland
Treillage Gallery, New York, NY
Daniel Blaise Thorens Fine Art Gallery, Basel, Switzerland

2002 Galerie Trittligasse, Zürich, Switzerland
Daniel Blaise Thorens Fine Art Gallery, Basel, Switzerland

2001 Salander-O'Reilly Galleries, New York, NY

2000 Art First, London, UK
Daniel Blaise Thorens Fine Art Gallery, Basel, Switzerland

1999 Galerie Trittligasse, Zürich, Switzerland
Treillage Gallery, New York, NY
Daniel Blaise Thorens Fine Art Gallery, Basel, Switzerland
Galerie Reygers, München, Germany
Kleine Galerie, Regensburg, Germany

1998 Kreonidis Art Galleries, Athens, Greece

1997 Daniel Blaise Thorens Fine Art Gallery, Basel, Switzerland
Galerie Ausstellungsraum Klingental, Basel, Switzerland

1996 Ursula Wiedenkeller Gallery, Zürich, Switzerland

Galerie Trittligasse, Zürich, Switzerland
Kleine Galerie, Regensburg, Germany
Andre Zarre Gallery, New York, NY

1995 Daniel Blaise Thorens Fine Art Gallery, Basel, Switzerland

1994 Daniel Blaise Thorens Fine Art Gallery, Basel, Switzerland
Kreonidis Art Galleries, Athens, Greece

1993 Stubbs Books & Prints, New York, NY
Daniel Blaise Thorens Fine Art Gallery, Basel, Switzerland

1992 Montgomery Gallery, San Francisco, CA
Cooley Gallery, Old Lyme, CT
David Anderson Gallery, Buffalo, NY
Ursula Wiedenkeller Gallery, Zürich, Switzerland

1991 Daniel Blaise Thorens Fine Art Gallery, Basel, Switzerland
Stubbs Books & Prints, New York, NY

1990 Ursula Wiedenkeller Gallery, Zürich, Switzerland
Galerie Trittligasse, Zürich, Switzerland
Nahan Contemporary, New York, NY

1989 Roger Ramsay Gallery, Chicago, IL
Fota Gallery, Alexandria, VA

1988 Daniel Blaise Thorens Fine Art Gallery, Basel, Switzerland

1987 Vorpal Gallery, New York, NY

1986 Cumberland Gallery, Nashville, TN
Daniel Blaise Thorens Fine Art Gallery, Basel, Switzerland

1985 Vorpal Gallery, New York, NY

1984 Daniel Blaise Thorens Fine Art Gallery, Basel, Switzerland
Vorpal Gallery, San Francisco, CA

1982 Daniel Blaise Thorens Fine Art Gallery, Basel, Switzerland

1978 Ursula Wiedenkeller Gallery, Zürich, Switzerland

1977 Galerie Riehentor, Basel, Switzerland
Ausstellungsraum Klingental, Basel, Switzerland

1976 Ursula Wiedenkeller Gallery, Zürich, Switzerland

1972 Sibyll Kummer-Rothenhäusler Gallery, Zürich, Switzerland

1971 Flaten Art Museum, St. Olaf College, Northfield, MN

1970 Galerie Stampa, Basel, Switzerland

1969 Sibyll Kummer-Rothenhäusler Gallery, Zürich, Switzerland

Selected Private and Public Collections

The Metropolitan Museum of Art, New York, NY
David Anderson Gallery, Buffalo, NY
Accel Partners, San Francisco, CA
Union Bank of Switzerland, New York, NY
Papier Union, Frankfurt, Germany
Commerzbank, New York, NY
BHF-Bank (Schweiz) AG, Zürich, Switzerland
Lonza Group AG, Basel, Switzerland

Bibliography

2013 *The Greek House* (Farrar, Straus and Giroux)

2007 *Homage: Encounters with the East* (Glitterati)

Bunny Williams is a celebrated interior and garden designer, known for her eclectic style of harmonizing the old with the new. Born in Charlottesville, VA, Williams has parlayed her refined taste and entrepreneurial spirit into her award-winning design business, Bunny Williams Home. She is herself a published author of many bestselling home and garden books, and her forthcoming title, *Love Affairs with Houses* (Abrams Books), is expected in 2019. She currently splits her time between her homes in New York City and Connecticut.

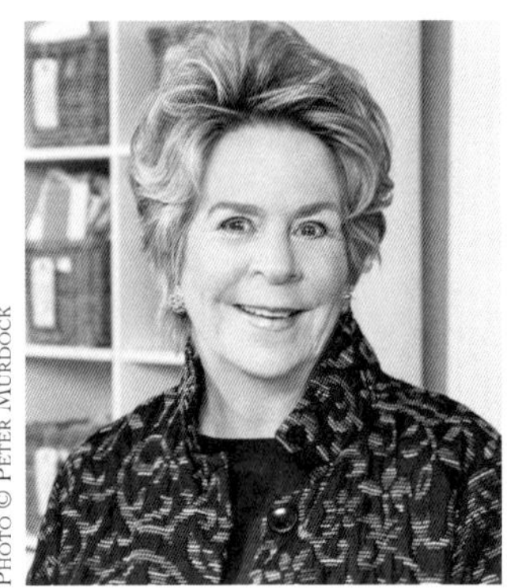

Photo © Peter Murdock

Regarded as one of America's most preeminent art critics, **Donald Kuspit** is the Distinguished Professor Emeritus of Art History and Philosophy at the State University of New York at Stony Brook. He has received numerous fellowships, including those from the Ford Foundation, Fulbright Commission, and the National Endowment for the Arts. Most notably, he is the author of *The End of Art* published by Cambridge University Press in 2004. Kuspit is based in New York.

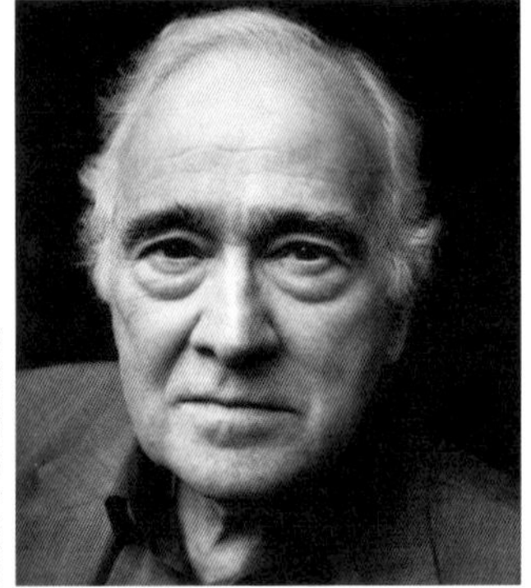

Photo © Chris Felver

Acknowledgments

Without our property in Whalebone Cove on the Connecticut River Delta, this book would not exist. It was my husband Tim Lovejoy's vision and designs for our garden in this magical place that inspired me almost 30 years ago to focus on the garden, to go in there, and start painting. I am forever grateful to Tim for the garden and for loving me.

After a wonderful and exciting collaboration over ten years ago with my book, *Homage: Encounters with the East*, the ever positive and enthusiastic Marta Hallett threw herself into this project, and with everyone at Glitterati on board, including Rocky Choi and the very talented and patient Liz Trovato leading the design team, we came up with this quite stunningly beautiful book, *Into the Garden*. Thank you all.

Special thanks to Donald Kuspit for his amazing, profound, and frankly sexy essay; Mac Griswold, whose early enthusiasm gave me a lot of confidence and who introduced me to Sylvester Manor on Shelter Island; and Ambassador Andre von Graffenried, who took me under his wing in Sri Lanka over three visits and introduced me to the late great Geoffrey Bawa and his garden, Lunuganga—to this day my favorite place in the world.

To my sculptor friend, Marina Lascaris, who opened all the doors for me in Mexico; Bea and Bob Guthrie, who hosted both Tim and me so many times at Casetta Rossa in Venice; my dear friend, Kathy Rayner and her late wonderful painter husband Billy Rayner, who opened their house for me so many times and allowed me to paint there in their magical Woodyhouse dune garden; and to Peter Wooster for putting up with me for a whole week while I painted there.

To Angus Wilkie and the late Will Harmon; Jimmy and Gretchen Johnson; the late Jeffrey Williams and his wife Hsing Mei; David White and the late Joe Erwin; Odile Maillet; Sunnie Evers; Jean-Christophe Eeckhout and Jean-Louis Lu Yen Tung; and the late Barone Alessandro Albrizzi, all dear friends whose generosity and kindness encouraged me to paint in their gardens.

To Hans-Peter and Suzette Loeffler-La Roche for their never wavering support, generosity, trust, and enthusiasm; Jeff and Betsey Cooley; and Jane Kelly Stubbs and John Stubbs who showed my garden paintings for the very first time in their eccentric, magical gallery on East 18th Street, one flight down from my own loft in New York in the late eighties.

To my art dealers and wonderful friends in Zürich, Enrico Bauer and Claudius Ochsner; the great stylist and dear friend, Howard Christian, who always makes my work look its best; everyone at the Bunny Williams Home showroom, where my work is constantly on display; Suzanne Rheinstein and Priscilla Wright at the former Hollyhock store in LA; and to my close friends and art dealers over forty years Daniel Blaise and Riitta Thorens in Basel who have enriched my life with their spectacularly beautiful gallery, their generosity, kindness, and loyalty.

Above all, thank you Bunny Williams for all your support and friendship over forty years, for your wonderful, kind, and loving foreword, and yours and John Rosselli's legendary hospitality, be it in La Colina in Punta Cana or Falls Village, both places with your enchanting, magical, and inspiring gardens I was lucky enough to be able to paint in so many times.

And, as always, my late parents, Axel and Dita, for opening my eyes to beauty, art, music, nature, and to love.

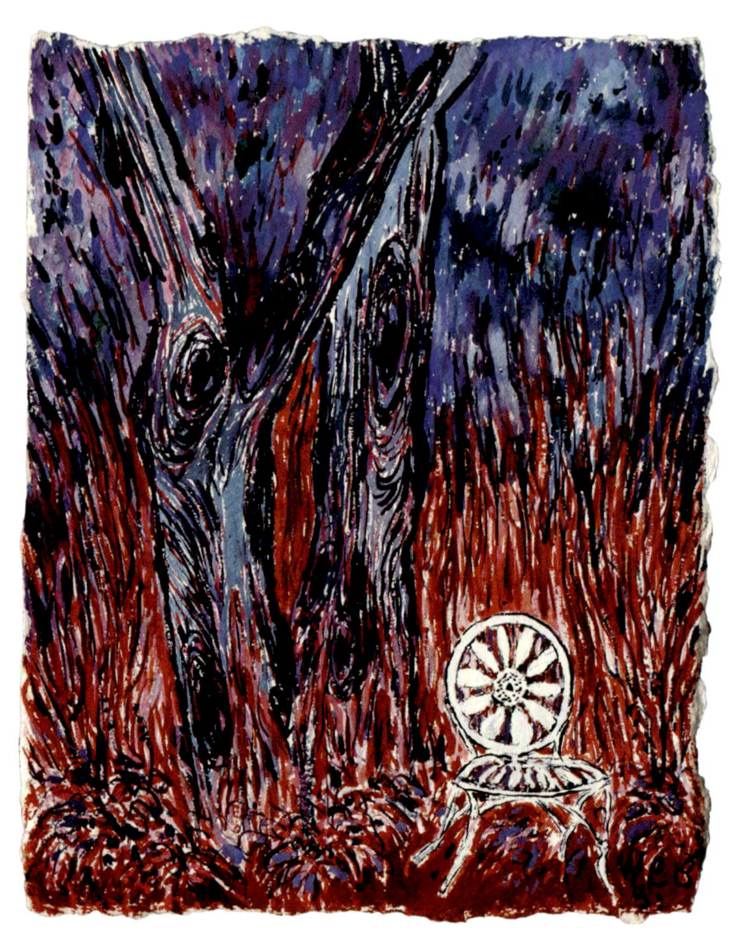

To plant a garden
is to believe in tomorrow.

~Audrey Hepburn